Arthur Morgan

A Progressive Vision for American Reform

Arthur Morgan

A Progressive Vision for American Reform

AARON D. PURCELL

THE UNIVERSITY OF TENNESSEE PRESS / KNOXVILLE

First Edition.

Library of Congress Cataloging-in-Publication Data

Purcell, Aaron D., 1972–
Arthur Morgan: a progressive vision for American reform / Aaron D. Purcell. — First edition.
pages cm
Includes bibliographical references and index.
ISBN 978-1-62190-058-0 (hbk.: alk. paper)
1. Morgan, Arthur E. (Arthur Ernest), 1878–1975.
2. Social reformers—United States—Biography.
3. Tennessee Valley Authority—Biography.
4. Tennessee Valley Authority—History.
5. Hydraulic engineers—United States—Biography.
6. Educators—United States—Biography.
7. Antioch College—Biography.
8. Bellamy, Edward, 1850–1898—Influence.
9. Community development—United States—History—20th century.
10. United States—Social conditions—20th century.
I. Title.

E748.H78 2014
370.92—dc23
[B]

2013047056

FOR SAMUEL SENET "BUB" PURCELL JR. (1910–1989),
A SELF-MADE FARMER, ENGINEER, AND GRANDFATHER

I am thankful that I am an engineer, because dreams are what the engineer works with. Always his structures exist first in imagination before he gives them substance in brick and steel and concrete. The engineer tells what and where he plans to build. "See, a great tower is to rise there. Can you not see it against the sky?" Some see nothing but dirt and stones and say, "It is just a dream." But sometimes others not only see what he sees, but add to and refine his vision, and so help bring it into being.

—ARTHUR MORGAN, 1924

We should not give up our visions, but we should examine them objectively, test them, and educate them in order that they will conform to the actual nature of things.

—ARTHUR MORGAN, 1948

Arthur Morgan was the most famous and important person you've never heard of.

—JEFF BIGGERS, author of *The United States of Appalachia: How Southern Mountaineers Brought Independence, Culture, and Enlightenment to America* (2006)

Contents

Illustrations

Acknowledgments

Over a decade ago I presented a paper at one of many Ohio Valley History Conferences. Arthur Morgan formed the basis for my presentation topic, but it was not a memorable conference for that reason. The dinner speaker that first night spoke about a number of Civil War projects he had undertaken and announced his upcoming biographical survey of a famous Confederate officer. As he segued into that announcement and as I finished my dry chicken dinner, his explanation of how he approached biography resonated above all distractions. He said, "Writing a biography is like your first marriage, you need about ten years to give the person a fair chance." Not many people laughed at the wry joke, but the idea of needing time for study and distance to do a biography stuck in my mind.

Indeed I have spent a decade and over a half of another one thinking about and, as my wife Laura would say, living with Arthur Morgan. My journey began in the fall of 1994 while working on a master's thesis on the early Tennessee Valley Authority (TVA). Arthur Morgan's leadership struck me as a crucial part of understanding the first years of the TVA and the New Deal itself. That realization led me to Morgan's papers held at Antioch College in Yellow Springs, Ohio. That collection formed a steady rock of research support for this and many other projects. I made well over a dozen trips to Antioch to work on various articles about other components of Morgan's life and career, some of which form parts of this book. At Antiochiana, Scott Sanders and Nina Myatt proved indispensable sources of information over many years. Without their assistance and encouragement I doubt this journey could have been possible.

Along the way I am met friends, descendants, and associates of Arthur Morgan. Although their recollections struck a chord with me, I have purposefully avoided relying on their stories as the backbone of my understanding of Morgan. Instead, I depended on Morgan's papers, published sources, manuscript collections, and official government records to provide a balanced picture of such a complex person. A number of archivists and librarians helped me locate a disparate lot of scattered primary documentation. Secondary to my work at Antioch, I spent numerous hours locating and digesting sources of information on Morgan's diverse legacies at the archives and libraries of the following institutions: the National Archives and Records Administration (in Georgia, Maryland, and Washington, D.C.); the University of Tennessee; the TVA libraries in Knoxville and Chattanooga; Princeton University; the University of Louisville; the Louisville Presbyterian Theological Seminary; Vanderbilt University; the University of Maryland, College Park; the University of Florida; Harvard University; Wright State University; and Virginia Tech.

Support from colleagues at several academic institutions gave me the strength to move forward with Morgan. History professor Thomas C. Mackey at the University of Louisville has read more of my early drafts on Morgan than he would admit or prefer. His encouragement to "press on" and dissect Morgan's "vision thing" gave me a challenge that I could not ignore. My dissertation advisor at the University of Tennessee, emeritus history professor Bruce Wheeler, gave me ample training to tackle the complexities of Morgan. Emeritus history professor Paul Bergeron has become a good friend over many years and during our chats back in Knoxville he encouraged me to explore the connections between Morgan and Edward Bellamy.

Progress on this project encountered numerous professional interruptions, including the brief closure of Antioch College, writing other books, and taking a position as director of special collections at Virginia Tech. Despite my tardiness in completing this manuscript, Scot Danforth, the director of the University of Tennessee Press, offered unwavering support over many years. His advocacy and careful reading of the manuscript made the editorial road much less rocky. I must also thank the outside reviewers of this manuscript for their insights and recommendations. There were numerous eyes and ears at both the University of Tennessee and Virginia Tech that led to improvement of the text. Most importantly, I could not have completed this book without the unyielding support of my family—my wonderful wife, Laura, and our two perfect children, Sam and Caroline. My parents Rodney and Betty Purcell supported this project in many ways, including storing many linear feet of research notes and photocopies in their basement and listening to me talk about TVA for so many years. I dedicate this book to my grandfather Samuel Senet Purcell Jr., who, like Arthur Morgan, came from humble beginnings to become a self-made engineer through years of hard work and patience. These and other parts of family life have given me deeper perspective on my subject, his motivations, his accomplishments, his shortcomings, and his legacies.

I have previously published several journal articles on components of Arthur Morgan's life and career. Thanks to the editors of the following journals for granting permission for portions of those articles to be part of this book: *The Journal of East Tennessee History, Tennessee Historical Quarterly, The Historian, New York History, Florida Historical Quarterly,* and *Ohio History.*

INTRODUCTION

On December 14, 1975, senior minister Donald S. Harrington addressed the members of the Community Church of New York City. He began the sermon with a simple question: "Who will history record as having been the greatest American of our age?" After a discussion of what constitutes greatness and how to measure significance, he concluded that, "the greatest of them was a man whose name you may never have heard. He died last month in the little village of Yellow Springs, Ohio, where he had lived most of his life, and he was in his ninety-eighth year." Harrington continued, "there are some who would consider him to have been a failure, for he lived to see some of his dreams discarded or damaged and distorted by less able, less honorable men." Then Harrington proclaimed that "the greatest American of our time—his name was Arthur Ernest Morgan." During the hour that followed, the minister described and celebrated the life and legacies of a largely forgotten figure in American history. Harrington closed the sermon saying, "Of all the gifts that he had left behind, there is nothing more powerful or more beautiful than his life itself, which shines like a great star in the dark skies of our time. He was, in all truth, the greatest American of our time."[1]

It is likely that few people outside of the church would have guessed Arthur Morgan as the greatest American of the twentieth century, and today it remains a safe bet that probably no one would choose him. So who was Arthur Morgan? That question was more common in the early 1930s. In spring 1933, with the eyes of the nation focused on the relief, reform, and recovery promised by the New Deal, Morgan took the national stage. On May 19, 1933, President Franklin D. Roosevelt told reporters that Arthur Morgan, a water-control engineer and college president from Ohio, would be the chairman of the Tennessee Valley Authority (TVA). Morgan was a familiar name to many engineers, educators at liberal arts colleges, and residents in central Ohio, but this appointment brought national attention and notoriety. One day prior to the announcement, Congress approved the creation of TVA and gave the agency broad powers to transform the poverty stricken Tennessee Valley. The flurry of activity during the coming months kept Morgan and TVA in the spotlight for much of the 1930s. Morgan's idealistic and visionary plans for the Tennessee Valley drew all kinds of attention, from support to criticism. Despite Morgan's accomplishments with TVA, his time in the spotlight faded, especially after being removed from TVA by Roosevelt in 1938.[2]

In the decades that followed, Morgan had an active career as a writer, social planner, educator, and international engineering consultant. Morgan maintained a following, especially abroad and in the Ohio Valley, but he never returned to the same level of national prominence and recognition that he had during the early 1930s. When Morgan died in the fall of 1975 at age ninety-seven, some took note. His lengthy obituary appeared in the *New York Times* and President Gerald Ford sent a telegram offering condolences to the Morgan family. The largest response to Morgan's passing came from friends, family, and associates who remembered and celebrated the somewhat forgotten engineer, educator, and reformer.[3]

Morgan emerged from a context of late-nineteenth-century values and culture. By the early twentieth century, he had become a socially conscious Progressive reformer with a vision. Morgan believed that the way to control and organize the rapid changes of the early twentieth century was through building small communities, one individual at a time. To build this enlightened society, Morgan stressed morality, character, practical education, non-competitive industries, and eugenic practices. Morgan's vision reflected the influences of the scientific thought of the late nineteenth century, Progressive Era reform, and the utopian writings of Edward Bellamy, but his ideas were uniquely his own.[4]

Morgan's idiosyncratic vision and social philosophy matured throughout his lengthy professional career. He found great professional successes and attracted international attention. Morgan recorded a significant public life before and after his six-year stint with TVA. Throughout his numerous flood control projects, most notably in the Miami and Tennessee River valleys, Morgan experimented with social and regional planning. Morgan inspired and built small communities across the globe, carried out innovations in higher education while president of Antioch College, staged several national battles against government agencies, wrote books and essays at a prolific pace, and remained a national public figure for nearly seven decades. Strikingly, after his TVA years, Morgan experienced perhaps his greatest successes as a community builder, social philosopher, and educational consultant. It was during his post–TVA years that Morgan got closest to achieving his vision of creating small self-sustaining communities, based on strong character, ethical standards, cooperation, and practical education. A more thorough and balanced analysis of Morgan, examining his strengths, weaknesses, accomplishments, and work beyond TVA is sorely needed.

Morgan's vision was complex and scholars have avoided dissecting the methods and results of his reforms. The words vision and visionary have somewhat negative connotations, including the quest for perfection, trying to achieve the unattainable, or exhibiting the quixotic. Morgan developed a social vision, and during the attempts to achieve his vision, he revealed many flaws. It is also important to note that, unlike most visionaries, Morgan produced tangible results that still exist. This study examines Morgan's vision and offers insights into how he hoped to improve society.

Only a few writers have tackled Morgan, and these biographical works focused on specific periods or aspects of his life. The first of these biographical treatments was his wife Lucy Morgan's *Finding His World: The Story of Arthur E. Morgan* (1928), a book about Morgan's earliest years, written before Morgan took bold steps in the Tennessee Valley. Another round of analysis came in the 1970s with a psycho-biography of Morgan written by Antioch College psychology professor Clarence Leuba, and then a biography by Walter Kahoe, a long-time friend of the Morgan family. These works were heavily sympathetic, celebratory to their subject, and relied on uncritical and personal sources.[5]

Beginning in the late 1960s a handful of scholars took note of Morgan. They interviewed Morgan and many of his associates, and had access to an enormous collection of personal and professional papers that Morgan had amassed over many decades. The resulting books and articles focused on his TVA years, the board struggles between Morgan and fellow board member

David Lilienthal, and some of the agency's engineering accomplishments.[6] Later, a few other scholars took interest in Morgan's administration of Antioch College during the 1920s.[7]

The most significant of these scholarly works was Roy Talbert's *FDR's Utopian* (1987), which examined Morgan's origins, his administration and view of TVA, and his relationship with Roosevelt. Talbert characterized Morgan as part Progressive reformer and part utopian, which equaled a style and a plan that did not work well in the second half of the New Deal. Talbert acknowledged the influence of utopian thought on Morgan's development but he did not fully explore the importance of Morgan's fascination with novelist Edward Bellamy. And because the book was focused on TVA, Talbert's study devoted less than ten pages to Morgan's post–TVA career. Talbert's book offered only glimpses of Morgan's larger vision of social reform and presented a partial and sympathetic portrait.[8]

A broader view of Morgan's long career is needed to fully evaluate this complex reformer. Talbert and other scholars have explored Morgan as TVA chairman, but Morgan's leadership during the New Deal needs a fresh assessment. Unlike most New Dealers, Morgan was not a bureaucrat; he abhorred politics, and embraced the reforms of the period as a continuation of earlier efforts. In his clash with board member David Lilienthal, Morgan was more concerned with differences in philosophy than policy. The significance of the New Deal in light of modern day discussions about government intervention in the economy, business, and regional development points to the importance of the early leadership of TVA and public works projects. At the same time, Morgan should not be judged on just his brief TVA career. His accomplishments before and after the 1930s have not received adequate attention.

A new assessment of Morgan must also address Morgan and his strain of utopianism. Talbert and other historians argued that Morgan exhibited utopian characteristics and attempted to build perfect communities. Morgan did take a strong interest in ideal societies, and during his career he founded a number of small communities. However, it is more accurate to describe Morgan as an admirer of utopian philosophy, writing, writers, and ancient societies. Morgan was not a utopian in the historical sense of the term; instead, he was a social reformer with a vision of how to improve society. His vision, rather than his utopianism, is the key to understanding his social plans and his approach to community building.

This book is a focused study of Arthur Morgan and his vision. It reviews many of his personal and professional accomplishments and limitations, but it is not a traditional biography tracing all of the details of Morgan's life. This book is based on published and unpublished sources, government records, manuscript collections at over a dozen repositories, Morgan's writings and research notes, and other sources that are part of the Morgan Papers at Antioch College. His voice, his contemporary writings, and other primary source documents are crucial to understanding and evaluating Morgan. In an effort to present Morgan in a scholarly and unbiased light, this book selectively uses sources that were created by many of Morgan's close associates and family, as well as Morgan's later recollections of events, simply because many of these sources were un-objective, unsubstantiated, and seldom found fault with Morgan.

This book fills several important gaps in our understanding of Morgan. His early influences and preparation during the Progressive Era are keys to understanding Morgan's vision. As his TVA tenure revealed, Morgan was more interested in community building than politics, public service, or popularity. Morgan had a unique and flawed vision, originating from late nineteenth-century culture, or what Julian West, the main character in Edward Bellamy's utopian novel *Looking Backward,* described as a "former time."[9] Morgan embraced the concept of social evolution, the creation of small communities, a rekindling of American character, and taking scientific steps to reform and improve society. With the right focus and resources, Morgan believed that a more enlightened society was possible. However, Morgan's vision relied on gradual changes in society, which conflicted with the pace of the dramatic changes taking place during the twentieth century.

This book analyzes Arthur Morgan's life and career within the context of larger social and cultural events of the first half of the twentieth century. It also addresses how Morgan was influenced by author Edward Bellamy and the utopian novel *Looking Backward.* Bellamy's influence on the reformers of the Progressive Era is often neglected in discussions of the sources of twentieth century liberalism. The book takes a chronological approach, starting with the larger themes of each period, and then analyzes Morgan's development, accomplishments, and attempts at reform. He held on to many of his Progressive Era tendencies, long after the spirit of that reform movement had faded, but unlike many Progressive leaders, Morgan remained an active reformer well into the second half of the twentieth century. Further, Morgan carried forward a Progressive vision for American reform decades after his contemporaries had faded into obscurity or lost interest.[10]

The first chapter explores Morgan's origins, his family, and upbringing. During this important transitional period in American history, Morgan absorbed the major scientific, religious, and political debates of the time. Watershed moments in his development included a visit to the 1893 World's Fair in Chicago and his reading *Looking Backward* when he was fifteen. Several threads from that book are evident throughout Morgan's life and work. In 1897, Morgan made a three-year journey to Colorado in search of a future and himself. Unsuccessful as a college student, Morgan learned the importance of practical experience as education. He returned to his boyhood home in St. Cloud, Minnesota, just months before the turn of the century a changed person. These events and influences shaped Morgan's thinking about the twentieth century, modern American society, and his life.

Chapter two focuses on Morgan's early professional successes as an engineer and as a budding Progressive leader. As a water-control engineer and drainage expert, his occupation fit well with the growing need to harness the physical landscape in efficient and productive ways for the benefit of society. During a brief stint working for the government, Morgan became aware of a potential land swindle in the Florida Everglades and demanded an investigation. The experience left him wary of unethical politicians, land promoters, and government work. During the first two decades of the twentieth century Morgan established himself as an innovative engineer with numerous projects in the South. His work to establish the Miami Conservancy District (an early example of regional planning and natural resource management) and to organize the construction of the massive undertaking was an early high-water mark for Morgan. By 1916, Morgan had found his niche as a water-control engineer with a clear Progressive voice and purpose.

The third chapter examines Morgan's work as chief engineer of the Miami Conservancy District. While completing the construction, Morgan demonstrated strong social concern for his workers. He built elaborate worker towns, instead of temporary quarters, which included schools for the children of workers. His Progressive tendencies to control, reform, and build were on full display with the Miami Conservancy District. Morgan's success in Ohio during the 1910s led to increased civic involvement and a chance to reform higher education. He became involved in civic groups such as the League to Enforce Peace and raised awareness for President Woodrow

Wilson's League of Nations Covenant. While balancing these numerous demands, Morgan reflected on educational reform. He and several other Daytonites found the nationally acclaimed Moraine Park School in Dayton.

Morgan's notoriety as a budding professional and educational reformer led to the presidency at Antioch College in nearby Yellow Springs, Ohio. His dozen years as president at Antioch resulted in a revolutionary work-study program and a complete revitalization of the school. He envisioned the college campus much like the ideal community of his dreams. The fourth chapter covers Morgan's Antioch experience and his involvement with professional organizations such as the Progressive Education Association.

The next two chapters cover Morgan as the first board chairman of the Tennessee Valley Authority. Initially Morgan had limitless opportunities and resources to revitalize the seven-state region that the agency served. During those first years, 1933–1935, Morgan represented the leading voice of TVA and introduced unique social programs and approaches to government administration. He also designed and championed the model TVA worker town of Norris, Tennessee. Chapter six traces the second part of his TVA tenure, 1936–1939, including his struggles with his fellow board members and President Roosevelt. The fate of private power companies and government ownership of utilities resulted in internal discord and contributed to Morgan's distrust of his colleagues. Morgan's staunch personality, rigid leadership style, and inability to compromise or deviate from his original plans are most evident in this period of his career.

Following his departure from TVA, Morgan focused on writing. His first major contribution was a biography of Edward Bellamy—a project that he had started in the early 1930s. That work led Morgan to publish several other books related to Bellamy and utopian thought. The seventh chapter covers Morgan's writings on Bellamy's role in the development of the American utopian tradition. His methodical research notes and early drafts for these works reveal much about Morgan's approach to Bellamy. Moreover, Morgan's interpretation of Bellamy and *Looking Backward* provides insights into the overall influence of Bellamy on Morgan's vision of the postwar world.

The eighth chapter reviews Morgan's work as a global community builder, educator, and engineering consultant. Upon returning to Yellow Springs in the late 1930s, Morgan founded Community Service, Inc. This organization became the centerpiece of his community outreach efforts. In the late 1950s, he befriended a young Indian student named Viswan. Morgan raised money and support for an experimental community called Mitraniketan in Kerala, India. Mitraniketan represented the perfect community that Morgan had tried to achieve throughout his long career. Morgan continued to write and lecture about the small community, development of the third world, peace during the Cold War, and regional development, which only increased his notoriety as an expert in multiple fields. Morgan's international influence and reputation resulted in his involvement in the 1950s with the Seneca Indian Nation. He worked with the Seneca in a bold attempt to prevent the Corps of Engineers from building a high dam and a resulting lake on their New York state reservation.

A conclusion provides an overall assessment of Arthur Morgan. It presents and analyzes Morgan's unique vision for improving society. While Morgan's character is discussed throughout the chapters, this last section summarizes several components of Morgan accomplishments, outlook, and personality. Morgan achieved great things in several professional fields, but in other areas his style and personality hampered his judgment. He founded many communities and local industries. However, he seldom remained an active member or supporter of his own initiatives. Morgan was a skilled engineer and manager of construction projects, but he often misunderstood the politics and local demands of those directly affected by his work. As an educator, Morgan inspired other college and university presidents, but he isolated his own faculty and students in the process.

Most importantly Morgan's vision was full of dichotomies. He wanted to build a series of small communities, but he ignored the importance of the industrial output and labor force that came from urban areas. He preached inclusion and diversity in society, yet he held on to eugenic principles decades after scientists had labeled the theory as racist and reminiscent of Nazi atrocities. Finally, his dream of centralized leadership and governance to regulate society was akin to the industrial army from Edward Bellamy's utopian or dystopian tomorrow.

Morgan was complex, and more than just an early leader of the Tennessee Valley Authority. At many points in his career, Morgan believed the best way to move forward was to rely on the lessons of the past, and that assumption often led him astray. Morgan created a vision of social improvement. While this vision did not consume him, throughout his various writings, speeches, projects, and proclamations, Morgan returned to his principles for building a stronger society.

Apart from scholars and admirers, few recognize the name Arthur Morgan. Further few would describe him as one of the greatest Americans of our time, as Donald S. Harrington proclaimed in 1975. Despite the lack of instant name recognition, Morgan has modern day significance and a reappraisal of his life, accomplishments, and career is long overdue.

This book argues that Arthur Morgan's contributions were complex and uneven, occurred over many decades, and were grounded in a vision of social reform for the modern world. His vision of community and character building for the twentieth century came from the culture and traditions of the late nineteenth century, which makes Morgan a man of a former time trying to improve a rapidly changing society that he often misunderstood or miscalculated. More simply, twentieth century society changed rapidly, while Morgan and his vision changed slowly. This book places Morgan squarely within a strain of liberalism and reform from the early twentieth century, which was not entirely forgotten but overshadowed by a more mainstream bureaucratic liberalism that followed. Morgan spent his life working to build a more enlightened society, one individual and one small community at a time. Throughout his quest, Arthur Morgan recorded a significant legacy of social reform, innovations in engineering, community building, and attempts to define a new American character and morality firmly rooted in the past.

1

A PERILOUS JOURNEY

On August 17, 1900, Arthur Morgan recorded in his diary a turning point in his life. Writing from the high altitudes of Fort Collins, Colorado, the twenty-two year old reflected on his past three years of independence in the Rocky Mountains. He began, "I am going home. [But] I feel that I am going away from home. It is here [in Colorado] that I have become a man." Morgan continued, "I have dreaded to leave these pleasant people, these grand mountains, these solemn plains, the flowers, birds, sunsets, trees, and little brooks. I love them all and my heart aches at parting. But perhaps I need not mourn. Perhaps it is I who am different." A few days later a changed young man began the return trip to St. Cloud, Minnesota.[1]

Morgan was not the same person returning to his boyhood home that summer. He had met failure as a college student at the University of Colorado, as a traveling bookseller, and as a coal miner. But during his three years in Colorado, he embraced Christianity, came to better understand his parents, found love but left that behind, discovered the beauty of the natural environment, and nursed a growing social consciousness for his fellow man. His fickle health had not improved during the extended stint, but Morgan gained a robust energy for life itself. Morgan's journey and realizations were not uncommon for his generation. The late nineteenth century world of Victorian culture, morality, and scientific thought that had shaped Morgan stood on the brink of a new century—a modern era that Morgan and many others attempted to define.[2]

The last three decades of the nineteenth century proved transformative for the United States. A once isolated and predominantly agricultural nation emerged as an industrial giant with a worldwide presence. By 1900, the percentage of Americans living in urban areas approached nearly half of the number of those living in rural parts of the country. The United States had become an industrial superpower, and recent immigrants, largely hailing from eastern European countries, formed the basis for the industrial workforce. These new Americans brought with them different religions, languages, and traditions. At the same time, a strong middle class emerged as an economic and political force. Overseas, the United States ended decades of isolationism and acquired a number of territories. Most notably, the United States earned control of the Philippines following the brief Spanish American War. In just a few decades, the United States had politically, socially, demographically, and economically redefined itself, and its role in the world.[3]

The year 1900 served as an appropriate capstone for the previous century. In 1900, Americans witnessed fantastic new modern innovations and challenges. In the period following Arthur Morgan's return home, a number of tremendous events occurred. Late that year, Orville and Wilbur Wright began a series of glider experiments near Kitty Hawk, North Carolina. On Christmas Day, Americans placed the first overseas telephone call from Key West, Florida, to Havana, Cuba. The geographic expanses of land and sea had become less of a challenge to communication and transportation. But 1900 was also plagued with instability. In September, a hurricane deluged Galveston, Texas, killing at least 6,000 people and destroying one-third of the town. On the world stage, an anarchist assassinated King Humbert of Italy, which heightened fears in the United States that President William McKinley would be the next victim. In the November elections, Eugene Debs received 96,000 votes for the Socialist Party in the presidential race. Union violence and mining disasters claimed the lives of workers in Utah, Pennsylvania, and elsewhere. Race relations between blacks and whites were dismal, with over 100 reported lynchings that year. In November, the last African American congressman of the Reconstruction Era, George Henry White, a Republican from North Carolina, chose to not run for third term. While many Americans claimed overall progress, many others could only see losses.[4]

Perhaps the most poignant example of the beginning of the modern period occurred on December 30, 1900, only two days before the twentieth century began. With little fanfare, that day the city of Boston decommissioned the last horse-drawn trolley and replaced it with an electric powered trolley. The United States had reached a point of departure, full of untold challenges but also limitless possibilities. As Americans looked backward on the enormous accomplishments of the nineteenth century, they also looked forward with a growing sense of optimism to the future.[5]

When Morgan arrived back at his family home in St. Cloud that August, he had had glimpses into a new century. During the 1890s, he had been surrounded by the marvels of electricity at the 1893 World's Fair in Chicago, had experienced the wonders of the natural world, had tasted adventure in the wilds of Colorado, and had followed the intellectual and scientific debates of the period. But those influences only partially prepared him for success in the modern era. During this time, Morgan read Edward Bellamy's utopian book *Looking Backward* (1887), which offered a model of a possible and achievable future. In late December 1900, as the Morgan family celebrated the arrival of the twentieth century, there were many indications of the perilous journey that lay ahead for young Arthur, and other modern Americans.[6]

Arthur Ernest Morgan began his life where, many decades later, he ended it, in the state of Ohio. Born on June 20, 1878, in Cincinnati to John D. and Anna Wiley Morgan, Arthur was the fourth of five children. John, who worked as a railroad surveyor, and Anna, a former school teacher, spent nearly a decade in Cincinnati. While there, the Morgans lost two children to epidemics and found little economic stability. John suffered from tuberculosis and sold notions on the streets of the Queen City to supplement their income. In 1879, the Morgans moved to St. Cloud, Minnesota, where they had been married ten years prior. They found temporary quarters in an old farmhouse far on the outskirts of town.[7]

Today, St. Cloud is about seventy-five miles from Minneapolis and is the third largest city outside of the Twin Cities metro region. But during the 1870s, St. Cloud lay on the edge of undeveloped parts of the state. European immigrants, including Germans, Poles, Slovaks, and Swedes, dotted and defined the surrounding area. Also known as the Granite City, St. Cloud offered quarries and steamboat access to the Mississippi River. With help from

John Morgan. Antiochiana, Antioch College.

extended family, the Morgans built a new house just south of St. Cloud. To support the family, John found work as a surveyor, while Anna took in normal school boarders and raised their children.[8]

Poor health plagued Arthur Morgan's earliest years. In 1880, the then two-year-old developed a severe case of cerebral meningitis. A local St. Cloud doctor diagnosed the condition as "congestion of the brain." Later accounts claim that infant Arthur suffered so badly that his mother hoped that he would die to cease the intense pain. He survived the episode, but upon his recovery doctors warned that another infection might be fatal. Morgan developed into a sickly child, suffering from common diseases such as measles and struggling with poor eyesight and other ailments possibly due to a poor diet.[9]

Decades later, Morgan pointed to his early bout with meningitis as creating a lifelong disability. He explained that during times of stress or concentration, blood rushed to the front part of the head, resulting in intense headaches, insomnia, nervousness, and restlessness. As a young adult, Morgan told his family that he expected to have a short life because of his condition. Morgan's frequent comments about his poor health led some scholars to claim that he developed lifelong hypochondria. More likely, Morgan was an inattentive and hyperactive child. As an adult, Morgan suffered some residual effects from the early case of meningitis, but by the time he burst on the national scene in the 1920s and 1930s other real, and not just imagined, health problems emerged.[10]

His mother, Anna Frances Wiley, served as a profound influence on Arthur Morgan's life. Originally from Massachusetts, Anna valued the natural world, insisted on demonstrating high moral standards, and practiced a rigid brand of Puritanism. She emulated many of the traits of the Victorian Era, including prudishness, strict adherence to religious faith, and a strong work ethic. Such high expectations created a lofty burden for her children, especially for young Arthur. Years later, he explained that his mother "doggedly hung on to her principles and her pride through every discouragement." This thread became a constant for his life, as well. His efforts to please her while a child grew into a lifelong attempt to uphold her values of honesty, Godliness, and even stubbornness (a trait shared by her husband, John Morgan). She often took in boarders, not only to help financially support their family, but also to teach others the Christian values of right and wrong. Morgan's social consciousness that blossomed in the Progressive Era grew from his mother's concern for those less fortunate.[11]

Upon graduation from high school in the late 1860s, Anna headed east toward the Minnesota frontier to teach grade school. While in St. Cloud, she met John Morgan and, in 1869, the couple married. Once out of the New England environment, Anna demonstrated some flexibility (molding her Puritanism into a Baptist church setting), but remained a solid Victorian in thinking and practice. Arthur Morgan later explained that "she was sincerely, narrowly, and devoutly religious." Anna exhibited "streaks of liberalism beyond the standards of her religious associates, as in her refusal to believe in eternal punishment," as well as an implicit belief in the Bible. Her attempts at perfectionism were clear in everything she did and said. Arthur spent much of his life trying to attain the same level of Christian morality and rigidity, while

Anna Morgan. Antiochiana, Antioch College.

sometimes sacrificing tolerance, flexibility, and respect for differing opinions. Anna proved to be the polar opposite of her spouse, John Morgan, and their ongoing family discord left a lasting impression on young Arthur.[12]

While Anna Morgan gave her son a moral compass, John Morgan provided his son with alternative ways of dealing with others, a more scientific view of the world, and later an occupation. Descended from some of the first Quaker settlers in Pennsylvania, John Morgan spent his early years in the small town of Bright, Indiana, just a few miles west of Cincinnati. The twelfth of thirteen children, John learned the blacksmithing trade from his father. As a young man, he found success as an oil well driller in Pennsylvania, but chose more formal education. During the mid-1860s, he attended the Lebanon Academy, in Lebanon, Ohio, studying mathematics and science. Although he could recite "Shakespeare from memory by the hour," as Arthur Morgan later recalled, John Morgan focused on surveying as a profession.[13]

The next two decades proved tumultuous for John Morgan. Just after the end of the Civil War, he and several of his siblings relocated to St. Cloud, Minnesota. In 1867, twenty-two-year-old John Morgan began an appointed position as County Surveyor of Pope County, the county adjacent to Stearns County, and its county seat, St. Cloud. Shortly thereafter, he met and married Anna Wiley, and they spent most of the 1870s struggling in Cincinnati. With the family's return to Minnesota in 1879, John Morgan secured work as a surveyor. Unlike his work in Cincinnati, in Minnesota, Morgan successfully worked for small firms, served out political appointments, and ultimately ran his own surveying business. But the transient and sporadic nature of John Morgan's work intensified an already difficult home life and marriage.[14]

John Morgan's outlook on life differed from his wife's. He had little concern for social graces, drank alcohol, and chewed tobacco. Most significant, John Morgan was skeptical of religion. Arthur Morgan later described that his father "was a true agnostic—open minded, curious, as slow to deny as to affirm, and temperamentally unwilling to commit himself beyond the evidence." Such a polarity on faith created a huge wedge between John and Anna, leaving the children in the middle. Young Arthur gravitated toward his mother's religious piety, but over time he better understood his father's scientific inquiry and religious skepticism.[15]

During his frequent travels as a surveyor, John Morgan enjoyed meeting settlers, who were often recent European immigrants offering their hospitality in the form of sharing alcoholic drinks—a custom not practiced in the Morgan household. John and Anna were constantly at odds. Arthur Morgan remembered his "father as the ill-natured inconsiderate man" who often kept "his shoes unlaced and his hair uncombed, his feet on the table, reading a book, and forever spitting tobacco juice in the general direction of the stove." When reprimanded by his wife for his slovenly appearance and actions, John showed her little respect. Young Arthur later noted that his father was "seldom considerate or courteous to her," and arguments erupted "almost every mealtime."[16]

By young adulthood, Morgan became more sympathetic towards his father. In his twenties, Morgan began accompanying his father on surveying trips and found him to be "an entirely different person." In the field, Morgan discovered that his father "was genial, tolerant, considerate, understanding," and respected. That discovery prompted Morgan to reassess his opinion of his mother and father. But during his youth, marital discord and family strain (compounded further by living in a small house with four family members and sometimes four boarders) led young Arthur to explore the outside world on his own.[17]

From his mother, Arthur Morgan developed a love of the natural world. "She was interested in birds, animals, and flowers, and introduced me to them," Morgan later recalled. That appreciation grew as he retreated to the outdoors in order to escape constant family discord. During family arguments, at night, and in the early morning, he would climb out of his bedroom window and spend hours exploring the nearby woods. Underneath the canopies of oaks, he found untouched ecosystems. Morgan took great joy in collecting samples of unique specimens, which he first shared with his mother and later with other budding naturalists.[18]

In addition to exploring areas of nearby primeval forest, the Mississippi River was only a few miles east of his house. At a bend in the mighty river, Morgan spent many hours observing the rise and fall of the water, the changing of the seasons, and how civilization grew along the banks, usually with negative effects. He also recognized geologic formations on the banks of the river and observed how the path of the great stream had deviated. Morgan recalled that "after some years, the woods along the top of the bend were cut out for lumber and fuel, and the city chose the place where the forest had been for a city dump."[19]

Just west of the Morgan house, young Arthur explored a tamarack swamp. While traipsing through the shallow water, he discovered and collected mosses, lichens, and orchids affixed to the base of the towing conifers and evergreens. Morgan later compared the swamp, with its trees rising like pillars, its crystal pools of water, and its pervading silence, to a European cathedral. Just like the forests on the riverbank, the swamp became a victim of human development. Ironically, while an adult, Morgan oversaw the reclamation of thousands of acres of swampland. These early experiences in the nearby wilderness connect well to Morgan's devotion to preserving natural areas (later called the conservation movement) and his professional ambitions to control the natural environment through reclamation and water-control engineering.[20]

Arthur Morgan, 9 years old. Antiochiana, Antioch College.

Morgan took greater interest in his self-education in the woods than in practical schooling. He attended public school and recorded lackluster grades. Morgan found rote memorization contrary to his short attention span, and he had difficulty sitting still. As one result, he repeated the fourth grade and earned average scores during his elementary school years.[21] His poor health and hyperactivity contributed to his below average performance, but it is also clear that Morgan was not a visual-verbal learner, as the majority of people are. His numerous explorations and discoveries in the forest hint that Morgan functioned best as a kinesthetic learner, one who thrives with hands-on activities and practical learning exercises—a style of teaching that would have been largely absent from the St. Cloud schoolhouse and even from most schools today. Morgan also demonstrated an aptitude for visual–non-verbal learning, such as interpolating raw data, maps, graphs, and charts. This trait is even more apparent when, as a young adult, Morgan digested complex engineering texts full of visuals, and even later when he authored engineering reports with scores of graphics and tables—all without any formal engineering training at the collegiate level. Further, Morgan's own pattern of learning during these developmental years formed the basis for his conceptualization of how to structure secondary and higher education. The precocious Morgan thrived best and learned the most through practical hands-on experience, full of moments of discovery.[22]

In addition to the schoolhouse, St. Cloud offered young Arthur other chances for learning. Religion played an important role in lives of the town's residents. Throughout his childhood Morgan attended Baptist church services with his mother and siblings. Attendance at these functions also became a social outlet for Morgan. At age eight, Morgan joined the Christian Endeavor Society, a group of mostly young adults from the nearby state normal school who discussed the Bible and theological questions. At first and understandably, Morgan joined the group, which held meetings in the late evening, to avoid his mandated bedtime of 7:00 p.m., but over time he found great intellectual companionship with the other members. At age ten, Morgan joined the Baptist church as an official member through baptism. But at this early age, Morgan challenged many religious doctrines held dear by the congregation. In particular, he questioned the omnipotence of God and argued that the search for truth through objective inquiry was the cornerstone of religious faith. Even before his teenage years, Morgan pondered the meaning of life and the church's role in his theological quest.[23]

Morgan discovered a great deal about himself, his burning religious questions, and the world around him during a family visit to the 1893 World's Fair in Chicago. In early September, the fifteen-year-old Arthur, his father John, and his older sister Jessie each bought a round-trip train fare from St. Cloud to the Windy City. They joined twenty-seven million others that summer and fall to pay tribute to American ingenuity and the four-hundredth anniversary of the landing of Christopher Columbus. The World's Columbian Exposition heralded electricity as the engine of technological change that would revolutionize the United States in the looming twentieth century. That summer, Chicago became the known as the White City, as 90,000 incandescent bulbs lit up the fairgrounds each night. Electricity powered nearly everything at the fair, including elevators, cash registers, automatic door openers, an elevated railway, a moveable sidewalk on the pier, and a gigantic wheel with passenger cars, designed by George W. Ferris. Although Thomas Edison developed the first system to control electricity, called direct current, his close rival George Westinghouse outbid him for the contract to illuminate and power the fair. As a result, Westinghouse's alternating current system, on full display at the fair, proved safe and reliable, and became the norm for electric power distribution in the nation and throughout the world. Other than three visits to an electrified Swiss Alpine panorama, Morgan recorded no other impressions on the use of electricity at the fair. [24]

The Morgan family lodged less than a mile from the fairgrounds and spent ten days as tourists. Arthur Morgan recorded in his diary seeing a massive telescope, original documents written by Columbus, the Liberty Bell, Native Americans, and as many as twenty-five buildings each day. He specifically mentioned visiting pavilions devoted to mining, transportation, fisheries, and government. During a visit to downtown Chicago, Morgan also noted seeing enormous grain elevators and a storm on Lake Michigan. Like most family trips, the experience proved exhausting and overwhelming. Morgan complained of headaches and longed to return to St. Cloud. Morgan later recalled that he had been most impressed with the World Parliament of Religions, where religious leaders representing nearly every faith discussed important social and theological topics. Morgan took particular interest in a presentation made by H. Dharmapala, a Buddhist from Ceylon.[25] Later that year, Dharmapala embarked on a national speaking tour which took him to the St. Cloud Unitarian Church with Morgan in attendance. That talk made an even deeper impression on Morgan, who later declared that Dharmapala's description of Buddhism exposed him to the importance of tolerance for other beliefs and traditions.[26]

Discussion of evolution, the most controversial issue of the Victorian Era, occurred at the fair. Charles Darwin's theory of natural selection, as described in his *On the Origin of Species* (1859), led to intense decades-long discussions of human evolution. The idea that mankind had evolved for millions of years, rather than mere thousands, brought scientists at odds with religious leaders. By the 1890s, many sociologists and reformers applied the principles of evolution to solving the social ills caused by rapid industrialization.[27]

A Congress on Evolution operated as part of the fair's World Parliament of Religions, and not through the various congresses on science. Key figures in the field of evolution, including English scientist Thomas Huxley and English philosopher Herbert Spencer, did not attend, but their papers were read by other presenters. Mirroring the rising interest in urban reform and the education of recent immigrants, Spencer's paper explained that social evolution depended on the altruism of others, mostly notably from the upper and middle classes. Some Parliament speakers argued that social evolution would result in more rights for women and changes in family structure. Presenters connected evolutionary thought to diverse fields of economic, ethics, and philosophy. Although the Congress on Evolution focused its attention on the religious implications of evolutionary thought, papers also discussed topics related to social reform, the theory of Social Darwinism, and the eugenics movement.[28]

Speakers presented on topics in evolution through other forums at the fair. Henry Drummond, an English writer and natural scientist, represented a middle ground in the evolutionary and creationist debates. His work encouraged religiously minded people to use scientific inquiry to unlock the mysteries of the history of humankind. Drummond delivered a paper entitled "Evolution and Christianity" to the audience at the World Parliament of Religions. Drummond celebrated science as a way to better understand religious thought, and emphasized that the concept of human evolution had not changed the doctrines of creation, the origins of life, and the existence of God. He encouraged fair goers to use scientific thought to better understand religious thought.[29]

Morgan searched for more information on the debates about evolution. In 1894, Morgan read Henry Drummond's just published *The Ascent of Man*, which argued many of the same points made before the 1893 World Parliament of Religions. In the book, Drummond asserted that "evolution is after all a vision—which is revolutionizing the world of nature and of thought, and, within living memory, has opened up avenues into the past and vistas into the future such as science has never witnessed before." Morgan later recalled that before reading that book he had been taught that evolution was "an evil concept," which had misled sincere people. Drummond's ideas about the value of scientific inquiry, and not necessarily the topic of evolution itself, drove Morgan to further question his own religious beliefs. Morgan recalled that "I was advised in religious matters to believe, and not to question." But by his teenage years, Morgan found scientific explanations for the natural world informative, comforting, and necessary to "make order out of chaos."[30]

In addition to reading Drummond's influential work, as a teenager, Morgan satisfied his growing intellectual appetite by immersing himself in books. St. Cloud "had a small but very fine library," and Morgan spent much of his free hours roaming its stacks. In the 1850s, the first residents of St. Cloud started a free public school by private subscription and named it after Edward Everett, an influential antebellum orator, politician, and president of Harvard University. So honored by the designation, Everett sent about 130 volumes of British and American literature to form the core of the school's library. That collection grew, and in the 1880s that library served as the city's public library, where teenage Morgan discovered scores of books.[31]

Beginning in 1893 and until he left for Colorado in 1897, Morgan recorded in his diary an annual list of books that he had read. Morgan recalled reading "in every field, including much that was beyond my understanding," and the list of complicated texts is evidence of his lofty reading breadth. He devoured the classic works of Charles Dickens, Mark Twain, Nathaniel Hawthorn, William Shakespeare, Henry David Thoreau, Homer, and Leo Tolstoy. These booklists reveal that Morgan learned much about the fields of natural science, history, geology, and botany. Besides Drummond's book on evolution, Morgan also noted reading J. W. Draper's *The Conflict between Religion and Science.* Most certainly Morgan familiarized himself with the writings of Charles Darwin, but his booklist only mentions reading Darwin's final work on the effects of earthworms on the soil. Morgan's reading of William R. Alger's *The Solitudes of Nature and Man* reinforced his introverted nature, while reading a biography of Christian mystic Emanuel Swedenborg further confused his religious outlook.[32]

More importantly, Morgan read theoretical texts dealing with the advances and subsequent problems of the late nineteenth century. His reading of Max Nordau's *Degeneration* hints that Morgan was becoming aware of the reactions against modernism and industrialization. While the book focused on new art and literature, Nordau also addressed the social effects of rapid urbanization. Morgan called it the "best book I have read," as it addressed so many of the issues relevant to modern society. But even more significant than Nordau's work, in 1893, Morgan read Edward Bellamy's utopian novel *Looking Backward, 2000–1887.* First published in 1888, the book addressed issues of modernization, urbanization, and class stratification, while offering possible future solutions to social ills. Although the fifteen-year-old merely recorded the author and title at the end of his diary with no further explanation, Bellamy left a lifelong impression on Morgan.[33]

Edward Bellamy came from a long family line of free-thinkers, pious eccentrics, and intellectuals. His distant ancestor, Captain Joseph Bellamy took notoriety as an orator and a pirate. During the 1720s, Captain Bellamy sailed off the Atlantic coast between the Carolinas and New England, capturing ships and cargo. He often addressed captured crews as being mere supporters of the wealthy capitalists that employed them, and claimed to be returning the cargo to the people. His piracy ended in 1726, after he ran aground near Eastman, Massachusetts, and made a subsequent trip to the gallows.[34]

The thread of religion in the Bellamy family began in the eighteenth century. The Reverend Joseph Bellamy, the great-great-grandfather of Edward Bellamy, developed his religious outlook during the Great Awakening of the mid-eighteenth century. He graduated from Yale at age sixteen, was ordained in 1740, preached near Bethlehem, Connecticut, and later studied under Massachusetts theologian Jonathan Edwards. A prolific speaker, the Reverend Bellamy delivered 485 sermons in the two-year period from 1741 to 1742. From the pulpit, the classroom, and through his pen, Joseph Bellamy spread the importance of cooperation, a non-competitive society, and the eradication of poverty.[35]

Rufus Bellamy, the grandson of Joseph Bellamy and father of Edward Bellamy, also chose the pulpit. A graduate of Middlebury College, he was ordained as a minister in 1838. The next year, Rufus married Louisa Putnam, the daughter of a Baptist minister. Unlike most preachers of the time, Rufus refused to threaten his congregations with eternal damnation and questioned the existence of hell. Such controversial theology led to his dismissal from four churches in the nine years that followed. However, in 1848, he accepted the pastorate of a Baptist church in Chicopee Falls, Massachusetts, a position that he held for thirty-four years. When the Bellamys moved to Chicopee, the town was in the middle of a transformation from a sleepy New England village to a manufacturing center. As part of that change, recent immigrants moved to Chicopee in search of work and encountered the old-line residents, as well as new arrivals to the growing middle class, including the Bellamys.[36]

In Chicopee Falls, Rufus and Louisa Bellamy raised a family of four boys. The youngest, Edward Bellamy, was born on March 26, 1850. From his mother, Edward Bellamy learned the importance of activist altruism and social reform, while his father kept him close to the pulpit. He took particular interest in reading texts on economics, character building, and sociology, while recording his thoughts in a diary. At age seventeen, he applied to the United States Military Academy at West Point, but was rejected because of physical inadequacy. In the fall of 1867, Bellamy enrolled at Union College in Schenectady, New York, where his brother Frederick was a senior. Bellamy stayed at Union College for a year, studying the works of French philosopher Auguste Comte and texts on socialism. The next fall, Bellamy accompanied his cousin, William Packer, on a two year stint to live and study in Germany. While there, from 1868 to 1869, Bellamy immersed himself in the theories of German socialism and how social reform and altruism could remedy poverty. Bellamy returned to the United States in 1869 with a renewed outlook on American society.[37]

Edward Bellamy began his writing career after a short-lived interest in law. He passed the bar examination with distinction in 1871 and opened a practice in nearby Springfield, Massachusetts. However, Bellamy's interest in writing led him to journalism and away from law. Bellamy worked as an editorial contributor for the *New York Evening Post* from 1871 to 1872 and then landed a more stable position as a book reviewer and writer for the *Springfield Daily Union*. He remained with the Springfield newspaper for the next five years, while writing his own fiction and philosophical texts on the side. Bellamy's most significant writing from this period was an unpublished 1873 essay entitled "The Religion of Solidarity," which largely outlined his social religious philosophy.[38]

"The Religion of Solidarity" essay is vital to understanding Bellamy's view of society that came out more eloquently in *Looking Backward* fifteen years later. In the essay, the twenty-four-year-old Bellamy wove elements of science, religion, mysticism, cosmic forces, and nature into a formula for human progress. While he argued that individuality and personality impeded the development of human society, he also found that uninformed altruism and self-sacrifice were just as negative. Instead, he called for a social outlook based on personal and communal motives. This combination of self and group, or universal solidarity as he called it, would led to greater social morality, improvement, and knowledge. Bellamy later admitted that the essay was "crude and redundant in style," not to mention difficult to parse, but the text encapsulated much of his philosophy on life and humanity's relationship to the universe.[39]

By the 1880s, Edward Bellamy found success with his fiction and left the newspaper world entirely. His short stories appeared in magazines such as *Scribner's, Appleton's Journal,* and *Lippincott's.* Bellamy also published several novels, including the philosophical *Six to One,* the psychological *Dr. Heidenhoff's Process,* the historical *The Duke of Stockbridge,* and the dramatic *Miss Ludington's Sister.* Readers took interest in Bellamy's complex characters, deeper symbolism, and socioeconomic discussions in these texts. In 1884, Bellamy resigned from the *Springfield Daily Union* to focus his energies on writing fiction.[40]

In 1885, Bellamy began work on a new novel to address social and industrial issues that had gripped Chicopee Falls and the rest of the nation. The mid-1880s were a period of significant upheaval, as the nation became more urban, less rural, and lurched toward a new definition of America. High unemployment, economic downturns, large-scale strikes and labor disputes, a massive influx of European immigrants, and ostentatious displays of wealth from owners of unregulated industries (such as railway and steel companies) threatened any stability or gains since the end of Reconstruction. Intense partisanship, massive political indifference, and ineffective layers of federal bureaucracy created a disconnect between elected officials and the people they served. Solutions to such complicated social, economic, and political problems were nowhere in sight. Some turned to political bosses, others to labor organizers, while many found no advocate for their cause. In Chicopee Falls, entire families of recent immigrants worked twelve hours a day in the mills, while residents in the more established upper and middle classes ignored the plight of the lower class. Edward Bellamy wanted to address these and other issues in a new book.[41]

Bellamy drew great inspiration from the classic writings of Plato, Plutarch, and Sir Thomas More, and from his contemporaries including Henry George and Henry Demarst Lloyd. However, his greatest influence may have come from the writings of his younger brother Charles. In the early 1880s, Charles Bellamy published two books dealing with issues of labor and economics. In *The Breton Mills* (1880), the younger Bellamy discussed the relationship between the owners and the workers of a mill in a recently industrialized town in the United States. Four years later, in *The Way Out: Suggestions for Social Reform* (1884), Charles Bellamy discussed a number of legislative and social proposals to redesign the nation's economy. The sweeping ideas suggested a more even distribution of wealth, an eight-hour work day, an end to private ownership of land, elimination of monopolies, and complete government ownership of industries. The two books embraced these possible remedies as creating utopian solutions in a more modern society.[42]

By 1886, Edward Bellamy developed a rough outline for a utopian novel with a serious message. Bellamy built his story on the dichotomy of fantasy and reality. Similar to the premise of "The Religion of Solidarity," he wanted to present duality of personality (individualism versus dedication to the common good), but this work would demonstrate the unevenness of society and point to remedies. He embraced the literary mechanism of time-travel to compare the world of the late nineteenth century with expectations of the future, modern America at the end of the twentieth century. His manuscript, first entitled "Looking Backward: 2000–1887, A Tale of the Twentieth Century," followed the experiences of an upper class Bostonian from the 1880s who wakes up in the year 2000 to find a more utopian America, free of capitalism, class struggle, and competition. A year after publishing the book, Bellamy declared that he had not been influenced by social reformers in developing the story. But as the book gained phenomenal popularity, Bellamy later admitted that he had initially set out to offer a new method of economic and social organization with his book. Whatever the influences and purposes of the novel originally were, the book itself offers fascinating insights into the late nineteenth century and also into the later development of Arthur Morgan's vision.[43]

In 1888, Ticknor and Company published the Edward Bellamy's *Looking Backward, 2000–1887*. The book is centered on the narrator Julian West, an upper-class Bostonian, who in 1887 has become engaged and is waiting for the couple's new home to be completed. West comments that a series of labor strikes had slowed the construction of their home and contributed to deteriorating conditions between worker and employer. He later mentions the fear that a political uprising, possibly led by anarchists, could certainly disrupt the world that he knows. But at the beginning of the book, West speaks of this class struggle, political upheaval, and industrial malaise in the past tense, as if those problems could be and would be eradicated through simple reform.[44]

To escape the unsettling realities of 1887, the narrator often retires to a subterranean room of his family's home, far away from the noises and violence of the city. But after two sleepless nights, he invites a "Professor of Animal Magnetism" to put him into a deep sleep trance and leave him behind in the sleep chamber. West instructs Sawyer, his African American servant, to wake him the next morning. However, West awakens from his deep sleep to meet, not Sawyer, but a Dr. Leetee. Leetee informs West that, while digging in his backyard, he discovered the corner of a crumbling vault and inside that buried tomb he found West. With the help of fellow doctors, Leetee resurrected West from the deep trance. Most troubling to West, instead of sleeping for a few days, he had in fact slept for 113 years and found himself transported to the year 2000.[45]

The core of *Looking Backward* revolves around Dr. Leetee introducing his nineteenth century friend, Julian West, to Boston during the final days of the twentieth century. West first learns that a social and ethical revolution, without bloodshed, had brought about a recalibration of American society. Leetee explains that in the early part of the twentieth century, the period of monopolies and trusts ended with the creation of a government-controlled "great trust," which absorbed and nationalized all the private corporations and businesses. The creation of a single industrial workforce, or army, eliminated all labor struggles between employer and employee. As capitalism, competition, and a credit system gave way to a new kind of nationalized economy regulated by the government, a classless society of equals emerged. The new government, led by a president who had steadily moved from the lowest to the highest ranks of the industrial army, shunned political parties, dissolved all war powers, and eliminated corruption. The government focused on supporting its citizens through universal education, providing services, eliminating poverty, and generally equally distributing the nation's great wealth to its citizens.[46]

These drastic changes in governance and centralized production led to significant social recalibrations. Without a free-market economy, lawyers, merchants, retailers, agents, bankers, and many other occupations had become obsolete. Instead, people worked for the industrial army doing the tasks that best fit their strengths and talents. West is most shocked to learn that money and credit do not exist in twentieth-century Boston. Leetee explains that, "buying and selling is considered absolutely inconsistent with the mutual benevolence and disinterestedness which should prevail between citizens and the sense of community of interest which supports our social system." West also learns from Leetee that all other nations have abandoned money and credit in favor of exchanging goods to meet their mutual needs. Human energy, instead of capital, is the most important resource of the twentieth century.[47]

West's discussions with Leetee's daughter, Edith, who he later discovers is the great-granddaughter of his fiancée from 1887, tackles other significant social questions. Leetee explains to West that women in twentieth-century Boston have vital roles in society. Women are not dependent on their husbands or fathers, they hold important roles in the industrial army, and members of society applaud and support them if they choose to have or not to have children.[48]

Near the end of the book, Julian West briefly returns to the nineteenth century. After experiencing two days of dazzling discoveries of the modern world, West retires to his unearthed chamber to sleep. When West wakes the next morning, his servant Sawyer greets him. Suddenly, West has returned to May 1887. With the vision of the twentieth century still fresh in his mind, West walks the streets of Boston and notices the "squalor and malodorousness of the town." West observes extreme waste, corruption, poverty, and inhumanity. At the end of the day, West visits the home of his fiancée for dinner. He chides the dinner guests for ignoring the human suffering that surrounds them and suggests a new world based on mental enlightenment, moral elevation, and the common good. Furious by the display, West's future father-in-law orders his servants to remove West from the dining room. Sobbing, panting, and groaning, West resists the forced removal, and then suddenly wakes up in a room in Dr. Leetee's house in Boston of the year 2000. At the end of the book, West reflects on the inequities of the nineteenth century and refers to himself as "a man of that former time." West then fully embraces the realities of the nearly utopian twentieth century.[49]

The interconnected tenets of community building, morality, government oversight, and social reform are buried deep within the text of *Looking Backward.* Bellamy suggested that a better society could be achieved through regulation, both at the personal and communal level. While some feared total government control of industries and the economy, Bellamy believed that government ownership was a nearly inevitable force of social, political, and economic evolution. A transparent government, controlled by many, had the advantage of providing all members of society with basic needs, employment, and perhaps opportunities for personal fulfillment. But instead of a violent overthrow of capitalism, Bellamy believed that once those in positions of political and economic power surrendered their positions in society for the greater good, a natural and bloodless transition would occur. The bourgeoisie and proletariat would literally reach a common understanding and unite their efforts. Efforts at social reforms and improving society would precede this revolution, and continue long after to ensure equality. The resulting community, or series of communities, would be self-governed by a Christian morality of right and wrong and a shared government with the sole purpose of protecting its citizens.

Despite his extreme predictions of the future (especially the overthrow of capitalism, elimination of private property, and a seemingly omniscient industrial army), Bellamy shared an important vision in *Looking Backward.* Bellamy combined his call for social, political, and economic reform with the importance building a strong moral base at the community level. Education at the grassroots level, cooperation, and self-awareness served as core values for a future society. His resulting blueprint of a more efficient and regulated society appealed to people in all classes.

Bellamy's social commentary found an audience far beyond the casual reader. More than just a utopian parable with lofty predictions, *Looking Backward* offered real hope for human progress in the coming decades. Further, the first-person narrator approach and clear writing make the book accessible for many readers. During its first year of publication, *Looking Backward* sold 60,000 copies, and the following year sales of the second edition soared well past 100,000 copies. Editions appeared in England, France, and Germany. The book soon became only the second American novel to sell over a million copies, with Harriet Beecher Stowe's *Uncle Tom's Cabin* (1852) the first.[50]

Sales of *Looking Backward* transformed Bellamy from a mildly successful writer into a social and political activist. In the fall of 1888, a group of Boston intellectuals, journalists, and reformers founded a "Bellamy Club" to share and discuss the ideals of *Looking Backward.* The club served as the genesis for a political movement known as Nationalism, which spread across the country. Bellamy defined the policies of the movement as "the progressive nationalization and municipalization of industries by substituting public control for the public advantage, in place of already highly centralized forms of corporate control for corporate advantage." The characteristics of Nationalism, as defined by Bellamy, included unselfishness, tolerance toward opponents, patriotism, and a spirit of conservatism. On that latter point,

Bellamy argued that the Nationalists represented the equalitarian spirit of the American Revolution and sought to return the nation back to its roots and away from private interests who had staged a revolution against the founding principles of liberty. Instead of inspiring a radical revolution, the Nationalists were merely counter-revolutionaries keeping the greedy capitalist enemies of the republic at bay.[51]

By May 1889, leaders of the movement published the first issue of *The Nationalist,* a monthly magazine describing club activities and the principles of Nationalism. Dozens of reformers, including Bellamy, contributed essays to the magazine, which during its peak reached about 9,000 subscribers. But Bellamy did not play an active role in editing *The Nationalist* (which ceased publication in 1891); instead, he planned for a successor publication to refine his arguments and the goals of the growing political movement.[52]

By 1890, Bellamy took greater control of the Nationalist movement. Since 1888, detractors charged that Bellamy's industrial army represented state communism and that the post-capitalist world of *Looking Backward* was an anathema to democracy and freedom. Bellamy addressed these charges with the publication of *The New Nation.* This magazine focused more on practical social reform and political action needed to improve society. *The New Nation,* published from 1891 to 1894, discussed topics including labor strikes, high consumer costs due to private utilities, and swelling urban crime rates—all resolvable problems in a Nationalist society. At the same time, Bellamy sought support for the Nationalist cause from politically mobilized American farmers, who by the 1890s coalesced as the Populist Party.[53] Like other social reformers of the period, Bellamy found the third party movement of the 1890s full of great potential. Bellamy rallied for the Populists and Nationalism until 1894, when he began work on a sequel to *Looking Backward.* The result, *Equality,* published in 1897, found a receptive audience but the sequel could not match the popularity or sales of *Looking Backward.*[54]

In the mid-1890s, Arthur Morgan stood on the brink of adulthood. His diary entries and experiences demonstrate that Morgan was fully aware of the political, social, scientific, economic, religious, and moral issues of the period. His interest in the natural environment, education, social reform, and finding an occupation were foremost on his mind. By the end of the

Students at St. Cloud High School, 1896. Arthur Morgan second from right. Antiochiana, Antioch College.

nineteenth century, Morgan had determined much of his own personal course for the twentieth century.

Morgan's boyhood interest in collecting specimens while wandering in the woods blossomed into a more serious endeavor as a teenager. In 1895, Morgan and two other friends founded the Granite City Geologists Club. Their informal group held regular meetings, made field visits to nearby unique geologic formations, examined fossils, and discussed published bulletins from the state geologic office. The next year, Morgan had an essay published in *Popular Science News* describing the Weesitchia, an unusual plant found in Africa. Although not a groundbreaking piece, Morgan went on to publish a half-dozen other essays for the journal. A recognized naturalist, Morgan intensified his efforts to collect botanical samples, including rare lichens.[55]

In June 1896, Arthur Morgan graduated from a three-year high school in St. Cloud. Unlike his early years in the classroom, Morgan flourished in high school. Just a month before graduation, Morgan noted that he had "passed final (college entrance) examinations in Plane Geometry, English

History, Essay, Biology, and Geology," while recording perfect attendance for that year. He also developed strong relationships with a few of his teachers. Before high school, Morgan found that his teachers emphasized discipline over teaching. He once referred to his seventh grade teacher as a "driving tyrant" only focused on distributing demerits to inattentive students. However, Morgan found his high school teachers more focused on cultivating different opinions on subject matter than having pupils sit upright. He even noted that the principal of the school demonstrated honesty, integrity, and encouraged intellectual freedom. Those positive high school experiences were influential in Morgan's developing educational philosophy.[56]

Morgan's high school success and interest in teaching led him to try his hand as an educator. A few weeks after graduation, Morgan learned that a nearby school in the same county needed a teacher for a three-month term. In late August, Morgan visited the school, in Brockway, Minnesota. The school board offered Morgan a salary of $22.00 a month, with a room and board charge of $6.00 a month. He accepted the offer, secured a teaching certificate, and began teaching on September 2, 1896. Morgan taught four pupils in a one-room schoolhouse for the next three months, trying a variety of methods and subjects. Morgan recorded only mediocre results at the school and returned to St. Cloud with an unclear future as a teacher. To improve his teaching skills, the next year Morgan took a course in English literature at the high school and enrolled in summer classes at the nearby state normal school in St. Cloud. At the same time Morgan took odd jobs in the Granite City, including delivering milk and farm work.[57]

At the end of the normal school's summer session in August 1897, Morgan embarked on a new journey. Morgan planned for an extended trip to find stable work and, on the morning of September 11, 1897, packed a small bundle. Morgan filled the bag with personal belongings including "a small Testament, a copy of [Thomas] Gray's *Elegy,* a cyclopedia of universal information, writing paper, pencils and envelopes, pair of socks, shoe strings, diary, and handkerchiefs." After walking about a mile, a farmer gave him a ride in a wagon. During the short wagon ride, Morgan symbolically passed by the farmhouse where he had spent the first year of his life. Several miles later, Morgan left the wagon and went on foot in search of work. For the next two weeks, Morgan cut corn and did odd jobs for several farmers. But Morgan's jaunt through nearby Minnesota counties looking for work soon expanded in time and space.[58]

On October 1, 1897, Arthur Morgan reached the banks of the Mississippi River near Clearwater, Minnesota. After eating lunch, he bound several logs with clothesline rope into a makeshift raft. He then launched himself into the river and traveled to the outskirts of Minneapolis. Morgan spent the next three weeks rafting, walking, or generally tramping across Minnesota and into Iowa. He found intermittent work on farms, but intended to move further west and stay with a cousin in Denver while searching for work. In Charles City, Iowa, he took a train to Sioux City and then on to Omaha, Nebraska. Morgan's parents forwarded him enough money to buy a train ticket to Denver, and in November he arrived in the Mile High City. For the next three years, Morgan worked and tramped his way across Colorado.[59]

During the first part of 1898, Morgan only found short-term employment. Dissatisfied with prospects in Denver, in February he went to the gold mining town of Central City. In addition to the tight job market, part of Morgan's difficulty to secure work was his resolution not to accept a job if the result of his labor would be ethically undesirable. This trait, of only accepting work that would not violate Christian principles, lasted throughout his life. For instance, Morgan quit a job chopping logs that winter after he discovered that the timbers would be used to build a gambling hall. Central City featured many casinos and other institutions of ill social repute. Still, Morgan managed to find odd jobs, including work on a ranch and as a baker's assistant. In late June, he moved to the town of Boulder and found work as a typesetter in a printing office. In September, he enrolled in the preparatory school at the University of Colorado. Morgan wrote his sister saying: "Expect to start to the University tomorrow. Think that I shall take one subject less than a full course. I don't want to break down if I can help it." Although he had only a few dollars, the over-eager student took courses in Literature, German, Art, and Geometry. Despite his irregular attendance, Morgan completed the school year.[60]

Morgan developed friendships and possible roots in Boulder. He found room and board at a nearby ranch, where he could pay for his lodging by selling the farm's products. Morgan and a fellow preparatory student, Ward Foster, earned extra money by selling fruits and vegetables to people living in nearby mining camps. Because of their friendship and business partnership, Morgan met Foster's sister Lois. Her religious intensity intrigued Morgan, and the two regularly attended church services. After a brief courtship, the two were engaged in early 1899. During their engagement, Morgan renewed his sense of religious awareness and the importance of leading a Christian life. But by the end of the summer, Morgan became uncertain about the marriage and broke off the engagement.[61]

In September 1899, with preparatory school courses behind him, Morgan enrolled as a college student at the University of Colorado. He registered for courses in English, Latin, and Biology, and found himself a frequent visitor of the university's library. His past track record indicated that somehow Morgan would find a way to finish a least one term if not a degree program, but after only six weeks Arthur Morgan withdrew from the University of Colorado. It is unclear exactly what fate befell the young college student. Morgan later claimed that his non-stop reading had damaged his eyes and forced him to leave. The added pressures of insufficient funds, poor grades, and perhaps even social backwardness also may have led to his sudden departure. Most surprising, the three month stint as a college student in Boulder represents Arthur Morgan's only formal higher education. His later professional successes well obscured this fact, so much that Morgan even became a college president in the 1920s without actually holding a college degree of his own. While Morgan's professional ascendancy was not uncommon at that time, professions like engineering and faculty or administrative positions in higher education began to require credentials in the early part of the twentieth century.[62]

In late October, eager to escape Boulder, the home of his former fiancée and the location of his failed educational aspirations, Morgan wandered further into the Rocky Mountains. He collected about two dozen books and decided to peddle the volumes to miners and woodcutters. He put the books on a cart and set off into the mountains looking for isolated people interested in reading books by John Ruskin, Thomas Carlyle, Johann Wolfgang von Goethe, Ralph Waldo Emerson, and Rudyard Kipling. After three months in the field, Morgan had not sold a single book. In desperate need of work, Morgan tried his luck as a coal miner. He found the safety conditions so appalling that he resigned before the end of that first day. Morgan next found equally dangerous work in a lumber camp. While in the high altitude, Morgan also earned a small amount of extra money by collecting rare lichens for botanists.[63]

By the spring of 1900, Morgan had nearly run out of options and possibilities for staying in Colorado. He headed north toward Fort Collins and spent several months working in orchard, followed by temporary work as a librarian. Throughout his three years in Colorado, Morgan recorded a great deal in his diary, but during his stay in Fort Collins he became particularly introspective and reflective. In August, he noted that while in Colorado he had learned to be a Christian, to become acquainted with and more understanding of his parents, and to understand the plight of his fellow and often less-fortunate man. Despite Morgan's poor performance as a college student and his inability to develop any professional talents, he had broken out of the shell of his youth. In the short-term, his three years of intermittent employment did not result in great financial returns, but in the long-term Morgan learned the importance of hard work, practical educational experiences, friendship, and respect for others. Morgan realized that it was time to return home, and by September he was back in Minnesota.[64]

During the fall of 1900, Arthur Morgan reacquainted himself with St. Cloud. He took a job cutting cordwood and continued contemplating his future. His health had not improved after three years away from home, but his personal determination to do something significant with his life remained steady.[65] His influences were strong and varied. From his parents he had developed a strong sense of Christian morality, social concern, and the importance of education. An appreciation for the natural world only grew as he explored parts of the disappearing American frontier. Although Morgan had limited formal schooling, his self-education and immersion in advanced topics like evolution and higher mathematics made him fully aware of the intellectual world around him.

Morgan's early exposure to Edward Bellamy's *Looking Backward* is especially significant. Concepts of morality, social reform, education, government oversight, and community building are central to the novel's narrative. Those values influenced Morgan's thinking about creating a more perfect society and the possibilities for modern America. But in 1900, Morgan was far from clear on his theories about education, social and regional planning, and the small community

On December 31, 1900, Arthur Morgan recorded nothing unique in his diary about the passing of the nineteenth century into the twentieth.[66] But the twenty-two-year-old understood that a modern era of great possibilities was on the horizon. In just his short lifetime, the United States had become more urban, ethnically diverse, economically uneven, socially stratified, and significant on the world stage. These larger forces could affect the future just as they had the last decades of the nineteenth century. New technologies, a seemingly endless supply of natural resources and cheap labor, and uncontrollable hubris fed the American imagination for a limitless tomorrow. However, at the same time, many Americans sensed that the nation teetered on the brink of a possible social, cultural, economic, and psychic collapse.

The combination of optimism and fear in the late nineteenth century led to larger reform efforts to adjust, monitor, and control a changing society. Several reform movements, such as the Populists and the Nationalists, emerged during this period, but it would be a more generalized movement, known as the Progressive movement, that dominated the first few decades of the twentieth century. In just a few years, Arthur Morgan became one of these Progressive reformers, with a near desperate need to enact social reforms and improve society as they saw fit.

2

FINDING HIS WORLD

On March 23, 1913, heavy rain began to fall on the Miami River Valley. Located in the southwestern part of Ohio, centered near the city of Dayton, the Miami River basin absorbed over ten inches of rain during the next four days. As the waters of the Great Miami River rose, affected residents moved vertically, up into the second floor of their homes, then to their attics, and some to their roofs. When the water finally receded, it left behind 400 dead and over $100 million in damages. This flood of near Biblical proportions marked an important moment for those living in the Dayton area. Residents formed a flood prevention committee to raise money and explore solutions to repel another such cataclysmic event of nature.[1]

A few weeks later, on May 3, 1913, Arthur Morgan spent a quiet Saturday morning tending to his backyard garden. Then president of his private engineering business headquartered in Memphis, Tennessee, Morgan was responsible for dozens of reclamation projects throughout the South. Within only a decade of largely self-directed training and work, Morgan had become a leader in the new field of water-control engineering. That morning Morgan's wife, Lucy, interrupted his gardening. She told him that "Dayton was on the telephone" and wanted him to solve their flood problem. The invitation and subsequent acceptance constituted a turning point for Arthur Morgan.[2]

The Morgans visited the Ohio hinterlands that spring, and for the next decade, Morgan served as the chief engineer and director for the massive undertaking, known as the Miami Conservancy District. This project ranked just behind the building of the Panama Canal and improvements on the Mississippi River as one of the most significant building projects of the early twentieth century. During the 1910s, Morgan set out to protect the residents of the region through a series of earthen dry-dams and river improvements. With the Miami Conservancy District, Morgan recognized the power of large-scale regional development and planning.[3]

In the 1910s, Morgan embodied a spirit of Progressivism that swept the nation. Morgan's accomplishments during this period mirrored the influence of nationally known Progressive leaders such as Hull House founder Jane Addams, the founder of the theory of scientific management theory Frederick W. Taylor, educator and intellectual John Dewey, U.S. senator from Wisconsin Robert La Follette, President Theodore Roosevelt, and even muckraking journalist Ida Tarbell. During this period he relied on the power of the press to expose corruption, expected government officials to practice civic responsibility, assumed a moral responsibility for those less fortunate, and embraced the credo of efficiency. Morgan seized opportunities to promote morality, launch social reform, encourage government oversight, and plan intentional communities. It is within this larger social and political context of the period that Morgan's actions must be viewed.

Progressive reform reached a high water mark in the first two decades of the twentieth century. Scholars remain split on the origins, motivations, and effectiveness of Progressive reformers. Whether a rural, urban, or class phenomenon, progressivism was a reform movement that sought to temper and improve an industrial society plagued by modern problems. Some of the reformer's methods included making the political process more open and responsive to its citizens, creating new educational and housing opportunities for those less fortunate, and exposing corruption through investigatory journalism. Many reformers demonstrated a strong sense of Protestant morality, based more in the values of their Victorian Era parents and Republican Party leaders like Abraham Lincoln, and less on the traditional ministry. Reformers came from professions such as social work, journalism, politics, engineering, and the law. These reformers possessed a strong faith in improving the environment and conditions of life through purposeful action.[4]

The combined work of reformers from the 1890s through the 1910s represented a larger period collectively known by historians as the Progressive Era. During that time, an astonishing number of reforms took place.

By the early 1920s, women could vote in elections; the purchase or sale of alcoholic beverages was a federal crime; voters directly elected senators, and citizens had increased participation in local, state, and national lawmaking; and, through legislation, the role of government in the economy and culture increased. Despite such advances, numerous unresolved issues existed in this period, including declining race relations, the revitalization of nativist groups such as the Ku Klux Klan, limits on immigration, few assurances for workers, international discord, a widening economic gap between classes, and limited regulation of the financial sector and large corporations. Uneven, incomplete, and sometimes contradictory reforms cloud the legacies of the period.[5]

Progressive reformers varied in their methods and focus. Morgan exhibited atypical traits for a middle-class Progressive reformer. Building and controlling small orderly communities, instead of cleaning up already existing communities such as slums, appealed to Morgan. He also focused his attention on rural, and not urban, reform. He favored Americanizing the immigrants, not restricting their arrival on American shores, but at the same time he feared a decline in the hereditary quality of the next generation. Morgan's elitist attitude toward race and heredity contradicted his belief that, through hard work and moral actions, anyone could improve themselves. While relying on government leaders to accomplish reforms through legislation and exposure of corruption, Morgan took an apolitical stance on most issues. Throughout this period Morgan refined his thinking about establishing a more organized society, through reform, moral uplift, government oversight, elimination of competition based on economic gain, and community building. By 1916, with the work of the Miami Conservancy District just beginning and Progressivism at high tide, Morgan had a voice, career, vision, and purpose.

The first year of the twentieth century, 1901, marks the beginning of the modern era and a jumping-off point for Progressivism. The assassination of President William McKinley by an anarchist, Leon Czolgosz, in September 1901 led to the ascendancy of conservationist, imperialist, and Progressive leader, then–Vice President Theodore Roosevelt. During Roosevelt's presidency, 1901–1909, Progressive reform took root through legislation and civic organizations. At the same time, middle-class reformers embraced a strong faith in human improvement and set out to regulate an industrial society in need of organization. This wave of reformers established larger objectives, such as prohibition, suffrage, and political reform goals, which would not be fully realized for another decade.[6]

In 1901, Arthur Morgan was literally miles away from urban reformers and emerging Progressive efforts. That winter and spring he worked cutting cordwood in the forests near Stearns County, Minnesota. The laborious work took a toll on Morgan, and he turned to the St. Cloud public library and his diary for solace. Despite his isolation Morgan remained current with modern developments and recorded some of his deepest thoughts on society, reform, and progress. Most notable, and foretelling of his future, were Morgan's diary entries on the great potential for improving America in the new century.[7]

In January, he read Edward Bellamy's book *Equality* (1897) and declared it "A great book—great in its dreams. Let all the people read it." The follow-up to *Looking Backward*, *Equality* continued the story of Julian West and his adjustment to life in the year 2000. The book criticized the profit-system and called for government regulation of the economy, society, and industries. But the Nationalist movement that Bellamy launched in the 1890s was all but dormant by the end of the nineteenth century. Bellamy's death from tuberculosis in 1898 effectively ended Nationalism as a political movement, and what did survive became absorbed into other reform and political movements of period. Twenty-two-year-old Morgan found great truth in Bellamy's ideals, and revisited them for many decades.[8]

Morgan followed political movements and took great interest in the platform of the Social Democratic Party, a predecessor to the Socialist Party of America, founded in July of that year. In January, he declared that "I have been finding myself for the last two or three years inclining toward socialism. It seems right to me that cooperation of production should succeed the present system of competition." Morgan recognized the growing gap between the elite and working class, and pointed to the extreme waste generated by a capitalist society. Instead, Morgan believed in the creation of a "new and higher order of society" without class distinctions and based on cooperation.[9]

Morgan reflected on social problems and attitudes of the modern era. He found society full of waste, competition, and lacking a moral compass. His solutions were thrift, restraint, and what he called "social purity." In January, he explained that "we must be true . . . simple . . . orderly and economical" and leave behind the "diplomacy, policy, and expediency" of the nineteenth century. According to Morgan, collectivism needed to displace individualism as the driving force in society. In particular, Morgan took issue with vice and leisure spending, saying, "one ninth of the wages of American labor are spent for alcoholic drink. To this if we add tobacco, coffee, tea, spices, meats, frivolous food, frivolous clothes, bad literature and the loss through other leak holes perhaps more than half of the workman's wages are thrown away." He applied those objections to reformers, even criticizing Bellamy's utopian characters in *Looking Backward* for smoking cigars. His displeasure at the consumption of alcohol, tobacco, coffee, and tea continued for decades—no one ever accused Morgan of being the life of any party.[10]

Morgan also took issue with the disjointed nature of reform and offered his solutions. He charged that reformers were too individualistic and narrow in their approaches to progress. Morgan believed that unified reform would bring social purity and progress. Controlling the environment lay at the heart of Morgan's reform philosophy. Like other reformers, Morgan embraced scientific approaches to solving social ills. In February, Morgan wrote that "my life has been lived in possession of the scientific temperament. I try to rule life by system and by brain." Morgan's scientific mind embraced the theory of social Darwinism and natural selection as part of social evolution. He stated that the ideal environment will nurture the ideal man, and that "the man approaching nearest to the ideal is the man to be selected to perpetuate the race." Further, Morgan added that it was immoral and cruel to perpetuate the lesser races through their unfortunate inheritance. Morgan's racial attitudes, which would later align him with the eugenics movement, were common for a majority of white, middle-class Progressive reformers. Although Morgan upheld the tenet of Christian morality to improve society, he did not embrace religion or the Social Gospel movement as an avenue to effective reforms. Instead, in the coming decades, he found strength among other learned professionals who were consumed with control, efficiency, and plotting designs for a better tomorrow.[11]

In 1901, Morgan delivered his reform message to local audiences. In August, he founded the Granite City Club, a civic organization that promoted and publicized "reform experiments" to St. Cloud citizens. Through the meetings and publications of the group, Morgan expressed great optimism for reform. He noted that "America is capable of producing anything" and stressed the importance of having differing and common interests (or "faculties" as Morgan called them) within the members of society. While commercial faculties were an expected part of society, Morgan believed that other common faculties would "attract the nation's attention first." Morgan then expected that the higher faculties, those which might benefit the most people, would prevail over the more individualistic or lower faculties.[12]

In September, Morgan wrote a contemplative diary entry about the assassination of President McKinley and a memorial service that he attended at the St. Cloud Unity Church. He noted that "I doubt if ever before during the history of government were so many people drawn together voluntarily to mourn their chief as were together today at the memorial services of McKinley." The outpouring of sympathy for McKinley moved Morgan to note that "only liberty can produce such unity and such love." Although the assassin, Leon Czolgosz, was in custody, many unanswered questions existed about anarchists. In his diary, Morgan emphasized the importance of reforming society in order to suppress anarchists and the atrocities that they cause. He stated that "it was a long, long while before people found out what mosquitoes mean, but now they are beginning to drain the swamps. Not until we drain some other swamps will assassination cease." In spite of such an unimaginable act committed by a dangerous anarchist, Morgan's asserted that the overwhelming national unity "testifies well for McKinley and for present civilization."[13]

The assassination of President McKinley in the fall of 1901 set in motion a number of changes in American society and politics. As the able-bodied Theodore Roosevelt took the reins of leadership, a wave of Progressivism began to build. Riding the crest of this reform phenomenon were emerging leaders in their fields and communities. During the first decade and a half of the twentieth century, Morgan and many others set the tone for reform and carried America into the modern era.

By the fall of 1901, Arthur Morgan had convinced his father John Morgan to allow him to learn the surveying trade. John Morgan, then the County Surveyor of Stearns County and City Engineer of St. Cloud, agreed for his son to accompany him as a laborer. The twenty-three-year-old spent long hours in the field and in the office with his father. Morgan later recalled, "I watched his every action, how he appraised evidence, how he mediated disputes, how he used his instruments, made notes, handled his crew of helpers, made charges for his services, and overcame difficulties." For the next six months, Morgan learned from his father not only the technical aspects of surveying, but how to handle clients and settle boundary disputes. The precision of the work and the ability to set controls on the environment appealed to Morgan. While John Morgan had never made a comfortable living as a surveyor and discouraged his son from following his footsteps, Arthur Morgan believed that with initiative he could find success.[14]

After about six months as an apprentice to his father, in the spring of 1902, Morgan started a surveying business on his own. He secured work locally, mostly divining property lines, sewer lines, and street grades. The work proved steady, but that fall Morgan secured a position as a timber cruiser in the Red Lake Indian reservation in northern Minnesota. The position, which involved measuring and selecting prime hardwoods for harvesting, paid $8.00 per day, nearly twice what surveyors made. Morgan secured endorsement from his congressman, and in November 1902, Morgan joined a four-man timber crew. He spent the next nine months surveying and measuring virgin timber. Morgan resigned in July 1903, largely because he objected to reporting full days of work when only half of the day had been worked, to return to surveying.[15]

Morgan's return to St. Cloud in the summer of 1903 prompted an important business decision. Because of the great overlap in their work, John and Arthur Morgan decided to jointly incorporate their surveying business as "Morgan and Morgan." They agreed to handle their incomes and projects separately. John Morgan benefited by having his son organize scattered business records covering several decades, while Arthur Morgan gained new contacts and improved his reputation by the simple association. Administrative support from Jessie Morgan, John's daughter and Arthur's older sister, further bonded the family business.[16]

As a young surveyor, Morgan took a particular interest in drainage work. He explained, "I considered sanitary engineering, water supply engineering, structural, railroad, bridge and other special fields of engineering, and settled upon land reclamation and flood control because little was known of these fields, and I was not much worse off than other engineers." The ability to reclaim unproductive and thus wasted land through scientific calculations and

Arthur Morgan as a timber cruiser, 1902. Antiochiana, Antioch College.

public works projects (installing drainage tile, building contoured ditches, and draining swamps) embodied one facet of Progressivism. Drainage work also figured into efforts of conservationists, like Theodore Roosevelt, to preserve pristine areas while improving others. Morgan recognized the demand for drainage work far exceeded the supply. From 1900 to 1904, engineers reclaimed seven million acres of land in the United States and during the following four years the number skyrocketed to eighteen million acres. With such a market open for drainage engineers, Morgan expected that practical experience would be more important than formal education in the burgeoning field. In fact, colleges offered no formal courses in drainage engineering, which put Morgan in an equal position with educated engineers also hoping to break into the field.[17]

Morgan took great responsibility for furthering his self-education. During the winters, slow periods for surveying, Morgan traveled extensively to visit drainage projects. He spoke with engineers, contractors, professors, and the common laborers about the issues of drainage work. During his fieldwork, Morgan devoted evenings to studying drainage engineering texts while his laborers played cards. Morgan bragged that he had never learned to play cards and did not even know the names of the cards or suits. His sobriety and concentration paid off. Morgan expanded his surveying and drainage work far beyond Stearns County into other parts of the state.[18]

While the openness of the drainage field attracted self-educated engineers like Morgan, there were few regulations and standards to regulate such public works. By 1904, Morgan had completed about a dozen reclamation projects. But he found that the state's drainage codes were antiquated and unable to meet the demands of the modern era. As an example, if a swamp straddled city or county boundaries, conflicting codes had to be resolved by the state legislature before any drainage work could take place. At that time, almost all state legislatures passed individual drainage laws as new needs arose and projects were proposed. John and Arthur Morgan realized the need for a more universal approach to codifying drainage laws. Both men understood that river and drainage systems must be treated as an entire unit, regardless of political boundaries.[19]

In 1904, the Morgans attended the annual meeting of the Minnesota Engineers and Surveyors Society to discuss this issue with other professionals. As a result, the committee on legislation added John to their committee to help draft a preliminary bill for the legislature to consider. However,

Minnesota Engineers and Surveyors Society Meeting, 1905. Arthur Morgan, standing far right. Antiochiana, Antioch College.

Arthur became the active behind-the-scenes voice for his father. The younger Morgan immersed himself in the existing legislation and court decisions related to drainage work. He wrote to county commissioners, local attorneys, engineers, surveyors, and members of the legislature informing them of the committee's work. Morgan also offered any interested parties the chance to read a preliminary draft of the proposed bill. As a result, about one hundred people accepted the invitation and returned their comments to Morgan for consideration.[20]

In January 1905, after nearly a year of work on the drainage bill, the Morgans traveled to St. Paul for a meeting of the Minnesota Engineers and Surveyors Society. The society focused its entire meeting on the work of the legislative committee and the draft bill on drainage codification. To increase communication with the state's legislatures, the society secured meeting space in a room in the capital building nearly adjacent to the house chamber, where legislative sessions were underway. At the end of the society's meeting, the legislative committee submitted their draft bill to the state House of Representatives for consideration. By February, the Minnesota legislature passed the bill into law. The 1905 drainage laws relaxed the restrictions on drainage projects that crossed county lines. The law acknowledged the great need for this revision by insisting that reclamation projects would result in public health benefits, road improvements, recovered lands, and improved infrastructure.[21]

Arthur Morgan's involvement with the 1905 drainage bill marked an important professional and political plateau for the young engineer. Morgan's work on the project fully took him out of the giant shadow cast by his father. Members of the Minnesota Engineers and Surveyors Society appointed Morgan as their secretary-treasurer and editor of their annual publication. His close work with drainage control engineers, most of whom had the academic credentials that he lacked, improved his professional reputation. But perhaps most important, Morgan's work with politicians also solidified his name at the state level as an emerging figure in land reclamation. As evidence of this notoriety, in the summer of 1905 Minnesota Governor John Albert Johnson offered Morgan the position of State Engineer (Morgan declined in order to spend more time with his family). The following year, Johnson asked Morgan to represent the state as a delegate to the National Drainage Congress, which he attended and at which he presented a paper on the costs of land reclamation. By 1907, the twenty-nine-year-old managed thirty reclamation projects and dozens of employees. In particular, the company completed improvement projects on several Minnesota river systems, including the Clearwater, Sauk, Long Prairie, Watab, Crow, Chippewa, and Elk rivers. By that time, Morgan and Morgan had become the largest drainage engineering company in the state. As Morgan found great professional success, he also focused on his personal life and family.[22]

When Arthur Morgan returned to St. Cloud in the summer of 1903, after his work as a timber cruiser, he met a young osteopath named Urania Jones (whom he called "Ranie"). Her family had moved to the small town the previous year. Urania, the oldest daughter in the Jones family, held a Doctor of Osteopathy degree from the Still College of Osteopathy in Kirksville, Missouri. While a student, she studied under Andrew Taylor Still, the founder of osteopathic medicine. Still based his holistic approaches to medicine on the importance of the musculoskeletal system to human health. Urania established herself in St. Cloud's medical community and opened her own osteopathic practice in 1904. An ambitious professional, Urania planned to attend medical school and earn a M.D.[23]

Arthur Morgan and Urania Jones, 1904. Antiochiana, Antioch College.

Urania's ambitious temperament and emphasis on natural ways of healing (such as not prescribing medicine) appealed to Morgan. He once described her as "a modern American woman with self reliance, strength, intelligence, will and all those qualities which go to make strong womanhood." The two began dating in the fall of 1903 and the next year became engaged. In September 1904, while Morgan focused on researching drainage laws, the two were married. While tending to her medical practice, Urania also provided secretarial support for the Morgan and Morgan firm. In July 1905, she gave birth to a son, Arthur Ernest Morgan Jr., who they called Ernest. At nearly the same time, Governor Johnson offered Morgan the position of State Engineer. Morgan declined the appointment in order to spend more time with his young family.[24]

Tragedy struck the Morgan family that fall. A few months after giving birth, Urania contracted typhoid fever, and, in November 1905, she died. She left behind a four-month-old infant and a grieving husband. Arthur immediately took Ernest to live with his parents, John and Anna. The loss of his wife led Arthur to revisit his own fragile health. Afraid that his meningitis would return and leave Ernest an orphan, he began writing lengthy letters and notes for Ernest to read at later points in his life. During the following year, Morgan also dealt with his grief by increasing his workload and travel. In 1906, he initiated dozens of reclamation projects across the state. Although Morgan's family life was difficult, by early 1907 he achieved enormous success and established his reputation as a drainage control engineer.[25]

In 1907, Morgan embarked on another professional challenge. During the early part of that year, Charles Elliott, a government engineer, contacted Morgan about government service. Elliott heard Morgan speak at both the January 1905 meeting of the Minnesota Engineers and Surveyors Society and the 1906 National Drainage Congress. Impressed with Morgan's skill and precision, Elliott offered Morgan an opportunity to be a Supervising Drainage Engineer with the Department of Agriculture's Drainage Investigations department. To qualify, Morgan needed to take and record a high score on the Civil Service Examination, cease any competing work with his private firm, and move to wherever survey work might take him. The professional opportunity and the transient lifestyle (which might distance him from memories of Urania) appealed to for Morgan.[26]

Apart from private firms and small state efforts, since the 1890s the United States government led the way in identifying and funding irrigation and drainage projects. In 1887, Congress passed the Hatch Act which created the Office of Experiment Stations within the Department of Agriculture. This department authorized cooperative federal and state agricultural research programs. Besides establishing agricultural offices in all states and territories, this bureau was responsible for addressing nationwide agricultural concerns. The use of water for irrigation was one of these concerns, and in 1898, Congress appropriated to the Office $35,000 towards irrigation research. To manage this work, the Office created an Irrigation Investigations Division. This branch provided direct technical aid for irrigation programs throughout the country. Local money had to pay for the actual construction of the projects, but the federal government provided free analysis and planning. With help from the state experiment stations, the Division studied the irrigation laws for each area, determined the amounts of water available, and analyzed acceptable irrigation methods.[27]

In 1902, the Department of Agriculture assigned special agents for drainage in the Office of Experiment Stations. The work of the drainage officers expanded and in 1904 the Division officially became the Irrigation and Drainage Division. For the next three years, drainage and irrigation work progressed. The Division conducted surveys throughout the western

Drainage Investigations Staff, 1908. Arthur Morgan is seated on front row, second from left. Antiochiana, Antioch College.

states, including California, Nevada, Utah, and Arizona, and across the eastern states such as Maryland, Massachusetts, Arkansas, and Florida. Congress supported their research, and yearly appropriations jumped from $67,500 in 1904 to $150,000 by 1907. With such growth, in July 1907, the Office of Experiment Stations separated the research areas into two specific divisions: the Irrigation Investigations Division and the Drainage Investigations Division.[28]

Charles Elliott served as the first chief of Drainage Investigations. Before his government tenure, he worked as a civil engineer for twenty-five years, mostly completing farm drainage projects in the north central states and geologic investigations in western oil fields. Elliott was a pioneer in agricultural drainage and, in 1895, prepared the Department of Agriculture's first bulletin on the subject. In 1902, he became a special agent for drainage for the Office of Experiment Stations, and in 1904 headed the drainage activities for the Irrigation and Drainage Division, under the supervision of Elwood Mead. Then, in the summer of 1907, Elliott became chief of the newly created Drainage Investigations Division.[29]

That spring Arthur Morgan and about two hundred others took the Civil Service Examination for employment with Drainage Investigations. He and three others (two of those three were Elliott's staff and had actually written the exam) scored high enough for an appointment as a Supervising Engineer. These engineers would oversee the fieldwork for projects proposed by boosters, state governments, or even real estate agents, and write feasibility reports. With the position, Morgan hoped to gain a good deal of technical knowledge that he lacked. In early 1907, John Morgan retired from Morgan and Morgan, and his son found an able partner, Walter Wilson, to run their new enterprise in his absence. Morgan traveled to Washington, D.C., that summer, leaving his infant son with his parents to nurture and Wilson to oversee the engineering business.[30]

After some orientation work in the nation's capitol, Morgan received his first assignment for Drainage Investigations. Morgan requested that he be given work in an area familiar to him, but the division assigned him a three-month study of the alkali lands and their reclamation in the San Luis Valley of Colorado. Morgan later revealed that initially he did not fully understand the definition of "alkali land." But following his own process of studying texts, searching for case studies, and talking with people, he became an expert on the topic. At the end of the project, Morgan concluded that too much irrigation had resulted in soil with an excess of mineral salts. His report led to the reclamation of about 5,000 acres in the San Luis Valley.[31]

For the next two years, Morgan traipsed across the swamps, marshes, and river valleys of the South. He completed surveys and wrote reports for sites across the states of Louisiana, Arkansas, North Carolina, and Mississippi, and provided plans for the reclamation of 1.1 million acres of unimproved land. Morgan learned that the government had not allotted enough funds for a thorough examination of each project, and thus he began submitting incomplete expense reports and paying the remainder from his own out-of-pocket funds. The thorough young engineer also worked additional days on projects, far beyond what the government expected or would pay for. In fact, Morgan often refused to take his next assignment until he had completed work on the task at hand. During trips back to Washington to write the final reports, Morgan learned that financial allotments were based, not on drainage needs, but on the wishes of influential congressmen and special interests. He also realized that many of his Drainage Investigations colleagues were swayed by financial promises of landowners and speculators. Even in a period of a government openness and reform, Morgan discovered a great deal of dishonesty and corruption.[32]

Morgan found his government fieldwork grueling and lonely. Often traveling by canoe or horseback in low-lying areas, Morgan contracted malaria and had frequent bouts of sickness. During his times of illness, Morgan wrote detailed letters to Ernest about the realities of his adventures. In a letter dated May 31, 1908, from Newport, Arkansas, Morgan explained that he had been "technically dishonest" in submitting his bills to the government. But, Morgan assured his son that "I did more for my money and gave the people better service for the money" than the regular allotment would have provided. Everywhere Morgan looked, he told his son, there was grafting and dishonest people trying to make a profit. Unlike Morgan's positive recollections of traveling through Colorado a decade before, he wrote Ernest saying that "traveling is demoralizing . . . seldom do I meet a man who is large minded and intelligent and yet is pure and holy in his life and loves his fellow man." He closed the letter reminding Ernest not follow in his footsteps of professional and moral failure.[33]

Despite Morgan's depression and self-loathing about government service, he managed to record significant and even happy personal moments during this period. While he was in Washington, D.C., writing final reports, Morgan's family often visited him. In May 1908, he recorded a fascinating diary entry about one of those visits. On May 17, Morgan wrote that "As Ernest and I were taking a walk, we met President Roosevelt going to church. His big silk hat was on the back of his head and he had a stride like a giant. He smiled at the boy as he passed and waved his hand at him." The next year, while in the Boston area, Morgan visited a friend at Wellesley College. The friend introduced Morgan to Lucy Middleton Griscom, an instructor of chemistry and home economics at Wellesley. A staunch Quaker, she held a master's degree in the chemistry of nutrition and impressed Morgan with her intellect and concern for social issues of the time. The three friends spent a sunny April day canoeing along the Charles River and ended their excursion with a picnic. Morgan returned to the swamps of Arkansas smitten by Lucy; the couple married two years later.[34]

In 1909, the same year that Morgan met his future wife, he rekindled his interest in writing non-technical pieces. While working on a drainage survey in northwest Arkansas, Morgan befriended relatives of Abraham Lincoln's stepsister. Morgan had extended conversations with the descendants and learned a great deal of obscure information about Lincoln's boyhood and family. After this discovery, Morgan developed a lifelong fascination with Lincoln and began accumulating research material. In a February 12, 1909, letter, Morgan stated: "My boy, get acquainted with Lincoln . . . try to catch his sprit. It is like the spirit of Christ." Morgan explained that, unlike most men, Lincoln "was not unmindful of the past and the lessons it taught; but he did not limit his life by the experience of the past." He upheld Lincoln as the ideal leader, citizen, and man. Twelve years later, Morgan's conversations with Lincoln's forgotten and undiscovered family members appeared as an article in *Atlantic Monthly* with the title "New Light on Lincoln's Boyhood."[35]

Morgan's fieldwork in Arkansas during 1908 and 1909 represents the largest and most significant engineering project he directed while a Supervising Engineer for Drainage Investigations. A million acres of fertile land, located in the St. Francis River drainage basin in eastern Arkansas and Missouri just behind the levees of the Mississippi River, were ripe for reclamation. Timber companies requested the survey, but farmers, real estate agents, and other small industries would also benefit from the recovery of this land. Despite Morgan's "dishonesty" with the government's time and money, his detailed reports put him ahead of more qualified Supervising Engineers. Starting in the fall of 1908, the thirty-year-old supervised six survey parties totaling nearly fifty workers. The cost of the project totaled $13,000, and at that time it was the most expensive project undertaken by Drainage Investigations. The fieldwork ended in March 1909, and Morgan retreated to Washington, D.C., with six months of data to begin work on the report.[36]

As with many large-scale surveys that affected so many, Morgan released a preliminary report of his findings and recommendations. In July, the Government Printing Office published a thirty-one page preliminary survey, or circular, to the public. The document presented a plan to reclaim 4,000 square miles of land in Missouri and 1,500 square miles in Arkansas. Morgan recommended construction of new flood channels, guarded by dikes or levees, to divert excess rainwater. The cost amounted to nearly $7 million, or about $8 per acre, which would be less than ten percent of the cost needed to improve natural channels for the same purpose. The preliminary report satisfied many of the interested parties and that summer Morgan focused on completing the full report. That document appeared two years later and totaled 158 pages of detailed text and charts. With the St. Francis River survey and its report, the self-taught Morgan had earned his stripes as a thorough, precise, and methodical engineer. Morgan's growing reputation as an expert

Arthur Morgan (seated at far right) with survey crew working for Drainage Investigations, 1908. Antiochiana, Antioch College.

on large-scale reclamation studies resulted in his accidental involvement in another and even more significant Drainage Investigations project taking place in Florida.[37]

During the spring and summer of 1909, Morgan stationed himself in the office of Drainage Investigations in Washington, D.C., to work on his full report of the St. Francis River survey. The work was tedious, but Morgan found diversions while in the nation's capital, such as watching an airplane flight demonstrated by Orville Wright. That summer Morgan was the top-ranking engineer in the office, and he assumed responsibility for reviewing incoming time-sensitive reports. In early August, with division chief Charles Elliott absent, the assistant chief A. D. Morehouse assigned Morgan the task of reviewing page proofs of a Drainage Investigations report on the reclamation of the Florida Everglades. Morgan knew nothing about the survey and little about the Everglades, but he realized the ramifications of such a government-endorsed plan and postponed work on his St. Francis River report.[38]

The origins of the Florida Everglades survey report helps clarify Morgan's sudden role with the project and the later controversy. At the dawn of the twentieth century, the Department of Agriculture considered the Everglades an important area worthy of reclamation study. In 1904, Charles Elliott, with support from Florida governor William S. Jennings, cousin of William Jennings Bryan, made a preliminary survey of the region. He explored an area from sixty miles north of Miami to twenty-five miles south and west into the Everglades. Elliott never questioned whether the area could be improved, and suggested a plan of gradual reclamation, beginning with relatively small units near the coasts. He estimated that reclamation would cost $50 per acre, but stressed that more detailed studies of the region were still needed.[39]

Reclamation became an important issue in Florida's 1904 gubernatorial campaign. Napoleon Bonaparte Broward won the election and announced that the drainage of the entire Everglades region would result in new heights of prosperity and greatness to the state. In February 1905, he and a group of engineers made an inspection tour of the Lake Okeechobee region. Broward's investigation attracted attention from Elliott, who informed Broward that the government would assist their efforts to drain the Everglades. Broward responded to Elliott's inquiry and declared that the Division of Irrigation and Drainage Investigations would "be of great assistance" to their endeavor. In January 1906, Elliott met with Broward in Tallahassee to discuss the division's role in reclamation efforts. After this first encounter, Elliott reported that the governor "has a sort of plan of his own and is evidently the engineer as well as the promoter and pusher of the whole drainage scheme." Following the meeting, Secretary of Agriculture James Wilson endorsed the division's involvement with the project. Later that summer, Wilson ordered a lengthy examination of the region.[40]

Despite such assurances, Wilson only designated $11,000 for the Everglades survey (an amount less than Morgan had been given for the much smaller St. Francis River project). Elliott, who had previously made a survey of the region, scoffed at the project, saying that an adequate study of the Everglades region would cost approximately $150,000 and require considerable time, perhaps a year, to complete. Elliott announced that the proposed survey would be inaccurate, and he refused to take the project. Wilson then asked James O. Wright, one of Elliott's supervising engineers, to undertake the work. Wright accepted and planned for the first complete engineering survey of the Everglades.[41]

Wright oversaw two surveys of the region during the winters of 1907 and 1908. During the second survey, Wright created a good deal of publicity for the project. While in Miami, in February 1908, he addressed three hundred land owners and growers about the possibility of draining the Everglades. Wright reported that his message was well received and "generally discussed in the streets the following morning." He believed that his efforts would help support Governor Broward's reclamation mandates during the 1908 elections. However, reclamation opponents claimed that Wright was indicating the conclusions of his forthcoming report before the surveys were completed.[42]

In March, Elliott reprimanded Wright for the public statements. Elliott advised that prematurely releasing engineering data related to an issue that had created sharp differences of opinion throughout the state was unwise. He explained to Wright that, "the object of our work is to quietly investigate the facts relating to the physical, economic, and engineering features of the situation," and not to endorse or denounce plans for the area. Elliott ordered Wright not to make any public statements without consent from the Department of Agriculture, until his report had been delivered to the division. Wright responded two weeks later, explaining that his talk was only to educate Miami landowners and growers interested in their work. He agreed with Wright and explained that his lecture was "in no sense a premature discussion of our report, or a statement of what it will contain." In May 1908, Wright ended his survey and started work on the final report. Wright completed a draft for Elliott to review on February 25, 1909.[43]

At that same time, political pressure forced Secretary Wilson to allow release of information from the draft report, before it had even been approved by the division. The extracted data recommended building new canals and other improvements at a cost of $2 million, or a little less than $1 per acre. Florida governor Albert Gilchrist distributed the information to the members of the legislature and declared that through publicity he could secure enough federal funds to complete the drainage project. By this time, Elliott had completed a review of Wright's report and offered a number of suggestions. Elliott warned that Wright's plans and estimates were tentative, and called for additional review before the final printing. In August, the government board of censors returned page proofs back to the division for further review or final endorsement.[44]

Thus, in August 1909, with both Elliott and Wright absent, assistant chief Morehouse gave the top engineer in the office, Arthur Morgan, the page proofs of the Everglades report to review. Morgan's role expanded because of the constant flow of letters to the division that summer from interested entrepreneurs, usually of small means, asking about the merits of the project. Some of the writers stated that they were prepared to invest their life savings in small tracts of soon-to-be-reclaimed Everglades real estate already being advertised by land companies. During the middle of Morgan's review, Morehouse asked Morgan to speak with Harold Wheeler, a land company representative. Armed with a copy of Wright's excerpt, Wheeler questioned the accuracy of cost estimates and evaporation levels. Morgan supplied Wheeler with few answers, but assured him that the final report issued by the division would be accurate.[45]

As the entire reclamation plan hinged on the report, Morgan knew that the correctness of the Wright's findings would have great ramifications on the area's future development. Following Wheeler's visit, Morgan finished reviewing the draft and concluded that "the engineering was greatly inadequate, that the favorable conclusions which were stated were entirely unjustified, and that anyone buying a small tract of land would probably lose his entire investment." Therefore, he suggested to Morehouse that the report be reexamined by Elliott before final publication approval. Morehouse agreed, and Morgan wrote Elliott explaining the inaccuracies of the report and suggested that the publication should be postponed. Perhaps because of political pressure, Elliott disagreed, insisting that the draft should be published despite the errors. Elliott explained that he had added qualifying statements to some of the chapters and that urgency demanded the release of the long overdue report.[46]

Morgan and Morehouse understood Elliott's arguments but still refused to approve the report. They believed the inaccuracies were too serious to publish, so again they wrote Elliott, this time stating that the report would remain on hold until his return. Although Elliott preferred immediate publication, the actions of Morehouse and Morgan demonstrated to him that a closer review was necessary, and he telegrammed them saying that he endorsed their decision. Elliott returned to Washington on October 13, 1909. After a conference with Morgan and Morehouse, Elliott reexamined the report only to discover "serious faults and discrepancies." Elliott agreed with their conclusions and officially withdrew the manuscript from the publication process. To rectify the situation, Elliott scheduled a meeting with Wright.[47]

Morgan's actions with the Wright report may seem of little consequence to his life and career. He had merely drawn attention to a report that needed additional review and raised somewhat ordinary objections about an official government publication. But the Everglades project proved to be the largest and most important survey done by Drainage Investigations up to that time. The economic ramifications of the Everglades report far eclipsed Morgan's St. Francis River work. By the fall of 1909, it appeared to Morgan and many others in the division that the situation with the Wright report was finished. Morgan expected the report to be rewritten with accurate data and cost estimates, whether or not such information would make draining southern Florida a feasible reality. For the remainder of 1909, Morgan finished writing his St. Francis River report and largely forgot about the Florida Everglades survey. Two years later, however, he once again found himself knee-deep in the controversy.

Morgan's dissatisfaction with government service began almost as soon as he began work for Drainage Investigations. The realities of patronage appointments, dishonest reporting, and insufficient allocations of both time and funding proved too much for his moral temperament. Yet the experience gave Morgan newfound confidence in his ability. During his two-year stint, he managed large field teams scattered across hundreds of miles, collected and interpreted vast amounts of mathematical data, and wrote detailed reports for publication. Through this work, Morgan expanded his administrative skills and learned how to direct complex engineering projects. Past surveys in the southern states of Arkansas, Louisiana, and Mississippi demonstrated to Morgan the need for reclamation in the region. In 1909, Morgan decided to return to private practice, this time focusing only on the reclamation of swamp lands. He resigned his position as supervising engineer in late 1909, but retained his status as a consultant for Drainage Investigations.[48]

On New Year's Day 1910, Morgan and Leroy L. Hidinger, a fellow Drainage Investigations supervising engineer, founded the Morgan Engineering Company. They based their enterprise in Memphis, Tennessee, to have close access to the swamps of the lower Mississippi River Valley. Their first brochure announced that the company was "prepared to take entire charge of drainage engineering projects of whatever size; to make surveys, to prepare plans and estimates, and to superintend construction." The Morgan Engineering Company offered farmers and speculators the opportunity to reclaim lands that were overflowed, damaged by erosion, or in need of irrigation. Morgan added to his team other experts in the field of hydraulic and drainage engineering, as well as other professionals familiar with water power development.[49]

During the next two years, Morgan Engineering Company prospered. The company secured contracts in Arkansas, Missouri, Louisiana, and Tennessee. By 1912, Morgan's team completed surveys and drainage work for over 2 million acres of unusable land across over 100 drainage districts. The most notable projects included work on the Forked Deer River system in west Tennessee and the Little River Drainage District in southeast Missouri. The company often collaborated with Drainage Investigations during the survey phase, but thereafter the company became the chief engineer on projects, setting construction schedules and arranging for the various contractors to complete the work. By 1912, Morgan Engineering Company had secured contracts to be chief engineer for projects totaling nearly $7 million.[50]

While in Memphis, Arthur Morgan added a great deal of stability to his life. Success with his engineering company resulted in financial solvency, which would last throughout his life. His ascendancy in the water-control engineering profession, all without formal education, brought his admission as an associate member to the American Society of Civil Engineering in 1910. But more importantly, in 1911, he married Lucy Griscom, and the two settled in a modest Memphis neighborhood. Morgan's son Ernest joined them, and, in 1912, Lucy gave birth to another son named Griscom and, two years later, to a daughter, Frances. As president of an expanding enterprise, Morgan maintained a hectic travel schedule for the business, but during this period he managed to spend a good deal of time with his growing family. Missing from Morgan's diary were fears of ill health and a sense of aimlessness; in their place were happy entries of a satisfied home life.[51]

Morgan adapted well to living in Memphis. At the time, Edward H. Crump began a term as mayor and set about improving the city. Crump represented the bossism and cronyism of the past, as well as the Progressive spirit of the time. Morgan's entry into the professional middle class brought him in contact with other successful businessmen. He became close friends with Memphis investment banker Bolton Smith, who spoke against lynching. Smith founded a group called "The Egyptians" to discuss scientific, religious, and economic issues of the time. The club, which Morgan joined, consisted of other influential middle and upper class Memphians. Morgan tried Unitarian church services, but shifted his religious allegiance to a Society of Friends branch attended by his wife Lucy. In 1912, Morgan discovered that his new Progressive friends in Memphis could help him with a smoldering issue.[52]

In January 1912, Arthur Morgan learned that his former supervisor, Charles Elliott, faced serious charges. The Department of Agriculture alleged that Elliott submitted false expense vouchers during 1909 field expeditions for Drainage Investigations. Elliott faced termination as chief of the division and reached out for Morgan's help. At the heart of the issue lay Elliott's suppression of the Florida Everglades report, penned by Charles Wright back in 1909 and first held up by Arthur Morgan. By 1912, a group of politicians and speculators with great financial interest in reclamation of the Everglades resurrected Wright's original report, despite Elliott's opposition. As an engineer in private practice, Morgan had little to lose by helping his colleague and a great deal to gain as a Progressive reformer by exposing corruption.

After Morgan left Drainage Investigations in late 1909, Wright's Everglades report remained a political hot potato. In early 1910, Elliott significantly reworked Wright's report and submitted a "second version" to Secretary of Agriculture James Wilson for publication. But at the same time, Florida's Drainage Commission hired James Wright as their chief drainage engineer to implement the plans originally described in the first version of the unpublished report. The division distanced itself from Wright and the report, keeping the latter from the printer, and focused on other reclamation projects.[53]

In fall 1911, because of the growing interest from potential investors, lawmakers took issue with Wright's suppressed composition. On August 7, Utah senator Reed Smoot (R) introduced a resolution to have an omnibus of material on the Florida Everglades published as a Senate Document. The Senate approved the resolution, and Florida senator Duncan Fletcher (D), a pro-drainage activist, took on the responsibility to prepare the document. As to Elliott's changes, Fletcher ignored the revisions and ordered that the Senate document include the original 1909 Wright report. The Government Printing Office published an omnibus of Everglades-related material in December 1911. Drainage Investigations issued a memorandum explaining that Fletcher had ignored Elliott's revisions. Elliott later stated that the inclusion of Wright's original 1909 report as part of an official government publication revealed the enormous political influence of those selling un-drained Everglades lands. Fletcher denied his connection with land companies, and claimed that when he took responsibility for compiling documents for the Senate Document, he knew nothing about the complicated history of the Wright report.[54]

In early 1912, while the national press circulated rumors about the controversial Wright report, the Department of Agriculture charged that Charles Elliott had submitted false expense reports. The department prepared to remove Elliott from his position and stated that their actions had nothing to do with the Everglades matter. Florida congressman Frank Clark (D), representing the anti-drainage camp, demanded a full investigation of the Wright report and the accusations against Elliot. Clark and others charged that Department of Agriculture officials had been influenced by land promoters to suppress any reports that showed reclamation of Everglades to be unfavorable. He also argued that any attempt to remove Elliott was because he had refused to suppress any unfavorable reports.[55]

In January 1912, Arthur Morgan reappeared on the scene of the unfolding Everglades controversy. Morgan doubted any impropriety by his former supervisor, and once stated that Elliott was so "punctiliously honest . . . that he carried two lead pencils, one for official and one for personal use." At the end of January 1912, Morgan wrote Secretary Wilson. In the letter, he reviewed the engineering inadequacies of Wright's report and asserted that "the suppression of the document was a proper move." He mentioned that he had contacted other professional engineers with "national reputation[s]" who also verified that Wright's report was flawed. Morgan knew that Wilson was under great pressure to explain his reasons for suppressing Wright's report, but he stated in the letter that the push to remove Elliott resulted from real estate promoters attempting to prevent Elliott from speaking.[56]

Morgan's first effort did little to rectify the situation, and a few days later Wilson removed Elliott from his position. Elliott's removal and the building publicity for the Everglades work led Congress to begin hearings before the committee on expenditures that February. While the lengthy proceedings began in Washington, Morgan defended Elliott elsewhere. He first wrote Representative Clark about Elliott's difficult situation. Morgan explained that suppression of the report had been an embarrassment to the higher officials of the Department, especially Wilson, and therefore Elliott could not defend himself from attacks by land companies without incriminating Wilson. Morgan agreed with Clark that the Department of Agriculture had concocted false charges against Elliott in order to silence him.[57]

Morgan next took the matter to the local press in Memphis. In February 1912, with Wright testifying in Washington, Morgan called a press conference. Several Memphis area newspapers ran articles summarizing the event and reprinted parts of Morgan's letter to Clark. Morgan was quoted saying "for two years Mr. Wilson, has suppressed Mr. Elliott's report and has allowed the land companies to use the other report for advertising purposes." As to Elliott's dismissal, Morgan announced that it was "reprehensible" to saddle "a man of this character" with the burden of Wilson's failure by claiming that he had misapplied funds.[58]

Morgan then appealed to the professional engineering ranks with an editorial to *Engineering News.* Morgan's brief missive, titled "Does the Punishment Fit the Crime?" questioned the circumstances surrounding Elliott's dismissal. The editorial challenged the engineering community to ask how the profession should react when the profession's reputation was endangered through unjust attacks upon one of its members. The article and a follow-up by Morgan the next month drew several positive responses. The editors and readers of *Engineering News* agreed that a commission of competent engineers should review Wright's plan and that Elliott's dismissal was unjust. The journal printed a letter of support and suggested that readers "cut it out, sign and mail it to his Senator or to the President" to let the country know where the engineering profession stood in the matter.[59]

On February 26, a few days after Morgan's first editorial appeared, he took the witness stand in Washington, D.C., to recount his involvement with the Wright report during the summer of 1909. Although his respect for Elliott and contempt for Wright was obvious to the committee, during his three days of testimony he focused more on the engineering fallacies of Wright's plan. When asked whether Wright's plan would work, Morgan called it a "decided failure" and suggested that a board of engineers review the design before progressing with the reclamation. He believed Wright to be an "incompetent engineer" who had ignored findings and miscalculated cost estimates. Morgan then stated that the division suppressed the Wright report because of the inaccurate data and not because of an elaborate conspiracy with land promoters.[60]

Hearings in the Everglades matter concluded in August 1912. The final report of the committee declared that Wright's report was full of inaccuracies, the suppression of government documents was not influenced by outside interests but caused by internal disagreements, Elliott's mismanagement of expense vouchers was a minor offense, and that Wright had inappropriately colluded with land companies while a government official. As a result of the hearings, the Department of Agriculture reinstated Elliott, Wright decided to resign from his position with Florida's Drainage Commission, and one period of Florida Everglades land speculation reached a conclusion.[61]

In 1912, Morgan played an important supporting role in the investigations of the Florida Everglades reclamation matter. His defense of Charles Elliott through the press, professional organizations, correspondence with government officials, and government investigating bodies, demonstrated the traits of a Progressive reformer. While not all the rumors connecting politicians with speculators were proven true, some were verified, and his efforts helped expose government corruption, human greed, unethical business practices, and impropriety. Morgan's sudden and successful appearances before reporters and investigating bodies on Capitol Hill hinted at his ability to succeed in a more visible public role. More than just a self-taught engineer, by 1912 Morgan had established himself as a public face of energetic reform. His work to expose corruption in Florida represented Morgan's first real social activism and first active participation in an effort to reform government.

When the Dayton Flood Prevention Committee called Arthur Morgan in 1913, they discovered a young engineer in search of a new challenge. After only a few years of practice, he owned a successful engineering firm in Memphis and had earned the reputation as one of the top reclamation experts in the region. Morgan accepted their offer to develop a plan to prevent future flooding for the city of Dayton and other communities in the Miami River basin. That spring, Morgan left his Memphis work in the able hands of his associates and relocated to Dayton to complete a survey. Morgan's team of fifty surveyors scoured the region during the summer, and on October 3 he delivered a preliminary report to Dayton's Committee. He concluded that the construction of five storage reservoirs, or "dry-dams," along with standard improvements of the river channel, would protect Dayton from all future flooding. These earthworks would only hold water behind them during times of flooding; during most of the year the land in the flood basin would be useable for farming or recreation. Morgan's report drew considerable opposition from Dayton citizens, engineers, and local leaders, but in January 1914 the Committee upheld the elaborate plan.[62]

Morgan worked closely with former Ohio representative John A. McMahon (D) to draft legislation to establish a multi-county flood control district. The resulting Ohio Conservancy Act went before the state's general assembly in January 1914 and passed the following month. Although Morgan had been involved in preparing bills for water-control laws in Minnesota, Arkansas, and Mississippi, the passage of the Ohio Conservancy Act established the nation's first regional flood control and watershed district. The district covered some four hundred square miles of the Great Miami River's drainage basin. He would use this same regional model for later water-control projects.[63]

But not all residents of the Great Miami River Valley were pleased with Morgan's elaborate engineering schemes. Beginning in 1914 and lasting until construction officially began in 1918, a number of community and city-based groups emerged to oppose the Conservancy Act and the chosen plan of flood protection. Their chief concerns were that the dry-dam method was untested, that many landowners would lose their property, and that the money raised after the 1913 flood would be squandered on the ideas of a novice engineer. Morgan took the moral high ground and agreed to numerous public speaking engagements during this period. Building on the experience of his first press conference in Memphis to defend his former supervisor, Morgan became more comfortable with newspaper reporters and public appearances. He became a public figure in Dayton, gained the trust of community leaders, and refined his ability to make and defend his arguments.[64]

To resolve many of the legal challenges surrounding flood control plans in the region, in March 1914 the state created a Conservancy Court. Consisting of ten judges, this court of common pleas convened in Dayton and served as the first level of judicial review. Their proceedings were open to the public and often drew so many attendees that they met in a large auditorium of the Dayton Memorial Hall. Its first task would be to consider the constitutionality of the Ohio Conservancy Act, brought forth as a petition from a group of five hundred anti–flood control advocates. Proceedings before the Conservancy Court began on March 31, 1914, and concluded in mid-April. On April 18, the court ruled in favor of the constitutionality of the Conservancy Act, and the plaintiffs filed an appeal. In June, the court of appeals upheld the lower court's decision.[65]

With approval from the courts, in June 1915 the state officially organized the Miami Conservancy District, which covered territory in nearly a dozen Ohio counties. Ohio funded the Miami Conservancy District almost entirely from tax revenues and donations, and appointed a three-member Board of Directors to operate the agency. At their first official meeting in July, the Board appointed Arthur Morgan as chief engineer for the Miami Conservancy District. Although Morgan had fallen into ill health after having an appendectomy and blood poisoning, that summer he resolved that the Morgan Engineering Company would oversee the majority of the work. Upon his recovery, he opened a branch of the company in Dayton. While employees set up the Dayton Morgan Engineering Company and planned for the recruitment of workers, Morgan focused on preparing the final survey report on the Miami Conservancy District.[66]

The provisions of the Ohio Conservancy Act called for the adoption of an official plan for flood control and reclamation in the district. Morgan's final report, released in February 1916, detailed the construction plans for the improvements on the Great Miami River and its tributaries. He estimated that the entire project of five dry-dams and multiple river improvements would cost approximately $23 million and take about three years of concurrent construction work to complete. Morgan offered the opportunity for Dayton and other Miami River Valley towns to be flood-proof. The Board released the final report to the public and held open hearings to discuss the plan. At these open sessions, several city-based groups objected to the plan, arguing that the plan was too expensive, and offered alternative approaches to flood control, including channel improvements and levees. Other groups representing "upriver towns" not heavily affected by the 1913 flood, argued that they did not need flood protection, and built support by organizing anti-Conservancy rallies. Following the open hearings, these opponents filed litigation and initiated another round of legal challenges to the Miami Conservancy District.[67]

In the fall of 1916, the Conservancy Court met in Dayton's Memorial Hall to hear legal objections to the official plan for the Miami Conservancy District as submitted by chief engineer Arthur Morgan. For five consecutive days in October, Morgan appeared before the Conservancy Court to defend his plan. The *Dayton Daily News* reported that Morgan demonstrated a firm grasp of the subject. While on the witness stand, Morgan emphasized that his engineers had explored every conceivable option for flood protection, even studying the plans offered by opposition groups. The public appearance gave Morgan yet another chance to describe his flood control plan, how the dry-dams would operate during times of flooding, and how construction would be completed. His convincing testimony filled over six hundred typewritten pages. Just as he had done during his Florida Everglades testimony, Morgan embraced public hearings as a way to expose the "truth" to all.[68]

In late November 1916, the hearings before the Conservancy Court concluded. On November 24, the court formally approved Morgan's engineering plan for the Miami Conservancy District. The court declared that "the combination of dams and dry detention basins together with channel improvement is the only practical and efficient method of protecting the Miami Valley from the results of destructive floods." Morgan's somewhat experimental dry-dam design had won out over mere channel improvements and levees. While perhaps a more expensive option, Morgan's claim that the improvements of the Miami Conservancy District would make the region and the city of Dayton flood-proof was convincing to most. But the legal battles against the Miami Conservancy District were not quite finished. While answering the engineering issues, the Conservancy Court did not fully address the issues raised by groups from upriver towns who did not want to sacrifice their tax dollars and land for the improvements. Further, the construction plans called for the displacement and removal of residents in certain areas.[69]

As Miami Conservancy District advocates expected, the plaintiffs filed new appeals against Morgan's plan and during the following year made further attempts to weaken the Ohio Conservancy Act. However, by late 1916, the courts upheld Morgan's report and the Board of Directors of the Miami Conservancy District instructed him to proceed. In the middle of these important legal battles, Morgan began building up his company for the massive work that lay ahead. The implementation of his plan would be an enormous task, but at the end of 1916, Morgan embarked on one of his most significant engineering projects and perhaps his greatest professional challenge.[70]

When Arthur Morgan visited Dayton, Ohio, in the spring 1913, he was a few weeks away from his thirty-fifth birthday. In a dozen years, he had overcome the challenges of a limited education, poor health, and a restless spirit to become a recognizable leader in a new field of engineering. Along the way, he demonstrated many of the characteristics of a Progressive reformer. While learning and defining the work of water-control engineering, he assisted in the drafting of legislation, exposed corruption through the press and the profession, contributed to official government investigations and committees, and excelled in private enterprise. He and other Progressive reformers took steps to regulate a complicated society in need of order and a moral compass.

Morgan was a modern American who exemplified the spirit of progress and improvement, but at the same time he was still grounded in the past. It was during these important formative years that Morgan embraced the concepts of government oversight, minimizing the economic motives of competition, practical education, and moral uplift to solve social problems. With the Miami Conservancy District, Morgan exhibited regional planning, which emphasized societal rather than individual needs. Morgan expanded his emerging vision for the small community and practical education in the coming years, but in 1916, with Progressivism at high tide, Morgan established himself as an emerging professional with a voice and social conscience.

3

REFORM IN PROGRESS

On a sunny June day in 1919, Arthur Morgan walked down the streets of Dayton, Ohio, on his way to a meeting. Along the way, his friend Arthur Hauck stopped to talk with him. Hauck, a teacher at the Moraine Park School (a school that Morgan helped found), congratulated Morgan for being elected as a college trustee at nearby Antioch College. Surprised to learn this news, Morgan and his wife, Lucy, traveled to Yellow Springs (just a few miles southeast of Dayton) the next weekend to inspect the nearly bankrupt school. After their first trip to Antioch, Morgan reportedly said to his wife, "I believe it is near enough dead to start over in the form I dream of." In mid-1919, Arthur Morgan's challenge of educational reform arrived.[1]

In the few years prior to his arrival at Antioch, Morgan registered notable engineering improvements, fostered the development of small communities, and became a civic leader. The late 1910s were some of the most fruitful, hectic, and publicly visible years of his professional life, second only to his tenure with the Tennessee Valley Authority. During this crucial time, Morgan's work as chief engineer of the Miami Conservancy District established him as a preeminent leader in the fields of water-control engineering and flood control. While directing the monumental undertaking, Morgan built elaborate workers' villages at the dam construction sites in order to improve the lives of the laborers, mostly recent immigrants seeking the American dream. From that work, Morgan refined his vision of a small community where local business enterprises and high morals would sustain its residents. Morgan's civic involvement during this period also reflected his conceptualization of a war-free world, without political boundaries.

Morgan's growing notoriety led to opportunities for education reform. His once undefined ideas for offering students a practical education crystallized into a more specific course of school reform for secondary education. For the first time, he sketched out clear plans for teaching students real-life skills such as economics, carpentry, manufacturing, and ethical business practices. While launching his own school in Dayton, the Moraine Park School, Morgan demonstrated his understanding of the educational theories of the late Progressive Era and his maturity as a reformer. He arrived at Antioch with some experience as an educator and administrator. Morgan's challenge was not to create a new curriculum, but to adapt his student-centered practices to meet the needs of college and university students. Like his engineering projects, Morgan's educational reforms could result in new communities and promote high moral standards. During the last years of the Progressive Era, Morgan transformed from a successful water-control engineer with a penchant for reform into a leader in higher education.

The year 1916 represents an important milestone for Progressivism and for understanding Morgan's world. Democratic President Woodrow Wilson won reelection by a narrow margin over Republican candidate Charles Evans Hughes. Wilson campaigned on the platform of keeping the United States out of the growing war in Europe, but his other planks focused on Progressive reforms. He signed legislation to create modern-day entities such as the Federal Highway System and the National Park Service. Under Wilson's leadership, many of the demands of Progressive reformers came to fruition that year.[2]

In 1916, Congress approved several crucial pieces of Progressive legislation, including the Keating-Owen Child Labor Act, the Workmen's Compensation Act for federal employees, and the Adamson Act to establish an eight-hour work day for railway employees. Congress also established the Farm Credit System for farmers in need, while the U.S. Supreme Court ruled federal income tax constitutional. Many states took matters of reform into their own hands. That year, Montana, South Dakota, Nebraska, and Michigan adopted statewide prohibition. At the local level, hundreds of cities adopted a commissioner or manager approach to governance. Other reforms created social welfare programs, reduced party influence, and made services more effecient. Progressive leaders, such as Margaret Sanger, also pushed forward with their reforms. That fall she opened the nation's first birth control clinic in Brooklyn, only to see it closed a week later and be arrested for operating a contraceptive center. Other Progressive women in Chicago formed a pro-suffrage group called the National Women's Party.[3]

While many Progressive leaders rejoiced in their gains, the year also brought great challenges and setbacks. In March, Mexican general Francisco "Pancho" Villa raided the border community of Columbus, New Mexico, burned most of the town, and killed nineteen Americans. Federal troops pursued Villa far into Mexico for the next year, but did not capture him. War in Europe escalated to new heights. From February through December, the Battle of Verdun in northern France claimed almost one million lives. War abroad heightened nationalist spirit at home and increased violence against immigrant and minority groups. Many Progressives took comfort in eugenics as a way to scientifically justify their supposed racial superiority. Because of this movement, by 1916 a number of states adopted sterilization laws to limit the reproduction of those whom the Progressives considered unfit and racially impure. The war also led to new economic opportunities in the industrial North. At the end of 1916, massive numbers of African Americans, in search of greater opportunity and hoping to escape discrimination in the South, relocated to northern cities, in what historians would later call the "great migration."[4]

In 1916, water-control engineer and Progressive reformer Arthur Morgan experienced a series of pivotal transitions. At the end of that year, his work as chief engineer for the Miami Conservancy District shifted from planning to implementation. The most unique facet of the Miami Conservancy District was a series of worker camps, where the laborers would receive education while they built the earthen structures to protect the region from flooding. These untested designs, for both flood and labor control, could either make or break Morgan's reputation as a chief engineer. At the same time, because of his public notoriety and professional reputation, he could no longer be an anonymous citizen in the bustling city of Dayton, Ohio. Morgan became involved in a number of civic organizations that waved the flag of Progressivism and Nationalism. Through his work with the League to Enforce Peace, Morgan promoted the idea of a war-free world.

But perhaps even more important, in 1916 Morgan explored his interest in education reform. He absorbed the discussions and writings about education from other Progressive Era reformers, such as John Dewey. In 1916, he and wife Lucy considered starting their own school in Massachusetts, but passed on the opportunity. Demand for better education in the local public schools led him and other influential Progressive leaders in Dayton to found the Moraine Park School that same year. As the hidden hand of the school, he experimented with his practical education strategies. Combining his work on the Miami Conservancy District with the school, Morgan's early writings on the school referred to his work as educational engineering. He explained that, "The object of education is not primarily to impart information, but to insure to the child the qualities, character and accomplishments he will need when he is a man." Morgan envisioned a scientific and controllable way to produce graduates with strong character, morals, and community spirit. His experiences at Moraine Park served Morgan well as he moved on to direct Antioch just a few years later.[5]

During this period, Morgan refined his plans for practical education and the components of his small community. His conceptualization of an enlightened society, similar to the future described by Edward Bellamy, would be possible through the process of building strong communities, morality, education, and a social awareness. These transformative years are crucial in understanding Morgan's conceptualization of the modern world, how he enacted social change, and his emerging vision.

In 1916, Arthur Morgan had become a household name in the Dayton area. His engineering plans for the Miami Conservancy District created both notoriety and controversy. While his detractors were many, his supporters included influential business and civic leaders, which made Morgan's entrance into their ranks much easier. Morgan kept quite notable company in Dayton, including strong friendships with co-inventor of the airplane Orville Wright, inventor of the electric car starter and head of research at General Motors Charles F. Kettering, president of the National Cash Register Company John J. Patterson, vice-president of the same company and board chairman of the Miami Conservancy District Edward Deeds, and wealthy department store owner Frederick Rike. These colleagues would have signif-

Morgan in his Miami Conservancy District office. Antiochiana, Antioch College.

icant influence on Morgan's career as an engineer, educator, and public figure during this period, and far beyond.[6]

While in Dayton, Morgan gained appointments to several civic and official groups, including a membership in the Engineers' Club of Dayton and the chairmanship of the Ohio Mental Hygiene Committee. But in early 1916, just as Morgan submitted his final plans for the Miami Conservancy District, Frederick Rike encouraged him to take a leadership role a new organization with national significance called the League to Enforce Peace. His work with the league demonstrated Morgan's leadership potential at the state and even national levels.[7]

In 1915, Hamilton Holt, editor of the *Independent* and leader of the New York Peace Society, in collaboration with Theodore Marburg, minister to Belgium in the William Howard Taft administration, founded the League to Enforce Peace. This organization raised funds, influenced politicians, and cultivated public interest for the cause of peace. The League to Enforce Peace was not a pacifist organization or an anti-war group. Instead, it was more focused on creating a postwar organization to encourage peace between nations. Over the course of World War I, the organization expanded nationwide to become the preeminent sponsor of a postwar league of all nations—the first group to endorse such a conception. Headed by Taft, the League to Enforce Peace prepared the plan that served as the backbone for President Woodrow Wilson's League of Nations Covenant.[8]

The League to Enforce Peace had support from nearly every state and maintained a strong following throughout the Midwest. In early November 1915, a small committee of influential Dayton citizens, including Morgan, met and expressed their interest in launching an Ohio chapter of the League to Enforce Peace. The next month, Frederick Rike assumed the role of temporary state chairman and began organizing the state's chapter. Shortly thereafter, Rike asked Morgan to raise awareness for the group in Dayton and Montgomery County and bring a delegation to the chapter's first official meeting in March 1916. Morgan met the challenge and on March 2, 1916, he brought fifteen civic leaders to the chapter's initial gathering in Columbus. The group elected permanent officers, a finance committee, and a twelve-member state executive committee consisting of judges, deans, and college presidents. It was at this meeting that the group elected Morgan as the chapter's state secretary.[9]

In May, state secretary Morgan arranged for fifty members of Ohio's branch to attend the national meeting of the League to Enforce Peace in Washington, D.C. The event attracted 2,000 interested supporters and featured presentations by William Howard Taft, newly appointed Secretary of War Newton D. Baker, Henry Cabot Lodge, and Woodrow Wilson. The business section of the meeting dealt with matters of national and state organization. During the selection of new officers, the group's leaders appointed Morgan a member of their national executive committee, a group of thirty national league leaders, one of whom was Morgan's Memphis colleague Bolton Smith. Morgan returned to Dayton with new vigor to raise money for the national organization. He pledged an annual $10,000 contribution for the Buckeye State and divided the fundraising responsibilities among individual communities. Fundraising efforts in Ohio's cities and town commenced, but the fall presidential election attracted the most attention from league leaders, members, and supporters.[10]

With his sudden involvement in the League to Enforce Peace during 1916, Morgan demonstrated his ability to lead and raise funds, but he also showed his disinterest in politics and holding elected office. Despite the local opposition to his engineering plans, he could have easily retained his job as chief engineer of the Miami Conservancy District while earning a spot as a state representative or in a city government position. But instead of building on his influential connections in Dayton and across the state for political gain, Morgan turned to an earlier fascination with education.

Lucy Morgan had a great deal of influence over her husband's educational outlook. In fact, their first meeting revolved around a possible educational opportunity for both. While a government engineer and recovering from a bout of malaria, Morgan stumbled upon an isolated part of the Buffalo River, in the Ozark Mountains of Arkansas. Morgan envisioned establishing a small school in that area, but needed to first locate suitable educators who could share his idea. A friend in Boston suggested he meet Lucy Griscom, who taught at Wellesley College. Thus his introduction to Lucy in April 1909 was at least partially a business meeting. Although plans for the Arkansas project did not materialize, the Morgans shared a vision of establishing their own school. Morgan later said of his wife, "I found her to have a more ranging concept of education than anyone else I had known. . . . She introduced me to some unusual schools and teachers," including influential educators such as Charles Eliot, president of Harvard University, and Ellery Sedgwick, editor of *Atlantic Monthly*.[11]

Together the Morgans formulated plans for their school. To begin, they wanted to "recruit a small number of intelligent, imaginative people of various ages, some mature research persons, and older people in training," as the nucleus of the student body. They visualized that "the students would spend from five to twenty years together studying, working, and experimenting." In addition to standard academic subjects, the imagined curriculum would include physical development, practical industrial skills, civic awareness, and exposure to the natural world. Their school would combine practical education with traditional instruction, but at this stage the Morgans had not found a suitable site for their endeavor.[12]

During the early stages of the Miami Conservancy District planning, the Morgans, then with residences in Dayton and Memphis, decided to purchase a home that would serve as a haven between engineering jobs and as a place for their children to spend summers. Arthur wanted a location where he could cultivate a variety of cranberry bush, the *Viburnum Americanum*, or highbush cranberry, while Lucy longed to return to the East. The new residence would also be the location of the school that the Morgans longed to establish. The Morgans wanted their school to be in an isolated rural area, preferably in the mountains with access to a lake, but close to transportation routes and civilization. In 1914, after intensive study of geologic survey maps, the Morgans sent a young engineer on a six-month search, via bicycle, to New England and northern New York looking for possible sites for their Xanadu.[13]

The Morgans put all of their plans on hold in the spring of 1915. In May of that year, while the Miami Conservancy District was being officially organized, Morgan underwent an emergency appendectomy and suffered from blood poisoning. Morgan's doctor suggested that he take a lengthy vacation to recover. That summer, the Morgans bought a car and set out to examine the one hundred or so possible sites targeted by the young engineer. They started their search in Vermont and by August found themselves in rocky counties of western Massachusetts. In Shaw Pond, near the town of Lee, in Berkshire County, the Morgans discovered an available farm on Jacob's Ladder Road that met their needs. They purchased about four hundred acres, which included a house, three barns, stands of timber, and open fields suitable for fruit growing, and named it "Jacob's Pillow." During the excursion, Morgan had recovered from his illness, and that fall he resumed his work on the Miami Conservancy District with the expectation that he and Lucy would soon return to Jacob's Pillow to start their school.[14]

The engineering work in Dayton kept the Morgans from visiting Jacob's Pillow, but not from thinking about it. In early 1916, Morgan began work on a prospectus for the school. Reflecting his educational background, Morgan made clear that the school would emphasize practical over traditional education. He called the Jacob's Pillow approach a reproduction of living "on a New England farm" while learning the values of self-reliance, individual responsibility, and community involvement. The prospectus emphasized the importance of self-sufficiency, sustainability, and even making small profits. Students and teachers would maintain the physical plant, thus eliminating the need for custodial staff, while tending to the farm. Morgan believed that these basic responsibilities offered great learning opportunities "without the loss of idealism or culture." Through simple cooperation and shared contribution it would be self-sufficient and self-sustaining school.[15]

Morgan's discussion of creating small industries to help financially support the school represent an important component of Morgan's philosophy on community building. At Jacob's Pillow, Morgan recognized the great potential of the "200 acres of timberland." Morgan believed that the manufacture of wood products from the timber could financially sustain the school while teaching students lessons on business and economics. Specifically, Morgan found that when the students were responsible for the purchase of food and sale of school products, they learned the importance of "being solvent, the functions of a budget, the principles involved in credit, simple methods of accounting, and the custom and spirit of business organization." Morgan's plan allowed students to generate some profits for the school, but any dividends would be tempered by boundaries. He called for an ethical basis for any business practices and shunned mere profits as the primary motivational factor in business. Instead, he encouraged fair prices for quality products. The call for developing small industries in his intentional communities would be repeated for decades to come.[16]

Despite such lofty intentions, the Morgans found little time to devote to their Jacob's Pillow project. The location proved far too many miles from Morgans' growing nest in southwest Ohio. By summer 1916, Morgan settled on a more realistic educational project in Dayton. The Morgans briefly rented the Jacob's Pillow property to the Lincoln School of the Teachers College at Columbia University. But in the 1930s, the Morgan's sold the property to Edwin "Ted" Shawn, who established the Jacob's Pillow Dance School and Festival. This program remains the oldest dance festival in the United States, and presently the ten-week summer season attracts well over 50,000 visitors to see performances on three stages. Certainly the Morgans picked a fruitful location for some kind of school, but the educational concepts of Jacob's Pillow were even more important in the progression of Morgan educational philosophies.[17]

In 1916, Morgan realized an opportunity to launch a smaller version of the Jacob's Pillow school in the Dayton area, and he had little problem finding a receptive audience. Many of the leaders of the Miami Conservancy District new to the region and Dayton's business elite had school-age children. These people found the area's public schools lacking. Morgan shared his ideas for a private school with his closest friends and support for his practical-based education plan followed. In the summer of 1916, Edward

Deeds, Charles Kettering, Orville Wright, and Frederick Rike pledged their financial commitment to Morgan's school and joined the institution's board of directors. With that promise, Morgan recruited staff for his private school in Dayton.[18]

Morgan first searched for a qualified headmaster to run the proposed school. He reworked his Jacob's Pillow prospectus into an extended outline for his Dayton school, which would be mailed to potential applicants. The document described the objectives of the school as educating "six to twelve boys, from ten to seventeen years old," in traditional subjects, business skills, self-reliance, and manners. Morgan wanted the students to develop a greater appreciation for the natural world and their fellow man. Much like a Montessori school, Morgan's program featured individualized instruction, self-directed learning, and student mastery of subjects through discovery. Morgan's inspiration for the curriculum came from three important sources: Lucy Morgan's understanding of educational theory and practice; his own experiences of practical education; and reading the works of education reformers, including Johann Heinrich Pestalozzi and Charles Hanford Henderson. He concluded the lengthy outline with a list of twenty-nine questions (two concerned alcohol and tobacco use) for interested applicants to answer and return to his attention.[19]

That fall, Morgan mailed out over 2,500 of his outlines to principals, school administrators, college and university professors, and known education reformers. One of Morgan's outlines made its way to the inbox of Charles Eliot, the president of Harvard University. In September, Eliot wrote Morgan to congratulate him for such an innovative approach to education. By the end of 1916, Morgan screened the hundreds of applications for the headmaster position. In early 1917, Morgan selected Frank D. Slutz, the superintendent of schools in Pueblo, Colorado. Once in Dayton, Slutz coordinated nearly all of the school's work. He hired teaching staff, including Arthur Hauck, a high school principal from Idaho; refined the mission of the school; and worked with the school's board of directors to open the school.[20]

The Moraine Park School, located near a wooded glacial moraine about four miles south of Dayton, adjacent to the community of Moraine City, began operations in June 1917. That first term commenced in a renovated greenhouse donated by Charles Kettering. Slutz screened the applications and accepted thirty-three boys for grades five to eleven. A majority of students were children of Dayton's business elite or were related to the leaders of the Miami Conservancy District work—for example, Ernest Morgan and Charles Deeds appeared on the class rolls—but Slutz did not limit the admittance of students from lower income households. The curriculum encouraged independent learning, practical application of knowledge, self-discipline, and outdoor recreation. Students were free to progress through their courses at their own pace. Slutz developed an elaborate system of non-graded evaluation, which measured students in areas such as congregating, languaging, cosmologizing, and self-realizing. He issued reports to parents covering the student's strengths and weaknesses. The school encouraged self-sufficiency and taught practical skills such as carpentry, managing budgets, gardening, and printing. Upper level students developed projects that would demonstrate their business prowess, while serving in self-appointed supervisory roles.[21]

Moraine Park expanded its offerings. By 1922, the school enrolled over two hundred boys and girls from first through twelfth grades. The physical plant grew to include new class buildings, a library with biological samples, an electrical repair shop, a chemical laboratory, an indoor gymnasium, and a wading pool. Although the school did not issue grades to its students, graduates found entrance into a number of reputable colleges and universities. Moraine Park graduates attended nearby schools such as Miami University, the Ohio State University, and Denison University, with some attending institutions farther afield, including Rice University, the University of Minnesota, and the University of Pennsylvania. The leaders of Moraine Park School heralded their creation as Progressive education at its best. Its success brought great improvements to the Dayton public school system. The bright flame of the Moraine Park School flickered briefly; the school closed at the end of the 1927 school year, because of improvements in local schools and the withdrawal of financial support from most of its original founders.[22]

The successes at Moraine Park brought Arthur Morgan some attention from Progressive educators. In 1918, Morgan accepted an offer from *Atlantic Monthly* to write an article about his educational philosophy. In "Education: The Mastery of the Arts of Life," Morgan argued that standard subjects had displaced the importance of practical skills, leaving students with little ability to function in the modern world. He found traditional schools drab in their appearance and curriculum, and thus unable to excite creativity in their students. Morgan believed in lifelong education, saying that "education is not an institution . . . kept alive by ceaseless vigil," but rather "it is an innate process of human life." Morgan wanted to encourage "independence, originality, and initiative" by re-injecting practical skills and exposure to real-life situations into the traditional structure of primary and secondary education. Like other education reformers of the time, Morgan recognized the importance of the inherent spontaneity and interests of the students, which made education more protean and less static. Morgan's article and his success with the Moraine Park School led to other opportunities for education reform.[23]

Although Morgan devoted only a small amount of his energy to the Moraine Park School, his blueprint for education reform crystallized during the planning of the school—an education so practical that students could learn real business skills and life lessons that contributed to the growth of small industries and communities. Morgan shared Edward Bellamy's utopian dreams of universal education with practical applications, which is evident in the experimental nature of Moraine Park. The self-governing feature of the school, which put the students and not the headmaster in charge of supervision, mirrored the principles of Bellamy's apolitical society regulated by shared responsibility for the common good. Morgan brought his plans for education reform to higher education and to professional groups just a few years later. But at this time, the challenges of the Miami Conservancy District consumed Morgan.

After the 1916 approval of Morgan's engineering plan by the Conservancy Court, additional legislative motions and individual lawsuits from affected residents challenged the work of the Miami Conservancy District. During 1917, courts, judges, and state legislators extinguished these smoldering threats, with the last legal barriers disappearing the following year. During these disputes, chief engineer Arthur Morgan, with full confidence from the board of directors, planned for construction of the massive undertaking.[24]

Morgan's plan called for the construction of five earthen dry-dams at strategic sites in the Great Miami River basin. Three of the sites were close to Dayton: Englewood to the northwest on the Stillwater River, Huffman to the east on the Mad River, and the Taylorsville site to the north of the city on the main branch of the Great Miami. The other two locations were more remote and rural. The Lockington site was to the north of Dayton, near the town of Piqua, and regulated parts of the upper Miami River. Germantown, to the southwest of the city, would control flooding in communities below Dayton. On the average, the structures rose one hundred feet from their bases, with the largest stretching over 6,000 feet in length. Unlike concrete dams, Morgan's innovative design made the dams self-regulating and nearly free from maintenance. During normal weather conditions, water would naturally flow through a spillway. However, during flooding, the specially designed outlet conduits slowed the rushing water for exit, while the excess water waiting to escape formed a lake behind the dam, which would naturally empty by gravity. Inside the dams, an impervious core prevented water seepage, while an outside layer of sand, gravel, and dirt built at sloping angle minimized erosion. Other river improvements were part of the plan, but building the five dry-dams was the greatest engineering challenge.[25]

Morgan resolved that the Miami Conservancy District would do nearly all of the construction with its own workers and not rely on contractors. Because of legal and administrative delays, he estimated that construction of the five dry-dams and other improvements would take about five years to complete. That timetable, however, depended on his ability to hire and manage hundreds of common and skilled laborers. In his earlier engineering work, Morgan had not worked on multi-year projects of such scale—this kind of regional planning had previously been undertaken by only the federal government. While Morgan respected the need for efficiency during the construction, he also recognized an opportunity to ensure quality work by providing optimum living conditions for the workers. Although the original submitted plan did not include details and costs, by 1917 Morgan developed specific plans for worker villages adjacent to the dam sites. These elaborate villages—complete with sewer, electricity, and water systems, streets, community centers, stores, and schools—would be a far cry from the shantytown construction camps of the time.[26]

During the 1910s, workers on large outdoor construction projects received few comforts. Employers housed them in tar-paper bunkhouses, shacks, or construction cars. Quite commonly, houses of gambling, drinking, and prostitution arose nearby to separate the workers from their wages. Under these conditions, laborers had become a type of migrant construction worker, often homeless, thriftless, uneducated, and wandering from job to job. Furthermore, workers with families had an even more difficult time adjusting to the harsh camp life and the constant moving.[27]

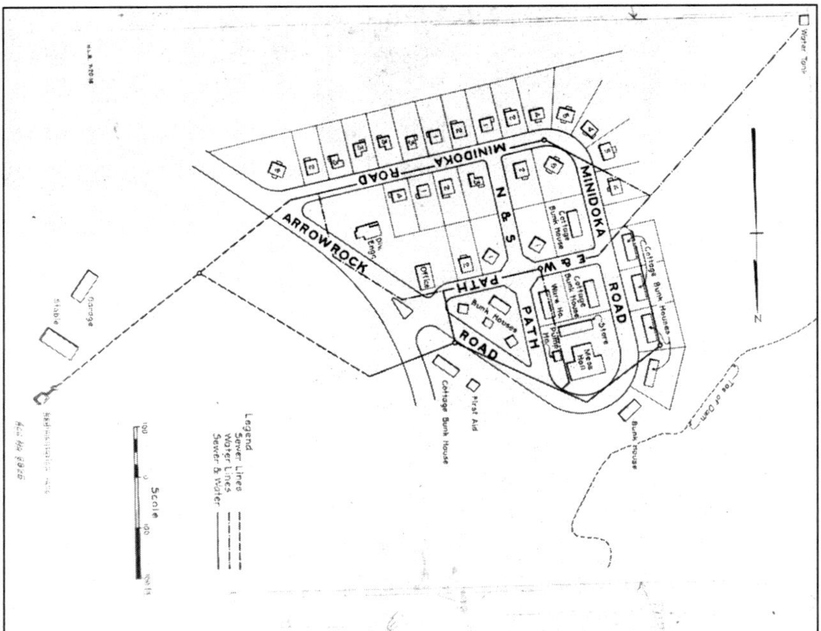

Fig. 1A
Plan of Germantown Camp

Plan for Germantown Worker Community. Antiochiana, Antioch College.

These lackluster conditions were well explained in the 1917 publication *Preliminary Survey of Labor Camps in Ohio.* This report examined 108 construction camps in the Buckeye State and outlined general conditions. The report found most of the camps to be unsanitary, overcrowded, and lacking a sense of community. The survey offered simple suggestions for improvement that could be implemented “at very slender expense,” and suggested that these changes would encourage worker efficiency through better living and thus increase the employers’ prosperity.[28]

Hoping to change these conditions, Morgan demanded decent living conditions for his workers. In late 1917, Morgan revealed his plans for the worker camps to the district’s board of directors. He explained that “Godd [*sic*] housing, good meals, opportunity for wholesome community and social life, and educational advantages are held to be due the workers.” He argued that the camps were “good business” because the desirable camp conditions would keep the “best men on the job.” In January 1918, the board of directors approved Morgan’s bold ambitions and authorized construction of a labor camp at each of the five sites.[29]

The idea of building five near-permanent worker villages for the Miami Conservancy District reveals Morgan's conception of what he later dubbed the small community. Much like the communities of the future described in Bellamy's *Looking Backward,* Morgan believed that the development of character was best cultivated in a controlled environment. Although Morgan believed that close-knit communities could exist in large metropolitan areas, for the most part he encouraged the advancement, and often rebirth, of small rural localities. Within these communities, Morgan encouraged the development of small industries, localized cooperative ventures, and cooperation (instead of competition) between all of the residents of the community, regardless of their age. Morgan believed that with hard work and dedication, the individuals of small communities developed respect for others and for the self-sustaining community itself.[30]

Each labor camp, or small community, encouraged democratic principles, provided the residents with diverse opportunities for betterment, and fostered improved character. Morgan believed that workers with a strong Christian character would improve a society that he and many other reformers saw as plagued by low moral standards, inadequate labor conditions, uneducated immigrants, inefficiency, and few opportunities for personal or professional advancement. The labor camps surrounded his work force with a climate of morality, community, and cooperation, while they built the massive structures needed to protect the Miami River Valley from flooding.[31] The level of detail in Morgan's Miami Conservancy District worker villages is important for understanding his later community building with TVA, especially the planned town of Norris, Tennessee.

Morgan gathered information on labor camps from officials from other large construction projects, housing associations, and sociology professors, and then hired city planner John Nolan to design the camps. With Nolan's guidance, Morgan and his staff laid out the infrastructure of the five sites. The camps contained decent, attractive homes with different floor plans (from designs by Lucy Morgan), and modern amenities such as running water, electricity, and a sewage system.[32]

To supervise the camps, in January 1918, Morgan hired C. W. Porter-Shirley, a specialist in labor economics and sociology, to serve as the head camp inspector and employment manager. He told Porter-Shirley that he wanted an overseer "to do more than simply manage the men adroitly for the sole purpose of preventing industrial unrest." Instead, Morgan hoped that the camp manager would further the lives of the workers by promoting social, cultural, and educational opportunities. By February, Porter-Shirley took up the search for similar minded individuals to serve as camp overseers. Under Porter-Shirley's supervision, construction of the camps commenced in late February, and by early May all five were nearly complete.[33]

Each of the five camps housed and supported from 150 to 300 people. For families of two to eight people, each camp contained forty to sixty cottages with three styles and various floor plans. The first style featured three rooms with dimensions of 24' x 24', while another model featured four or five rooms with sizes as large as 26' x 34'. A third style featured a second floor and a choice of floor plans. The exteriors of the cottages were painted and had screens on doors and windows, while the interiors were ceiled and stained. Each house was equipped with a stove for heating, a kitchen range, water heaters, indoor plumbing, shower baths, and electric lights. Rent for cottages ranged from $13 to $21 per month; there was no charge for water or electricity.[34]

The single men were housed in two different styles of bunkhouses. The first kind provided separate sleeping rooms and accommodated eight, twelve, or twenty-four workers. Each house had a porch, sitting room, toilet, shower bath, wash room, and sleeping rooms accommodating either one, two, or four men each. Rent prices ranged from $0.50 to $1.00 per week, and most residents ate at the camp mess hall. The second type of bunkhouse was more of a dormitory style with one large common chamber for sleeping, which accommodated twenty-four, thirty-two, or forty-two men. These structures featured stoves where men did their own cooking. The district charged a rent of $0.50 per week to live in the larger communal bunkhouses. As part of the rent, the district provided the laborers with cots, springs, mattresses, and blankets.[35]

For the workers who did not cook, each camp had a mess hall that fed about two hundred people. Meals were $0.35 each. Morgan's company outfitted the kitchens with modern equipment such as ranges, steamers, roasters, dishwashing machines, and refrigerators. A large bakery and meat-cutting plant at the Taylorsville site delivered fresh breads and meats daily to each camp. Gardens for growing other foods were also popular, and at each of the five camps there were private plots and large communal tracts available for planting.[36]

The villages contained other public buildings. For social events and assemblies, the Huffman, Englewood, and Taylorsville sites had large community centers that seated over 120 people. The district also built schools at

Germantown Worker Community, 1921. Antiochiana, Antioch College.

four of the camps, where district educators taught both children and adults. Except for the Lockington site, each camp had a fully equipped first aid hospital where minor injuries and ailments were treated by a district physician. Finally, a general store in each community offered the laborers a full line of groceries, work clothes, candy, and tobacco products (even though Morgan opposed the latter).[37]

Within the communities, workers determined their neighbors and neighborhoods. With a diverse population of workers, stratified social living arrangements based on ethnicity and race developed. Reflecting domestic living patterns of the time, self-segregation by different groups of workers was commonplace and the camps of the district were no different. Although the district's records were vague, there were "black" sections of camps, as well as other areas grouped by ethnic background, such as Polish, Italian, Greek, and Mexican. Whether clustered by street, house, or room, these divisions were typical for the time. With a large number of families in the camps, women were common. Camp records reveal that nearly all of these women were married to workers and served domestic roles.[38]

During the course of the Miami Conservancy District construction, Morgan hired more than 1,000 employees. He was particular about how each person would contribute to the project. To select the skilled engineers, Morgan wrote to his acquaintances, placed advertisements in trade journals, informed engineering societies of his needs, and wrote those near the end of other large construction projects. The district received more than 400 applications for these positions, and by 1917 Morgan's careful selection process resulted in employing only about 50 engineers.[39]

Morgan also wanted talented and socially concerned skilled laborers. To perform the complex construction, he needed draftsmen, electricians, machine operators, mechanics, painters, riggers, rodmen, carpenters, and foremen to supervise the workers. Morgan's employment staff received nearly four thousand applications for these varied positions, and by early 1918 the district had hired 325 skilled laborers.[40]

Finally, Morgan planned for the recruitment of the common laborers. By early 1918, Morgan estimated that, to complete the project, a force of about 2,000 would be needed over the course of about 5 years. In February 1918, Morgan's assistant chief engineer, Charles W. Paul, announced that the district would soon "sound out the labor centers of the United States" to secure enough labor to bring the work to completion. Paul, like other project leaders, believed that the comfortable nature of the camps, as well as the promise of "good food and plenty of it," would attract a large number of high-minded and dedicated workers.[41]

But the demands of the European war created problems with securing labor teams. Because of the restrictions on domestic workers, Morgan turned to recent immigrants in Detroit and Chicago for the bulk of his common work force. These largely unskilled laborers hailed from various parts of Eastern Europe. Even more than other district employees, Morgan was concerned with the character of these "new Americans." If possible, he wanted to hire unskilled laborers who would "be helped in their desire to find themselves socially and economically." Morgan wanted to mold the foreign laborers into responsible workers and American citizens, fully capable of contributing to society. With the model camp communities, Morgan provided the "foreign laborers a fair chance to make favorable acquaintances with American standards of living." He further believed that carefully selected administrators would promote American social principles and political traditions throughout the work force.[42]

By April, employment recruiters and professional bureaus were well aware of the project, and by April 18, Porter-Shirley estimated that from 1,000 to 1,200 laborers could be secured from reliable sources. These recruiters provided the district with employees of varying ethnic backgrounds. Employment agent H. L. Hopwood promised to supply the district with between 500 and 1,000 Greek employees, while other sources could secure for the district about 100 "White, Colored, Macedonian, Italian, Rumanian, and Armenian laborers." By late April, the district listed 322 common laborers and 325 skilled workers on their payroll.[43]

In April, Morgan hired Dr. W. M. Smalley as the district's doctor and director of camp hygiene. Smalley had been a country physician for ten years and, with assistance from Ohio's State Department of Health, he maintained the sanitary standards of the five camps. As public health director, he was responsible for attending to all cases of accidents, conducting physical examinations, and maintaining the sanitary conditions of the camps. For his first assignment, Smalley worked hard to eradicate lice, vermin, and bedbugs from the camps and from the workers.[44]

By the middle of May 1918, construction of the dams had begun, and Porter-Shirley posted pay rates. For unskilled laborers, the wages were $3.00 per day for the eight-hour work day, but the district allowed workers up to ten hours for $3.85. As a comparison, unskilled laborers working in nearby Cincinnati made approximately $0.03 less per hour. The camps and wages attracted large numbers of workers, and during that month the total number employed by the district reached 1,250.[45] By the early summer, the United States government took control of all private employment agencies to better supply the American forces on the European fronts. But even with the restrictions, the availability of foreign born labor was hardly affected.[46]

During June, Morgan formulated a labor policy. He estimated that 28 different skilled labor unions in the area could claim jurisdiction on segments of the construction. To avoid future conflicting claims and possible union disagreements, he researched labor practices for the area and incorporated them into a Miami Conservancy District labor policy. Released in mid-June 1918, Morgan's decree stated that all employees, including high- and low-skilled workers, would receive the same treatment, and that "a man's character and workmanship shall be the sole basis on which his employment shall rest." The policy established the recognition of an eight-hour work day, time-and-one-half for overtime, approved Saturday weekend work, and wages based on skill level. His code recognized the right of all workers to organize or join trade unions to challenge the district's policies, but forbade employees from using coercion to induce persons to join any labor organization.[47]

Later that month, Morgan met with the Trades and Labor Council of Dayton to discuss the policy. He stressed that his open-shop plan fostered union organization within the district's construction ranks, thus adding to the prominence of the unions. According to Morgan, the labor representatives supported his proposals; however, the union leaders later disagreed with Morgan's account saying that they had rejected the open-shop policy. Despite the difference of opinion, on June 21, 1918, the district's board of directors adopted Morgan's mandate as the organization's official labor policy. In the succeeding weeks, membership drives brought a large part of the district's workers into appropriate unions.[48]

Once organized, the unions challenged the district's policies and pay wages. On July 11, the union of carpenters and electricians requested the district's board of directors to revoke the open-shop policy. The board did not cooperate and during the next week, about 125 workers, mostly carpenters, plumbers, and electricians at the Huffman, Taylorsville, and Englewood sites walked away from their jobs. Strikers charged that they were not being paid the same rate as skilled laborers working for contractors in Dayton and that payment for overtime weekend work, promised in the plan, was not being rendered.[49]

The district denied the striker's claims and declared that the false accusations were concocted to force a closed shop. Morgan released a statement saying that, "as the work is of a public nature, the directors feel that they have no right to close employment to men who are not members of the union." Assistant chief engineer Paul reported that some difficulty was encountered during the first few days of the strike, but within a week new workers (mostly all non-union) had replaced the lost labor. By the following week the strike, the only one significant labor uprising during the entire project, ended, leaving the district's open-shop policy intact.[50]

The strike resulted in additional criticism. Dayton labor leaders charged that the district hired foreign workers simply because they were unaccustomed to American work traditions and less likely to complain. Further, opponents argued that the remote locations made transportation difficult for qualified skilled American laborers, unwilling and financially unable to uproot their families. Morgan, however, argued that the wartime restrictions and immediacy of construction made it necessary to recruit foreign labor. He also stressed that the camps were especially designed for families and that nearby rail spurs created adequate access to each of the dam sites.[51]

By 1919, each camp developed its own community government. Although Morgan played an important role in designing the camps, his hands-off approach allowed the workers to improve their communities with only minimal interference. Morgan believed that the governmental and social life of employees should not be controlled by those in charge of construction. Similar to the educational principles at the Moraine Park School, he stressed to the camp supervisors that the workers should carry on all activities of community life through self-governance.[52]

The Taylorsville site was the first community to form a governing body. In late November 1918, elected individuals wrote a constitution and bylaws to "promote the social, physical, and intellectual development of the residents at the Taylorsville Dam site." They approved the document, which outlined five areas of jurisdiction: Community Service; Social Service; Education; Records and Finance; and Community Safety. Residents also elected a chairman and five officers, called commissioners, to head each of the departments.[53]

The other four camps followed the lead of the Taylorsville Association, and within two months each had adopted similar self-governing systems. By early 1919, the five camp associations had committees on schools and libraries, entertainment, religious activities, fire prevention, law and order, health and sanitation, transportation, and gardens. These groups led the way in developing the social, recreational, and educational character of the communities.[54]

These associations supported a number of entertainment choices. The camps held weekend dances, usually twice a month, and for those unfamiliar with dance steps, classes were held once a week. The classes were well attended by the younger residents of the communities, and at each of the camps the nominal fee was put toward purchasing player pianos. The three camps with community centers were opened nightly and featured a game room with pool tables. Despite the barroom atmosphere created by dancing, music, and competitive games, only soft drinks were available. Even with a general wartime prohibition, alcohol was available outside of the camps, so Morgan hoped to somehow keep alcohol out of the reach of the district's employees. Thus, on June 28, 1919, Morgan issued a "dry" edict for all the construction camps. By banning alcohol, he hoped to attract a larger number of employees with families to the camps. Despite a handful of incidents, the dry mandate was successful, and Morgan reported that after June, the absence of alcohol led to better labor turnover rate, a decreased number of accidents, fewer employees on district credit, and less "trouble" after Saturday night dances.[55]

School at one of the Miami Conservancy District Worker Communities. Antiochiana, Antioch College.

Education of all employees was a major part of camp life. Except at the Lockington site, where there was a village school nearby, each camp had its own school and educated about thirty to fifty children. The district made a careful search for competent and practical-minded teachers. Morgan was interested in teaching the students both standard academic subjects and practical working skills. Some of the classes covered domestic science, gardening, and skilled work such as carpentry and plumbing. The schools represented high quality elementary education, and the Montgomery and Greene county school systems upheld the curriculum by granting high school certificates to conservancy students.[56]

Four of the camps offered free night classes to adult employees. The subjects included advanced mathematics, industrial arithmetic, penmanship, mechanical drawing, English for foreigners, and first aid. Each class met two evenings a week, and ran for twelve weeks. Morgan encouraged foreigners to attend these classes and recruited volunteers from his staff to teach. The courses were well attended, with average of twenty-seven pupils for each class. According to Morgan, the expense to run the schools was minimal.[57]

Even with the varied European backgrounds, workers in the camps largely supported the country's involvement in World War I. With Morgan's endorsement in May 1918, the district formed a "regiment of the Community War Chest Association." This philanthropic organization backed American soldiers with donated funds from various sources. By June, their group had collected over $12,000 in donations for the organization, and with the end of the war in November, War Chest members took part in a Victory Parade in downtown Dayton.[58]

Leaders of the Miami Conservancy District took full notice of Morgan's support for the war effort. However, they criticized him for connections to a pacifist sounding organization, the League to Enforce Peace, and for having German workers on his projects. In late February 1918, Morgan received an alarming letter from Edward Deeds, the chairman of the district's board of directors. Deeds informed Morgan that within the board "there have been several criticisms lodged against you and your relations to some peace or pacifist movement." Further, Deeds reported that some members recommended that Morgan be dropped from the Engineers' Club of Dayton because of his "German tendencies." Deeds stressed to Morgan that the Miami Conservancy District should take precedence over all of his outside endeavors and suggested that Morgan keep himself out of all public issues as his opinions might reflect upon the district's work in and around Dayton. Although Deeds stated that he did not share the opinions of the other board members, he wanted to caution to Morgan of the danger.[59]

Morgan heeded the warning from Deeds and planned to resign his position as state secretary of the League to Enforce Peace. His departure became more difficult after his reelection to the league's national executive committee in May 1918. He accepted the position although he knew that his continued involvement with the league at any level might be detrimental to his work on the Miami Conservancy District. While Morgan searched for a replacement at the state level, the Ohio branch experienced a renewed interest in league activities. Morgan coordinated the chapter's activities that summer, with the intention of passing the torch to a suitable successor at an October state meeting. However, the deadly Spanish influenza epidemic that fall forced postponement of the meeting and halted a decision on replacing Morgan as state secretary.[60]

The end of World War I in early November increased national interest in the League to Enforce Peace. In January 1919, President Wilson arrived in Versailles, France, just outside of Paris, to represent the United States at a peace conference consisting of leaders from twenty-seven countries. Meanwhile, the League to Enforce Peace focused its attention on the United States

Senate. Leaders of the organization knew that Wilson's League of Nations or any similar agreed-upon peace accord would have to be ratified by the Senate. To prepare for such a treaty, league leaders prompted the state branches to inform their senators of the league's principles. In Ohio, the organization's branch opened up channels of communication with Senators Atlee Pomerene (D) and Warren G. Harding (R).[61]

In the spring of 1919, Morgan finally resigned his position as state secretary of the League to Enforce Peace. His successor, Daniel Ryan, began coordinating the state's efforts to support Wilson's League of Nations platform. After the resignation, Morgan kept his place on the national executive committee and remained a member of the Ohio branch. Even though the Miami Conservancy District project remained his top priority, he developed a more subtle role in the league, which allowed him to be part of its activities without attracting attention or criticism.[62]

While President Wilson negotiated the last points of the peace accord in Paris, the League to Enforce Peace sponsored state ratifying conventions that spring. These meetings were designed to unite all pro–League of Nations sentiment for the impending Senate battle, to show support for senators favoring the league, and to demonstrate how strongly Americans wanted the League of Nations. The Ohio convention took place on May 27 in Columbus and featured A. Lawrence Lowell and William Howard Taft as speakers. Over 1,800 attended the event, and the group adopted a resolution calling for a prompt ratification of a peace treaty with Wilson's League Covenant intact.[63]

On the morning of May 27, Morgan attended a meeting of the Miami Conservancy District's board and later that day he traveled to Columbus to attend the evening league sessions. During May and June, Morgan did quite a bit for the League to Enforce Peace, considering his need to "refrain from active propaganda on every issue where there is a party alignment." To raise money for the state convention, he arranged for other prominent Dayton leaders not affiliated with the Miami Conservancy District to carry out that campaign, using their names so as not to reveal Morgan's involvement. Financial records also indicate that throughout the summer Morgan collected league funds for the Dayton area and made several small personal donations. Although not an active member publicly, Morgan remained involved, while cleverly avoiding direct association with the league and any potential criticism.[64]

Morgan's work with the League to Enforce Peace largely ended in the summer of 1919. He favored the ratification of an unamended peace treaty with the League of Nations Covenant intact, but thereafter he confined his efforts to a handful of letters, various Dayton newspaper advertisements supporting the League of Nations, and several small personal donations to the chapter. Morgan remained a member of the league's national executive committee, although he did not attend any of their meetings, until finally severing his affiliation in the summer of 1920. Most impressive was his civic organizing and fundraising, while managing the construction projects of the Miami Conservancy District.[65]

The League to Enforce Peace experience stayed with Morgan for decades. In 1963, some forty-five years after his involvement with the League to Enforce Peace, Morgan declared how important the organization had been. In a bold statement that year, Morgan suggested that had he been able to continue working with the league, his efforts might have influenced enough senators to change the Senate's November 1919 vote on the League of Nations Covenant. Although quite overstated, Morgan's ability to inspire, to lead, and to manage an organization came shining through with his service as state secretary of the League to Enforce Peace. Those skills served him well during his next challenge as an educator and college president.[66]

In the spring of 1919, Arthur and Lucy Morgan first stepped on to the grounds of Antioch College. Located in the sleepy hamlet of Yellow Springs, just a few miles from Dayton, Antioch had deep roots in education reform. Famed Massachusetts congressman and educator Horace Mann served as Antioch's first president during the 1850s. By that time, Mann had revolutionized approaches to education in Massachusetts and his influence spread to other regions and abroad. Mann sought to improve the quality of the common schools, which he believed should be open to all children, regardless of socio-economic status. While Secretary of the Massachusetts Board of Education, 1837 to 1848, he launched a system of normal schools for teacher training, he pushed for standardized textbooks and strong school libraries, he added a regiment of physical exercise and health education to curriculums, and he lobbied for legislation to limit child labor. Following his 1852 defeat as the Free Soil candidate for governor of Massachusetts, Mann seized an opportunity to preside over a new nonsectarian, biracial, and coeducational college in rural Ohio.[67]

Horace Mann served as the president of Antioch College from 1853 until his death in 1859. Mann's attempts to keep the school free from religious affiliation ran counter to the aims of the school's trustees, who wanted to operate a Christian college. The college faced bankruptcy several times during his presidency. Just after the 1859 commencement, Mann collapsed from exhaustion and died a few months later. Mann's legacies and constant struggles over finances became part of Antioch's ongoing traditions. During the rest of the nineteenth century, Antioch closed on multiple occasions and graduated only a handful of students (usually less than ten students each year). By 1910, the budget hovered around $10,000, which supported only thirteen employees, funding to purchase sixteen books for the library, and services for just over 150 students. Somehow, the situation worsened in the next several years. The school's unpaid president, Siemon Fess, who at the time served also served as a representative from Ohio, resigned in 1917. Two years later Antioch's trustees, faced with mounting debts and dwindling matriculates (somewhat due to the demands of World War I), attempted to turn the school into a national YMCA college. The failure of that proposal led the trustees to consider complete closure.[68]

In early 1919, members of Antioch's board turned to the American Unitarian Association, one of their largest benefactors, for advice on recovery. Samuel Eliot, the president of the group and the son of former Harvard president Charles Eliot, suggested that the board appoint notable Unitarians to their dilapidated ranks. Eliot, with the advice of his father, recommended engineer Arthur Morgan, who by this time identified himself as a Unitarian. He also recommended Unitarian reverend John Malick of Cincinnati as an ideal board member. The additions were a logical choice: Morgan's work with Moraine Park School and his regional popularity made him an ideal candidate, while Malick would draw the school closer to the Unitarian community in the Queen City. The board agreed and, at their annual meeting on June 17, voted to fill their two empty seats with Morgan and Malick.[69]

A few weeks later, Morgan "discovered" that he had been appointed to the board, and he visited the campus with Lucy. The legacies of Horace Mann, his dreams of education reform far beyond his imagined Jacob's Pillow project and the Moraine Park School, the close proximity to Dayton, and submerged insecurity about not holding a college degree meant that Antioch offered Morgan innumerable opportunities. He found enormous potential with the rundown campus and the adjacent natural area known as Glen Helen. Most importantly for his educational objectives, the other board members were desperate for solutions to save the school from its imminent demise. When Morgan began as a board member, Antioch's budget was less than $15,000 per year, with only about fifty students enrolled. The board lacked the energy to develop their own escape plan, and offered Morgan a free hand to resurrect the school. In the summer of 1919, twenty years after dropping out of college, Morgan returned to the doorstep of higher education, this time as the leader and not as the student or the teacher.[70]

At the dawn of the 1920s, Morgan had matured into a nationally known engineer, reformer, and educational theorist. In particular, Morgan refined his plans for practical education and the components of his small community through several significant initiatives. His worker camps of the Miami Conservancy District exemplified the ideal community of his dreams, which stressed morality, education, and cooperation. As a state and national representative for the League to Enforce Peace, Morgan rallied for Wilson's League of Nations Covenant and the idea of a war-free world. Finally, Morgan's development of the Jacob's Pillow school and the launching of the Moraine Park School represented his interest in reformulating education as a practical experience. Through these areas of reform, Morgan exemplified the tenets of community building, morality, and social change, all key concepts in Bellamy's predictions for the future. These transformative years are crucial to understanding Morgan's approach to reforming higher education at Antioch.

The following decade challenged Morgan and other Americans to understand the changing social climate of the postwar world. The reforms of the Progressive Era—women's suffrage, national prohibition, changes in the election of officials, and a national income tax—created innumerable alterations to society. While reforms continued into the 1920s, the heyday of the Progressive Era passed into a period dominated by modernist thought. Many reformers, including Morgan, did not adapt to the shifting winds and found the decade a difficult time of unintended changes and setbacks for progress. Morgan countered these social and cultural forces with a moral rigidity that harkened back to the late Victorian Era. Ironically, Morgan rejected many of the components of the modern society that had contributed to his successes. While at the helm of Antioch, he turned inward and refocused on the principles of building small communities, promoting practical education, and developing character. Those traits served him well in revitalizing the college and facing other challenges of the decade.

4

EDUCATING THE COMMUNITY

On Sunday, 17 August 1919, Arthur Morgan penned a rare letter to his mother about his sudden involvement with Antioch College. He wrote, "It is the biggest job outside of [the Miami] Conservancy [District] I ever undertook, and I think it the most important as well." Recounting the events of the past weeks, Morgan wrote, "I was elected to the board of trustees before I knew they were thinking of me. I looked over the situation and told the trustees I thought the situation was hopeless as a standard small college, but that there might be some hope if it could be doing something other colleges were not." Morgan described his emerging plan to allow students to work in nearby industries to both learn practical business skills and pay their way through college. The trustees were favorable to the revitalization strategy and as Morgan explained to his mother, "they approved my suggestion and practically turned the college over to me for me to reorganize and finance." To lead this important transition, Morgan expected to "let go of other interests," such as the League to Enforce Peace and the Moraine Park School.[1]

But Morgan couched his excitement with the reality of his limited experience with higher education. He wrote, "I would not want to be president of the college, for that job ought to go to a man of long experience in school work." However, Morgan admitted that he wanted "to pick the president and the faculty, and arrange the courses," and develop relationships with nearby industries willing to host the students. His wife Lucy would help him with those enormous short-term goals, as she "has lots of practical ideas on college affairs having gone to college, taught in one and having run a college dormitory and fed college girls." He closed the letter saying that "we have not got far enough yet to make sure of anything, but I feel encouraged" with progress at Antioch.[2]

Much of Morgan's letter dealt with one proposal to make his practical educational package a reality. The day before he wrote the letter to his mother, Arthur Morgan and Gordon Rentschler took a short field trip from Dayton, Ohio, to inspect the Antioch College campus. Rentschler, one of the original board members of the Miami Conservancy District and close associate of Henry Ford, planned to build a Ford automobile plant next to the campus. Rentschler saw the proposal as a strong business investment, while Morgan envisioned a way for the college's students to work their way through school. The marriage of practical work experience and a liberal arts education seemed a practical way to revitalize the ailing school and reinvent Antioch's reputation.[3]

While plans for the Ford plant in Yellow Springs evaporated, the concept of students working part-time to learn practical skills and spending the other half of their time in traditional coursework stuck with Morgan. That plan formed the centerpiece of Morgan's "Antioch scheme," as journalist H. L. Mencken called it two years later. Morgan's plan dominated the institution's growth throughout the 1920s. Some components of Morgan's Antioch were not too distant from the future described in Edward Bellamy's utopian writings. Antioch became his first opportunity to build an idealized and self-sufficient community, to institutionalize moral standards, to encourage the growth of small industries, and to test practical educational methods in higher education. But more than just resurrecting a failing college, Morgan hoped that success at Antioch would demonstrate to others his brand of reform and how tangible social change could occur by building one small community at a time.[4]

The predominance of the automobile and the Ford Motor Company in American life during the 1920s is a good starting point to understand that crucial decade. During the 1920s, Henry Ford's company produced half the cars in the world and became the largest industry in the American economy—using 20 percent of the steel produced in the country, 75 percent of the nation's plate glass, and 80 percent of its rubber. Ford's assembly lines produced vehicles quickly, efficiently, and in such large quantities that the cost (just over $260 for a Model T) was within reach for most Americans. Installment and credit plans further eased the financial burden of buying a car. During the decade auto ownership tripled, and motor vehicles became a commonplace part of society instead of an unusual invention reserved for only the wealthy. Some of the ripple effects of automobile ownership included road paving projects, gas stations, automobile clubs, driving tours, and a general sense of independence from regimented transportation schedules. The automobile literally and psychologically created an open road for Americans, who were now more urban than rural, to explore.[5]

Great economic prosperity in the 1920s made it easier for Americans to support a consumer revolution. In addition to buying their first car, many Americans became first-time homeowners. Low interest loans and installment credit increased homeownership and spurred new home building, including houses bought as kits through mail-order catalogs. To fill those new homes, manufacturers developed new kinds of inexpensive electrified kitchen appliances to reduce household drudgery. But appliances were just the beginning of new offerings; never before had Americans had access to so many new consumer products, which were advertised on a national scale through radio and motion pictures. Games and children's toys, health products, retail clothing, and household electrical appliances were just a few of the options for Americans. New mass produced food products included Baby Ruth candy bars, Wonder Bread, and Eskimo Pies.[6]

In the 1920s, most Americans had more time for leisure and entertainment. Unlike previous decades, during this period many blue and white collar workers enjoyed a shortened work week, a paid vacation, and higher wages. As a result of having more disposable income and more free time, Americans spent over $4 billion a year on recreation activities such as attending baseball games, watching auto races, betting on horse racing, playing miniature golf, and buying wind-up children's toys and erector sets. Amusement parks and family vacations had replaced ceaseless work schedules for many workers. No longer were leisure activities and pastimes reserved for wealthy Americans.[7]

Economic prosperity, consumerism, and increased leisure activities were directly tied to larger changes of the period. While the nation returned to a peacetime normalcy after World War I, drastic cultural shifts transformed the American landscape. At the national level, the work of Progressive reformers brought national prohibition and women's suffrage. American voters, including women, elected three presidents from the Republican Party to guide the nation through the decade. Warren G. Harding, Calvin Coolidge, and Herbert Hoover promoted a path of economic deregulation and laissez-faire policies at the federal level. Victory in World War I spurred a confidence in American business, farming, and ingenuity. War-torn European nations demanded American crops, steel, and capital to rebuild their economies and feed their citizens. Throughout the 1920s, American businesses boomed and stock market prices skyrocketed to unimaginable heights. Between 1921 and 1929, the gross national product increased by 59 percent to 103.1 billion, the gross national product per capita rose by 42 percent, and personal income grew by nearly 40 percent. Most white Americans benefited from this era of great prosperity, which appeared to have a limitless ceiling.[8]

After over two decades of Progressive reform, many Americans believed that society had greatly improved since the first days of the twentieth century. Legislation and reforming crusades had brought greater order to a predominantly urban and a generally more complicated society. Other Americans, including African American soldiers returning to segregated society and a reborn Ku Klux Klan, recent immigrants struggling to make ends meet in the face of labor inequality, and suspected radicals accused of un-American activities during the Red Scare, were not so sure about the successes of the Progressive Era. Some Progressive reformers remained active as civic leaders and elected officials, but most scholars argue that the movement stalled during the early part of the decade.[9]

The activities of Progressive reformers such as Arthur Morgan during this period refute the notion that the Progressive ideals withered just as Americans reaped the fruit of reform. While he was president at Antioch College, Morgan's Progressivism matured, and he refined his plan for achieving an enlightened society. Morgan's ideas about community, education, and morality came into sharper focus while at Antioch. At this time, Morgan also imagined the world 100 years into the future and those predictions reveal the strong influence of Edward Bellamy. The eugenics movement, in many ways an outgrowth of Progressive Era reform, became an important cornerstone of Morgan's plan for social betterment. During a period of rapid cultural change, economic speculation, and national prosperity, Morgan developed his skills as a college administrator, publicist, fundraiser, and educational expert, well on his way to the national spotlight. To build Antioch, Morgan needed funding and attention; both came easily for the budding professional, and during this period he enacted notable educational reforms and achieved personal milestones.

In the weeks following Arthur Morgan's appointment to Antioch's board of trustees in the summer of 1919, he crafted revitalization possibilities for the bankrupt college. He first turned to his colleague and self-picked headmaster of the Moraine Park School, Frank D. Slutz. Morgan asked Slutz to develop a rough outline of a curriculum combining industrial employment and standard instruction. On June 30, 1919, less than ten days from the time Morgan discovered his appointment, Slutz delivered to Morgan a four-page plan for transforming Antioch. Much like the qualifications for an engineering position, Antioch would measure applicants "upon the *ability to do the job,* instead of upon previous preparation." The courses, or norms, would each last for an entire academic year, but the "quality and content" of the sessions would determine the number and frequency of the class meetings. Standard subjects such as English, economics, sociology, chemistry, and biology were placed alongside courses in shop work, factory office work, and business administration. Slutz suggested that each student work a four-hour shift each day as part of the latter category of courses, and earn a salary to offset tuition and expenses. The outline estimated that after four years of study and work, students would have accumulated the twenty courses required for graduation, would have paid for their education, and would have gained enough practical experience to qualify for decent jobs. Most amazing about the document was that Slutz compiled the outline so quickly and that all subsequent documents related to Antioch's reorganization, which bear Morgan's name, follow the same basic structure of combining work and traditional instruction.[10]

During the next month, Morgan gathered administrative and curricular information from other small liberal arts colleges. He discovered that schools such as Berea College in Kentucky taught students practical skills alongside traditional academics, but Morgan wanted to go another direction. To resurrect Antioch from financial ruin and an outdated reputation, he added to Slutz's outline a clear plan for students to receive "industrial education." Even

Bird's eye view of Antioch College. Antiochiana, Antioch College.

though most educators of the time classified industrial education as reserved for African Americans, there is no indication that Morgan's choice of words triggered any kind of racial backlash or incorrect assumptions. Morgan was clearly focused on white students. While there had been African American students at Antioch since the school's founding, the first significant enrollment of African Americans came in the 1940s. Instead of having students work on campus directly for the school, Morgan planned to place students in actual positions with nearby companies, whether large corporations like the Ford Motor Company or small enterprises making handmade products. He also hoped that the school would launch and operate its own industries. His brand of practical education would give students real-world experience and the option to adjust their curriculum to better prepare them for working after graduation.[11]

Morgan moved rapidly with his planning for Antioch. On August 3, 1919, the Antioch College Board of Trustees met to discuss new directions for the school. Morgan officially presented to the board his reorganization plans. In essence, the program of work and study would make academic life more holistic. The finalized plan called for students to alternate every five weeks between work and school. While based on ideas from other colleges (including the nearby University of Cincinnati), Morgan's work-study program was one of the first of its kind in the nation. One additional result would be closer ties between the school and private enterprises, which meant possible sources of income and support. The board encouraged Morgan to refine the details of his plan, and that month he set off to evaluate the immediate needs of campus. By September, Morgan completed a thorough survey of the campus buildings, existing faculty, and connections to the town of Yellow Springs. He estimated that repairs of the preexisting buildings (president's house, main building, and dormitories) would cost $150,000, nearly the amount he expected for an annual operational budget, which Morgan placed in the $170,000 range. From these early surveys Morgan consistently remarked on the great value of Glen Helen, the wooded park adjoining the campus.[12]

In early 1920, Morgan expanded his reorganization plan by supplementing the work-study program with curricular changes. Simply put, Morgan wanted to limit the number of programs, courses offered, and number of faculty, while expanding the coeducational student body to about 500. In his view, fewer teaching positions meant higher salaries and the ability to recruit top-notch faculty, who would teach larger overview courses and then have the freedom to design "autonomous courses" for smaller group of students interested in a specific area of study. Using that methodology, Morgan hoped to improve the overall academic quality of Antioch without decreasing enrollment. That winter, Morgan strengthened his work-study component by meeting with owners of several companies, and he tested the development waters by meeting with several potential financial supporters. But at the same time, Morgan admitted to the board his limitations for reorganizing Antioch.[13]

By early 1920, Morgan was in great demand throughout the region. He still had responsibility for completing the engineering work of the Miami Conservancy District. Other obligations, such as appointments to the boards of the Moraine Park School and the League to Enforce Peace, could be ignored, but his reputation depended on the successful completion of his engineering work in the Miami River Valley. As another factor, by early 1920 Morgan had come up empty in selecting a potential president for Antioch. Morgan's claim that he originally had no interest in becoming president was genuine, largely because he knew that academic credentials were a prerequisite for higher education administration and he possessed none. But by the spring of 1920, unable to attract potential presidential candidates and in the spirit of his practical education mantra, Morgan reconsidered his ascension to the post.[14]

To make such a bold leap and to continue to rally Antioch's flag in lieu of his other duties Morgan needed encouragement from the board. On April 1, 1920, Morgan wrote the board on his progress and asked for more authority to proceed with plans for reorganization. He reported that he had undertaken a full survey of the campus grounds and buildings, had developed a preliminary budget, and had plans for ensuring the school a stable water supply and sewage services from Yellow Springs. He next listed the daunting challenges that lay ahead, the largest of which included launching a $500,000 fundraising campaign, recruiting faculty, making building repairs, and securing support from private companies for his work-study program. The board responded positively to Morgan's objectives and at a meeting on May 3, 1920, the group adopted Morgan's preliminary plans for reorganization. But not all members of the board supported Morgan's ideas, and some made a fast exit. At the annual meeting in June, several members of the board resigned, and Morgan replaced them with friends, associates, and supporters. That summer Morgan situated himself as the leader of the board, and at a meeting on July 6, the board of trustees unanimously elected Arthur Morgan as the fourteenth president of Antioch College.[15]

Morgan's unlikely rise to the presidency of a small college represented yet another significant jump in his development. By that time, he had mastered the art of delegation and surrounding himself with competent associates. Better than a juggler, Morgan had a network of associates and underlings who could help him manage projects and maximize his time. While Morgan walked into a dire situation at Antioch, he did not assume a leadership role overnight; it was a more gradual process. He convinced the Antioch board of trustees of the validity of his ideas by presenting a clear plan of action, innovative approaches to education, and impressive connections to funding opportunities. After a few years at Antioch, Morgan made it clear that morality would serve as a guidepost for the students and the school.

Morgan's style of administration was an unusual combination of project management and moral rectitude. Whether he was building a dam or leading a college, Morgan began each project with an attitude of flexibility, adaptability, and openness to innovation. However, once he had established his design, Morgan dictated a rigid set of rules to those working for him that could appear idealistic, paternalistic, and sometimes close-minded to new ideas. This pattern reoccurred during his larger projects, including the Miami Conservancy District, Antioch, and the Tennessee Valley Authority. However, his administrative style often attracted more followers than detractors.

Even though Morgan claimed only a handful of educational influences and asserted that he had been thinking about approaches to practical education his entire life, he absorbed the larger discussions about educational theory during the 1910s and early 1920s. At Antioch, Morgan incorporated emerging educational theories into his programs. He also became active in a national organization aimed at reforming the nation's school system.

By 1920, educational theorists and reformers had much to celebrate. John Dewey, perhaps the most recognizable educational theorist of the first decades of the century, led the way toward connecting education reform with the advances of the Progressive movement. He blamed rapid industrialization for many of the problems in the educational system, and called for education that emphasized practicality, democratic principles, community, and the centrality of the student in the learning process. Dewey and others defined progressive education as a way to create an enlightened and adaptable citizenry capable of making informed choices and adjusting to the new social roles of the modern era. A more progressive educational system offered Americans practical skills and prepared them for the ever-improved society that reformers had imagined. Even though his theories shifted over time, by 1920 Dewey's educational approaches were part of the reforms of the Progressive movement.[16]

Dewey's reforms brought significant shifts and mixed opinions. Progressive educational methods appealed best to the middle or upper middle class. By 1920, a large number of primary and secondary schools, often in comfortable white communities, adopted Dewey's methods. Administrators in higher education took careful note of these trends and developed more "practical" programs needed to fill important white collar positions, such as in the professional fields of teaching and business. As one result, traditional courses such as Latin, Greek, algebra, and rhetoric declined in enrollment, while typing, civics, law, engineering, and chemistry courses filled with interested students. Critics contended that progressive methods of education actually limited democracy and instilled the future workforce with the concepts of scientific management and efficiency standards.[17]

While Dewey took much of the credit and criticism for the principles of progressive education, other proponents consolidated the ideas of the movement into a national organization. In 1919, Stanwood Cobb, a teacher at the United States Naval Academy, called a meeting of progressive-minded educators at the District of Columbia Public Library. At this gathering, which featured speeches and discussions about the "new education," Cobb and others founded the Association for the Advancement of Progressive Education. Leaders of the group collected membership dues of $1 each from all eighty-seven attendees. Cobb and others in the Washington, D.C. area continued small gatherings during the fall and winter, to plan for fundraising, publicity, recruitment of new members, and a large annual meeting set for the spring of 1920.[18]

The 1920 annual meeting of the group in Washington, D.C. established the budding organization. At that April meeting, leaders shortened the name of their group to the Progressive Education Association (PEA), recruited new members, defined their educational principles, and appointed officers. Members of the group defined practical education and their mission with the following seven themes: allowing students the freedom to develop naturally; application of learned knowledge to real world situations; teachers as guides and not task masters; scientific study of student development; attention to the health and physical development of students; cooperation between the school and the home; and the progressive school as a leader in educational movements. To build national attention, Cobb filled the PEA's advisory council with well known authors such as H. G. Wells, Floyd Dell, and Angelo Patri, and notables including Mrs. Alexander Graham Bell. The advisory council offered retired Harvard president Charles Eliot the presidency of the organization. Eliot, who was eighty-five, declined the honor for health reasons and accepted the role as honorary president. Arthur Morgan, who did not attend the meeting, became their second choice for the presidency of the Progressive Education Association.[19]

Morgan success with the Moraine Park School attracted great attention from the PEA. His Progressive reforms, insistence on practical education for elementary and secondary school students, and growing notoriety made Morgan a perfect fit. Just after the appointment, Morgan wrote an introductory letter to the other leaders of the PEA. He announced a series of meetings to be held that fall in Washington, D.C., Philadelphia, Boston, and New York, where members could discuss policies of the organization and other aspects of the progressive education movement. At the Boston meeting on August 6, 1920, Morgan addressed the audience not as an educator but as a product of the "old regime" educational system. He emphasized the practical nature of education in preparing students for economic and social responsibilities of adulthood. For Morgan, the development of character was the most important part of primary and secondary education. Through these and other early meetings, Morgan formulated principles and generated publicity for the PEA. In appeal letters, he explained that better pay for teachers, smaller classes, an emphasis on the individuality of each student, and new or renovated school buildings were the central to the PEA's mission to improve the national system of education. The organization published bulletins about achievements in progressive and practical education projects, including a detailed history of the Moraine Park School.[20]

By the fall of 1920, Morgan tempered his involvement with the PEA. In a November 18, 1920, letter to PEA founding member Gertrude Stevens Ayres, Morgan admitted that personal and professional factors had led him to consider resigning as president of the PEA. Morgan explained that "my doctors, Mrs. Morgan, and my friends are insistent that I carry less work." But his professional obligations were just as important. Morgan's letter continued, "My engineering work takes much of my time, and Antioch takes nearly all the rest. I *must* make Antioch go." Leaders of the PEA understood the preexisting demands on Morgan's time and allowed him to continue as their president on a more limited basis.[21]

During the early part of 1921, Arthur Morgan organized and presided over the second annual convention of the PEA, held that April in Dayton. As the highlight, the PEA advisory board elected John Dewey as a vice-president. While scheduling his close acquaintances as speakers, including Charles Kettering and Frank Slutz, Morgan took an opportunity at the meeting to promote his work at Antioch. Morgan explained, "It takes both theory and art to make a master of a calling, and our colleges have been so concerned with the theory of the calling that they have had no time for the art of the calling. We are planning to combine the two at Antioch." By 1921, Morgan's focus on higher education reform set him apart from the other leaders of the

PEA, who were most concerned with national policy for primary and secondary schools. Morgan agreed to serve as president of the PEA for another year, but clearly his ambitions lay in higher education reform at Antioch.[22]

Had the timing been different, Morgan might have steered the organization toward higher education, but he later admitted that Antioch work kept him away from the organization. Still, Morgan served as an important early cheerleader for the PEA and the movement. His close work with education reformers of the period, and not specific parts of his PEA leadership, represents the scale of his expanding network of influential associates—many of whom would fund reorganization at Antioch. Morgan recalled years later that the early leaders of the PEA were unrealistic in their approaches to education reform and needed to be less evangelistic and more critical. But even without Morgan's contributions or direction, the organization prospered during the next three decades. Beginning in 1924, the PEA published the influential journal *Progressive Education* and, by the 1930s, expanded their reach into educational research. After World War II, PEA membership declined, as other professional educational groups gained momentum, and the Progressive Education Association finally dissolved in 1955.[23]

Arthur Morgan accepted the presidency of Antioch College at the July 6, 1920 board of trustees meeting, and at that very same gathering he distributed an updated reorganization program for the school. The four-page document began with historic assets of the school, including the legacy of Horace Mann and the claim that Antioch was the first college to equally admit men and women, even though Oberlin College in northern Ohio admitted women twenty years earlier. Morgan then explained that Antioch would be a small liberal arts college focused on the individuality of its students, which could teach practical and technical skills alongside standard academic subjects. His work-study concept would allow students to pay for their education, while they gained industrial experience. The anticipated period of study would take students six years to complete. But Morgan still needed time to attract quality faculty members and students, secure financial support, and promote his plans at a national level. The preexisting curriculum would continue that fall and next spring, but Morgan told the board that he expected to launch his "Antioch Program" the following year, in September 1921.[24]

Following the meeting, Morgan spent the rest of the summer traveling through the northeast searching for Antioch supporters. He first secured a number of new members for the depleted board of trustees. The new board of twenty members (thirteen were fresh to Antioch) included educators, bankers, lawyers, journalists, and other influential businessmen. The most noteworthy members included *Atlantic Monthly* editor Ellery Sedgwick, General Motors vice-president Charles Kettering (who later pledged $250,000 to Antioch and doubled that figure by the end of the decade), and former dean of the Harvard University School of Business Administration and president of the *New York Evening Post* Edwin F. Gay. The new members brought with them national connections, ideas for fundraising and publicity, and clear insights on education reform. When Morgan joined the Antioch board of trustees in 1919, seventeen out of its nineteen members were from Ohio, but by 1920 Morgan had filled the spots with thirteen from Ohio, four from New York, two from Massachusetts, and one from Michigan. By 1930, nearly half of the board members at Antioch were from states other than Ohio. During the early 1920s, the refreshed board of trustees wholeheartedly supported Morgan's initiatives.[25]

Morgan did even more house-cleaning by building a new staff and faculty group at Antioch. He inherited thirteen full-time employees, with only two holding a Ph.D. By 1921, Morgan had expanded the staff to twenty-five teaching faculty, the president (himself), two librarians, and a dean of women. Only half of the previous employees remained on the roster. Even more dramatic, Morgan brought in another twenty new employees by the beginning of classes in 1922. He searched nationally for faculty, staff, librarians, and administrators. As his most ambitious recruitment, in early 1921 Morgan worked with Charles Eliot on the prospect of hiring John Dewey to teach at Antioch. While Dewey decided not to come to Yellow Springs, other nationally known educators and experts did, including social science professor and children's author Hendrick W. Van Loon, and Northeastern University professor Philip Nash, who served as a dean. However, Morgan faced the problem of retaining high quality faculty, especially when many of his new recruits left urban areas such as New York and Chicago to move to Yellow Springs. Van Loon and many other top recruits came to Antioch, but nearly all departed within a few years. Adding to the struggles of moving to a small academic environment, Morgan cast a heavy shadow over those he administered. Once his plans were in place at Antioch, Morgan exhibited a much more rigid and moralistic approach to leading the school. Morgan required his faculty and staff to embrace his vision for Antioch—a devotion that drove many faculty to other pastures.[26]

Morgan faced an additional challenge of attracting quality students to begin an untested six-year program that required them to work far outside of the traditional classroom. Journalist H. L. Mencken summarized this problem best, saying that Morgan "will get plenty of applicants, but most of them will be, not the superior fauna he dreams of, but simply boneheads unable to pass the entrance examinations at Yale, Amherst, and Ohio Baptist University." Morgan first approached the issue by arranging for diverse options for student work-study. In addition to having students work for Antioch directly, as library assistants or workers in a campus print shop, he anticipated that five hundred private industries within a thirty mile radius of Yellow Springs would agree to host working Antioch students. By fall 1921, with help from Philip Nash and Frank Slutz, Morgan had arranged work assignments at nearly forty off-campus enterprises. As the number of participating corporations grew, so too did the geographic range of the program; within the first few years, Antioch students worked in Philadelphia, Detroit, Miami, Cleveland, and New York City.[27]

Much like his criteria for hiring new faculty, Morgan had in his mind the "model" Antioch student. He valued character, personality, intelligence, physical health, and maturity. Unlike other schools, Morgan admitted students without high school diplomas. He explained in a 1921 curriculum guide that some of the highest quality students might not be able to complete a high school program, but might still possess exceptional qualities of character and experience. Although Morgan had graduated high school, this requirement indirectly referred to his background of limited educational opportunities and taking the personal initiative of practical self-education. Morgan also disregarded any kind of standard college entrance examinations to measure the quality of the applicant. His curriculum guide described the purpose of Antioch more as a trade school to train successful business owners, administrators, professionals, and public officials than as a lofty institution of higher education to train academic scholars. Morgan's appeals for somewhat non-traditional students brought a huge response. In the summer of 1921, Antioch received over eight hundred applications, with two hundred of those enrolling in the fall. Over forty percent of the 1921 student body at Antioch hailed from states other than Ohio. Never before had the student body and the campus been so diverse.[28]

Morgan built national interest for his Antioch program through a variety of networks. In early 1921, he announced his reorganization plans to a familiar audience, professional engineers. His first article, "The Antioch Plan," appeared in the January issue of *Engineering News Record*. It stressed the groundbreaking nature of the school's work-study program and how Antioch would prepare the managers and factory owners of the future. Morgan asked for criticism of the plan from his fellow engineers to help him perfect the vocational and near-factory programs at Antioch. Before classes began that fall, popular audiences learned about Antioch through the work of journalists writing for periodicals such as *The World's Work, The New Republic,* and *The Nation.* Each of those articles stressed the importance of technical education for college students and applauded Morgan's designs for work-study at Antioch. By the fall of 1921, journalists and educational experts praised Morgan's Antioch plans as a revolutionary, although untested, experiment in higher education.[29]

As excitement for the beginning semester of Morgan's Antioch grew, Morgan spent equal time fundraising for the school. During early 1921, Morgan unofficially received financial pledges from a number of businessmen and philanthropists. On May 11, 1921, Morgan launched a $200,000 campaign for the school, and by July supporters pledged half of that amount. Morgan solicited potential donors through mass mailing, local presentations, and his preexisting network of associates. He even donated a good deal of his own money to the cause. That year, Morgan actually doubled the expected figure by raising $400,000 for Antioch, but these funds were for immediate needs and were not used to start an endowment. Morgan used much of the start-up money to purchase the nearby Glen Helen property, build homes adjoining the campus, renovate the campus buildings, and attempt to attract high-quality faculty by offering competitive salaries. He reserved the remainder for operating expenses and anticipated purchases for the next two years. Ongoing fundraising and promotion for Antioch consumed much of Morgan's time as president. When he came up short, Morgan resorted to borrowing from supporters, especially Charles Kettering.[30]

In September 1921, the reorganized Antioch College opened its doors to students. Just over two hundred students matriculated that fall and received their various work-study assignments. Morgan reported great success with student placements and expected to expand work options in the coming year. Most of the campus improvement projects ended that fall, including renovated male and female dorms, a new campus sewer system, a new chemistry laboratory, and new homes for Antioch faculty (and Morgan) on nearby property. Morgan also reported purchasing athletic equipment and building tennis courts, although intercollegiate sports such as football and basketball did not last through the decade. Flush with cash, new faculty, a refreshed board of trustees, a more diverse student body, and physical improvements to the campus, Morgan ended the 1921 school year on a positive note.[31]

Morgan's next few years at Antioch built on his initial success by gradually expanding the work-study programs and striking a balance between liberal arts and technical education. He later added self-directed study courses for all students and used existing connections to build small campus industries. Awareness for Antioch had never been higher, including laudatory articles in *The Outlook, The New Republic,* and perhaps the most significant a positive article by Ida Tarbell in *Collier's.* She described Arthur Morgan's life as an American success story of overcoming limitations to lead engineering projects and educational advancements for the good of humanity. At the same time, Morgan maintained his own promotional activities by speaking and writing articles on developments at Antioch. Using his PEA connections with Ellery Sedgwick, Morgan contributed a 1922 essay on the collegiate experience to *Atlantic Monthly.* His article dealt with the educational philosophy of practical education and how Antioch offered a new way to prepare college graduates for the realities of the modern working world. Morgan wanted to create socially conscious professionals, more concerned with improving society than making profits.[32]

As Arthur Morgan's devotion to Antioch College grew in the early 1920s, he cast off many of his other responsibilities to focus on education reform. Not only did he exit from national organizations such as the League to Enforce Peace and the Progressive Education Association, but Morgan also kept a distance from his own engineering company. He headed up a handful of consulting projects during the 1920s, including drainage work in Colorado and New Mexico, but Morgan delegated most the work of the Morgan Engineering Company to his business associates. The theme of Morgan as a planner and builder, but not necessarily a man with longevity to see the work to the end, emerged during his first years at Antioch. In more modern-day terms, Morgan had mastered the ability to multi-task and delegate responsibilities to others. The most obvious example of these attributes can be seen

Arthur Morgan and Lucy Morgan at their Yellow Springs Home, 1921
Antiochiana, Antioch College.

with Morgan's minimal involvement with the Miami Conservancy District after 1920. Morgan made careful selections for his top administrators, and he made sure that they embraced his vision for each project. Morgan later recalled that assistant chief engineer Charles Paul and superintendent of construction Charles Locher "were so much more competent and experienced in large construction that I was largely without any necessary function." Morgan continued, saying that "For the last two or three years [of the Miami Conservancy District] I felt somewhat like a parasite on the job."[33]

The last stages of work on the Miami Conservancy District did not require Morgan's guiding hand, and he was absent from the glory of its completion. The major work of the district included the building of five dry retarding basin dams and the deepening and widening of the Miami River channel through the affected cities. Unlike the most notable dams built during the twentieth century, the district's structures were primarily made of earthen materials and concrete was only used for the conduits and spillway area—an untested design invented by Morgan and his engineers. In September 1921, with the project nearly seventy-five percent complete, Morgan resigned as chief engineer of the Miami Conservancy District to focus on Antioch and assigned assistant chief engineer Charles W. Paul the position. In 1922, the district began selling construction equipment and camp buildings (part of the model villages that Morgan had designed) at public auction. In early 1923, after five years of work, the construction officially ended with the completion of five enormous dry dams and a score of river channel improvement projects costing $34 million.[34]

With the fulfillment of the Miami Conservancy District, the city of Dayton and other cities on the Great Miami River were forever safe from flooding. Despite the national attention, Morgan remained focused on Antioch and not on engineering. Further demonstrating Morgan's newfound role as an educational innovator, in 1923, the University of Colorado awarded Morgan an honorary Doctor of Science degree. The college dropout turned college president had then become Dr. Morgan—a title he frequent wielded. As Morgan enjoyed the notoriety of Antioch during the mid-1920s, he began committing to paper more specific ideas about morality, character, human behavior, and heredity.[35]

In 1923, Morgan launched *Antioch Notes*, a semi-monthly journal devoted to promoting the programs at Antioch and, more specifically, to sharing his morally infused educational philosophies. The essays in *Antioch Notes* offer stunning and even contradictory glimpses of Morgan throughout the 1920s and 1930s. Through the pages of *Antioch Notes,* Morgan provided students and nationwide subscribers (reportedly 20,000 recipients) with his unique take on the world and education. Morgan's opinions on student behavior reflected his values and cures for the ills of the modern world. He spent many pages of *Antioch Notes* discussing the importance of morality, which he defined as one's individual traits or behaviors learned from associates or personal experience. Morgan emphasized that strong individual morality would solve the complex problems of modern society and "keep open the road to progress and well-being." At that higher level, Morgan's definition of morality bordered on middle- and upper-class *noblesse oblige* for those less fortunate. College educated students with practical business skills would be ripe for professional positions and economic opportunity, making it crucial for them to understand their moral duty to others. At the individual level, Morgan's morality encouraged his students and other responsible members of society to follow a path of restraint, Christian living, and furthering the general good of society. In particular, Morgan chided Antioch students to avoid tobacco, alcohol, stimulants, coffee, and tea, as they weakened one's moral fiber. By choosing not to indulge in personal vices, Morgan preached that students could exhibit high levels of social morality. Such a blueprint of conservatism and social responsibility, recognizable in Edward Bellamy's futuristic predictions, would lead to the enlightened character that Morgan wanted to produce at Antioch and further afield.[36]

In a similar fashion, Morgan wrote incessantly in *Antioch Notes* on the even broader topic of ethics and ethical standards. Morgan believed that the negative, neutral, and positive forces of society determined a larger set of governing ethical standards to follow. Ethics, according to Morgan, defined the overall beauty, economy, fitness, and conduct of a society. The most intelligent and innovative in a society (who also possessed the highest moral standards) would improve the quality of life by exercising ethical discrimination and set the tone for others. Morgan later wrote that, "My *one* business in life is to have an ethical philosophy, changeable tho it be, and to inforce [*sic*] it everywhere." As a true Progressive reformer, Morgan equated change with improvement and thus progress, but ignored any negative consequences resulting from near-paternalistic decision making. By building solid students with an ethical and moral conscience, Morgan hoped to bring about social uplift at a gradual pace. Morgan's larger view of ethics, as an almost uncontrollable force comparable to the weather, made the role of individual morality paramount in changing the lackluster American character, which he believed had drifted toward selfish individuality, materialism, crass commercialism, and economic motives.[37]

Morgan's words reached the desks of many educational and social reformers outside of Yellow Springs (later including Eleanor and Franklin Roosevelt). He reassured readers of *Antioch Notes* that his students were of the highest caliber, but faced the same societal temptations. He judged incoming freshman for intelligence, scholarship, and evidence of solid character. "Most Antioch freshmen have good personal standards," Morgan explained, "but they have twilight zones between good and bad, within which conduct is determined by prevailing custom." Such a diverse set of standards and collective experiences challenged the students' ability to arrive at a suitable moral middle ground. Morgan approached faculty recruitment in the same manner. He believed that faculty with impeccable character, sound scholarship, intelligence, and a desire to teach would be the greatest positive influence on impressionable young minds in need of a moral compass. The faculty's real job, according to Morgan, would be to build character in their students through demonstrating high moral standards. Morgan's idyllic view of Antioch, its students, and its faculty grew in the pages of *Antioch Notes,* making Yellow Springs sound like a benevolent community reminiscent of *Looking Backward* or even the never-realized utopian community of New Harmony, Indiana. Some students and faculty found Morgan's moralistic ramblings too much to take and departed, while others were drawn to Yellow Springs.[38]

By the mid-1920s, Morgan tightened his grip over the moral and ethical standards at Antioch. Because the negative and neutral forces of ethical improvement far outnumbered the smaller group of positive forward-thinking reformers, Morgan concentrated more on improving moral standards one individual at a time. But to achieve that massive task, Morgan decided that moral codes, devised by the most intelligent, were necessary to enlighten the masses. In the December 1926 issue of *Antioch Notes*, Morgan tried his hand at a moral code of conduct for students. He boldly prefaced the code with the assurance that "the following is an effort to formulate a statement which will find approximately universal acceptance in principle, and will cover almost every circumstance of life." The short list emphasized the importance of the whole over the individual, in the form of good will toward others. Honesty and integrity were integral to demonstrating a moral life.

DECEMBER 1, 1926

Morality

MORALITY is conduct which is good in the light of all of its consequences. Immorality is conduct which, though pleasing or desirable in its immediate results, in its total consequences is bad. Native intelligence, educated to enable people to see the whole result of their conduct, is just as essential for the highest morality as is right motive. Stupid and ignorant men depend upon leadership, yet cannot distinguish between good and bad leadership. In a democracy, the demagogue achieves his purposes through them.

Arthur Morgan's thoughts on morality in Antioch Notes, 1926. Antiochiana, Antioch College.

He addressed the health dangers of smoking, drinking, and sexual promiscuity by encouraging students to stay fit in mind and body. While Morgan often found difficulty in accepting the views of others, his code emphasized the importance of inquiry, considering the values of others, and aspiring to influence others. The publicized but never enforced code provided students important moral and ethical guideposts, but, perhaps more importantly, the document revealed much about Morgan's thinking on administration, controlling behavior, and how to improve the moral lapses of modern society. A similar moral code for employees would appear a few years later in Morgan's next assignment in Tennessee.[39]

Morgan's 1926 moral code for Antioch students listed eugenics as a key part of living a moral life. He defined eugenics simply as "the best lives should be perpetuated." In one article for *Antioch Notes*, under the heading "race suicide," Morgan decried the improper balance between growing non-white races and intelligent white Americans who had chosen not to have families. It was the duty, Morgan proclaimed, of the most intelligent, pure stock Americans to raise educated children and limit the growth of less desirable populations who were "too uncontrolled or too stupid to exercise birth control." Another document written about the same time predicted that, in the future, "the feeble minded will not be allowed to propagate. They will be isolated on self supporting farms, or sterilized." In today's terms, Morgan's statements sound cruel, racist, and xenophobic, but the concept of eugenic science was part of the Progressive mindset of the early twentieth century. Morgan was certainly not alone and not extreme in his beliefs about perpetuating the most intelligent and racially pure in favor of the weak of mind, character, or heritage. In fact, Morgan adopted eugenics later than many of his contemporaries, but Morgan continued to promote eugenics long after most had abandoned it as a scientific justification for anything.[40]

Eugenic thought developed in the second half of the nineteenth century as an outgrowth of debates on Charles Darwin's *On The Origin of Species* (1859). Darwin believed that higher forms of life evolved from more primitive organisms through natural selection and survival of the fittest. Scholars and scientists applied Darwin's evolutionary theory of natural selection to social, political, and economic development. The derivative theory of "social

Darwinism" served as the backbone ideology of the eugenics movement. In the 1880s Darwin's cousin Sir Francis Galton coined the term "eugenics." Defining eugenics as the theory of scientific improvement of the human race by better breeding, eugenicists believed that heredity largely determined success and development. Thus, they encouraged the perpetuation of those with the most desirable traits, while limiting those with the least desirable traits. Eugenicists determined the "unfit" largely on racial and class lines, favoring those with a western European, or Anglo, heritage. They believed that, by deemphasizing and gradually eliminating the weaker segments of society, a more enlightened civilization would result.[41]

The opportunities and challenges of the early twentieth century brought the eugenics movement to the forefront of Progressive reform efforts in the United States. Eugenics provided many reformers a scientific justification to limit the influx of immigrants. Since the end of the Civil War, increased numbers of Asians and eastern and southern Europeans had come to the United States in search of brighter futures. Many well-established citizens opposed the growing foreign population and demanded a return to Anglo-American Protestant values and workers. The publication of Madison Grant's *The Passing of the Great Race* in 1916 had tremendous influence on popular audiences. Grant's data asserted that the Northern European races that had founded America were of superior hereditary stock. If the new immigrants were the cause of the nation's problems, then restricting those huddled masses would result in the return of a more pure generation of Americans. Eugenics leaders were also concerned with limiting the perpetuation of the feeble-minded, the insane, the dangerous, the mentally ill, and the physically disabled. Sterilization of these "unfit" groups, according to eugenics supporters, would strengthen the gene pool of American society.[42]

The eugenic plan for "race betterment" attracted many followers during the first decades of the century. Prominent and influential figures, including Presidents Theodore Roosevelt and Woodrow Wilson, birth control advocate Margaret Sanger, and inventor Alexander Graham Bell, supported components of eugenics. The work of these and other progressive reformers spurred state and federal action to achieve their purposes. During the Progressive Era, eugenics leaders influenced the passage of state laws for sterilization and IQ testing. The growing acceptance of the eugenics movement assisted the creation and passage of the Immigration Act of 1924. Spearheaded by Washington congressman and president of the Eugenics Research Association Albert

Johnson, the law established an immigrant quota system based on country of origin and remained in effect until the 1960s.[43]

Eugenics leaders of the early twentieth century organized a number of professional groups, meetings, and publications to promote their efforts. The first, the American Breeders Association, founded in 1903, featured leadership from Secretary of Agriculture James Wilson and geneticist Charles Davenport. In 1913, the organization became the American Genetic Association and began publishing the *Journal of Heredity*. The movement gained momentum in the 1910s with a series of national conferences on race betterment and the founding of the Galton Society in 1918. Another significant eugenics organization emerged in the wake of the successful Second International Congress on Eugenics. The American Eugenics Society advocated sterilization, segregation, and marriage restrictions for the mentally ill or disabled. During the 1920s and 1930s, the organization was the largest and most effective eugenics group, with notable scientists, public health officials, urban planners, philanthropists, and engineers as its members.[44]

While many of Arthur Morgan's writings of the 1920s and early 1930s mentioned the importance of eugenics, his involvement came late in the movement. In 1929, he served as chairman of a symposium sponsored by the Ohio Race Betterment Association, which represents one of his first professional contributions to the eugenics movement. He wrote the foreword to the published proceedings announcing the goals of conference, which included the importance of proper birth and spacing of children, prenatal and childhood health, education reform, and restriction of parentage to those with serious hereditary problems, low intelligence, and social diseases. He closed the piece by comparing his scientific work of educating students at Antioch to scientifically determining the traits of future generations.[45]

Morgan returned to the eugenics movement several years later, in 1935, when the American Eugenics Society asked him to be honorary president. By that time the group dealt more with issues of birth control and sterilization efforts than immigration restrictions. During the heart of the Great Depression, the American Eugenics Society attempted to connect their eugenic programs with democratic principles. Combating the nation's economic woes, they argued, could be accomplished by limiting the size of families, especially curbing the arrival of children to the destitute or mentally unfit. At the time of the generous offer to be their honorary president, Morgan was well consumed with designing dams and social improvements for the Tennessee

Valley Authority. He declined their post, but did agree to address the membership at their annual meeting in New York in early May 1936.[46]

Attendance at the 1936 annual meeting of the American Eugenics Society swelled, largely due to having the chairman of the Tennessee Valley Authority as the keynote speaker. Morgan spoke on the importance of eugenics to social inheritance, especially related to how the work of the eugenicist could solve social problems and perpetuate cultural values. By this time, Morgan's view of eugenics had moved away from a strict adherence to sterilization of the unfit to solve problems. Instead, he endorsed programs that focused on the most fit in society, by encouraging them to reproduce, transmit their cultural values to the next generation, and take a leadership role in their communities. Still the educational theorist, Morgan emphasized that education was really the "process of eliminating negative values, of appraising values, comparing values, selecting the greatest values, of putting them in order, and of transmitting them to the next generation." His talk challenged the audience to focus on the social conditions (including education, family, and other environmental influences) which favored genetic improvement and inherited cultural traits.[47]

The leaders of the organization were pleased with Morgan's 1936 talk and his appearance at their annual meeting. However, Morgan's hectic schedule and massive responsibilities in Tennessee made it impossible for him to devote time to the organized eugenics movement. Much as he had during his early period of devotion to Antioch, during the 1930s Morgan eliminated involvement in most ancillary efforts or organizations to focus on the Tennessee Valley Authority. Morgan would return to the eugenics movement in the 1940s, long after the principles of the "science" had fallen out of favor because of the similarities of eugenics and Nazi atrocities based on genetics and ethnicity. But during the 1920s the concepts of eugenics (preserving culture, heredity, and engineering the future) fit well into his plans for the perfect community, character, and morality at Antioch.[48]

Morgan believed that eugenic practice improved character and increased character development with each successive generation. Edward Bellamy's writings also promoted the concept of eugenic science as a way to improve society. In his later biography of Edward Bellamy, Morgan explained the importance of eugenics to Bellamy's future society. In *Looking Backward,* Bellamy wrote that a stable social and economic order depended on a sound eugenics program. In other works, Bellamy suggested that the unfit in society would not be allowed to reproduce, and some of the most violent or deviant individuals should be isolated from the rest of society. During the 1920s, Morgan expanded his ideas on genetic improvement, most of which involved eugenic practice.[49]

By the mid-1920s, Morgan registered a number of successes at Antioch. Due to effective publicity and fundraising campaigns, new buildings, including a library named after Horace Mann, dormitories, and administrative offices dotted the campus. In 1924, the school completed the purchase of the Glen Helen property. In 1925, thirty-two students graduated from the school making it the largest graduating class in Antioch's first seventy-two years of existence. Total enrollment crept to nearly six hundred students, even more than Morgan had wished for. After just a few years in place, Morgan's reorganization plan created a stable curriculum and a balance between working and studying. The work-study program allowed students to train for careers in business, industry, government, education, engineering, medicine, publishing, and architecture, while taking liberal arts courses. In the first years of the program, nearly all students worked in Ohio, but by the end of the decade, only about half of the student work placements were in the Buckeye state.[50]

Morgan also faced challenges and criticism as Antioch's chief representative. In the fall of 1925, he struggled with an important decision on whether to admit an African American student to Antioch. While Morgan expected to open Antioch's doors to African American students, he believed that the prevailing public opinion and possible negative publicity would damage progress at the school, and he therefore denied the student admission. Students, faculty, and writers for the school's alternative newspaper, *The Blaze,* took issue with Morgan's action. That fall, several faculty members challenged Morgan's growing claim that Antioch offered courses and programs of study on par with Ivy League schools. While the faculty praised certain programs, they argued that many improvements were needed. The paternalistic Morgan, who initially operated with a sense of *carte blanche,* struggled during the mid-1920s. Ironically, many of the challenges from students and faculty were the result of the growth and success of the school, which Morgan cultivated.[51]

Morgan's public and private writings of the mid-1920s reveal a decided shift in his vision for Antioch. During the reorganization period, Morgan emphasized offering a practical education for future business leaders and entrepreneurs; simply put, students would get the advantages of a liberal arts school while getting real on-the-job training in an actual work setting. But after several years at the helm, Morgan upped the ante, proclaiming that Antioch would build students of character to impart social change. His offerings on morals and ethics, through the pages of *Antioch Notes* and during student addresses, made it clear that he wanted Antioch students to have a social conscience. According to Morgan, improving America's failing culture would take place by building one person (or Antioch student) at a time, building one small community (starting with Yellow Springs) at a time.[52]

Based on Morgan's past record in engineering and education, infusing an ethical component into a building project sounds almost predictable. Morgan attributed his moral principles as a necessary part of success with his private engineering firm, the completion of the Miami Conservancy District, and the reorganization at Antioch. By exercising the principles of honesty, cooperation, and social concern for others, he believed his projects could help take the nation to a more perfect cultural level. But what Morgan did not account for at Antioch during the mid-1920s were critical reactions from faculty, students, and financial supporters. As Morgan's initiatives moved closer to attaining the moral perfection that he sought, and drifted further from the practical concerns of running a small college, he found himself isolated and dissatisfied with progress at Antioch.

As Morgan attempted to refocus the moral compass at Antioch, he also looked to the future for a path to ethical and moral bliss. In January 1924, Morgan wrote a lengthy list of predictions for the world of 2024. His list of 105 specific changes during the coming one hundred years relied on the heavy influence of Edward Bellamy's writings and the tenets of the eugenics movement. Despite Morgan's prolific publishing of articles during the following decades on a diverse set of topics, the list, simply entitled "One Hundred Years from Now," never made it to the printed page, and has gone unstudied by scholars. The document, a fascinating example of utopian literature, reveals Morgan grappling with the issues, practical applications, and potential of the world of the 1920s and far beyond.[53]

Similar to the beginning to Bellamy's *Looking Backward,* Morgan prefaced the document with an explanation how he gained access to a glimpse of the future. He explained, "Calling on our family medium one day I asked for a message from my great, great grandfather. Through an accidental reversal of the time control, she put me in touch instead with my great, great grandson."

In no particular order and with different levels of explanation, he listed 105 changes in the coming one hundred years. Morgan's predictions fit well into about a dozen themes, all of which pointed to gradually building an ideal society. In 2024, hunger, poverty, war, and immorality were largely eradicated, through invention and an ethical evolution. Many insights reflect the influence of *Looking Backward,* including the elimination of wealth in favor of economic redistribution, global governance based on a larger body called the League of Nations, the assignment of individuals to occupations that best suited their talents and interests, women having the freedom to pursue professional careers while managing their families, better use of natural resources for recreation and energy production, and, instead of large urban areas, the world of 2024 consisted of small close-knit communities and specialized industries.[54]

In the document, Morgan spent the most space talking about the topics of agriculture, education, ethics, and eugenics. Agricultural developments were a necessity for supporting a growing world population. In an effort to feed the world, Morgan believed that future generations would harvest foods from both tropical and arctic regions, with a strong reliance on the oceans for meat, especially whales. To improve existing agricultural practices, Morgan explained that soils would be sterilized to kill unwanted plants and then replanted with high-yield crops. Terracing, crop rotation, and tree farming were other methods used to reclaim unusable farmland in the twenty-first century. Agricultural research would result in the discovery of new medicines and the eradication of diseases. Advances in agricultural practices related to the greater management and conservation of natural resources, such as coal and other ores, water, sun, and the wind—all necessary elements to support a world of perhaps billions of people.[55]

Holistic education played a heavy role in the structure of Morgan's future society. Teachers commanded respect from all members of society. Education had become a lifelong process, especially in the case of industries making sure that their workers were given significant opportunities to learn new skills and follow their interests. In fact, most industries took responsibility for educating their employees, which made specialized technical and vocational training schools obsolete. With wealth not an important part of the future society, Morgan believed that business education would be more about teaching ethics, employee management, and how to develop new skills, rather than focusing on how to make profits. Similar to the pages of *Antioch Notes,* Morgan stressed that an ethical education—consisting of honesty, loyalty, inquiry, and restraint—was at the core of a more enlightened, intelligent, and refined society.[56]

Morgan hoped to achieve a more advanced civilization through an ethical revolution, but he also relied on eugenics to weed out the less intelligent in society. His predictions suggested that careful selection of mates, propagation by those with high levels of intelligence and character, sterilization of the feeble minded, and emphasis on only the most intelligent children would bring about a more perfect order. In rearing children, Morgan combined the importance of physical health and genetics saying that "every child grows up under the care and periodical examination of a qualified surgeon," but "if during this process very serious inherited defects are discovered, the person is advised to never have children, and serious consequences follow the ignoring of this advice." By targeting and then isolating those who possess less than satisfying inherited traits, Morgan saw the chance to build a society of quality instead of mere quantity. Morgan defined these inadequate traits (both inherited and learned) as social, cultural, educational, psychopathic, physical, and dietary defects. These tainted tendencies would be eliminated from humankind through simple birth control (careful selection and sterilization), holistic education, and an accepted moral code of behavior.[57]

Morgan's futuristic essay touched on his emerging world views about education, ethics, morals, art, culture, and reforming society. As before, he took the opportunity to chide users of immoral substances such as stimulants, narcotics, tobacco, alcohol and even hot spices used in cooking, saying that persons in the twenty-first century had discovered that those temporary satisfactions were empty and worthless. The reoccurring themes of practical education, moral superiority, ethical control, eugenics, and social evolution were in line with his writings in *Antioch Notes* and his frequent presentations to Antioch students. But by the late 1920s, Morgan noted a growing distance between his aspirations for Antioch and the actual results from the school.[58]

In just a few short years Morgan fully reorganized the mission and curriculum at Antioch College. Increased student enrollment, national attention, financial donations, and cooperative work agreements for students in a variety of locations and industries marked Antioch during the second half of the 1920s. It is debatable how innovative and original Morgan's programs were, but he clearly revitalized the school and set it back on its feet as a notable liberal arts school. In hindsight, it is unfortunate that Morgan rejected early

Arthur Morgan (standing at right) with Antioch Students, 1927. Antiochiana, Antioch College.

offers from Kettering to establish an endowment to keep Antioch financially sound. He long argued that the school needed the ongoing challenge of fundraising and awareness to stay relevant.[59]

His greatest admitted miscalculation at Antioch was the speed at which campus-operated industries developed. Morgan wanted about a dozen small campus industries to provide the school with basic services, employment and training for students, and income for the institution. These small industries would solidify the concept of the small self-sufficient community full of scholars, teachers, students, and enlightened residents. Morgan understood that other parts of the reorganization, especially the work-study program, had to be in place before launching small industries. But his implementation of small industries in the late 1920s was plagued with instability and, in the case of the Antioch Shoe Company, complete collapse. He did find success with several small industries including the Antioch Press and the Antioch Bookplate Company, but those accomplishments did not live up to his first expectations and took far too long to prosper. In a similar fashion, Morgan's plans for instituting self-studies (or autonomous courses) for every Antioch student stalled. The lukewarm faculty response to this change in the curriculum further upset Morgan.[60]

Despite the early successes at Antioch, Morgan's obsession with moral behavior and the demonstrated lack of ethical standards among the faculty and students brought him the greatest dissatisfaction. In a March 7, 1928, letter, he confided to his wife Lucy that "seven years is long enough to try out the method we have been working on [at Antioch]. If we are going to fulfill our hopes we must change our plans." As one possible solution, he considered a yearly dismissal of the students not committed to his moral vision. By keeping about half of the student body, Morgan stated that "disciplinary problems would then fade away, and we would begin to set new standards." Morgan never introduced this plan of moral rebirth. Frustrated with a campus unwilling to adapt to his high levels of morality, Morgan avoided many college activities and took a series of official leaves of absence to regroup. However, the national financial collapse of 1929 intensified the need to keep Antioch afloat through fundraising. Morgan resumed his role as chief development officer, but his effectiveness was plagued by his internal dissatisfaction with the moral and academic quality of Antioch.[61]

By 1931, Morgan faced a perfect storm of disappointment with Antioch. He believed that the faculty, students, and supporters had all but abandoned him, leaving any successes to founder. In June, he and Lucy left for an extended European retreat. While staying in the small town of Cintra, Portugal, Morgan penned a detailed letter to the Antioch faculty to express his concerns. The letter first described his failings as a leader and person. Morgan called his leadership "inadequate" due in part to his "lacking educational and cultural background, with a strain of petty bitterness and a tendency to make believe, with unstable temperament and bad judgment." He next railed against the fact that "there are too many colleges in America," with not enough good students and faculty to go around. Thus, Morgan believed that Antioch could only survive the storm of mediocrity by demonstrating its moral spirit and commitment to a purpose greater than just granting college degrees. He observed that students and faculty at Antioch had chosen to settle for less and give in to society, instead of taking the hard road of moral righteousness and purpose. Morgan explained that to have strong character and purpose, students and faculty must follow a moral code, take eugenic responsibility, exhibit scholastic excellence, and serve as role models for the small community. Morgan closed his lengthy missive emphasizing that Antioch was an excellent institution worthy of perpetuation, but because of its moral deficiencies, he admitted that, "Antioch is not the fulfillment of my hopes."[62]

Morgan intended to share the letter only with Lucy, but the lengthy note quickly circulated around the Antioch community, eventually taking a published form. In response, a group of Antioch faculty requested that Morgan provide specifics on how to resurrect the moral purpose of the school. They expressed support for Morgan but also outrage for not being consulted. Morgan returned to campus in early 1932 with a newfound vigor. He confided to Lucy that, if reorganized, Antioch would be "the job we have dreamed about." But if the school were reorganized, he must have full support from important financial backers, especially Charles Kettering. To answer the demands of the faculty, in January he sent them a lengthy essay on his outlook and life purpose. The meandering document emphasized the importance of human "validity" in one's work, social consequences of one's actions, hereditary and learned inheritance, pursuing a life that creates progress and value, and commitment to a greater common good. Morgan charged that progress at Antioch had been most hampered by only a "half-hearted" attempt to accomplish his moral and ethical goals. The patient faculty asked for more specifics and explained that they, too, were concerned with the issues Morgan raised.[63]

In May, Morgan provided the faculty with suggestions for curricular improvements at Antioch. He wanted to make courses less autonomous and more conforming to a set of teaching standards. Morgan asked for the formation of committees to determine these instructional practices, but more importantly he wanted each faculty group to compile a set of life aims and purposes to guide the academic lives of Antioch students. Almost counter to those goals, Morgan also asked that faculty commit to working with students on an individual basis and construct a life program for each person. In the document, Morgan proposed a restructuring of Antioch's academic programs around seven areas of study, which focused more on moral and ethical behavior than actual areas of study. By mid-1932, Morgan saw an opportunity to focus Antioch on character building, while the faculty saw more value in maintaining stable and successful liberal arts and work-study programs.[64]

In 1932, Morgan sensed resistance from the Antioch faculty, students, and supporters and focused his energies elsewhere. During his numerous sabbaticals from Antioch, Morgan embraced the pen and typewriter for solace. Morgan brought back from Portugal a unique play that he wrote, entitled "Seed Man," about human triumph over evil through honesty, restraint, purity, and cooperation. In this morality tale, the main character John Smith mirrored many of the challenges from Morgan's life. John, the son of a spinach grower, learned from his strict mother a strong sense of ethics and social consciousness. He was faced with decisions about having premarital sex, working for a dishonest employer, denying his employees rights and a share of the profits, and spending his life savings to help a colleague from being fired by crooked administrators. Instead, Smith resisted temptation and took the moral high road. He married a reputable woman named Mary, he quit his job to start a garden seed company, he shared profits and responsibilities with his workers, and he took the public stage to defend a wrongfully accused friend. Morgan used *Seed Man* to highlight the importance of character, honesty, small industries, improving the lives of workers, and uncovering waste, corruption, and inefficiency in society. While the title of the play referred to a simple man who found success by selling seeds, it also conjured up images of sexuality and the importance of transmitting the most desirable traits to the next generation through eugenics.[65]

The play was an effort for Morgan to express his moral and ethical ideas to those at Antioch. In the preface of his draft, Morgan wrote, "Frequently of late I have heard the expression 'I am tired of your abstract philosophy. It leaves me cold. Let's get down to cases.' So be it." In 1932, Antioch Press published the play, making it readily available to already tense audiences in Yellow Springs. A 1932 review of the piece in the *Christian Register* explained that the play was not intended to be performed. The review suggested that the play could be used in religious education. Other than a mention of the book in the aptly titled agricultural journal *Seed World* in 1948, the play faded into obscurity.[66]

A workaholic at heart, Morgan became more involved in the activities of his still active engineering firm during the early 1930s. He spent the most time developing a plan similar to the Miami Conservancy District for eighteen counties in eastern Ohio. By early 1933, Morgan completed an elaborate engineering proposal to create the Muskingum Conservancy

District. Morgan's plan to control flooding on the Muskingum River called for building over a dozen dry-dams and eight lakes in areas south of Akron, Ohio. Much larger than the Miami Conservancy District project, the work on the Muskingum watershed would encompass a full one-fifth of the state. Morgan's work to pass the Ohio Conservancy Act fifteen years prior made it possible to undertake a multi-county regional flood control and watershed district project. However, the growing national depression in the early 1930s made funding the project from tax dollars nearly impossible.[67]

Morgan preferred to avoid political lobbying to accomplish his goals, but he recognized the potential for funding the Muskingum proposal with federal funding. In 1933, the emerging relief and infrastructure measures of newly elected President Franklin D. Roosevelt offered great possibility for Morgan's Ohio project. That spring, he traveled to Washington, D.C. to talk with Ohio's congressional delegation about the need to fund a water-control district along the Muskingum River. A few weeks later, Morgan got his answer; in late March, he received an invitation to the White House to meet with Roosevelt. Morgan, maligned president of Antioch College and reinvigorated water-control engineer, returned to the nation's capitol in early April 1933 expecting to discuss the details on the Muskingum Conservancy District. Morgan's fateful meeting with Roosevelt led to stunning new opportunities for both men and the programs of the New Deal. [68]

By the early years of the Great Depression, Arthur Morgan made the important transition from being a highly regarded engineer to a nationally respected educator. His triumphs at Antioch College included a forceful reorganization of an insular and bankrupt institution, raising funds and awareness at a national level, launching an early program of work-study, and recruiting high quality students and faculty. But his later dissatisfaction with lacking moral standards and no exhibited commitment to a larger social purpose from the school's students and faculty overshadowed many of those accomplishments. The faculty, students, and board members Morgan recruited for Antioch during the 1920s brought with them an interest in inquiry and academic freedom, unlike the faculty and board members that Morgan first inherited in 1919. Reorganizing the school according to Morgan's changing demands proved difficult in part because the academic community that Morgan did so much to build gradually began to challenge his own moralistic view of education.

During this period Morgan became more involved in national groups such as the Progressive Education Association, which contributed to his thinking and writing. While at Antioch, Morgan borrowed from the concepts found in Edward Bellamy's writings to run a college and build a real community. He promoted the tenets of morality, social reform, and community building to the students and faculty at Antioch. Morgan attracted many followers, but he also repelled many because of his strict oversight and lofty moral tenor. Of all of his projects, Antioch represented Morgan's best chance to build an idealized and self-sufficient community, to institutionalize moral standards, to encourage the growth of private industries, and to test practical educational methods in higher education. In many ways he accomplished those goals, but the gradual pace took far too long for the anxious engineer. Morgan's abandonment of that quest at Antioch for an even larger challenge in Tennessee led him to attempt the same kind of methods on a much grander scale. By the early 1930s, Morgan teetered on the verge of fantastic professional opportunities for reforming modern America, which he fervently hoped would be more to his moral and ethical liking.

5

VALLEY OF VISIONS

On April 6, 1933, Arthur Morgan arrived at the White House to meet with newly inaugurated President Franklin D. Roosevelt. The nation had just begun its first few weeks into what would soon be called the first hundred days of the New Deal. At the same time, the country faced the worst economic depression and unemployment figures in its history. Interestingly enough, Morgan voted for Herbert Hoover, an engineer, in the 1933 presidential election, but he was optimistic about the meeting with the charismatic commander in chief. Morgan prepared for a lengthy discussion about the need for the Muskingum Conservancy District project for the people of Ohio. The project would provide much needed jobs and ensure flood protection for the region. Morgan spent the first few minutes of their White House meeting talking about the potential for the Muskingum project, but then Roosevelt interrupted Morgan and shifted the conversation to a much larger proposed project located several hundred miles to the South—the Tennessee Valley Authority (TVA).[1]

With little if any warning for Morgan, Roosevelt asked him to be the chairman of TVA, a new agency still in the committee stages of Congress. Morgan responded to the offer saying "But Mr. President you do not know me." Roosevelt retorted, "Haven't I been reading *Antioch Notes* all these years? I like your vision." The two got along famously discussing the potential for TVA to tackle social, economic, and regional problems. Morgan expressed his distaste for governmental favoritism and partisan politics, to which Roosevelt responded by pounding his fist on the table and saying, "There is to be no politics in this!" By the end of their meeting, Morgan agreed to serve as the first chairman of the planned agency, to help write the federal statute to make the agency official, and to assist in selecting two other board members.[2]

Morgan's selection to head TVA emerged from two sources close to Roosevelt. Former governor of Ohio and 1920 Democratic presidential candidate James Cox suggested to Roosevelt that, of all the engineers under consideration, Arthur Morgan was by far the most qualified. Cox worked with Morgan during the implementation of the Miami Conservancy District. He found Morgan honest and capable of any engineering task, but Cox warned Roosevelt that Morgan had a stubborn streak. Eleanor Roosevelt also played an important part in choosing Morgan. She belonged to an Antioch fundraising group in New York, had visited the campus in 1931, and was a devoted reader of *Antioch Notes.* With successes nationally as an engineer and educator, Morgan stood well on his own merits and reputation.[3]

At age fifty-four, Morgan reached a career defining opportunity. His bold return to water-control engineering at the national level featured a heavy dose of social and regional planning. Morgan envisioned the rebirth of an economically depressed region through building small industries, controlling the rise and fall of an untamed river, offering the people job opportunities, teaching new agricultural practices, and bringing electricity to a largely darkened region. Instead of seeing multiple tributaries, states, and groups of residents, Morgan saw a single unified region and population that he could improve through his engineering, community building, and moral uplift. The first few years of Morgan's TVA tenure were highly productive. From 1933 until about 1935, Morgan was a New Deal darling, a national figure, and a shining example of American ingenuity. His planned community of Norris, Tennessee, served as another tangible example of his perfect small community of the future, and attracted national attention. At the same time, however, Morgan's patience and morals were tested by his fellow board members. Their early disagreements formed a rift that grew in the following years.

On July 2, 1932, New York governor Franklin D. Roosevelt took the podium at the Democratic National Convention in Chicago. Breaking from previous tradition, the Democrats asked their presidential candidate nominee, Roosevelt, to appear and address the delegates. Roosevelt delivered a powerful message of liberalism, progress, security, and, most importantly, hope in the face of great adversity. He closed his short speech with the uplifting promise, "I pledge you, I pledge myself, to a new deal for the American people. Let us all here assembled constitute ourselves prophets of a new order of competence and of courage. This is more than a political campaign; it is a call to arms. Give me your help, not to win votes alone, but to win in this crusade to restore America to its own people."[4]

Roosevelt handily won the election over Republican Herbert Hoover that November, but he faced the greatest challenges of an incoming president since Abraham Lincoln. The stock market crash in October 1929 precipitated a worldwide economic depression. Within a short period, the speculation and entrepreneurship of the 1920s evaporated, leaving failing banks, massive unemployment, and sheer panic. President Hoover had little success in stopping or even slowing the downward spiral with his government programs to maintain confidence in American business. By early 1933, incoming President Roosevelt faced harsh realities: a quarter of Americans were unemployed; the nation's industrial output had fallen by fifty percent in three years; scores of people were starving; foreclosures and dust storms forced thousands from their farms to seek opportunity in overcrowded cities; nearly two million unemployed people wandered aimlessly across the country, while millions more built ramshackle towns on the outskirts of cities; thousands of banks closed; stock prices hovered at record lows; and federal aid had been an ineffective antidote.[5]

During the first three months of 1933, Roosevelt prepared his economic recovery plans by relying on the advice of politicians, businessmen, intellectuals, and other colleagues. While sticking to his many campaign promises, he generally planned to aid agriculture, stimulate industrial production, support the banks, balance the budget, and lower the unemployment rate. Critics charged that Roosevelt's early plans and promises were no different than Hoover's measures. However, one area in particular set Roosevelt apart from his predecessor. While governor of New York, Roosevelt promoted the social and economic importance of public ownership of water power. On the campaign trail in 1932, Roosevelt demanded that inexpensive electricity be available to all Americans. During a speech to residents of Portland, Oregon, on September 21, he outlined his power policy, which called for standardized power rates through government operated power projects and closer regulation of private power companies. Roosevelt did not want to limit the expansion of private power companies, just their abuses.[6]

Roosevelt's right-hand man in the development of New Deal public power strategies was Nebraska senator George Norris (R). In fact, Norris had been promoting the idea of greater government control of electric power production since the 1910s. While serving on the Public Land Committee, Norris took an interest in flood control and multipurpose resource development. After studying flooding patterns on the Mississippi River, he concluded that federally funded dam projects would benefit the most people. According to Norris, reservoirs would control flooding, generate electricity, supply water for drinking and irrigation, ease navigation, and develop natural areas. He opposed private ownership of power because Norris believed that such interests would put profits above service to the millions without electricity. After World War I, Norris concentrated his national water-control policy on Wilson Dam, straddling the Tennessee River near Muscle Shoals, Alabama. Norris struggled for public ownership of Wilson Dam for the next decade and that victory would be the centerpiece in Roosevelt's New Deal plans for the Tennessee Valley.[7]

In February 1918, President Woodrow Wilson approved the construction of a dam at Muscle Shoals to generate electricity for a nearby nitrate plant producing explosives for the war effort. The resulting reservoir and locks on the dam would also provide greater navigation around the challenging shoals of the Tennessee River. Despite the end of World War I and the halting of work on the nitrate plant later that year, construction of the dam (named Wilson Dam after the president) continued until 1921. By that time, Norris was chairman of Senate Committee on Agriculture and took a devout interest in finishing the project. Norris wanted to close the gates of the dam and have the government sell the generated electricity to nearby communities, thus creating a competitor for nearby private power companies. Norris believed that private power companies formed a powerful monopoly that forced high power rates on their customers. Politically, Norris's timing was inopportune. The 1921 election of Republican Warren G. Harding as president, coupled with a majority Republican Congress, made it more likely that Wilson Dam and the nitrate properties would be sold to private interests.[8]

While several private power companies stepped forward to bid on the right to operate Wilson Dam, inventor and industrialist Henry Ford made the most stunning proposal. On July 8, 1921, Ford offered the government $5 million to purchase the nitrate plant and surrounding property and to lease the water power generated by Wilson Dam for 100 years. Ford wanted to build a sprawling industrial city, 75 miles long and 15miles wide, adjacent to Muscle Shoals and Wilson Dam. He announced that the Muscle Shoals project could be replicated to harness and develop the entire Mississippi River Valley, which would easily generate enough electricity for the entire nation. Despite the grand promises and Republican support, the offer stalled in Congress, largely due to the efforts of George Norris, who questioned the benefits of Ford's plan for the American people. In October 1924, Ford withdrew the offer.[9]

The fate of Muscle Shoals and Wilson Dam remained unanswered through the rest of the decade. The U.S. Army Corps of Engineers completed construction of Wilson Dam in 1927 at a final cost of $150 million. While Norris had kept private interests from seizing the upper-hand, his proposals for government operation of Wilson Dam also fell short. In 1928, Norris's joint resolution, which at that time also called for the development of the entire Tennessee River system, passed both houses of Congress, only to be pocket-vetoed by President Calvin Coolidge. Likewise, in 1931, President Herbert Hoover vetoed a revised version of Norris's Muscle Shoals proposal, on the grounds that the government should not enter into the electric power business. Hoover viewed Muscle Shoals from an engineering perspective, and in 1931 he established a commission to study the best uses of the facilities at Wilson Dam.[10]

By 1932, despite the setbacks, George Norris elevated the Muscle Shoals issue to represent the struggle between public and private power interests. Norris endorsed Franklin Roosevelt's candidacy for president and by October he began campaigning for the New York governor. Following the election, Roosevelt fulfilled his campaign promise to visit Muscle Shoals. On January 21, 1933, Roosevelt, accompanied by Norris and other congressional leaders, traveled to Alabama to inspect Wilson Dam and the nitrate plants. While there, Roosevelt declared that Muscle Shoals represented "an opportunity of setting an example of planning, not just for ourselves but for the generations to come, tying in industry and agriculture and forestry and flood prevention, tying them all into a unified whole over a distance of a thousand miles, so that we can afford better opportunities and better places for living for millions of yet unborn in the days to come." A few days after the visit,

Roosevelt outlined a detailed plan for regional planning throughout the Tennessee River watershed, including a coordinated plan of flood control, power generation, improvement of navigation, and industrial development. The president-elect's approach to the Muscle Shoals controversy was much larger than the scope of Norris's past proposals and hinted at the sweeping changes ahead for the nation.[11]

Following Roosevelt's March 4, 1933, inauguration, George Norris worked closely with the new president to draft a bill aimed at the revitalization of the Tennessee Valley. By early April, the two were ready to introduce their plan to Congress. At the same time, on April 6, 1933, Roosevelt invited Arthur Morgan to the White House to discuss the emerging vision for the Tennessee Valley. While stunned by the offer, within a few days Morgan fully confirmed his support for the proposal and offered his services to the new president. On April 10, 1933, Roosevelt announced to Congress his plan to create the Tennessee Valley Authority. This agency would not only manage the power generation and nitrate plants at Muscle Shoals, but would oversee regional planning for the entire Tennessee River Valley, including the conservation, use, and development of natural resources. The next day, Norris introduced the bill to the Agriculture and Forestry Committee for review. While committee debate on the bill commenced, Roosevelt reassured Morgan on April 18 that "there is no question that the [TVA] bill will pass at this session." With Roosevelt's encouragement, by the end of April, Morgan, who had no real authority to determine policy, launched an unofficial inquiry into some of the engineering components of the proposal and began working with congressional leaders on the fine-tuning of the TVA proposal.[12]

George Norris's Muscle Shoals bill reached the Senate floor on May 1, 1933. The comprehensive legislation authorized government operation of the facilities at Muscle Shoals, the construction of the Cove Creek Dam on the Clinch River just northeast of Knoxville, the building of electric transmission lines, and the operation of a public power system. During this period, Morgan worked closely with Senator Norris and South Carolina congressman John McSwain (D) to adjust the details of the emerging bill. Most of Morgan's nearly one hundred additions were small, but a few were significant to the founding principles of TVA. Morgan suggested that the new agency, not the U.S. Army Corps of Engineers, would construct its own dams using its own work force. He also encouraged stronger language in the bill to allow the agency to build transmission lines for the distribution of its electric power. Finally, Morgan verified that the agency would be administered by a three-person board of directors, with one director serving as chairman. Instead of the chairman receiving a higher salary, as first proposed, Morgan recommended that the three directors would be paid an equal annual salary of $10,000.[13]

Like other New Deal legislation of the first hundred days, the revised legislation, by then known as the TVA Act, took a fast-track through Congress. On May 16, the Senate passed the bill without debate. The following day, the House approved it by a large margin, and on May 18, 1933, Roosevelt signed the bill into law. The TVA Act defined the agency as a government owned corporation responsible for the overall revitalization of the Tennessee River Valley through improved navigability, flood control, reforestation, reclamation of marginal lands, industrial development, agricultural programs, hydroelectric power generation and transmission of electricity, and operation of government facilities at Muscle Shoals for national defense. TVA's operating area covered the entire Tennessee River watershed which included parts of seven states (Tennessee, Kentucky, Alabama, North Carolina, Virginia, Georgia, and Mississippi), but that Act also allowed the agency to control flooding in the adjacent Mississippi River basin. To enact this broad and vague mission, Congress appropriated $50 million for TVA. The Act designated that the agency had the right to hire its own employees without following Civil Service laws, and it strictly forbade any political appointments.[14]

The TVA Act established that a three-person board of directors, appointed by the president with consent from the Senate, would administer the agency. Each of the directors would serve staggered terms of service, and one of those directors would serve as board chairman. The Act also explained that Congress had the authority to appoint, reappoint, and remove board members. Arthur Morgan's early arrival on the scene as the promised board chairman of the agency made it possible for him to work with Roosevelt to select the other two board members. In fact, in mid-April, only two weeks after Morgan's first meeting with Roosevelt and before the passage of the TVA Act, Morgan began confidential inquiries of potential board members. With help from his staff at Antioch College, Morgan compiled a short-list of qualified candidates. Roosevelt encouraged Morgan to locate an electric power expert and an experienced agriculturalist for the board. He gave specific names to Morgan, who began in-person interviews in late April.[15]

At a press conference on May 19, 1933, just one day after signing the TVA Act, Roosevelt officially announced that Arthur Morgan would chair the new agency. Roosevelt introduced Morgan to reporters saying that: "He [Morgan] is President of Antioch College, but, probably more than any other man in this country, has carried through similar projects. He was in charge, for instance, of flood control on the Miami River up above Dayton after the Dayton flood in 1913. They spent on that one river alone, for flood control, about fifty million dollars. He has probably more experience in that line of work than anybody in this country.[16]"

By that time, Morgan had taken a leave of absence from Antioch and narrowed his selections for fellow board members. After investigating several southern agricultural experts, Morgan decided on Harcourt Alexander "H. A." Morgan (no relation), who was the president of the University of Tennessee. Morgan's search for a suitable utilities expert proved more difficult. In late May, Morgan followed the advice of Supreme Court justice Louis Brandeis and pursued David Lilienthal, a member of the Wisconsin Public Service Commission. Morgan met with Lilienthal at the Palmer House in Chicago, and the two had a lengthy conversation about the duties of a board member of the new agency. On May 29, 1933, Morgan forwarded the names of H. A. Morgan and David Lilienthal to Roosevelt. The President heartily approved the selections.[17]

Residents in the Tennessee Valley were already familiar with the work of H. A. Morgan. Although born in Canada, H. A. Morgan first made a name for himself in the South as a professor of entomology at Louisiana State University. At LSU, he developed his agricultural skills and became an expert on crop pests, especially boll weevils, army worms, cattle ticks, and grasshoppers. In 1905, H. A. Morgan came to Knoxville to serve as the head of the University of Tennessee's agricultural experiment station. Working in cooperation with southern farmers, H. A. Morgan lectured throughout Tennessee, cajoled his students into using progressive agricultural methods, and traveled on horseback recruiting young farmers to come to college in Knoxville. In 1913, he became dean of the University of Tennessee's agriculture college, and he served as Tennessee's Food Administrator during World War I. He became president of the University of Tennessee in 1919, and in 1927 he was elected as president of the Association of Land Grant Colleges and

Universities. On several occasions during the 1920s, H. A. Morgan was urged to run for the governorship of Tennessee, but he continually declined.[18]

Agriculture, not politics, formed the basis for H. A. Morgan's career. His approach to agriculture revolved around a more general environmental philosophy he called the "Common Mooring." According to H. A. Morgan, the Common Mooring placed humans as an equal part of nature. But when humans received undue attention, natural and ecological disaster resulted. Since the 1920s, such a disaster could be seen in the misuse of southern farmlands, which had set off an economic chain reaction that injured industry and commerce, as well as agriculture. Through his extension work, teaching, and lecturing across the Tennessee Valley, H. A. Morgan encouraged a better balance between farming practices and natural resources. In 1933, approaching his sixty-sixth birthday, H. A. Morgan accepted the offer to join the TVA board with the intention of further improving agricultural practices throughout the Tennessee Valley.[19]

On the other hand, David Lilienthal, at the tender age of thirty-three, was largely an unknown to Tennesseans. Lilienthal grew up in Valparaiso, Indiana, where his father operated a succession of retail stores. In 1916, Lilienthal enrolled at DePauw College in Greencastle, Indiana. During the next four years, he took great interest in labor conditions and social reform, and upon graduation in 1920 had set his sights on a legal career. Lilienthal decided on Harvard Law School, and once in Cambridge, he developed an admiration for Felix Frankfurter, who taught courses in public utilities law. In June 1923, Lilienthal graduated from Harvard Law School, and two months later he secured a position in Chicago with the firm of notable labor lawyer Donald Richburg. Lilienthal's three-year tenure at the firm provided him with lessons about the strength of private privilege in America as well as the power of the law. After leaving Richberg's firm, Lilienthal established his own successful practice in Chicago, but his commitment to public welfare led him to become increasingly interested in public utility laws.[20]

In the early 1930s, Lilienthal exchanged private practice for public service. In 1931, Wisconsin governor Philip La Follette offered Donald Richberg a position on the Wisconsin Railroad Commission. Richberg declined the position, but recommended David Lilienthal for the post. La Follette agreed, and on March 25, 1930, Lilienthal became a member of the Wisconsin Railroad Commission—in fact the youngest member in the Commission's history at age thirty-one. While on the Commission, Lilienthal broadened the group's regulatory powers, changed its name to the Wisconsin Public Service Commission, participated in hundreds of legal cases, and drafted legislation that encouraged greater regulation of electric power holding companies and their subsidiaries. Despite Lilienthal's dedication to utilities reform, the defeat of La Follette in the 1932 gubernatorial race effectively marked the end of Lilienthal's future on the Commission. With his appointment set to expire in July 1933 and reappointment unlikely, Lilienthal looked to the national stage. The election of Franklin Roosevelt as president that November opened new doors for Lilienthal. His meeting with Arthur Morgan in late May 1933 confirmed his hopes for public service at the federal level.[21]

Roosevelt's three board members brought different backgrounds, specialties, and expectations to TVA. Arthur Morgan believed that TVA should not only be an engineering project but should also be concerned with social, economic, and regional planning. Both Roosevelt and Morgan agreed that the agency could and must become a dramatic and conclusive demonstration, on an unprecedented scale, of what multipurpose regional planning could achieve in the way of harmony between man and nature. Morgan was also a moralist who called for a changed American character that stressed personal honesty and openness. He insisted on a moral revolution, based on his late nineteenth-century ideals, as a prelude to a social revolution. Morgan's firm ethical principles also fashioned a strong distaste for governmental favoritism and partisan politics, which he believed severely damaged the course of government.[22]

H. A. Morgan also took great interest in the harmony between man and nature, with his Common Mooring philosophy. To tackle the agricultural problems in the South—eroded hillsides, depleted topsoil, and uncontrolled flooding—H. A. Morgan believed that TVA's broad program of unified resource development would restore the balance and integrate natural and human resources. But unlike Arthur Morgan's approach to social and economic development, H. A. Morgan believed that changing farming practices and local acceptance of a government agency would be a slow process, achieved through careful publicity, planning, and education.[23]

David Lilienthal, the youngest member of the board, proved to have the most pragmatic plans for TVA. Through electric power production and sales, Lilienthal saw the potential of TVA to establish public control of power throughout the South. He well understood the need for greater local control, freer municipal management, and less reliance on bureaucratic direction in the utility business. Lilienthal knew that the region was economically stagnant, but he also knew that local prejudices and attitudes had to be respected. He believed that these attitudes would slowly change as cheaply produced electricity raised the region's standard of living, stimulated industrial development, and encouraged local industries. Similar to Arthur Morgan, Lilienthal held a passion for progressivism and social reform. Lilienthal also knew how the political system operated and carefully considered the strengths of his opposition.[24]

On June 3, 1933, the same day the Senate confirmed Arthur Morgan as chairman of the TVA board, Roosevelt announced that H. A. Morgan and David Lilienthal would fill the remaining two spots. News of their selection brought a positive response from those in Washington, D.C., Wisconsin, and, most importantly, in the Tennessee Valley. During the next week, while the Senate considered H. A. Morgan and Lilienthal for their posts, Arthur Morgan began the search for other top TVA employees and in the process uncovered one of the realities of politics.[25]

Morgan, Norris, and Roosevelt all agreed that TVA would be free of patronage appointments; instead, employees would be hired based on merit and efficiency. In fact, the TVA Act prohibited any politically based employment. On June 7, 1933, Morgan followed Roosevelt's instructions and scheduled an appointment with James A. Farley, the postmaster general and chairman of the Democratic National Committee. Morgan began the meeting by explaining to Farley the objectives of TVA. However, Farley quickly focused their conversation on appointments to the new agency. Throughout the brief meeting, Farley vigorously insisted that Morgan appoint Democrats to significant TVA positions so as not to embarrass the administration. Morgan replied by saying, "If there were two good men available, but the better man had no political influence, I should appoint him." Farley repeatedly warned Morgan that his apolitical philosophy would get him into a great deal of "trouble." The postmaster general further justified his position by saying that if Morgan applied non-Democratic hiring practices, President Roosevelt might lose control of Congress and the country.[26]

A distressed Arthur Morgan met with Roosevelt the next day to discuss Farley's suggestions. The president assured Morgan that Farley had meant no such implications of patronage. With Roosevelt's encouragement, Morgan returned on June 10 to confer with Farley. The postmaster general retreated from his earlier position, stating that TVA work should be non-political and

First Tennessee Valley Authority Board of Directors. Seated left to right, Harcourt A. Morgan, Arthur E. Morgan, and David E. Lilienthal. Antiochiana, Antioch College.

non-partisan. Farley then explained that all he wanted from the appointments was to protect the administration from congressional criticism. At the conclusion of the meeting Morgan agreed to consider Farley's recommendations for positions, as long as the individuals were well-qualified. Morgan's strong position against patronage appointments lasted throughout his tenure with TVA, with only a handful of recorded exceptions.[27]

On the afternoon of June 16, 1933, just a few days after Senate confirmation of H. A. Morgan and David Lilienthal, the TVA board held its first meeting at the Willard Hotel in Washington, D.C. Arthur Morgan led the meeting, but as board chairman, he retained no special voting or policy powers (each board member held an equal vote, and the board approved proposals and charted policy by majority). The initial excitement of the meeting evaporated when Arthur Morgan distributed an extensive agenda. H. A. Morgan and David Lilienthal, who met for the first time at the meeting, were not prepared for what resulted in eight hours of discussions. As a further distraction, Lilienthal was scheduled to return to Wisconsin for his son's surgery that very night. Despite the tight scheduling, the board elected H. A. Morgan vice-chairman, adopted the official seal of the agency, approved arrangements for surveys for a dam to be built around the Cove Creek site (later to be called Norris Dam after Senator George Norris) just northeast of Knoxville, and agreed to locate TVA's administrative headquarters in Knoxville. However, the issue of private power companies in the Tennessee Valley brought the greatest discussion and disagreement.[28]

Just prior to the meeting, Arthur Morgan received a letter from Wendell Willkie, the president of the Commonwealth and Southern Corporation (C&S), the holding company that owned most of the electric utilities in the Tennessee Valley. In the letter, Willkie invited Chairman Morgan to discuss the importance of C&S to TVA. The letter caused a long discussion over the agency's policy toward private power interests. Morgan suggested cooperation and a sense of good will between the new agency and already existing electric power enterprises. On the other hand, David Lilienthal encouraged caution with such negotiations, especially because the agency was still many months away from full operation and years away from electric power production. The discussions over TVA's power policy brought out a clear hostility between Arthur Morgan and David Lilienthal, even at this very early interaction, with H. A. Morgan acting as mediator. Eventually, Morgan convinced his two fellow board members that a frank and forthright discussion with Willkie was a necessary step for the budding agency. However, they cautioned the chairman against committing TVA to any kind of agreement.[29]

The first meeting of the TVA board of directors concluded at 10:00 p.m. that night, leaving behind three weary directors and a host of complicated issues still unresolved. The three directors reached some fundamental short-term agreement at the meeting, but their difference of opinion planted long-term seeds of distrust between Arthur Morgan and David Lilienthal. Morgan's authoritarian leadership style, which had brought him success on engineering projects and initially at Antioch College, further irritated relations with his fellow board members. His ethical dictates and moral standards would later lead Morgan to take issue with Lilienthal's character, motives, and ethics, and effectively force H. A. Morgan to side with Lilienthal.[30]

The strategy and tactics of dealing with private power companies was the most pressing and polarizing topic for the board. Lilienthal, who fashioned himself as the agency's expert on electric power policy, believed in government control and regulation of electric power. On the other hand Morgan, who took the early lead in launching all aspects of TVA, including its electric power program, believed in some level of cooperation between government and private power companies. Morgan was not simply giving in to the demands of private power companies by his policy of cooperation; rather, he expected that over time those private enterprises would conclude that government generated power was a better and more efficient model. Thus, Morgan's long-range power plan was for private power companies to adapt and become part of government-sponsored power programs.

Following the marathon meeting, the three directors scattered. Lilienthal returned to Wisconsin to be with his son and conclude his work with the Wisconsin Public Service Commission, H. A. Morgan returned to Knoxville to attend to presidential matters at the University of Tennessee, and board chairman Morgan stayed in Washington, D.C., to hire employees, design dams, plan for the move to Knoxville, and prepare for a meeting with Willkie. For the next six weeks, Lilienthal and H. A. Morgan concluded their non-TVA responsibilities, which in effect allowed Morgan to establish the early policies, daily workings, and overall objectives for the infant agency. During these important first weeks, Morgan charted the course of TVA largely by himself.[31]

After the first TVA board meeting, Morgan scheduled a meeting with Wendell Willkie. On June 28, the two met for dinner at the University Club in New York City to discuss the relationship between TVA and C&S. Morgan explained to Willkie that the TVA board had yet to make any firm decisions on the agency's power policy or how to work alongside private power companies. Willkie told Morgan that the goals of the TVA Act would be best fulfilled if the government generated power but private companies distributed it under government supervision. Morgan replied that he, the other board members, and Roosevelt thought otherwise, believing that the TVA Act committed the agency to both generate and distribute electric power. Their conversations were friendly, but reserved. At the end of the meeting, Morgan suggested that "all our dealings with each other be open and above-board—that we do not have underhanded or indirect gossip and propaganda." Willkie agreed to Morgan's suggestion.[32]

The good will between Morgan and Willkie continued into July 1933. In a July 12 letter to Willkie, Morgan reemphasized that the goal of friendly and cooperative efforts between TVA and C&S was necessary for ultimate success. Three days later, Willkie replied to Morgan saying that he subscribed to collaborative efforts, but added that the conduct of their business shall be "measured on the cold basis of its merits." Clearly, Willkie envisioned some kind of deal with Morgan and TVA. At the same time, Morgan believed that further negotiations would lead to the acquisition of C&S properties and customers for the agency.[33]

In mid-July, Morgan sent David Lilienthal an update on TVA's power policy. In the "penciled memorandum," Morgan explained that cooperation, and not competition, with private power companies was a necessary step toward establishing a basis for power rates. In this key document, Morgan suggested that TVA purchase electric power territory near Muscle Shoals and set up a demonstration electric power system there, which would be a tangible example of TVA's effectiveness and efficiency. He opposed the policy of seeking contracts for customers because that approach, Morgan believed, caused unnecessary competition with private utility companies and would prolong legal struggles between public and private interests. Morgan closed the letter by encouraging Lilienthal to help him develop an acquisitions proposal for the utilities. In addition to delivering his policy, Morgan also used the document to measure Lilienthal's reaction.[34]

Lilienthal fired back on July 21, 1933. While he respected Morgan's views, Lilienthal believed that the most constructive way to develop a sound power policy was "through the frank exchange of views between the directors. . . ." Lilienthal urged Morgan to refrain from any commitments to power companies, because he was doubtful of the legality of any formal agreement for a division of territory. The letter revealed Lilienthal's frustration with Morgan's negotiations with Willkie. He reminded Morgan that making preliminary agreements with private power companies exposed TVA to "the gravest hazards." Lilienthal's terse response to Morgan's missive further exacerbated disagreement between the directors.[35]

Shocked to receive such a dissenting response, Chairman Morgan interpreted Lilienthal's letter as a personal attack and turned inward. Instead of retaliating, Morgan decided that, to win over his fellow directors, he must first convince them of his vision for TVA. Morgan's plans for revitalizing the social and economic character of the Tennessee Valley started with the agency's own workforce. TVA's first non-board employee was economist and Antioch alumnus Paul David. In collaboration with Morgan, David spent the summer managing the agency's Washington office, which included printing 20,000 TVA job application forms for distribution. Morgan's concern for the moral and ethical fitness of the expected thousands of new employees led him to construct an ethical code for TVA workers. Similar to his Antioch code, the TVA version expressed Morgan's conviction that only ethical and moral actions could produce desirable ends.[36]

Morgan distributed his "Tennessee Valley Authority Code of Ethics" to H. A. Morgan and David Lilienthal at the second meeting of the TVA board on July 29, 1933. The code stressed professional honesty, company loyalty, and Christian/Protestant morality. It specifically prohibited employees from bribery, gambling, taking habit-forming drugs, pre-marital sex, large personal expenditures, and the receiving of gifts or favors. Morgan believed that the code encouraged friendliness, company enthusiasm, thriftiness, and would set high standards for personal, social, and business conduct within TVA. He expected that all TVA employees would be required to sign the contract. But Morgan's plan to convince his fellow directors of the need for such a personal code backfired. Lilienthal warned that ethical codes were inappropriate and regulated individual thinking and action too much. The code did not survive its first reading at the board level and never reemerged. The defeat of Morgan's missive further distanced the chairman from his fellow directors, and it alerted Lilienthal and H. A. Morgan to the chairman's strict allegiance to moral standards.[37]

At this second board meeting, Lilienthal and H. A. Morgan were now free from other obligations and able to fully commit their efforts to TVA. At this meeting, however, they discovered how much chairman Morgan had accomplished in their absence. They held lengthy discussions of engineering, electric power, and agricultural policy. One of their most significant decisions was to approve the building of a "model" village near the Cove Creek Dam site. Morgan had planned for such a demonstration town, similar to the villages of the Miami Conservancy District, to be an example of an efficient, modern, and electrified community. One of Morgan's assistants suggested the town be named New Deal, but he and the board voted to call it (and the nearby dam) Norris, in honor of the Nebraska senator.[38]

During the summer, Morgan assigned Earl S. Draper, a city planner who began as director of TVA's Division of Land Planning and Housing in June, to prepare a detailed town plan. Morgan stressed TVA's commitment to social planning and instructed Draper to plan a worker village which would combine agriculture, handicrafts, and small manufactures to supply local needs and possibly produce goods for a larger market. At this point, Morgan wanted a community that would allow the workers to have several acres for subsistence agriculture and shared common areas and buildings for the production of local products. Much as he had in the labor camps of the Miami Conservancy District, Morgan wanted to offer his workers and their families not only comfortable places to live, but educational and technical training opportunities. In August, the TVA board approved a location for the model town, a site four miles south of the future Norris Dam, and ordered the immediate construction of 250 homes for the workers (with a layout to support 1,000 total houses), scheduled to coincide with the building of the dam later that year.[39]

Morgan took his plans for building a permanent town to the local community. On October 21, 1933, he addressed the Knoxville Central Labor Union in about why such a town was needed and why he needed their support. He explained: "There was some talk of building temporary quarters to be used for three years and then thrown away—just torn down and done away with. It seemed to me that that was a waste, that we would be better off to spend some more money and build permanent houses that people could live in, such houses as most people ought to live in—not expensive, but good substantial houses. . . . But wages have gone up, materials have gone up. I need cooperation there; I need some friends; I need some help in getting the town actually built. Now here is where I think the building trades can help us. . . . I hope that in that work we can get hearty support. We hope that you will try not to make these houses too expensive."[40]

As Morgan pushed his Norris community forward, his two fellow directors began close collaborations. Unimpressed with the chairman's moral code and talks with Willkie, H. A. Morgan and David Lilienthal developed a strategy to focus all of their talents and effectively diffuse Arthur Morgan's reach. On August 3, 1933, H. A. Morgan and Lilienthal issued Morgan a memorandum that called for a division of responsibilities within the TVA board. Carefully constructed, the memo called for an allocation of initial responsibilities; Morgan would take charge of nine areas of TVA, while H. A. Morgan and Lilienthal would equally split six other domains. Chairman Morgan grasped the significance of controlling such a large number of TVA's programs while his fellow board members controlled so little and endorsed the idea. However, Morgan failed to realize that, when the division took effect, he would have no authority to intercede into either electrical or agricultural activities which were both necessary for his plans for the Tennessee Valley.[41]

At the third meeting of the TVA board on August 5, 1933, the three directors agreed upon the division of responsibilities set forth in the memorandum. H. A. Morgan commanded all matters dealing with agriculture, specifically fertilizer production. Lilienthal supervised all aspects of electric power, including legal matters of land acquisition and the economics of transportation. As chairman, Arthur Morgan became responsible for the overall coordination of each specific mission. The board agreed to give Morgan control of engineering, construction, training, regional planning, housing, flood control, forestry, and other matters relating to social and economic organization. While the division of responsibilities allowed the three directors new freedom to develop TVA programs in their fields of expertise, it also intensified their disagreements.[42]

Morgan made the first move to disrupt the temporary truce created by the division of responsibilities. On August 14, 1933, Morgan sent his co-directors a memorandum describing his views on TVA's power policy. First, and quite correctly, Morgan wanted the power program to promote the "orderly and well proportioned development of the economic social resources of the Tennessee River area." According to Morgan, this development also included the generation and transmission of electric power as a "beginning and as a laboratory of planned development" throughout the region. Secondly, Morgan wanted TVA's electric power rates to provide a "yardstick" by which to measure the effectiveness and economy of public and private ownership. This meant that TVA's electric prices would be the gauge, or yardstick, for other electric power producers to follow. The policy implied that TVA should cooperate with private power companies until the public realized the advantages of government-owned power and forced private power companies to succumb to TVA. Morgan further believed that TVA need not build its own distribution facilities and power lines. Instead, it would be more efficient for the agency use preexisting grids owned by private power companies.[43]

Lilienthal, surprised that chairman Morgan had already interfered with his domain, responded with a series of his own documents. On August 16, Lilienthal issued Morgan a memorandum opposing any cooperation with private utility companies. Lilienthal charged Morgan's proposal of being impractical, unscientific, not in the public interest, endangering the TVA project, and opposed by time-tested public men. On the same day, Lilienthal released his goals for a power policy. Lilienthal emphasized that generating and distributing electric power was a public business. Instead of signing distribution contracts with private companies as Morgan had suggested, Lilienthal preferred to build new transmission lines and power facilities in order to take TVA's electric service directly to the customers of the region. He explained that, through government ownership of electric power and distribution, utility customers would pay cheaper rates and escape private electric monopolies. On August 17, Lilienthal followed up with a plan of action for carrying out his power program. At the beginning of the document, Lilienthal reminded the board that they had delegated public power policy to him. He outlined his plans for constructing transmission lines, establishing rates, designating territory, and dealing with private power companies. Lilienthal concluded that, although several plans of organization had been prepared and presented, none were considered satisfactory by the electric policy director.[44]

Morgan objected to Lilienthal's actions and power policy because both reflected a great deal of competition—a trait which did not fit into his character-based small community of the future. In Morgan's mind, direct competition with private power companies reflected motives that were not in the public's best interest. He believed that building new transmission lines and facilities, instead of working with companies and using existing infrastructure and equipment, represented a great deal of waste and inefficiency. Further, Morgan wanted low TVA power rates to result in private companies either merging with the agency or matching the rates. He did not want to put private companies out of business by direct competition, but he was willing to indirectly put them out of business if the resulting model brought cheaper rates and more benefits to the people.

Competition at the personal and professional level had also increased with Morgan's TVA position. Morgan viewed this sort of competition as unethical and demonstrating a weakness of character. To him, a public servant on a quest for personal gain by outmaneuvering others was not in the best interest of the people they served. Quite simply, Morgan wanted the most beneficial and efficient idea, concept, or policy to prevail, not just the originator. At the same time, Morgan often believed that his approach was the only choice to consider, which meant that competition or criticism from others was unnecessary. With previous projects, Morgan diffused criticism and overcame challengers because of his higher administrative position and authority. He had also made effective use of a sympathetic press and professional literature to defend his position. However, Lilienthal was at a nearly equal level, and his style and personality was direct and competitive. Lilienthal, who had impressive legal credentials and experience, was also much more politically connected than Morgan and had the ear of many important New Dealers. Morgan was not prepared for this sort of professional competition, and in the months and years that followed he exhibited a wide range of reactions to Lilienthal's challenges.

In late August, the board met to vote on the two power policies. H. A. Morgan, who Morgan had largely alienated and ignored, sided with Lilienthal and cast the deciding vote for the electric power director's policy. On August 24, TVA released its official power policy, and from that point forward Lilienthal took command of the agency's power program, which included resuming negotiations with Willkie, launching a government-operated electric appliance company (Electric Home and Farm Authority), and later preparing the legal team for a hearing before the Supreme Court. Although largely excluded from electric power decisions after August 1933, Morgan maintained his vigor for social planning, assembled crews to build dams, and completed the designs for the town of Norris, Tennessee.[45]

Morgan's management of the Norris project represents one of the highlights of his TVA tenure, a highpoint for his engineering prowess, and offers another glimpse into the perfect community of his dreams. The building of the town was just one component of TVA's work on what would become Norris Dam and the resulting lake. On October 1, 1933, TVA began work at the Norris Dam site on the upper Clinch River. With much of the area to be flooded still inhabited, TVA began the complicated process of acquiring property, planning for the resettlement of the dispossessed families, coordinating archaeological excavations of areas to be flooded, and removing and reinterring over 5,000 graves. That work continued for the next three years, while construction crews built the massive concrete dam that stretched over 1,800 feet across the valley and at its highest rose up 250 feet from the waters of the Clinch River. The first workers at Norris built temporary dormitories to occupy, while the plans for a more stable community took shape. Initially, the goal of the model village of Norris was to house the approximately 2,000 workers needed to build the dam. However, by November, Morgan made it clear that the village—complete with roads, sewers, water lines, and electrified houses—would be a permanent community after the construction workers departed.[46]

That fall, the designs and purposes for Norris changed dramatically. While the construction workers and engineers would first live in Norris, after construction of the dam a more permanent group of residents would occupy the homes. Further, instead of serving as a demonstration town of subsistence farmers and local artisans, Norris would represent a modern electrified small community with ongoing training opportunities for its residents. In November, the TVA board approved the purchase of about 2,500 acres for the proposed town, just four miles from the dam site. At the same time, Morgan hired town planner Tracy Auger to finalize the plans laid out by Draper. Auger designed roads to follow the contours of the landscape, planned for publicly shared green spaces, placed dwellings in harmony with the natural environment, and selected architectural designs that reflected the structures of the region. Auger's designs for Norris were influenced by American and British city planners, most notably the use of a large greenbelt to surround the buildings of the new town. The undeveloped forest would provide a recreational and gardening area for residents, protect the town's water supply, deter real estate speculation, and serve as a clear boundary between the town and any other communities.[47]

The final plan for Norris, released the next year, included future phases of expansion to house up to 4,000 residents. In addition to the houses, the design included three central components of shared community spaces. The town center included a community school, a shopping center, and an outdoor commons area. Second, a shop area would support woodworking, ceramics, the town's maintenance area, and future small industries. Finally, after construction of the dam, the dormitories and boardinghouses would be converted into town offices and community meeting areas. Auger, Draper, Morgan, and others wanted to make the town accessible to traffic, but they purposefully kept the new freeway from bisecting the town. Instead, motorists driving north from Knoxville would skirt the edge of the community's protected greenbelt on their way to drive across the impressive Norris Dam. The final plan for Norris reflected a great deal of Arthur Morgan's approach to social planning and community building. Norris was far different in structure and layout from the urban utopian community described in *Looking*

Early plans for the town of Norris, Tennessee. Antiochiana, Antioch College.

Backward. However, the town of Norris reflected several of Bellamy's concepts, including the importance of shared spaces, educational opportunities for residents, and the need for equality, trust, and cooperation to govern the members of the community. And because the town would have some level of self-sufficiency, the community would downplay competition.[48]

While Morgan focused his energy on the engineering and social components of the Norris project, the discord on TVA board of directors became common knowledge within the agency. Although TVA officials publicly denied rumors of disagreements between its top leaders, in late 1933 an internal report revealed that many of the agency's employees were aware of the growing rift between Morgan and Lilienthal. The report came from a consultant working in TVA's Washington, D.C., office, within H. A. Morgan's agricultural division, and further confirmed the uneasy working relationship of TVA's board of directors.[49]

In the summer of 1933, H. A. Morgan hired chemist Dr. Harry A. Curtis as the agency's chief chemical engineer. In that role, Curtis served as the director and organizer of TVA's fertilizer program. In addition to his regular staff, Curtis hired independent consultants to complete detailed technical reports. In the fall of 1933, Curtis hired consulting chemical engineer, and his close friend, Russell S. McBride to complete several scientific reports for TVA. During October 1933, McBride completed a general five-page report on TVA, to highlight its significant engineering accomplishments and electric power policy. Despite the original intention, the first page and a half of his report dealt with the controversy within the board of directors. Upon discovering the document in early December, Curtis immediately shelved the report, labeled "confidential," and thereafter referred to it as the "fool report." When first confronted by Curtis, McBride claimed that his accusations were accurate and came from a variety of reliable sources near the problem.[50]

McBride's "fool report" alleged that the differences between the board directors were the most serious problem in TVA. First, the document accused Lilienthal of playing politics and appealing to President Roosevelt in order to undermine chairman Morgan and eventually become chairman of the board himself. Further, the report characterized Lilienthal as egotistical, overly aggressive, and manipulative. McBride's missive accused Arthur Morgan of having ultra-idealistic views for his "socialization" projects, being disagreeable with the other two board members, and referred to him as "an individualist to whom rightness was more important than convention." The document also offered a mixed view of H. A. Morgan. Although the report praised H. A. Morgan for his stability, thoughtfulness, decency, and his ability to see the whole project in proper perspective, a strong connection with the South greatly hindered the "Tennessee Morgan." Later documentation, such as board minutes, articles, and congressional testimony, verified what McBride reported in the fall of 1933.[51]

In December, Curtis collected and suppressed all copies of the "fool report." Despite Curtis's efforts to eradicate the document, however, the board of directors learned of its existence and its content. Realizing the implications of the statements, Curtis severely chastised McBride for his judgment in discrediting TVA and the board of directors. In a December 19 letter, Curtis called McBride a "purveyor of malicious and disgusting gossip gleaned from the gutters of Washington." He also told McBride that he knew of no "explanation that can be made to the Board which will improve the situation." McBride responded by drafting an apology letter to the board, but Curtis advised to suppress that document also, and it was never issued.[52] In the end, the "fool report" clearly identified the internal disagreements of personality and philosophy between board members Morgan and Lilienthal as the key problem, superseding their differing electric power policies. In the following year, the board members drifted further into their own realms of responsibility, with Morgan growing more distrustful of his TVA colleagues.

Apart from the burgeoning discord at the top levels of TVA's leadership, the year 1933 marked an important first year for the agency. After nearly nine months of incorporation, TVA had significant dam building projects underway at Norris and at the Wheeler site, near Muscle Shoals, Alabama. Early work on the planned town of Norris also caught the attention of those in Washington, the national press, and the people in the agency's operating region. Each director also lodged important accomplishments during that first important year. H. A. Morgan's agricultural programs, especially those related to fertilizer, registered a strong start in the Tennessee Valley. By the end of the year, David Lilienthal defined his role as the agency's electric power policy expert. Early negotiations with Wendell Willkie were tenuous, but Lilienthal established a clear mission and future direction for TVA's electric power program.[53]

But during 1933, Arthur Morgan registered the most noteworthy accomplishments and national attention. From the first days of the agency, Morgan set the tone for the daily operation of TVA, its personnel, its policies, and its mission. As chief engineer, Morgan directed the agency's numerous river improvement projects and had responsibility for supervising nearly 3,000 construction workers. In addition to the Norris and Wheeler projects, Morgan took full responsibility for planning and designing all of the dams and river control projects throughout the Tennessee Valley. He started with detailed surveys from the U.S. Army Corps of Engineers, mostly completed in the 1920s, and worked with his engineers to design a comprehensive water-control system for the Tennessee River and its tributaries. Beyond building dams, Morgan played a crucial role in developing an integrated plan for control of the entire Tennessee River system for power, flood control, and navigation. Within that plan, Morgan outlined plans for social and economic programs to deal with problem areas, such as soil erosion, education, agriculture, industry, and public health concerns like malaria.[54]

Because of his close work with Roosevelt and Norris during the creation of TVA, Morgan maintained national recognition as the central leader of the agency. He provided Americans with updates on progress in the Tennessee

Valley through radio programs, newspaper and magazine articles, and during numerous public speeches. His message focused on TVA's role in regional planning, economic recovery, employment, and social improvement. Morgan distinguished TVA as more than a temporary emergency relief measure like other New Deal agencies. Instead, Morgan explained that TVA's mission was to "build up the permanent social and economic prosperity of the Tennessee Valley."[55] While Morgan had his critics, because of his efforts the national media buzzed with interest about TVA. In late 1933, the *New York Times* announced that, because of the agency, the "Tennessee Valley Wakes From Dream . . . Harmony Is In Sight, Hum of Industry Heard, Money Pouring In." Likewise, *The New Republic* declared that TVA would be "the first large-scale experiment in economic and social planning ever undertaken outside of Soviet Russia."[56]

Sometimes, however, Morgan either misinformed the public about TVA or the press misinterpreted what he said. For example, in late 1933, the *Chattanooga Times* reported that Morgan's "grass roots" social and economic plans included creating a self-sufficient trading network and possibly even introducing a new system of coinage throughout the region. As another example, in the very same *New Republic* article that applauded TVA's work, journalist Jonathan Mitchell called Morgan's plans to preserve the local folkways by creating specialized industries "so much romantic mush." Mitchell argued that manufacturing (the very kind of kind of big impersonal industries that Morgan hoped to avoid) already had a firm toehold in the Tennessee Valley. Further, Mitchell expected that by generating a large amount of electricity, TVA would only attract more large industries and turn the remaining subsistence farmers into factory wage-earners. Nearly foreshadowing the events of the next few years, the journalists who criticized Morgan's social and economic plans were at the same time praising the efforts of David Lilienthal to break up the power trusts and regulate electric power costs.[57]

Despite the criticism, Morgan campaigned for the importance of social planning in the Tennessee Valley. To Morgan, TVA represented a balance between agriculture and industry which would preserve the small communities, where character could be best developed. He believed that with social development, economic development would occur. To start the process of improving the social structure of the Tennessee Valley, Morgan proposed to eliminate political patronage from government work, strengthen labor polices that favored the worker, consider the importance of race relations, provide new training opportunities for workers, and launch small cooperative industries. Such improvements, Morgan believed, would contribute to the larger plan of regional development. Further, he asserted that the programs of the New Deal were based on the idea of improving the social order.[58] In a 1934 article in *The Scientific Monthly*, Morgan explained that, "The President, I believe, sees this project [TVA] as one of seeking the cooperation of the region in eliminating the grossest wastes and in creating design, order and organization for releasing the creative capacities of the people and for the best use of natural resources of the region."[59]

During 1934, while Arthur Morgan spread his message of social and economic uplift, more detailed plans for the town of Norris emerged. Early that year, TVA completed enough temporary dormitories, cabins, and portable huts at Norris to house 1,000 workers. The agency also acquired more surrounding property to expand the town's footprint to about 4,200 acres. By the fall, the first 150 homes at Norris were completed and occupied by either workers or administrators. Tracy Auger's final town plans, released that fall, included the second stage of building for Norris. Along the street system, he included plans for more homes, duplex houses, apartments, a K-12 school for up to four hundred students, a multipurpose auditorium, a hospital, a firehouse, and a town library. The plans for the community of Norris far surpassed any of Morgan's labor camps of the Miami Conservancy District.[60]

The design and efficiency of the single-dwelling homes at Norris attracted great attention from the public. The cinder-block and wooden-frame homes ranged from two to six rooms, with screened porches, oak floors, plywood paneling on the inside, brick or wood shingle veneers, and, most importantly, electric power throughout the dwelling. To save on construction costs, none of the homes had cornices, moldings, or other ornaments. Showers took the place of bathtubs as they used less water and required less floor space. Lucy Morgan, who designed the floor plans for the cottages of the Miami Conservancy District, also offered suggestions for the dwellings in Norris. Local lore recounted that Lucy added a second bathroom door to some of the floor plans, to insure that no residents would be "exposed" to other housemates. Each home cost TVA between $2,300 and $3,100 to build. The agency charged rents that ranged between $14 and $18 per month, with an extra $5 per month for use of an electric range, refrigerator, water heater, and space heaters. As part of their rental benefits, TVA gave each family a four-acre garden plot on the outskirts of the town. For those residents who decided not to cook their own meals, the Norris cafeteria charged $0.25 per meal. Unlike other company-owned or construction towns with all homes of the same character, the planners of Norris decided to build their homes using alternate styles, colors, and building materials.[61]

The lack of churches in the town plan was one of the most discussed features. Morgan believed that denominationalism encouraged ownership of property and divided communities. His solution for Norris was that any religious group could worship in the community center or in the school, but that no separate church buildings would be built within the town's boundaries. The controversial mandate resulted in some backlash and charges that Norris was an example of New Deal socialism and, even worse, a hotbed of agnostic thought. Chicago reverend John Thompson charged that the churchless New Deal towns like Norris would breed street crime and immorality. By restricting religious worship in Norris, Thompson explained that TVA had created a "moral desert" in the Tennessee backcountry. In November, writers for the *Christian Century* reviewed the charges that TVA was inciting a social and immoral revolution. The journal found that TVA had not restricted religious services in Norris, and its writers expected that permanent residents would demand churches once the temporary construction workers departed. While Norris had its detractors, favorable publicity for the town continued through the decade.[62]

The first outside visitors to Norris had much acclaim for the buzzing community. The most important early visit came on November 16, 1934. While on a southern tour to inspect New Deal programs in action, President Roosevelt and Eleanor visited Norris Dam to examine the construction progress. Arthur Morgan escorted the Roosevelts and their entourage to a platform to view the dam construction in the valley below. Next, the group drove to the banks of the Clinch River, where Roosevelt addressed a group of workers. Roosevelt applauded their efforts and predicted that in the future TVA's builders would be regarded as "veterans of a new kind of war—a war to improve the conditions of millions of our American people." After Roosevelt's remarks, Morgan took the Roosevelts to the town of Norris for a quick inspection. The town, with its small and affordable homes, impressed the president. Other visitors to Norris found the town quaint, modern, and

President Franklin D. Roosevelt, Eleanor Roosevelt, and Arthur Morgan toured the Norris Dam project in November 1934. Antiochiana, Antioch College.

a refreshing approach to community planning. After a 1936 visit, architect Frank Lloyd Wright called Norris a wonderful worker's village, more pleasant and civilized than most summer resorts.[63]

Besides being heavily involved with building the town of Norris, in 1934 Arthur Morgan was also instrumental in funding and establishing a network of cooperatives in the Tennessee Valley region. Although the agency had no direct charge to promote cooperative organizations, the TVA Act called for the improvement of social and economic conditions in the region. In early 1934, with start-up funds from the Federal Emergency Relief Administration (FERA) and congressional approval, Morgan founded the Tennessee Valley Associated Cooperatives (TVAC), Inc. While only loosely tied to TVA, the new entity would promote, organize, establish, manage, finance, coordinate, and assist in the development of cooperative enterprises in the Tennessee Valley. Morgan concurrently served as board chairman of TVAC.[64]

During the spring and summer of 1934, TVAC organized four cooperative cannery associations in Western North Carolina and East Tennessee.

The next year, those cooperatives merged to form the Land O' the Sky Mutual Association and worked closely with TVA for regional development of cooperatives. Land O' the Sky established quality and price standards for local agricultural commodities including blackberries, beans, spinach, tomatoes, okra, and rhubarb. In addition to establishing canning associations, TVAC helped found cooperative ventures for mills, dairies, and producers of handicrafts. The early success of TVAC increased Morgan's expectations for building regional economies with locally produced products—part of his early TVA vision for preserving the region's folkways through building small but intertwined communities.[65]

The town of Norris remained central to Morgan's plan for the Tennessee Valley, although his "perfect" small community quickly revealed its flaws. In the spring of 1935, TVA completed construction of the planned homes, facilities, workshops, and other structures. The permanent residential section of Norris consisted of 152 electrified and insulated houses, 130 cinder block houses, ten duplex houses, and five apartment buildings. In addition, TVA remodeled some thirty existing farmhouses in the immediate vicinity and converted them to employee housing. The total cost of $3.5 million doubled the original estimate, but Morgan explained to the press that the permanence of the town justified the extra expenses. The timing of completion was fortuitous: that year employment at the dam site peaked at 2,500 workers and the town swelled to full capacity.[66]

Housing in Norris brought up the issue of race. The agency strictly forbade the practice of job discrimination of the basis of race and sex. Accordingly, and much to the dismay of many southerners, TVA hired African American laborers and paid them the same rate as other workers. The policy, however, did not cover discrimination in the workplace. African American workers at the Norris Dam site were housed in temporary housing and TVA reported that no black families lived in the permanent homes. Segregation was common in the South, and Morgan did not envision TVA as changing that course. He believed that TVA's work would improve the lives of African Americans, but he did not believe the government to be responsible for creating direct opportunities for all races.[67]

For the white employees and administrators living in Norris, Morgan seized an opportunity for continuing their education. A school building served as a centerpiece of education for Norris, by day educating the school-age children of Norris, by night educating adults in a variety of skills or providing

Homes in Norris, Tennessee, early 1930s. K-1878. Tennessee Valley Authority.

entertainment for the community. In addition, Morgan ordered construction of large trade shops where TVA employees received training in the electric, mechanical, and woodworking trades. The classes in machine-shop practice, welding, wrought-iron blacksmithing, electrical work, carpentry, and detailed woodworking were popular with employees. To accommodate the families living in Norris, TVA offered training classes including cooking, child care, home furnishing, and family budgeting. TVA's training section also developed an adult education program that ran concurrently with the specialized training classes. The agency later built a demonstration dairy and poultry facility on the outskirts of the town, to provide farm products to the town and offer its residents an opportunity to learn farm operations. Finally, Morgan attempted to educate his employees through reading. Initially, he sent boxes of books to the timber cutting crews clearing the reservoir bed stationed many miles from the town. Each crew received a waterproof box of fiction, non-fiction, and children's books to occupy their non-working hours. After the crews finished their work the volumes found their way back to the Norris library for all residents to read.[68]

Similar to his work with the Miami Conservancy District, Morgan took an interest in TVA workers and their rights. Some of his ideas about worker relations reflected a sense of benevolent paternalism, which included creating a moral code of conduct and a working environment free of worldly temptations. With the right conditions, Morgan believed, workers could improve themselves professionally and personally, while they completed their jobs efficiently and effectively. Unlike many leaders of engineering projects in the South, Morgan believed in the importance of unions, the right for workers to organize, and an open shop. By 1935, he crafted a labor policy for TVA workers that resembled the policy that he had used fifteen years prior in Ohio. The policy reaffirmed the open-shop approach to organizing, set wages according to location, held merit as the basis for promotion, outlined grievance procedures, established hours for the work week, approved authorized overtime, and recognized holidays. The policy was released to employees for their discussion in the summer of 1935 and approved by the TVA board on August 28, 1935.[69]

With the town of Norris, Morgan greatly expanded his community ideas first evident in the worker's villages of the Miami Conservancy District. Morgan's principles of the small community, which combined local industries, practical education, and self-governance, are all evident in his planning and building of the town of Norris. Concurrent efforts of other New Deal programs to build model small towns, such in as Greenbelt, Maryland, and Roosevelt, New Jersey, further strengthened support and interest for Morgan's Norris.[70]

Morgan found a national audience receptive to the Norris concept, but despite its successes, he was unable to convince Roosevelt and his fellow directors to build similar permanent towns at other TVA dam sites. That distance from his colleagues became clearer after the completion of Norris in 1935. While directing the engineering aspects of the agency, Morgan spent much of his first two years with TVA focused on social, economic, and regional development projects. But at the same time, David Lilienthal and H. A. Morgan charted their own direction and policies for TVA.

H. A. Morgan faced not only poor agricultural practices in the Tennessee Valley, but a reliance on nitrogen for crop fertilization. By 1934, H. A. Morgan focused TVA's agricultural program on the production of concentrated phosphatic fertilizers and abandoned the use of nitrogen-based methods. He ordered construction of a furnace at Muscle Shoals to produce triple superphosphate and began testing later that year. H. A. Morgan next launched a farm demonstration program, where participating farmers could freely use the new products and methods. In return, the demonstration farmers agreed to map and inventory their farms, adopt an intensive five-year farm management program, keep records of the results, and pay the freight cost on fertilizer used. By June 30, 1935, TVA had established 984 test demonstration farms in the region. H. A. Morgan's demonstration program led to other farmer cooperative groups and community cooperation. Demonstration farmers often pooled their resources to purchase equipment, livestock, and even land. While Arthur Morgan intentionally started agricultural cooperatives in the region, H. A. Morgan's cooperatives developed naturally.[71]

As one aspect of the farm demonstration program, TVA supplied participants with electricity and often appliances. Beginning in 1934, David Lilienthal's Electric Home and Farm Authority (EHFA) program expanded the market for TVA's power, simply by making electric appliances affordable and available. With help from General Electric and the National Electrical Manufacturer's Association, the EHFA developed low cost refrigerators, ranges, water heaters, and farm appliances. Lilienthal waged a successful marketing campaign for the program aimed at improving the lives of farmers. In Tupelo, Mississippi, the EHFA sponsored an appliance showroom where potential customers could examine the products before applying for installment purchase programs. Lilienthal's promises of cheap appliances and even cheaper electric rates caught the attention of residents of the Tennessee Valley, but larger external forces interrupted his administration of the EHFA.[72]

After establishing TVA's power policy in the fall of 1933, Lilienthal reached a preliminary accord with C&S president Wendell Willkie. They signed a five-year contract of cooperation on January 4, 1934, with the stipulation that the contract could come due earlier, specifically six months after the opening of Norris Dam. As part of their agreement, TVA purchased selected properties and transmission lines from C&S, while C&S purchased electric power from TVA's Wilson Dam. Further, C&S agreed to promote the use of electric appliances, while TVA agreed not to expand their power territory any further. Ironically, Lilienthal co-drafted and signed a cooperative agreement with a private power company just a few months after he criticized Arthur Morgan for wanting the agency to partner with Willkie. Despite the initial good will, after signing the contract, Willkie publicly criticized the agency, saying that it was a socialist experiment that would end after the election of a new president in 1936. While Willkie railed and rallied against the New Deal, the courts took issue with the agreement, Lilienthal's electric power policy, and, more importantly, TVA itself.[73]

In the early fall of 1934, a small minority of stock holders in the Alabama Power Company led by George Ashwander petitioned an Alabama court to invalidate the sale of fourteen of its municipal distribution properties to TVA. Those properties were transferred to TVA as part of the January agreement with C&S. The litigants wanted to prevent TVA from selling its electric power to anyone but them, thus limiting the agency's operating region. One of the larger questions of the *Ashwander* case was the plaintiff's assertion that TVA represented an attempt by the federal government, under the guise of promoting navigation, to engage in the electric power business without constitutional authority, thus violating the Tenth Amendment. In February 1935, federal district judge William I. Grubb decided in favor of the stockholders, declaring that government lacked the constitutional power to engage in the electric power business. His decree annulled the contract between TVA and C&S and effectively shut down the power division of TVA. But in the spring of 1935, the U.S. Circuit Court of Appeals reversed the lower court's decision. The next year the Supreme Court, which had annulled several New Deal agencies, heard the *Ashwander* case and ruled in favor of TVA. However, their decision applied only to TVA's power generation at Wilson Dam and not any of the agency's other facilities, which increased the chances for further legal battles.[74]

During these crucial legal attacks, the TVA board experienced further internal unrest. Arthur Morgan, whose own initiatives crossed into the areas of agriculture and electric power, believed that H. A. Morgan and David Lilienthal were intentionally de-emphasizing and ignoring his social programs. Morgan criticized the work of his fellow board members. In particular, he publicly accused TVA's agricultural program of being sluggish and ineffective. In the summer of 1934, he recommended that H. A. Morgan hire a larger staff and delegate more responsibilities. H. A. Morgan appeased the chairman and hired additional personnel, but he advised Chairman Morgan that the slow implementation of TVA's agricultural programs coupled with extensive research and testing was necessary to achieve regional acceptance and national success.[75]

Morgan next lashed out at Lilienthal and the agency's electric power program. In the fall of 1934, he directly criticized the principles of Lilienthal's EHFA program. Morgan believed that TVA was selling appliances to people who could not afford them and questioned the soundness of the EHFA's installment financing program. As a matter of principle, Morgan saw consumer debt as a burden and morally questionable. He feared that Lilienthal's over-promotion of untested electrical appliances would damage the already fragile reputation of TVA in the region. Despite the criticism, Lilienthal continued to direct the EHFA and promote the use of electric power and appliances in the South.[76]

Arthur Morgan and David Lilienthal displayed an early sense of isolated cooperation, but by 1935 their conflict of personalities and polices reached a crossroads. That summer, Morgan learned that Lilienthal had made as many as five patronage-based appointments. By violating the TVA Act's anti-patronage clause, Lilienthal was subject to immediate removal. However, Morgan chose a more indirect path to achieve the same result. Because of the staggered terms of board members, Lilienthal drew the shortest of the original three terms, and his term would expire in May 1936. If Morgan could convince Roosevelt not to reappoint Lilienthal for another term, he could take control of the agency's power policy. Morgan saw the opportunity to rid himself of Lilienthal, whom he deemed unethical, unscrupulous, and untrustworthy, and reset the course of TVA back to his own social and economic vision.[77]

In November 1935, Morgan visited Roosevelt in Warm Springs, Georgia, to discuss Lilienthal's pending reappointment to TVA's board of directors. Morgan explained that board harmony had been shattered by Lilienthal's poor policies, attempts to undermine his authority, and unethical actions. Morgan delivered Roosevelt the ultimatum that, if Lilienthal were reappointed, he would resign because of significant personal and political differences. Perhaps not fully understanding the severity of the situation and certainly caught by surprise by Morgan's challenge, Roosevelt tentatively agreed not to reappoint Lilienthal. In fact, Roosevelt asked Morgan for names of suitable replacements. Morgan responded with the recommendation of one of H. A. Morgan's assistants, Neil Bass. With Bass on the board, Morgan assured Roosevelt that harmony between the directors would return. The president agreed and authorized Morgan to speak with Bass, and, as Morgan left, he reporting hearing Roosevelt say, "Arthur, it seems to me that you and I see things together just about one-hundred percent."[78]

After the presidential meeting, Morgan returned to Knoxville and immediately told H. A. Morgan that Roosevelt had agreed not to reappoint Lilienthal. According to Arthur Morgan's account of this conversation, H. A. Morgan said that he would rather work with the board chairman than David Lilienthal. Further, H. A. Morgan referred to the chairman as the leading spirit in the organization, and stated that TVA should continue under Arthur Morgan's leadership. While Arthur Morgan began planning for the post-Lilienthal era of TVA, Roosevelt realized that removal of either board member would disrupt the future of all New Deal authorities. If Lilienthal was not reappointed, advocates of private power would win a major battle in the utility wars and, if Arthur Morgan resigned, the absence of his strict administrative policies and expert engineering skills would result in many TVA projects never being completed or coordinated properly. Considering that 1936 was an election year, Roosevelt needed to remedy the clash between directors as quickly as possible.[79]

Morgan's early TVA tenure brought him notoriety as a cutting-edge engineer, social planner, administrator, and national figure. His social and economic vision called for the building of small communities with self-sustaining industries. The town of Norris, the establishment of local food and handicraft cooperatives, and TVA educational programs exemplified his ideas of the perfect small community. Despite his successes, from the very first days of TVA, Arthur Morgan developed an uneasy working relationship with his fellow board members, especially David Lilienthal. While the three directors registered distinct accomplishments in their respective areas of authority, their work often overlapped and their policies conflicted. The issue of electric power policy and cooperation with private power companies was central in the rift between Morgan and Lilienthal, but a difference of personality and philosophy finally drove them apart.

By 1935, Arthur Morgan reached the end of his patience for his fellow TVA board members, and at the end of that year, he asked Roosevelt not to reappoint Lilienthal to the board of directors. As a man of ethics and morality, Morgan believed Lilienthal demonstrated unscrupulous actions, and his big-government approach to TVA was an example of America's economic, social, political, and spiritual inadequacies. Further, a leader with a lack of character in an important position threatened Morgan's longer term vision for building a more enlightened society. Morgan did have reservations about Lilienthal's approach to developing electric power policy, but by 1935 the struggle was more about personal and philosophical differences than disagreements over policy. Likewise, Lilienthal was irritated by Morgan's unrealistic and visionary views for the Tennessee Valley, which he believed were damaging to the agency's reputation, especially that of its power program. Lilienthal respected Morgan for his engineering and organizational skills, but he recognized that the chairman was not a politically savvy leader. Further, Lilienthal disliked Morgan rigid moralistic outlook in personal interactions, which he found off-putting and rude. By late 1935, the two board members reached an impasse, which became front page news during the following year—a critical year for the future of the New Deal and TVA.[80]

6

THE LONG ROAD CUT SHORT

At 2:00 p.m. on March 4, 1936, President Franklin D. Roosevelt pushed a gold telegraph key from his White House office to activate the closure of the lower sluice gates at Norris Dam five hundred miles away. As the final sluice gates fell to impound the waters of the Clinch River, the Knoxville High School band began playing "Stars and Stripes Forever." That moment signified the opening of TVA's first multipurpose project, which included the fourth largest dam in the world, a resulting 34,200 acre reservoir, and a unique worker town designed to outlast the flurry of construction. The day also marked the third anniversary of Roosevelt's assumption of the presidency and the one-month anniversary of TVA's legal triumph before the Supreme Court in the *Ashwander* case. Roosevelt seized the significance of the moment, declaring that "Norris Dam is a practical symbol of better life and greater opportunity for millions of citizens in our country." The agency, just like Roosevelt, overcame the adversities of the early New Deal, and by 1936 both had tangible evidence of their work for all to see.[1]

That afternoon at the Norris Dam site, TVA employees and supporters, local residents, school children, boy scouts, and other onlookers gathered to witness the well-timed spectacle. Entry-level TVA employee Howard Bridgman captured the moment of that day in his diary. He wrote, "Today Norris Dam was christened and we all had a half holiday." Bridgman and a handful of his mailroom coworkers drove out to the site at 11:45 a.m. to witness the ceremonies from the west bank of the Clinch River below the dam. From that vantage point they heard sirens and saw "the water being shut off, while the crowd of two thousand or more who had littered the Clinch Valley with scores of autos milled around on the wrongside [*sic*] and didn't see a thing."[2]

TVA board chairman Arthur Morgan was a central figure at the Norris Dam dedication. Following the closure of the sluice gates, Morgan addressed the crowd. He paid tribute to Roosevelt, Senator Norris, Congress, and "the loyal and honest workers." Morgan stressed the national importance of the dam and called it a monument to efficiency and progress. He had reason to tout TVA's first dam. Under Morgan's watchful eye Norris Dam was completed ahead of schedule with a minuscule injury rate for its construction teams (only six fatalities, compared to more than one hundred at Boulder Dam), and far under the allocated budget. In addition to finishing Norris Dam, by the spring of 1936, Morgan's engineering teams started construction on two more dam projects (Wheeler and Pickwick), he convinced Roosevelt and many others of the need for a permanent town adjacent to Norris Dam, he defined a labor policy for the agency's construction teams, and he completed designs for nearly all of the other dams on the Tennessee River and its tributaries. Morgan was still TVA's loudest voice, and he kept his plans for TVA as a top story in the nation's publications. Despite Morgan's centrality to the early TVA, by the mid-1930s, internal discord and growing mistrust of his fellow board members detracted from his ability to lead the agency.[3]

From 1936 until 1938, Morgan channeled much of his energy toward resolving internal board struggles. Morgan's first effort to remove David Lilienthal from the TVA board in late 1935 would be followed by two more years of similar attempts and accusations of unethical behavior by his fellow board members. Morgan's disagreements over policies (especially relating to electric power) with H. A. Morgan and Lilienthal deteriorated into a personal conflict. More importantly, Morgan found his fellow board members lacking in character, which was not only offensive to him, but represented a failure of the leaders of modern society. In numerous discussions, especially during the case of compensating Tennessee senator and union leader George Berry for his marble mines flooded by Norris Lake, Morgan questioned the morals, ethics, integrity, and honesty of his fellow directors. But, Morgan consistently offered little proof to support his charges, demonstrated

Norris Dam, the first TVA dam, completed in 1936. Antiochiana, Antioch College.

an inability to compromise, and ultimately passed the point of reconciliation with the other two board members. Retaliation by Lilienthal and H. A. Morgan, both of whom appealed directly to Roosevelt, did not improve the situation, and as a result the board room battles brought significant negative publicity for the agency.

The timing of the board's infighting could not have been worse for TVA. While Morgan and Lilienthal waged a war of words, many questioned the survival of TVA. During the mid-1930s, TVA lawyers prepared for two critical legal cases (*Ashwander* and *TEPCO*), both of which came before the Supreme Court—a court which had struck down several New Deal agencies of the first hundred days. Despite Roosevelt's clear-cut 1936 reelection, his administration suffered enormous setbacks during the next two years. In 1937, a significant economic downturn dealt a heavy blow to national recovery and confidence. At the same time, Roosevelt attempted to secure rulings more favorable to the New Deal by expanding the number of Supreme Court justices from nine to twelve. In the face of crisis, Roosevelt responded with adaptation, improvisation, and pragmatic approaches.

Roosevelt understood that, through practical programs, TVA had great potential to provide economic recovery to the Tennessee Valley. He and other New Dealers recognized that electric power for the region's residents and high-yielding soils were the key to the agency's future and the region's economic prosperity. Roosevelt carried this more practical TVA concept further in 1937, when he and Norris proposed creating "seven little TVA's" to cover the country with similar regional agencies.[4] That need for pragmatic economic solutions and a firm national electric power policy largely eliminated the possibility of federal support for another town like Norris, Tennessee, regional food cooperatives, and self-sufficient handicraft economies that Morgan championed since the early 1930s. As part of that shift, by the mid-1930s, Lilienthal's electric power division and H. A. Morgan's agricultural programs supplanted Morgan's TVA initiatives. While fighting with his colleagues and fighting for his TVA vision, Morgan demonstrated an inability to adapt to the national changes and regional demands for TVA's services.

Within a few short years, Arthur Morgan, an early New Deal architect, was out of touch with the very agency that he had helped design. In early March 1938, just two years after the dedication of Norris Dam—a clear vindication of his TVA vision and a shining example of his engineering prowess—Morgan arrived at the White House to explain his actions and accusations to an irate Roosevelt. The clash of personal philosophies and an inability to adapt resulted in the end of his TVA tenure later that month and a lengthy congressional investigation of the agency the following year. Controversy and discord marked the second half of Morgan's TVA tenure, and largely overshadowed his early accomplishments with the agency. While attempting to sustain, promote, and create his perfect small communities in the Tennessee Valley, Morgan ran afoul of the political realities of the Second New Deal and experienced the greatest disappointment of his career.

As Roosevelt activated the sluice gates at Norris Dam on March 4, 1936, a number of crises still gripped the nation. While some recovery measures of the New Deal were successful, in 1936 over nine million Americans (16.9 percent) were unemployed, farm prices and factory wages remained low, displacement of families from farms and urban areas was rampant, and the gross national product had not returned to pre-Depression levels. Outside of the Tennessee Valley, the natural environment seemed uncontrollable. That year, dust storms scattered topsoil from the blighted Plains to the New

England states, spring floods killed over one thousand and left hundreds of thousands homeless, and drought gripped large sections of the country. In 1936, after two hearings before the Supreme Court, legal proceedings for the nine accused Scottsboro Boys continued. Their ongoing plight revealed the realities of Jim Crow segregation and gaping holes in the nation's social fabric. Americans also turned their eyes to Europe, where Francisco Franco's fascists in Spain initiated a bloody civil war, Adolph Hitler marched 25,000 troops into the Rhineland and expanded his anti-Semitic programs, and Italian dictator Benito Mussolini invaded Ethiopia while allying his initiatives with Hitler's Germany.[5]

Like many Americans, Roosevelt had great concerns about the spread of fascism overseas, but in 1936 he largely continued the course of neutrality and focused his energy on domestic recovery. Besides political detractors to his programs, Roosevelt's greatest obstacle to achieving his New Deal goals came from the Supreme Court, which by early 1936 had halted a number of New Deal programs. Most significantly, the Supreme Court had nullified the National Industrial Recovery Act (NIRA) and the Agricultural Adjustment Act (AAA), two centerpieces of the first hundred days. Further, during that year important cases related to labor, electric power, and social welfare legislation headed to the nation's highest court. Roosevelt feared setbacks and a complete dismantling of the New Deal, but he postponed any action against the Supreme Court until after the crucial elections of 1936.[6]

Alongside the judicial setbacks of the NIRA and the AAA, TVA stood out as one of the few successes and survivors of the early New Deal. In 1936, the agency not only dedicated Norris Dam but it passed muster with the Supreme Court in the *Ashwander* case. While that decision did not specifically deal with the constitutionality of the agency, it ensured a continuation of the agency (at least until the next court case, which came at the end of the year) and its programs. As TVA moved forward, so did Morgan's efforts to replace Lilienthal on the board of directors.[7]

With implied support from Roosevelt to locate a new board member, in early 1936, Morgan met with Neil Bass, a former Knoxville city manager and assistant to H. A. Morgan, to discuss the possibility of replacing Lilienthal as the third director in May. Bass agreed that he would accept the position and

Morgan's terms, and, if appointed, he would be a fair and impartial third board member rather than a "yes-man" for his mentor H. A. Morgan. Delighted with the discussion, Morgan suggested that Bass discuss the arrangement with H. A. Morgan and President Roosevelt.[8]

Despite Morgan's early satisfaction with replacing Lilienthal and his more permanent plans for TVA, the reappointment issue was not finalized, mostly because TVA's future was tied directly to the young power director. The February Supreme Court victory for TVA in the *Ashwander* case marked an impressive validation of Lilienthal's power program. Further, the opening of Norris Dam in March set in motion of the expiration of the agency's contract with Commonwealth and Southern that fall. Thus, Lilienthal's experience in negotiating and prior work with Willkie became an important issue in deciding his reappointment fate. By removing Lilienthal from TVA, Roosevelt risked a great deal for the agency's power program and for his own political fortunes.[9]

In late April 1936, a month before his "presumed" reappointment, Lilienthal learned of Morgan's push to quell his chances for another term as TVA's electric power director. For the next month, Lilienthal lobbied and worked with New Deal leaders such as Felix Frankfurter, Senator Robert La Follette, and Benjamin Cohen to preserve his board status. As their first action, in a May 4, 1936, letter, Lilienthal and his team cleverly appealed to Senator George Norris. Instead of focusing on the TVA board's contrasting personalities, Lilienthal's letter emphasized that TVA's tactics with private utilities was the only difference between himself and Morgan. Lilienthal also explained that the completion of Norris Dam meant that the contact with Willkie would come due in November 1936—a contract that he had negotiated. Because of Willkie's indirect involvement with the *Ashwander* case (he served on the board of directors of the Edison Electric Institute, which financially supported the litigants), Lilienthal pointed out that he was hesitant to make further deals with any private power companies. As a point of strategy, Lilienthal knew that Norris was opposed to another deal with Willkie and made it clear that Morgan endorsed renegotiating a new contract with Willkie and cooperating with private power companies. Lilienthal closed the letter by stating that the power issue had caused board difficulties, which were based solely on matters of principle and not personality.[10]

As Lilienthal expected, Norris read the letter and immediately shared it with Roosevelt. The letter dispelled any rumors of personality issues and made it clear to Roosevelt that Lilienthal's power program and policy lay at the heart of TVA's and the New Deal's future. A few days later, Roosevelt received a personal communication from Morgan regarding Lilienthal. Morgan emphasized the personal and philosophical difference that he had with Lilienthal. Specifically he accused Lilienthal of "neglect and incompetence in administration, combined with great skill in personal publicity and political promotion." Lilienthal's unethical and unprofessional behavior, Morgan argued, discredited the agency, its skillful and honest employees, and the Roosevelt administration. Morgan concluded by saying that although TVA had been successful in many respects, he would "prefer some other job" if Lilienthal were reappointed.[11]

On May 12, 1936, Roosevelt met with Lilienthal to discuss board differences and the power director's reappointment. Roosevelt encouraged Lilienthal to compromise with Morgan and to reestablish respectable relations on the TVA board. Roosevelt believed the situation could be corrected if Lilienthal reassured Morgan that there was no plot or conspiracy undermining TVA policies. Lilienthal responded positively to Roosevelt's suggestion of cooperation but doubted if that approach would work. Still, Roosevelt believed that, without reassurance from Lilienthal, Morgan would either resign or protest the reappointment and perhaps disrupt the progress of the New Deal. While losing Morgan would be a significant loss for TVA, Roosevelt made it clear that, without Lilienthal, the private power companies would have the upper hand on the agency.[12]

A few days later, Roosevelt announced Lilienthal's reappointment to the TVA board, this time for a nine-year term. On May 15, 1936, Roosevelt wrote to Morgan about the change of plans. Roosevelt explained to Morgan that failure to reappoint Lilienthal would be regarded by the enemies of TVA as "the first victory against your fundamental beliefs and mine." Further, Roosevelt reassured him that TVA was still in a formative period and that the administrative methods for this new type of government agency were still developing. Upon receipt of the letter and the news, Morgan promptly resigned. During several phone conversation and a few White House meetings with Morgan, Roosevelt explained that, with an election in November, it was politically necessary to reappoint Lilienthal—who had become so closely identified with the battle for public power. According to Morgan's account, Roosevelt promised that after the elections he would move Lilienthal to another position in another New Deal agency. Within a few days, Morgan withdrew his resignation and announced plans to reorganize TVA's administration.[13]

On May 18, 1936, with Roosevelt's recommendation, the Senate reappointed Lilienthal as a TVA board member for nine more years. On that same day, Roosevelt received a TVA reorganization document from Morgan. His four-step plan recommended appointing a general manager, adding the power program to his engineering and construction division, creating a separate board for deciding power policy, and another separate board for agricultural policy planning. Morgan suggested that the board's chairman handpick a general manager and decide the make-up of these policy boards. Finally, he moved that all board measures be approved by a unanimous vote, which in effect would halt divisive issues from being approved. Upon first read of the document, Roosevelt concurred with Morgan's suggestions. However, after closer examination, he dismissed the proposed changes. More important TVA matters were on the horizon, and the agency and the New Deal once again found itself in court.[14]

In late May 1936, only three months after the positive *Ashwander* decision, nineteen private power companies entered into a lawsuit against TVA. Filed in the Chancery Court of Knox County, Tennessee, the suit charged that the federal government was unconstitutionally operating an electric power business, and the consummation of the project would irreparably injure their private business interests. The plaintiffs, including five C&S properties, sought an injunction prohibiting TVA from taking further steps to carry out its power program.[15]

Leading the pack of litigants was the Chattanooga-based Tennessee Electric Power Company, the largest power company in the Tennessee Valley. The company originated in 1910 and set up headquarters in Chattanooga, calling itself the Tennessee Power Company. During that decade, the company expanded their activities and power lines to the Nashville area. The company built other lines to Rome, Georgia; Knoxville; and to the Aluminum Company of America at Alcoa, Tennessee. By the 1920s, the company distributed electricity to approximately one hundred cities and towns in Middle and East Tennessee. To further solidify the organization, in October 1929 the company became a direct subsidiary of Wendell Willkie's Commonwealth and Southern.[16]

In May 1936, the Tennessee Electric Power Company (TEPCO) joined with eighteen other private power companies to challenge the constitutionality of TVA. The claimants operated companies in seven states and included: Georgia Power, Alabama Power, Appalachian Electric, Birmingham Electric, Carolina Power and Light, East Tennessee Light and Power, Franklin Power and Light, Holston River Power, Kentucky and West Virginia Power, Kentucky-Tennessee Light and Power, Kingsport Utilities, Memphis Power and Light, Mississippi Power, Mississippi Power and Light, Southern Tennessee Power, Tennessee Eastern Electric, Tennessee Public Service, and West Tennessee Power and Light. The directors of all the companies (Willkie owned five of them), the three TVA directors, and Roosevelt understood that the case would decide whether publicly or privately owned power would dominate the Tennessee Valley. In particular, Roosevelt knew how important the Lilienthal reappointment was for the future the agency's legal success and its power program.[17]

On May 22, 1936, the board reconvened for its first meeting since the numerous discussions surrounding Lilienthal's reappointment. While the board made some progress, there were still clear signs of disagreement between the directors. H. A. Morgan and Lilienthal agreed to Morgan's suggestion to create a general manager's position. The board's majority suggested appointing John B. Blandford Jr., one of Arthur Morgan's assistants, to the position. However, Morgan protested Blandford's appointment and insisted on setting up a committee of TVA department heads to pick a more qualified general manager. Lilienthal and H. A. Morgan agreed to Morgan's approach, but voted to appoint Blandford as the acting general manager and chair of that internal search committee. Infuriated by the turn of events, Morgan refused to sign the board minutes, kept by Lilienthal, claiming inaccuracies in the record. According to Morgan, the minutes did not reflect a majority of his suggestions and he demanded modifications. Lilienthal reworked the minutes, but upon review Morgan remained unsatisfied with the document and declined to sign. It is unclear why Morgan opposed the appointment of his own assistant to the position, but his declining health and high level of stress that had accumulated during Lilienthal's reappointment may have been at the core of his erratic behavior.[18]

Following the tense meeting, Blandford, the new acting general manager, took over many of the daily operations of the agency. Concerned that Blandford did not support his initiatives, Morgan encouraged Blandford to start the search for a general manager. However, before Blandford could initiate such a search, Lilienthal recruited him to prepare reports and supply figures for the electric power division. By that summer, Blandford's responsibilities grew to include submitting and monitoring budgets, working with the board to formulate policy, and serving as an important link between the agency's board of directors and its thousands of employees. In fact, Blandford was so proficient with these duties that the following summer, the board, over the objections of Morgan, appointed him as TVA's first general manager.[19]

With Blandford in a position to effectively manage the agency's internal activities, Morgan scheduled a much needed respite. The stress of the reappointment fiasco took a physical and mental toll on Morgan. He again considered the possibility of resigning, but Morgan needed clarity to make a decision. On June 4, 1936, Morgan announced to the board that he was taking an extended vacation from TVA activities. The summer of 1936 was a crucial time for the agency. However, Morgan announced to his fellow directors that no decisions concerning matters of major policy be made by the board in his absence, and that he should not be contacted. For the next seven weeks, Morgan recuperated in Yellow Springs with the assumption that his fellow directors would heed his instructions. During this period, Morgan wrote drafts of his resignation letter and letters demanding the dismissal of Lilienthal, but he never mailed them. His wife, Lucy, advised him to resign, but by July, Morgan had decided that he owed his service to TVA, the president, and his staff.[20]

The most significant matter to come before the incomplete board came from Tennessee labor leader George Berry. With Morgan absent, Berry contacted Lilienthal and H. A. Morgan to discuss greater compensation for his marble mines flooded by Norris Lake. Arthur Morgan previously denied the higher claim, but Berry, a friend of Roosevelt who closely followed the board struggle, now reached out to the other two members. The Berry matter, especially how his fellow directors responded, became a touchstone for the rest of Morgan's TVA career.[21]

Berry's case actually started before TVA began. In 1932, while Norris's Tennessee Valley proposal was still a bill, George Berry formed a partnership with W. H. Ford, C. A. Harris, and George Collins to lease mineral properties and mine marble in Tennessee's Union, Grainger, and Claiborne counties, near the proposed Cove Creek (Norris Dam) site. By late 1932, Berry's company started mining operations at two locations. The next year, as TVA became a reality, Berry emerged as an important New Deal figure.[22]

After humble beginnings in rural East Tennessee, George Berry spent his formative years in pressrooms as a newsboy and printer's devil. In 1899, the seventeen-year-old Berry moved to Missouri to work in the pressroom of the St. Louis *Globe-Democrat.* It was there that Berry began his lifelong association with labor unions, joining the International Printing Pressmen and Assistants' Union of North America. In 1907, the leaders of the union elected him president of the organization. Almost immediately, Berry moved union headquarters from Cincinnati to a site he named the Pressmen's Home, near Rogersville in East Tennessee.[23]

A lifelong Democrat, Berry also took a part in Tennessee politics. He unsuccessfully sought the nomination for governor in 1914 and United States senator in 1916, and in 1924 he was within three votes of receiving the Democratic vice-presidential nomination. Perhaps more importantly, at the 1924 Democratic national convention, he met Franklin D. Roosevelt. Their warm relationship continued, and during the first two years of the Roosevelt administration, Berry served as a divisional administrator of the National Recovery Administration.[24]

Work on Norris Dam triggered a survey and evaluation of Berry's properties. In the fall of 1934, TVA's chief geologist Edwin Eckel estimated that, when the Norris Dam was completed, Berry's two marble quarries and some of his leased properties would be flooded by the waters behind the dam. Early the next year, Eckel and a small marble committee surveyed Berry's properties and determined that the leases and the marble possessed no value. In late March 1935, Eckel issued the final report on Berry's claim to TVA's assistant chief engineer Carl A. Bock, who then delivered it to the TVA board. Bock suggested to the board that "if a settlement can be had for two or three-thousand dollars it should be taken," simply because Berry's claims were of very little value. On April 12, 1935, TVA wrote George Collins, one of Berry's partners, with an offer to purchase only the property below the flood line for a few thousand dollars. While TVA experienced several cases of resistance to removal, property compensation cases seldom resulted in lengthy negotiations or lawsuits.[25]

Ten days after receiving TVA's offer, George Berry wrote Morgan. Berry emphasized that his marble operations preceded any decision to build Norris Dam and that, instead of objecting to TVA's activities, he and his associates anticipated an "adequate and equitable settlement in the matter." In addition, Berry explained that, as the marble at the site was of unusually high quality, character, and value, he expected suitable compensation for estimated future losses. He named no specific sum, but shortly after the letter, one of Berry's representatives requested $1.6 million! A few days later, Morgan informed Berry that TVA had already made an offer to George Collins that was more than suitable. Morgan next ordered Bock to begin condemnation proceedings against Berry before the waters of Norris Dam submerged the properties in question. A number of reasons, however, prevented any progress in the Berry settlement until the summer of the 1936, well after the opening of Norris Dam.[26]

The next breakthrough in the Berry matter came just a few days after Arthur Morgan's announced hiatus from TVA. James S. Cullison, TVA associate geologist in charge of the Norris section, presented the board with yet another report concerning the Berry, Ford, and Harris marble claim, which suggested dishonest intentions on Berry's part. This report established that Berry secured the leases after the construction of the Norris Dam became a good possibility. Therefore, the claimants purchased the leases knowing that the properties would be flooded and the government would have to acquire them. As before, TVA geologists reported that Berry's marble and his other mineral properties were commercially worthless. Two weeks later, Arthur Morgan received Cullison's report in Yellow Springs, Ohio. On June 17, he wrote the board and advised that Roosevelt should be informed of the marble claim, "so that he may take any action or investigation . . . to assure himself as to the facts." Morgan also stressed that any action before informing the president would signify TVA's recognition of the validity of Berry's claim. However, Lilienthal and H. A. Morgan chose not inform Roosevelt of the issue.[27]

By the summer of 1936, George Berry was well aware of the TVA board's internal disharmony and believed that Morgan would soon resign, or be forced out, as chairman. On June 26, 1936, with Morgan still on extended vacation, Berry opened communications with Lilienthal. Berry believed that Lilienthal would be much easier to deal with, and he was correct. On July 13, 1936, while Morgan was still absent from TVA, the board entered into a conciliation agreement with Berry. The agreement ignored Morgan's instructions for the board to avoid agreements with Berry. Under this arrangement, both parties agreed to the appointment of a conciliator who would make an independent examination of the claims, receive confidential materials and documents from both sides, and serve as a mediator between parties at scheduled negotiations. By the summer of 1936, the acting TVA board and Berry were working together and clearly ignored Morgan's advice and directives.[28]

But even more damaging to board cooperation, during June and July, while Morgan rested in Ohio, Lilienthal began a campaign against the chairman and his policies. On June 12, just a week after Morgan's departure, Lilienthal spoke to a group of TVA employees at the First Methodist Church in Knoxville. In this harsh talk, Lilienthal was clearly opposed to Morgan's policies, philosophies, and personality. He first took issue with Morgan's social planning, saying that, "I am against 'basket weaving' and all it implies." While Lilienthal recognized the value of local traditions and cooperatives, he explained that Morgan's approach represented "the second coming of Daniel Boone." Lilienthal charged that if TVA forced residents to return to a simpler standard of living, the region would "retreat until it reached the level of the fourth century." Such retroactive and limited approaches, he believed, would be TVA's confession of failure. In the speech, Lilienthal also questioned Morgan's paternalistic style of planning, which ignored the voices of those most affected by the agency's projects. Lilienthal reassured the audience that he and H. A. Morgan would not "succumb to this Caesar complex."[29]

Next, Lilienthal reminded the employees of the importance of loyalty, humility, and public service, while overtly referring to failings of Arthur Morgan. He stated that "we should remember that this organization can be corrupted more quickly by a lack of a sense of proportion than perhaps any other way." Lilienthal stressed the importance of company loyalty, saying that, "there is no place for personal loyalty in this great enterprise," and that such subterfuge would lead the entire TVA to "intrigues, cliques, and petty scheming." He reminded the audience that the agency was designed to help people and through its programs, especially electric power production, TVA could spur recovery. Lilienthal announced that, since Chairman Morgan's sudden absence, he and H. A. Morgan had already taken steps to improve services and help people. Specifically, he discussed plans to open careful negotiations with private power companies, such as C&S, but he warned against Morgan's past plans for equal cooperation with Willkie. Lilienthal closed his speech to the stunned audience adding that because of suspected rumors of Morgan's resignation from the board, he had already developed a short list of possible replacements.[30]

Lilienthal later explained that the speech was not designed to discredit Morgan but to renew the vitality of the organization. A few weeks after the speech, Lilienthal reported to his mentor Felix Frankfurter that, "morale all through the outfit had improved, the excitement was over, we were again on our way."[31] Lilienthal continued his verbal offensive that summer, which questioned Morgan's policies and future with TVA. Newspapers took particular interest in the simmering story. A June 29 issue of the *National Whirligig* referred to Lilienthal as the "real boss" of TVA and humorously stated that Morgan has "about as much real influence on the agency's policies as Shirley Temple."[32]

Roosevelt took note of Lilienthal's conduct and reached out to Morgan. In a July 11, 1936, letter, he wrote Morgan, saying, "The best thing Alfred E. Smith ever said . . . was 'most problems can be resolved by reasonable men if they will sit around a table with a box of cigars and a few long drinks.' I am not certain about the necessity of the cigars and the long drinks but I am very certain about the sitting around the table." Two weeks later, Morgan returned from his vacation and wrote Roosevelt. Morgan made it clear that he would not resign from the board and expected his previous reorganization plans to be reconsidered. He informed the president that Lilienthal and H. A. Morgan had inappropriately made policy decisions during his absence. On the issue of board disagreements, Morgan outlined the corrosive effects of Lilienthal's summer-long "campaign of personal publicity" and concluded that the power director had allied himself with newspaper editors. Still convinced that Roosevelt would relocate Lilienthal after the fall elections, Morgan told Roosevelt that he would keep publicity about the board's disagreements to a minimum.[33]

Morgan's first post-vacation meeting with Lilienthal and H. A. Morgan happened in late July 1936. Their primary work was to consider Roosevelt's plan to host open conferences with private power companies that fall. This "power pooling" idea led to a temporary agreement between TVA and C&S that July. In exchange for halting construction on TVA projects, Willkie agreed to delay the *TEPCO* litigation against the agency. With encouragement from

Roosevelt, Lilienthal reluctantly agreed to the pact. Morgan relished the newfound spirit of negotiation with Willkie and saw an opportunity to promote his previous approach of cooperation with private power companies. However, his return to the board in July did not impress his colleagues.[34]

When Morgan returned to the board in late July, his animosity caught the attention of Lilienthal and H. A. Morgan. Lilienthal recorded his impressions of Morgan in a letter to Frankfurter: "Instead of coming back refreshed, his soul aired of its suspicions, jealousies and hatreds, he is worse than ever before. He looks like the wrath of God—dark bags under his eyes, nervously tight as a drum, thin. Been brooding and planning all that time. I think he is sick. He came into a conference attended by perhaps ten of the principal managers, after an absence of 6 weeks, and didn't pass a word of greeting, not a hand-shake, not a *word:* just walked in, sat down, with a dead pan face. The chilling effect on normal men is awful." At this first meeting, Morgan requested that consultants in the electric power division be part of the decision-making process. Lilienthal reluctantly agreed to the proposal, and the directors scheduled another meeting for the following afternoon.[35]

According to Lilienthal, at this second meeting, around July 30, 1936, Morgan then "piled into H. A. [Morgan], with an almost insulting condemnation and sarcasm on his whole agricultural industries program." For the rest of the meeting, the three directors argued over a number of issues, including the agency's upcoming budget. Both Lilienthal and H. A. Morgan voted to accept the proposed budget, but Morgan voted no, the first recorded dissent in the history of the TVA board. Morgan gave no reason for his opposing vote but explained that he would supply an extended statement for the minutes at a later time.[36]

Morgan continued his voting pattern and animosity for the August board meetings as well. At the August 3 meeting, Lilienthal proposed that if any differences arose within the board about electric power policies, Roosevelt would make the final decision. Although Morgan stated that the president's opinion was important, he believed that according to the law the board had to decide its own policies and voted against the proposal. Perhaps more importantly, at a meeting the following day, Lilienthal proposed a policy of territorial restrictions. This resolution stated that, in any future contracts with private power companies, TVA would not agree to territorial restrictions on the sale of power. Lilienthal and H. A. Morgan agreed, but Morgan cast a dissenting vote and oddly suggested that the issue be taken to Roosevelt for a final decision, which negated his objections from the previous day. Despite a lengthy break from TVA, when he returned, Morgan's erratic behavior became a near farce of his usual focused style. The pressure of administration, external criticism, and being outmaneuvered by Lilienthal had taken a toll on Morgan.[37]

One cause of Morgan's unusual tactics came from the emerging details of the George Berry case. When Morgan returned to the board in late July, he had concluded that Berry's commercial marble quarry claim was purposefully fabricated to defraud the government—not unlike the Florida Everglades land scandal that he had played a role in extinguishing nearly three decades prior. The conciliation agreement that his fellow board members made with Berry during his absence further irritated Morgan's moral and ethical sensibilities.[38]

Morgan first sought to resolve the Berry issue himself. In an August 9, 1936, letter to George Berry, Morgan referred to the marble claim as a "limestone deposit" and emphasized that reimbursement should be based upon land value and not estimated mineral worth. In addition, Morgan requested from Berry detailed information about the nature of the leases on all properties, the amount of the initial investment capital, and the sum previously spent to quarry the marble. Berry replied a week later and pointed out that his claims were for marble and not limestone, and that the matter of reimbursement and compensation was decided on June 10, 1936, (while Morgan was on vacation) at a formal meeting between himself, Lilienthal, and H. A. Morgan. Berry denied the chairman access to additional information on the leases, but he informed Morgan (incorrectly) that all properties had been obtained during the Herbert Hoover administration, before any rumor of flooding the area existed. Further, Berry explained that, although he intended to receive due compensation, his enterprise was not designed to defraud the government.[39]

Upon receiving the response, Morgan informed his fellow directors of Berry's scheme and demanded that a further investigation of the marble claims be undertaken by TVA. He again emphasized that any cooperation or agreement would only validate Berry's claim and connect TVA with possible fraud. However, Lilienthal and H. A. Morgan disagreed with Morgan's suggestion and pushed for the initial $1.6 million settlement with Berry. Morgan concluded that his fellow Board members were somehow connected to Berry and that they were looking for a share of the enormous settlement or some other political favors. These assumptions, which were never fully verified, significantly influenced Morgan's interactions with his fellow board members, especially during power policy negotiations.[40]

During early August 1936, both Lilienthal and Morgan contacted Senator George Norris for a sympathetic ear. In an August 7 letter to Norris, Lilienthal outlined the board's activities since May and noted Morgan's unwillingness to cooperate, especially in the area of power policy. Lilienthal emphasized the political importance of TVA's electric power activities. Six days later, Morgan sent Norris a letter explaining that his lack of personal confidence in Lilienthal, and not differing power policy approaches, had resulted in board disagreements. Further, Morgan stated that Lilienthal's effort to make it appear that the power issue was their primary difficulty was an example of one of the personal traits that Morgan could not respect.[41]

Morgan next took the offensive in the struggle. He appealed to newspaper reporters to document Lilienthal's deceptive tactics to undermine his authority. According to one newspaper source, Morgan planned to give Lilienthal "unshirted hell." While Morgan's campaign was not as effective as Lilienthal's speeches that past summer, he did deliver a different side of the story. Most notable, the *New York Times* reported that Lilienthal had single-handedly split the entire agency to such a depth that, after the November election, there would either be a "smash-up or an amputation" within the TVA board.[42]

With only a few months before national elections, Roosevelt again intervened. He advised the board members to first resolve their personal differences and then to work on negotiating a contract extension with Willkie and Commonwealth and Southern. On the latter suggestion, both Morgan and Lilienthal shared common ground. Lilienthal understood the need to extend the contract with C&S. His strategy emphasized the importance of protecting their existing investment, not creating a separate administrative unit to oversee any contractual agreements, protecting the consumer, continuation of the yardstick program, not agreeing to any territorial restrictions, and remaining cautious when dealing with private power companies. Likewise, Morgan liked Roosevelt's approach to working with Willkie and hoped to establish a reasonable power policy based on cooperation with private power companies.[43]

Morgan made it clear to Lilienthal that he supported Willkie's interest. In late September 1936, Morgan issued a memorandum to Willkie which outlined methods for cooperation. Largely drafted by George W. Hamilton, a TVA consultant and former vice-president of a private power company, the twenty-two page memorandum emphasized cooperation, mutual confidence, reasonableness, and the recognition of interests by both public and private power advocates. Morgan believed that his tactics for dealing with private power companies were more honest, open, and effective than Lilienthal's indirect dealings. But unlike during the first series of talks with Willkie, by this time TVA started building its distribution network and suffered a number of legal challenges from private power companies. Morgan's cooperative approach was no longer realistic, and Lilienthal seized the opportunity to explain how the board chairman was out of touch.[44]

Lilienthal noted that Morgan had "gone over to the power boys, hook, line, and sinker." Despite Morgan's newfound ability to become part of the power negotiations (an arena that Morgan had been away from since the fall of 1933) and to gain favor with Roosevelt, Lilienthal watched the chairman with great skepticism. In addition to reporting to Roosevelt about Morgan's inadequate policies, Lilienthal secured strong support from influential Senators Norris and La Follette.[45]

On September 30, 1936, Roosevelt hosted the first "power pool" meeting between private power company officials and public power advocates, which included Lilienthal to represent TVA. Although the conferences were planned to bring together the two factions, Louis Wehle, nephew of Justice Louis Brandeis, reported that, "There was no fraternization, no preliminary pipe of peace. Weapons did not seem to have been left outside." By the end of the meeting, TVA and C&S agreed to extend their soon-to-expire contract for ninety days or until a new contract could be negotiated. However, Willkie could not agree to Lilienthal's request that the *TEPCO* court case be suspended. Willkie, who owned five of the nineteen companies, explained that he did not have enough influence over the other litigants companies to stop the *TEPCO* case.[46]

During the next two months, informal power pool conferences continued between private and public power interests. Willkie and Lilienthal exchanged niceties, agreeing that their negotiations were all business and not personal. The two Indianans pledged that their professional negotiation and cooperation would continue in the future. However, without suspension of the *TEPCO* case, Lilienthal grew more skeptical of Willkie and agreements with private companies. Likewise, Willkie wanted to postpone any agreement until after the November elections, which he thought might change the very course of the New Deal and perhaps the presidency.[47]

Much to the dismay of Willkie and other Republicans, the Democrats swept the 1936 elections in convincing fashion. Roosevelt received over 27 million popular votes to Republican Alfred Landon's 16.6 million. He gained the largest presidential vote in history, the largest presidential plurality, the largest proportion of electoral votes since 1820, the largest House majority since 1855, the largest Senate majority since 1869, and gained nearly 5 million more Democratic votes than he had received in 1932. In other 1936 election results, Nebraskan George Norris was reelected to the Senate for an unprecedented fifth term. These victories meant a continuation and validation of New Deal programs.[48]

Following the elections, the *TEPCO* case against TVA resumed. At the request of the plaintiffs, the case moved to the federal district court for the Eastern District of Tennessee. In December, Judge John J. Gore of the Middle District of Tennessee issued a sweeping injunction against TVA. This mandate restrained TVA from enlarging or extending its electric power program. Specifically, TVA was not allowed to initiate any new construction, sign up any new customers, solicit or negotiate contracts with any of the plaintiff's customers, or supply service to any already existing rural lines. Gore based the issuance on his inability to see the constitutionality of the agency.[49]

The injunction proved a massive blow to the agency, but Gore's order did not put thousands of workers in unemployment lines. Although TVA was temporarily halted from expanding their power operations, Gore's action only applied to new projects. This narrowness allowed the agency to finish projects already underway, such as dams, transmission lines, and substations; provide electricity to their users; and let the board function as before. Although it was a major legal setback, TVA lawyers, led by Lilienthal, remained optimistic about overturning Gore's decree, and in early January 1937, they appealed Gore's decision to the Sixth Federal Circuit Court of Appeals.[50]

Even with the injunction and the court case, Wendell Willkie still believed that an agreement between TVA private power companies could be arranged. He hoped to solve the problems of electric generation and distribution with a pooling arrangement for the Tennessee Valley. Willkie pointed out that, with the 1936 elections over, key issues such as acquiring new capital, utility taxes, government purchase of individual companies, and yardstick establishment needed further discussion. However, the Roosevelt administration took the injunction as a major threat to government-owned power and TVA, and in January 1937, the president officially cancelled the power pool conferences.[51]

In response, Morgan vocalized his concerns about ending the meetings. Morgan urged cooperation with the utilities and stressed that an agreement between TVA and private utilities protected both public and private interests, as well as lead to the widest possible distribution of electric power at the lowest possible rates. In a January article in *The New Republic* titled "The Next Four Years in the TVA," Morgan discussed TVA's lack of social and economic planning and the agency's unjust power policies. Morgan made it clear that TVA should return to strategies of cooperation and social planning instead of advancing toward the next decade with Lilienthal's big business and bureaucratic approach to TVA's development.[52]

Lilienthal took his concerns about Morgan's statements and erratic behavior directly to Roosevelt. At a January 15, 1937, White House meeting, Lilienthal informed the president that because of Morgan's lack of administrative skills, many good employees had resigned and the internal situation on the TVA board was unbearable. Roosevelt explained that Morgan built good dams and that he was a competent administrator, but the president also told Lilienthal that Morgan knew nothing about electric power. Roosevelt then reassured Lilienthal that later that year he would reassign Morgan to a public works project to build and design dams—a pledge completely opposite to Roosevelt's earlier promise to Morgan that he would instead relocate Lilienthal. Throughout the entirety of the TVA board struggles, Roosevelt demonstrated an amazing level of political savvy and a mastery of negotiations. Somehow Roosevelt was able to convince both Lilienthal and Morgan that he supported their initiatives, even if their plans and his promises to them were contradictory.[53]

In the meantime, the Berry marble matter resurfaced and accentuated the differences between the TVA board members. On February 5, 1937, George Berry wrote Arthur Morgan to resolve his claim. Berry emphasized that he and his associates "suffered a very great loss" and remained patient while TVA had resisted a settlement. Morgan quickly responded and scheduled a conference but requested that Berry supply the board with information about the nature of the leases and various financial data in advance of the meeting. Berry agreed, but prior to the meeting sent none of the requested materials.[54]

Berry presented his case to the TVA board on February 24, 1937. Berry first established that he was not an enemy of TVA and only wanted fair compensation for his losses. He stated that "we are not willing to be sent to a Buddhist colony in the matter, and can prove that we have been damaged to a very great degree." Berry then informed the directors that he was "not accustomed to blackjacking, coercion, or intimidation" when it came to business or negotiations. As a political tactic, Berry mentioned that he was Roosevelt's advisor and that, if TVA did not want to arbitrate, he would sue the agency. Berry also pointed out that his associates had leased the properties before TVA existed and that "as sure as there is a God in Heaven" the agency had taken and flooded those lands. And on this property, Berry pointed out that he had proof that there was an ample supply of marble, which made substantial compensation from TVA necessary and fair.[55]

After Berry's appearance, Morgan pushed for a condemnation hearing against Berry without conciliation, while Lilienthal wanted to hire outside consultants to assess the situation. Morgan opposed the idea of outside investigators, and he also disagreed with Lilienthal's idea of taking the matter to Roosevelt, even though Morgan himself had suggested just that course in June 1936. However, Morgan's dispute with Berry was more than just the reimbursement issue; the chairman believed that investing in a scheme designed to defraud the government was "socially undesirable" and revealed a lack of character.[56] To Morgan, Berry represented the type of politician that he had encountered as a much younger man during the Florida Everglades investigation: an unethical public servant who relied on favors and was only interested in helping themselves, not the people they represented. To make matters worse, Berry's alignment with Roosevelt, Lilienthal, and H. A. Morgan made Morgan even more suspicious of TVA's inner circle.

The next day, Morgan issued a memo to the board. He reviewed the entire matter and stated frankly that, until Berry provided the requested information about the leases, he could not uphold the board's foregoing conciliation approach. Morgan also announced that his absence from the July 13 meeting invalidated the board's adoption of the conciliation agreement. On the same day, Lilienthal and H. A. Morgan responded to Morgan's memo. They argued that their July 1936 board decision to conciliate with

Berry was valid because the chairman instructed that he was not to be contacted on his vacation, and because decisions at previous board meetings had been made with one member absent.[57]

On February 27, 1937, despite all objections by Morgan, Lilienthal and H. A. Morgan reaffirmed TVA's previous conciliation agreement with Berry. Morgan protested verbally and in writing, as he believed that there was "almost conclusive evidence of bad faith." The accusation of "bad faith" instead of fraud revealed quite a bit about Morgan's mindset. Although Morgan opposed Berry's claim and the apparent scam, he objected even more to his fellow directors' willingness to participate in the intrigue and their potential bad faith.[58]

Morgan remained vocal about the Berry issue. On March 16, TVA's legal counsel James L. Fly reported to the board that no possibility of conciliation existed. Fly suggested that the board abandon conciliation and proceed with condemnation. With Fly's recommendation, and previous geologists' reports verifying the absence of high-quality marble on the submerged land, the board's majority reconsidered. On March 31, Lilienthal and H. A. Morgan finally agreed with Morgan, abandoned the conciliation approach, and voted to start condemnation proceedings against Berry.[59] Despite the board's agreement, the Berry matter further damaged the internal workings of TVA's board. Morgan could claim a small victory for his position, but he remained convinced that his fellow board members had their own self-serving interests at heart. By this time, any sense of trust and respect between Morgan and his colleagues had evaporated.

As the chilly atmosphere on the board grew colder, TVA faced a new round of legal proceedings with private power advocates. During mid-April 1937, TVA's legal team began arguments in the *TEPCO* case before the Sixth Court of Circuit Appeals. A month later, the appeals court reversed the district court's order and dissolved Gore's injunction. This court decreed that such an injunction was an inappropriate method for limiting a federal project under such a broad constitutional challenge. The case was then remanded back to the district court and Judge Gore for trial. But in the middle of the appellate process, another New Deal controversy erupted and dramatically changed the course of the case.[60]

With the successful election behind him, in early 1937, Roosevelt turned his attention to the federal judiciary. By that time, New Deal programs had suffered eleven defeats and five victories in the Supreme Court. In an effort to reform the courts, and presumably to appoint judges more sympathetic to his agenda, in February 1937, Roosevelt proposed to increase the number of justices on the Supreme Court with a judiciary reform bill. This suggestion, which became known as the "court packing" proposal, split the Democratic Party, undercut the New Deal majority in Congress, and cost the president an incalculable amount of public support. Critics believed that Roosevelt's proposal over-expanded the power of the executive branch and interfered with the judicial process. In an effort to reduce the criticism, in March Roosevelt appealed to the country in a fireside chat, the first radio talk of his second term. He explained that the courts tipped the balance of power in their favor, which contradicted the high purposes of the framers of the Constitution. Following the speech, the Supreme Court supported a series of New Deal measures, thus negating Roosevelt's accusation that the court was biased. By the summer, Roosevelt gave in to the opposition and offered an amended judiciary reform bill. Enacted in August, the bill said nothing about adding new judges, but it instituted a number of procedural reforms designed to expedite appeals of constitutional judgments by inferior courts. TVA lawyers drafted a section of the bill that required three judges, instead of just one, to rule on applications for injunctive relief in constitutional cases. For TVA's legal team, this important judiciary reform meant that Gore and two other judges would hear the *TEPCO* case that fall.[61]

During the summer of 1937, the TVA legal team also became part of the lingering George Berry claim, which became politically complicated. While Berry's demands from TVA were still unresolved, on May 6, 1937, Tennessee governor Gordon Browning selected Berry to fill out the unexpired term of United States senator Nathan Bachman, who died in April 1937. With Berry in the Senate and closely tied to the White House, he became an even more powerful political opponent. Despite Berry's political ties, seven days after the appointment, TVA filed a condemnation petition against Berry. TVA's legal team agreed that none of the directors would testify on their behalf, but Chairman Morgan opposed this decision, believing, typically, that he was being conspired against and ignored. Morgan showed his resentment by publicly accusing TVA lawyers in the Berry case of "soft-peddling" their efforts and announcing to newspaper reporters that the case was "not going to be fought very hard."[62]

During the summer and into the fall of 1937, Morgan further damaged TVA's reputation by renewing his publicity campaign against Lilienthal. The most harmful was a September 1937 article in *Atlantic Monthly,* which reviewed his opinions about TVA fostering a relationship with private utilities and questioned the ethics of his fellow board members. The article alleged that men with little or no ethical convictions had risen to political prominence by discrediting power companies through false accusations of overpricing and customer manipulation. Morgan further added that public officials who used inconsistent methods of action and false propaganda to achieve their purposes were undemocratic and should be removed from office. He argued that those ethically questionable individuals used their propaganda and unscrupulous tactics to gain an unfair advantage over, not only the private utilities, but also the public. While Morgan did not mention Lilienthal by name, the public, the directors, and the president made the obvious connection.[63]

Within a few days, Roosevelt scolded Morgan and informed him that H. A. Morgan and Lilienthal had passed a board resolution stating that the article had severely "impugned the integrity of the TVA and the honesty and motives of its Board of Directors," and attacked the government's present power policy. Roosevelt added that Morgan's article was "injurious to the project and to the public interest." Roosevelt encouraged Morgan to submit to the board any proof behind the charges of dishonesty. Instead of responding to Roosevelt's suggestion, Morgan took a sudden vacation, leaving H. A. Morgan as the acting chairman of the TVA board.[64]

Morgan's assaults and accusations during this period reveal his truly apolitical nature. He had no interest in mending fences to improve relations on the board, and he openly criticized President Roosevelt. Morgan explained to anyone who would listen that the administration of TVA was unsound, that his fellow board members could be swayed by political favors, and that the president needed to take action to focus the agency to its original principles. Morgan's strategy was intended to strengthen his position, but his actions revealed his inability to compromise and work with others who held differing opinions.

In November 1937, the *TEPCO* case began in a Chattanooga courtroom. Circuit judge Florence E. Allen from Cincinnati, district judge John D. Martin from western Tennessee, and Judge Gore made up the three-member court. As before, the chief issue was the constitutional basis of the agency and whether the agency was designed to be a government-operated electric power business under the guise of promoting flood control, navigation, and national defense. But Arthur Morgan's sudden involvement interrupted the proceedings. Although the legal team had forbidden the directors to testify in the *TEPCO* case, Morgan returned from his vacation in mid-November and further criticized the conduct of TVA's lawyers. While in Chattanooga, Morgan secretly interviewed witnesses, accused the legal team of presenting inaccurate engineering reports, and inquired about the possibility of declaring parts of TVA unconstitutional without rendering the entire agency powerless. On November 17, TVA's legal team reported that Morgan's criticism of the case came at a crucial juncture. During the proceedings, the legal team testified that Morgan was "severely disturbed" and his conduct "obstructive."[65]

In late November 1937, the TVA board again reacted to Morgan's activities. In a November 19 memorandum, H. A. Morgan and Lilienthal informed Roosevelt that Morgan's public and private attacks upon TVA and his relations with the private utilities exposed the administration to grave legal danger. Further, the memorandum pointed out that Morgan's public criticisms constituted legal admissions of many of the charges upon which the private utilities' case rested. For the moment, Roosevelt postponed taking any action until the district court returned a decision.[66]

Shunned from the *TEPCO* case, in December Morgan became an active participant in the Berry proceedings. By the fall of 1937, TVA attorneys discovered key documents that implied "bad faith" on Berry's part (as Morgan had long suspected). This new evidence indicated that, upon purchasing the mineral rights, Berry's associates prepared legal options (powers of attorney) in order to claim any future reimbursement on loss of property. Although Harris and Berry later testified that these agreements were secured in 1932 and 1933, TVA's legal staff had proof that the legal options were never officially filed until 1935. This and other data clearly indicated that Berry bought the leases with full knowledge of the area's soggy future. The condemnation hearing began on December 9 and featured George Berry as the first witness. Despite the documentary evidence and the geologic reports, Berry testified that his properties were valuable and requested an appropriate monetary compensation from TVA. Morgan decided that Berry's statements must be responded to and the "facts" as he perceived them, presented.[67]

Against the advice of TVA's legal staff, on December 20, 1937, Morgan made a statement before the condemnation committee. Morgan announced

In the fall of 1937, TVA Chairman Arthur Morgan took an active role in the Berry marble case. Antiochiana, Antioch College.

that Berry's marble claims were a direct attempt to "defraud the government," and further charged that Lilienthal and H. A. Morgan agreed to Berry's reimbursement claim even though they knew the marble to be worthless. Morgan also indirectly accused his fellow board members of having either monetary or political interests in Berry's large payoff, but he never substantiated those charges. Two days later, Lilienthal and H. A. Morgan responded to Morgan, saying that his charges were "unjust, unsupported by the facts, prejudicial in the interests of the government . . . and inconsistent with the responsibilities of public office." The two directors added that Morgan's accusations were designed to further his personal publicity campaign.[68]

Lilienthal and H. A. Morgan also took the opportunity to applaud TVA's legal team for their work on the Berry case. In a public statement, released the same day as their letter to Morgan, the two directors explained that the agency's lawyers had proven bad faith on the part of the investors, and had conducted vigorous cross examination of other witnesses. The document also stated that as Morgan's public statements were "so at variance with the record" that the public deserved to know the truth.[69]

Morgan responded with a late December memorandum alleging that H. A. Morgan and Lilienthal held numerous unannounced board meetings and made independent policy decisions. Morgan claimed that the meetings and decisions were perfect examples of their "conspiracy to interfere with the proper conduct of public business." Morgan also informed them that despite their treachery, conspiracy, and attempts to undermine his authority, he remained patient and supportive of Roosevelt's purposes for TVA. Morgan closed the document by stating that "the public interest demands that this conspiracy cease."[70]

The condemnation hearing against Berry ended in late December, and in early 1938 the agency shifted its focus to the *TEPCO* case. The plaintiffs intended to prove that TVA was primarily a power company evading state laws under the protection of a federal program. The litigants charged TVA with a conspiracy to injure their private business, to compete unlawfully, to breach previously existing contracts, and to compel complainants to sell their properties at distressed figures. TVA lawyers countered by arguing for TVA's constitutionality and congressionally mandated purposes. They established that the agency's projects were related to navigation and flood control. As to the generation and distribution of the secondary product, electric power, they argued that the *Ashwander* decision upheld the notion that electric power was property that the government could legally sell since it was generated while carrying out a constitutional purpose.[71]

During the first week of January 1938, Lilienthal and H. A. Morgan called a special board meeting to discuss the *TEPCO* case and Morgan's public statements. After some cajoling, Morgan agreed to the meeting in order to defend his actions. In an effort to discredit Lilienthal, Morgan made a number of negative statements about TVA's legal team. At this special meeting, Morgan explained that he had the utmost confidence in TVA's engineers who testified for the agency, but he believed that the legal team pressured them into making false calculations. Lilienthal countered by explaining that the legal team did instruct engineers with the specifics of the case, but that no employee was coerced into manipulating their testimony. The meeting then spiraled into a heated argument about the accuracy of the recorded court transcript, with Morgan declining to retract his charges of impropriety. Finally, with Morgan refusing to vote until he consulted the transcript, Lilienthal and H. A. Morgan approved a minute entry expressing complete confidence in the professional integrity and competence of TVA's legal and engineering staff. Lilienthal concluded the meeting by saying that Morgan's continued opposition to the policies of the agency made future decisions of the board nearly impossible.[72]

At the end of the special board meeting, Morgan promised Lilienthal and H. A. Morgan that he would address the reasons for his public statements and charges in a written report. He then announced that he would be taking a six-week Florida vacation to complete the report and to mentally recuperate. Just after Morgan's departure, the board's majority issued a nine-page update on board matters to Roosevelt. This statement outlined the democratic principles that governed board discussions and declared that, since the spring of 1936, Arthur Morgan had failed to accept, to cooperate, or to carry out provisions of the law and board decisions. In their attempts at reconciliation with Morgan, H. A. Morgan and Lilienthal reported that they had "maintained silence in the face of extreme provocation, in the hope that tolerance would lead ultimately to unity and loyalty." Instead, the board majority summarized, Morgan rebuffed their actions. Because of Morgan's frequent absences and general instability, Lilienthal and H. A. Morgan reported that they had slowly assumed full responsibility for all TVA programs. The report closed by saying that the working majority of the Board was dedicated to "never permitting any private agency to secure a monopoly over the public power resources of the Tennessee River." And finally, H. A. Morgan and Lilienthal stated that to surrender this principle would be a direct violation of the law and their oaths of their office—"too high a price to pay for internal harmony."[73]

With Morgan on hiatus, Lilienthal focused on the agency's legal battles. That January, expecting the worst from the district court in the *TEPCO* case, Willkie offered to sell TVA all C&S holdings in the Tennessee Valley if the agency agreed to permanent operating boundaries. Lilienthal rejected the offer, stating that TVA was not interested in territorial restrictions. A few days following the failed agreement, on January 24, the court filed an opinion in favor of TVA. The verdict declared that the construction of dams and improvement of navigation served the constitutional powers of national defense and flood control, and that producing electric power was merely a secondary activity. And because TVA served a legal and constitutional function by disposing of their power through electric sales, they were not entering into private business and thus not considered competition. Overall, the court, with Judge Gore dissenting on a majority of the issues, found in TVA's favor on virtually all of the counts. This ruling dissolved any chances of a permanent injunction against TVA and ordered the dismissal of the companies' complaint.[74]

One month after the decision, eighteen of the original nineteen power companies (the district court disqualified the standing of the Georgia Power Company) appealed the case to the Supreme Court. As a number of the companies were afraid that their appeal would go unfulfilled, Willkie pushed Lilienthal for some sort of settlement. After some encouragement from Roosevelt, Lilienthal began negotiations with his rival. Within a few months, Willkie agreed to transfer all TEPCO properties to TVA under the condition that Lilienthal would set up territorial restrictions. But negotiations came to a halt when the two sides could not agree on a selling price for the TEPCO properties—TVA offered $57 million, while Willkie asked for $90 million. The deadlock forced the two parties to suspend negotiations.[75]

In mid-February, while still in Florida, Morgan decided on a different path to resolve TVA board issues. In an effort to clear his thoughts with an interested party, he penned a lengthy letter to a TVA supporter, Texas representative Maury Maverick (D). In his February 14, 1938 letter, Morgan reported to Maverick that, since 1933 Lilienthal and H. A. Morgan had opposed additional dam construction and favored only power and fertilizer programs.

Then Morgan explained that, since their division of responsibilities in August 1933, the two directors invariably voted together, thereby controlling the TVA board. Further, he charged that, since 1933 the other two directors met privately to work out their policies and that they were involved in a conspiracy against him.[76]

Morgan then directed specific barbs against the character of the board's majority. In the letter to Maverick, he described Lilienthal as involved in "a practice of evasion, intrigue and sharp strategy, with remarkable skill in alibi and the habit of avoiding direct responsibility, which makes Machiavelli seem open and candid." Using the case of George Berry's "bare-faced steal," Morgan asserted that Lilienthal and H. A. Morgan knew about the plot and had hoped to profit either financially or politically from Berry's settlement. Overall, Morgan concluded that since the beginning of TVA, he had faced a campaign of propaganda that stated that he was the theorist and Lilienthal was the practical director. To resolve the complex board situation, Morgan suggested to Maverick that a congressional investigation of TVA was needed to promote the standards of openness, fairness, and honesty in government. Morgan closed the letter by saying: "It would be pleasanter to resign. . . . Yet, to surrender the chance to make some contribution to decency and effectiveness in government does not seem to be the right course." Morgan sent similar letters to other congressmen with the hope that an official investigation might result.[77]

The Maverick letter and other documents from this period indicated that Morgan knew his days with TVA were numbered. Instead of backing down or resigning, Morgan focused his efforts on finding an audience willing to listen to his charges of impropriety and unethical behavior against TVA's top leadership. Such erratic and destructive behavior hinted at Morgan's fragile mental state during the last few years of his TVA tenure.

Two weeks later, on March 1, 1938, the Berry condemnation commission officially concluded that the marble claims were "commercially worthless." The committee found no solid proof of fraud or "bad faith" on Berry's part, but their decision rested entirely on the failure of the claimants to establish commercial value. With this small vindication, Morgan publicly accused Lilienthal and H. A. Morgan of conspiracy, mismanagement, and obstructionism. He issued a statement to the *New York Times* declaring that TVA's internal difficulties were not based on differing power policies, but from his "efforts to secure honesty, openness, decency, and fairness in government. . . ." Similar to his Maverick letter, Morgan's statement pleaded with a national audience for a congressional investigation to resolve the uneasy situation.[78]

On March 7, 1938, Lilienthal met with Roosevelt to discuss Morgan's statements. Roosevelt's course of action would be to discuss all board issues at a White House conference where the three TVA directors could air their grievances against one another, with the specific purpose of allowing Morgan to explain his accusations. Roosevelt explained to Lilienthal that if Morgan began his "usual harangue," he would interrupt Morgan and ask for the facts behind the charges, instead of unsubstantiated personal opinions. Lilienthal agreed with Roosevelt's plan and he emphasized that without evidence or explanation of the charges, neither TVA nor the board could withstand further attacks from Morgan.[79]

The next day, Roosevelt sent messages to all three directors requesting their presence at a White House meeting scheduled for March 11, 1938. Lilienthal and H. A. Morgan immediately agreed to the meeting, but Chairman Morgan did not. The following morning, on March 9, Morgan replied to Roosevelt's invitation saying that, as the board difficulties were so extreme, he had been forced to resort to national publicity. Further, because of the public attention, Morgan demanded that the board difficulties be considered by a congressional committee rather than at a White House conference. That same afternoon, Roosevelt, in a telegram to Morgan, emphasized that the scheduled meeting was not designed to reconcile the differences between board members but rather for Morgan to present the facts behind his charges. Morgan once again declined the invitation but, after another message from Roosevelt, he reconsidered. The next morning, Morgan finally agreed to attend the meeting.[80]

On March 11, 1938, the three TVA board members met with Roosevelt in the White House. At the opening of the discussion, Roosevelt referred to his duty as chief executive to investigate when charges and accusations affected the proper functioning of an executive agency. Roosevelt then announced that he would call upon each of the directors to give specific facts to substantiate their charges. He then stated that the director or directors charged would then have the opportunity to respond.[81]

Roosevelt began by introducing a handful of Morgan's charges against his fellow directors for open discussion. One charge related to the George Berry fraudulent marble case, which asserted that H. A. Morgan and Lilienthal had prior knowledge of the scam and hoped to profit both financially and politically from Berry's windfall. Roosevelt then reviewed the more personal charge that Lilienthal and H. A. Morgan had demonstrated evasion, intrigue, sharp strategy, conspiracy, and dishonesty in their dealings with Morgan.[82]

The president gave Morgan the first opportunity to respond. However, Morgan stated that only Congress, and not the president, could conduct an appropriate investigation of TVA's internal conflict. Therefore, he refused to cooperate. Morgan lived up to his word and throughout the hearing he made only brief statements and failed to answer Roosevelt's questions. Morgan explained to Roosevelt that he was merely an "observer," and declined to present any of the "proof" behind his libelous charges.[83]

Conversely, when Roosevelt called upon H. A. Morgan and David Lilienthal to respond to Morgan's charges, the two directors answered with specifics and referred to supporting documents. Likewise, when Roosevelt asked the two directors about their own charges against the chairman, H. A. Morgan and Lilienthal presented their evidence to Roosevelt for examination. Specifically, H. A. Morgan and Lilienthal accused the chairman of challenging the integrity of close associates through numerous publications, interfering with constitutional litigation in two TVA court cases, and dealing with private utilities before, during, and after the 1936 power pooling conferences. But, most importantly, Lilienthal asserted that, since the spring of 1936, Morgan failed to carry out decisions of the board and that he had purposely removed himself from all TVA activities. Morgan refused to comment upon their charges against him.[84]

After six hours of ineffective and tense deliberations, Roosevelt adjourned the meeting and scheduled another conference for the following week. Roosevelt made it clear to the directors that the public interest could not be further jeopardized by internal dissension and announced that anyone not interested in upholding the principles of TVA should not remain on the board. While Roosevelt wanted to give Morgan another chance to explain his actions, Lilienthal pushed for Morgan's removal.[85]

On Friday, March 18, 1938, the three directors returned to the White House for another session. After Roosevelt's opening statements, Morgan asked to make a statement of his position that he claimed would last roughly ten minutes. Roosevelt complied but warned the chairman to strictly confine his declaration to evidence and not opinion. During his statement, Morgan did little more that review his vague charges against the other two directors. As promised, Roosevelt continually interrupted Morgan and demanded specifics. Morgan did not reveal of the proof behind his accusations and concluded that only Congress could fully investigate the matter. Dissatisfied with Morgan's excuses, Roosevelt offered the chairman one more opportunity to reveal his charges at a third White House meeting the following Monday. Roosevelt warned Morgan that he would be guilty of contumacy (a stubborn resistance to authority) if he did not attend the meeting or refused to present his evidence.[86]

At the brief gathering of the TVA board and Roosevelt on Monday, March 21, 1938, Morgan demanded a congressional investigation and informed Roosevelt that he could not participate in any further White House proceedings. Roosevelt responded saying that Morgan must either prove his accusations or withdraw them. Then the president stated that if Morgan took neither option, he would be forced to either remove or suspend him from the TVA board. Morgan, of course, announced that he would not resign and challenged Roosevelt's power to remove a board member without a vote from the Senate. Nevertheless, Roosevelt gave Morgan yet another day to resign, withdraw his charges, or produce the evidence behind his accusations. Morgan did not back down from the ultimatum and, later that day, announced that he had no intention of resigning.[87]

On March 23, 1938, Roosevelt removed Arthur Morgan as an employee and board member of TVA. Roosevelt made the decision on the grounds that Morgan made libelous charges against his fellow directors, obstructed the work of TVA, and refused to submit the evidence behind his various accusations. Initially, Morgan accepted the decree, but he quickly changed his mind and again challenged Roosevelt's authority to remove a member of the TVA board. Morgan contested presidential power to remove a member of the TVA board and, with the encouragement of several lawyers, he filed a lawsuit against TVA in Tennessee district court. TVA quickly issued an official statement upholding the president's authority to remove a board member, but Morgan was not satisfied with their explanations and again pushed for a congressional investigation of the agency.[88]

Perhaps because of the severity of Morgan's allegations or Roosevelt's seemingly drastic decision, a growing group of congressmen and reporters called for a congressional investigation of TVA and a chance for Morgan to present

Arthur Morgan during the TVA Investigation. Antiochiana, Antioch College.

his elusive evidence to the public. Maury Maverick supported the inquiry and declared that "no friend of TVA should fear the results." On April 4, 1938, Congress passed a bill which allocated $50,000 for a special joint congressional committee to investigate TVA. On the same day, Congress appointed Ohio senator A. Victor Donahey (D) chair of the nine-member committee and scheduled the hearings to begin in late May 1938.[89]

The first public hearing of the congressional committee to investigate TVA occurred on May 25, 1938, in the Senate Office Building. With a moderate crowd in attendance, Morgan took the entire first day by reading a series of prepared statements. During his testimony, Morgan accused Lilienthal and H. A. Morgan of conspiracy, mismanagement, and releasing inaccurate public reports. But, before leaving the stand, Morgan withdrew or explained away the majority of his charges against the other two directors. He explained that his accusations of corruption did not deal with bribery or financial gains, but were focused on a lack of ethics and values.[90]

H. A. Morgan took the stand on the second day of the hearings. He made a lengthy statement about the history of TVA's internal conflict, especially noting Morgan's inability to cooperate with his fellow directors since mid-1933. Following the statement, H. A. Morgan produced numerous documents as evidence behind his statements of the chairman's mismanagement and obstructionism. As one example, H. A. Morgan introduced into evidence differences in the chairman's voting patterns and increased absenteeism to demonstrate Morgan's complete change of attitude after Lilienthal's 1936 reappointment. H. A. Morgan explained that, after mid-1936, Morgan, through his own actions and initiative, removed himself from the cooperative participation in the agency's affairs by missing nearly one-third of the scheduled board meetings.[91]

After the lunch break on the second day, Lilienthal took the witness stand. In his opening statement Lilienthal announced that he would only discuss facts about TVA and not reply to Morgan's personal attacks. He argued that Morgan's close association with the private utility companies, his opposition to TVA's accepted power policy, his disruptive actions during the *TEPCO* proceedings, and his accusations against his fellow directors during the George Berry claims matter obstructed and sabotaged the integrity of TVA. Finally, Lilienthal concluded that Morgan, acting as board chairman, had proven a poor administrator, was gravely prejudicial to some TVA programs, and had violated elementary standards that govern both public and private officials.[92]

After two days of testimony, the congressional committee recessed the hearings until July. Despite the initial public excitement, when the hearings resumed in Knoxville on July 18, 1938, the issue lost its national appeal. Throughout the summer, Morgan continued his inconclusive statements before the committee and did not reveal the promised proof behind his various charges. Morgan slowed the hearings significantly by testifying about the George Berry marble case for thirteen days. Frustrated by the hearings, Lilienthal attacked Morgan's statements. On several occasions, Lilienthal uncovered inaccuracies in Morgan's testimony, thereby diminishing his credibility. For the most part, the summer hearings, held in Knoxville and briefly in Chattanooga, revealed to the committee a succession of TVA engineers and office workers who took the witness stand and embarrassed investigators with their familiarity of incomprehensible technical details. The last Knoxville session of the investigation ended in early September.[93]

The congressional investigation of TVA resumed in Washington, D.C., two months later. These sessions featured an appearance by Wendell Willkie as a witness. However, Willkie testified only about C&S's relationship with TVA, rather than his personal opinions of or his affiliation with Morgan and Lilienthal. Morgan also returned to the stand to present an extensive plan for

David Lilienthal during the TVA Investigation. Antiochiana, Antioch College.

reorganizing of the agency. He asserted that his past criticisms of TVA's leaders were well-grounded. In fact, Morgan commended his own past actions by stating that his ability to remain on a divided board so long demonstrated his capacity to operate under difficult circumstances.[94]

On December 21, 1938, chairman Donahey recessed the congressional investigation of TVA. After seventy days of hearings, the committee accumulated over six thousand pages of testimony, nearly six hundred exhibits, and a one-thousand-page document consisting of a TVA technical summary and majority and minority reports. During the six-month investigation, more than one hundred witnesses appeared; Morgan testified for ten days, Lilienthal for nine, and H. A. Morgan for four.[95]

Throughout the hearings, Morgan delivered to the committee long, rambling, and vague charges against his fellow directors. However, as Morgan produced none of his promised proof and as the other witnesses revealed nothing about TVA's alleged internal intrigue, the hearings provided little new evidence for the committee. In their defense, H. A. Morgan continued to supply the necessary documents to Lilienthal, who restated, challenged, and disproved nearly all of the chairman's charges. By disproving Morgan's statements, Lilienthal and H. A. Morgan depicted Morgan as an obstructionist. Clearly, the hearings revealed that any progress and cooperation on TVA's board had long since expired. The congressional committee began work on its final report, while the TVA board members finally went their separate ways; Arthur Morgan returned to Yellow Springs to regroup, while David Lilienthal and H. A. Morgan returned to Knoxville to lead TVA.[96]

During the congressional investigation, TVA lawyers took their *TEPCO* arguments before the Supreme Court. The hearing began in mid-November with fourteen of the original nineteen companies (nearly all C&S subsidiaries) joined in suit against TVA. The legal team argued that TVA was designed for the constitutional purposes of flood control, navigation, and national defense. The plaintiffs then presented their side of the case, arguing that Congress primarily established TVA to generate power from hydroelectric plants, and that navigation and flood control were incidental. On January 30, 1939, the Supreme Court, in a 5-2 decision, dismissed the case on the grounds that the complainants had no right to be free from competition and therefore had no standing to maintain the suit. Within two days of the ruling, Willkie announced that he would pursue no other legal actions against TVA. Negotiations between TVA and C&S resumed, and on February 2, 1939, Willkie agreed to sell TVA all of the TEPCO properties for just over $78 million.[97]

Two months later, on April 3, 1939, the congressional committee investigating TVA released its final report. The committee declared that Morgan's charges of dishonesty against his fellow directors were "without foundation, not supported by the evidence and made without due consideration of the available facts." Further, they added that Lilienthal and H. A. Morgan "acted with forbearance and dignity" during the long period of internal dissension before Roosevelt removed Morgan from office. After several years of controversy, the committee's report finally dispelled Morgan's charges of corruption and conspiracy against Lilienthal and H. A. Morgan. They concluded that the charges were exaggerated because of Morgan's propensity to attribute moral delinquencies to anyone opposing him.[98]

Morgan's lawsuit against TVA, which contested Roosevelt's authority to remove a member of the TVA board, was heard in the Tennessee district court in Knoxville in the fall of 1939. Morgan was listed as the plaintiff, but he did not testify or participate in any of the legal proceedings. In fact, following the congressional investigation, Morgan fully accepted his removal from the board and launched new initiatives. However, a number of attorneys with interest in testing the constitutionality of the removal led the charge against TVA and the executive office. They argued that the TVA Act designated the power of removal of a board member to Congress and made no mention of the president's role in such actions. Further, the lawyers for the plaintiff argued that TVA was an independent government agency responsible only to Congress and did not have direct connections to the executive branch. In August 1939, the district court ruled that the chief executive did have such powers of removal even if proscribed by the TVA Act. The lawyers for the plaintiff appealed the decision, arguing that TVA board members were not officers of the executive branch and that the TVA Act outlined the congressional process of removing board members. In December 1940, the Sixth Circuit Appeal Court upheld the lower court's decision, saying that the president had inherit powers to remove executive officers, and that TVA board members were in fact executive officers because they primarily exercised administrative and executive functions. In one final attempt, the lawyers for the plaintiff petitioned the Supreme Court to hear their complaint. But on March 17, 1941, the highest court denied the petition and ended all legal proceedings in the nature of Morgan's removal from TVA by the president.[99]

In 1939, Arthur Morgan reached the end of his TVA career and stood at a crossroads. After just a few years with TVA, Morgan achieved major accomplishments in engineering, flood control, cooperative enterprises, and social endeavors. As an early New Deal promoter, regional planner, dam builder, and town planner, Morgan demonstrated his Progressive Era tendencies of efficiency, organization, and administration. But at the same time, his ethical and moral principles were so inflexible that he became a victim of his own dictates. Instability marked the final two years of Morgan's TVA tenure and ended with his removal in 1938. The lengthy congressional investigation that he demanded did not validate his various charges or justify his strict adherence to moral principles.

Similar to his time at Antioch, Morgan experienced a significant setback for his vision during his TVA tenure. In both cases, Morgan exhibited incredible energy at the outset, offered innovative solutions, established a way of cooperating with diverse interests, and displayed considerable leadership and administrative skills. As time went on, however, he became, in some ways, a victim of his own success. As he gathered effective people around him, with their own ideas about success, his unbending moral sensibility and unwillingness to modify his essential vision reduced his effectiveness as a leader—and even awoke an almost paranoid tendency to reject the ideas of others. But unlike his experience at Antioch, at TVA, Morgan encountered much more significant opposition from others, especially David Lilienthal.

While Morgan's missteps with TVA were largely his own, Lilienthal, who was much more politically savvy, contributed a great deal to Morgan's downfall. The congressional investigation revealed that Morgan and Lilienthal represented two different ideologies and philosophies for TVA. First, "Progressive Era" Morgan wanted the agency to be a broad-based network of social endeavors and flood control, while "New Dealer" Lilienthal wanted the agency to focus on electric power production and government regulation of utilities. And, as the investigation focused more on Morgan's charges of intrigue, suspicion, and bad faith, rather than conflicting power policies, the philosophical, political, and personal differences between Morgan and Lilienthal became clear. The investigation represented the culmination of Morgan's and Lilienthal's differences—a conflict of governing philosophies and social analysis rather than only power policies, as previous interpreters have argued.[100]

During the external struggle for public over private power, an internal battle resulted in the removal of an important early leader of TVA. Morgan's departure from TVA in 1938 symbolized the end for any of the elaborate social programs that many New Dealers, including Roosevelt, had dreamed of just a few years prior. Morgan's first plans for TVA evolved into tangible results; however, many of his overall ideas for restructuring the region were much more idealistic than practical. By the beginning of the Second New Deal, Morgan's voice drew less attention and respect. His greatest political misstep was his approach to private power interests in the Tennessee Valley. Morgan favored cooperation instead of competition with private power interests, but Lilienthal's take-no-prisoners approach to TVA's electric power program ran counter to Morgan's plan to bring together the two factions.

But more at the heart of the problem, during their rocky six years together on the board, stark personalities and conflicting visions for the agency split the directors. Morgan, a moralist with Progressive Era values, clashed with the young, ambitious Lilienthal over large and small matters. The elder director found Lilienthal to be devoid of character, lacking in ethical conscience, and seeking to take the agency in the wrong direction. On the contrary, Lilienthal found Morgan to be a "befuddled old man" full of indecipherable moral standards who wanted to return the Tennessee Valley to an earlier, more primitive time.[101]

Their backgrounds revealed a sharp difference of experiences and motivations: Lilienthal was a politically connected lawyer with a great deal to prove; Morgan was a self-taught engineer who had recorded significant accomplishments across several decades. Each possessed a strong personality and a clear set of opinions, which made compromise and cooperation between Morgan and Lilienthal difficult from the very beginning of TVA. Unable to resolve their differences, the two directors struggled to work together, with Morgan becoming more erratic and near-paranoid in his behavior.

By the mid-1930s, Morgan lost touch with the changing times and was unable to recapture the reform spirit of his previous efforts. While TVA chairman, he emphasized strong character, community, and traditions of the past, but the audience for his type of social reform dwindled in favor of a different type of liberalism. By the end of the decade, Morgan and his generation of Progressive Era reformers and experts were largely become overshadowed by other public leaders, such as Lilienthal.

Morgan's departure from TVA removed him from the public eye. Out of the spotlight, Morgan entered the next phase of his career, one marked by international contributions to education, public works, and small communities. After leaving Tennessee, Morgan retreated to Yellow Springs, Antioch, and his typewriter to clarify his thinking about new approaches to building American character. He decided to revisit a lifelong interest in Edward Bellamy, utopianism, and imagining a more perfect and attainable society.

7

REDISCOVERING THE UTOPIANS

In early November 1933, Arthur Morgan received an unexpected letter from Ferris Greenslet, the director of publishing at the Houghton Mifflin Company. An established author and literary scout, Greenslet discovered such talented writers as Willa Cather. He wrote that "there is widespread, active, and increased demand for a short biography or book about Edward Bellamy and *Looking Backward.*" Greenslet explained that Mason Greene, an associate of Bellamy's, attempted such a work. Despite a fire that destroyed much of the original Bellamy material in his possession, Greene produced a draft manuscript. However, the Bellamy family and potential publishers did not believe that Greene's draft captured the essence of Bellamy's theories, and the manuscript remained unpublished.[1]

Greenslet had been working with Paul Bellamy, the son of the utopian author, to identify the most qualified author to tackle the life, theories, and legacies of Edward Bellamy. By 1933, Greenslet and Paul Bellamy agreed that Arthur Morgan was "the predestined author for a small book presenting the facts of Bellamy's life and the present application of many of his ideas." The letter offered Morgan a unique opportunity to revisit Edward Bellamy, exactly forty years since he first read *Looking Backward.*[2]

Greenslet well understood that time constraints and other obligations might delay Morgan in the writing of a biography of Edward Bellamy, but he was hardly worried. He explained in the letter that "if you want a job well and promptly done, the thing to do is to apply to the busiest man of your acquaintances to do it." A few weeks later, Greenslet wrote Morgan a second time with more details of a possible Bellamy book contract. He offered Morgan an advance of $500 and 15 percent royalties for a biographical work on Bellamy, which would be scheduled for delivery within a year. To speed the writing, Greenslet would allow Morgan complete usage of the unpublished Mason Greene manuscript and access to original material kept by Paul Bellamy. Greenslet hoped that Morgan's book could tap an even greater market of Bellamy followers. He reported to Morgan that Houghton Mifflin's $1.00 edition of *Looking Backward* had sold more than 10,000 copies in the previous eighteen months. Greenslet closed the letter saying that "we are confident that this is going to be a book of permanent importance."[3]

The sudden offer sounded nearly too good to be true to Morgan's ears. By 1933, Morgan had written scores of professional tracts, essays, technical reports, solicited pieces, a play, and a couple of short books, but this project represented his first large-scale commercial writing assignment. Over the Thanksgiving holiday, Morgan reviewed the Greene manuscript, a copy of *Looking Backward,* and Greenslet's book deal. On December 4, 1933, Morgan wrote Greenslet and accepted the offer to write a biography of Edward Bellamy. Even with the massive demands of TVA before him, Morgan relished the idea of having such a writing project, especially one that involved such an influential character in his own life and career.[4]

The writing of the book took far more time than Morgan or Greenslet projected—ten years instead of ten months. The work of TVA limited Morgan's ability to complete the book, but in early 1939, after the conclusion of the congressional investigation of TVA, he picked up the project with renewed interest and vigor. The final product, published by a different press in 1944, was a much lengthier study than Morgan and Houghton Mifflin first imagined. The delays in writing and publishing meant that the biography received a much different audience and response. During the Great Depression a newfound interest in Bellamy emerged because many believed that *Looking Backward* offered possible solutions to the social and economic problems of the period. Morgan's book missed an opportunity to connect with a brief reawakening of Bellamy's thought in the 1930s.[5] By 1944, in the last years of World War II, national interest in Bellamy declined. In addition to bad timing, Morgan's book was an extensive biographical and philosophical study of Bellamy, which did not appeal to popular audiences. Readers expecting the book to connect Bellamy's predictions with modern New Deal realities such as Morgan's own Tennessee Valley Authority were disappointed. Despite not meeting the intellectual and monetary expectations of literary scouts such as Greenslet, Morgan's detailed book became a definitive biographical source for Bellamy scholars. While working on the book, Morgan collected a voluminous amount of research material on Bellamy and utopian thought. During the early 1940s, Morgan wrote four other books that supported his larger work on the life and contributions of Edward Bellamy.

Even though Morgan began his book on Edward Bellamy while still with TVA, the majority of his writing on utopianism and *Looking Backward* occurred after his 1938 firing. For the next several years, Morgan entered a significant period of writing, researching, and theorizing about Edward Bellamy and the postwar world. By writing these five books and studying Bellamy, Morgan better defined his own conceptualization of the small community, ethical standards, social structures, and governance in a possible utopia. Although Morgan engaged in other projects during this period, as the next chapter will address, his research and writing on Bellamy deserves specific attention. To understand Morgan's motivations, character, and outlook (both before and after TVA), one must look backward to understand how Morgan interpreted the life and legacies of Edward Bellamy.

Morgan's writings on Edward Bellamy occurred during a tumultuous period in American history. As the final years of the Great Depression gave way to America's entry into World War II, cultural, social, and political shifts marked the landscape. Millions of men enlisted in the military, serving in a truly worldwide conflict. In their wake, millions of women found jobs in factories, on farms, and in government sectors. Combined, their work supported a military mobilization that sparked new life into a dismal economy that had been stagnant for over a decade. Wartime society at home also erased much of the desperation that had lingered throughout the 1930s. Suddenly employment, food, and opportunities became available to more Americans.[6]

In 1945, after years of fighting and millions of lives lost, Allied forces stopped the threat of Nazism and Fascism across Europe, Africa, East Asia, and the islands of the Pacific. In May of that year, the Nazis surrendered, and in August, following the dropping of two atomic weapons, the Japanese also surrendered to the Allied forces. The conclusion of World War II raised new questions about the fate of the postwar world and cast many new shadows. The use of atomic weapons to facilitate the end of the war with Japan began a lengthy Cold War and nuclear arms race between the United States and the Soviet Union.

World War II marked a significant turning point in American history. Military mobilization and the subsequent return to a peacetime society resulted in massive economic, political, and cultural shifts at home. These shifts redefined modern America and set the stage for a new era of American ingenuity, progress, and worldwide hegemony. However, many Americans, uneasy with such rapid changes, searched for earlier precedents for organizing postwar society. Morgan found answers to the challenges of wartime and the years that followed through the writings of Edward Bellamy. Similarly, Morgan and others believed that the only way to move American forward and not repeat the mistakes of two world wars was to look backward on the lessons of the late nineteenth and early twentieth centuries.

In the early 1930s and first years of the New Deal, the writings of Edward Bellamy attracted significant national interest. The Edward Bellamy Association of New York was the most active group promoting the ideals of Bellamy during the decade. Started in April 1932 as the "Edward Bellamy Group of Brooklyn," the organization believed that the Great Depression symbolized the nation's broken social and economic system. Their mission was to achieve a "social and economic system as advocated by Edward Bellamy in his 'Looking Backward' and 'Equality.'" They believed that the two books outlined a clear set of instructions, which they called the "Bellamy Plan," to transition the nation away from market capitalism to a system of utopian socialism. To achieve their lofty aspirations, the Bellamy Association wanted to build political power through a simple pyramid approach to sharing their plan—simply have one member distribute 10 pamphlets to 10 potential Bellamyites, who would in turn each distribute 10 more pamphlets to 10 others, until the group reached 30 million members of the voting public. With voting power, they believed that a non-violent transition, as described in *Looking Backward,* would occur in only a matter of years. To coordinate the massive effort, the organization planned for local chapters to reach new members, organize events, and distribute literature about the Bellamy Plan.[7]

The Bellamy Association made efforts to attract significant people to their organization. Honorary members of the group included educator John Dewey, historian Harry Elmer Barnes, journalist Heywood Broun, and founder of the American Civil Liberties Union Roger N. Baldwin. Articles on Bellamy by well-known authors, including John Dewey, boosted their efforts.[8] In late 1933, the Bellamy Association approached muckraking journalist Ida Tarbell with an interesting proposal. At the time, Tarbell was completing a book about the economic and social history of last two decades of the nineteenth century, and people expected her to comment on Bellamy's influence during this period.[9] The group asked Tarbell about writing a Bellamy biography to further their cause. Perhaps most significant was that the letter to Tarbell was dated November 3, 1933, the same date of the letter that Ferris Greenslet from Houghton Mifflin sent to Arthur Morgan for exactly the same purpose. It is unclear if the Bellamy Association sought to circumvent and compete with the efforts of Houghton Mifflin and publish their own biography, or whether they hoped to secure a potential back-up author for the press. As another possibility, correspondence with Tarbell later that month suggested that the Bellamy family made identical inquiries to the Bellamy Association and Houghton Mifflin about securing a notable and worthy author for a biography.[10]

Three days after receiving the offer, Tarbell declined the chance to write a Bellamy biography, because of a lack of time. However, she expressed interest in writing a magazine article about Bellamy, because he factored into her study of the late nineteenth century. With encouragement from the Bellamy Association and the Bellamy family, Tarbell completed on a short essay on Bellamy's modern day relevance. Later in 1934, the resulting article, "New Dealers of the 'Seventies'," appeared in *Forum and Century.* In the essay, Tarbell cast both Bellamy and Henry George as innovators of their day and as bright lights for the present economic crisis. She connected the emerging programs of the New Deal to the social programs and services described in Bellamy's writings. Her essay pleased the Bellamy Association and the Bellamy family, and it increased national interest in Bellamy and demand for a lengthier work on the utopian author.[11]

At the same time, Morgan began his detailed study of Bellamy for Houghton Mifflin. Time became the biggest challenge for the project, because in early 1934 Morgan was launching various TVA programs. Because of the massive responsibilities connected to TVA, Morgan hired a research assistant.

For the next five years, Grace Smelo, an Antioch College student, gathered material, spoke to Bellamy's acquaintances, and developed outlines for the biography. In early 1934, Morgan arranged for Smelo to complete research and interviews in Boston, New York, Philadelphia, and Washington, D.C. That summer, Smelo compiled a lengthy report on her research progress, which listed suggestions on the arrangement for the book and remaining sources of information on Bellamy. However, Morgan's professional responsibilities and occasional ill health delayed his work on reviewing the Bellamy research material compiled by Smelo. By fall 1937, Morgan explained to Houghton Mifflin that his TVA work made it nearly impossible to make progress on the book and he suggested that the task be given to another author. However, the publisher and the Bellamy family reassured Morgan that he was the only author capable of capturing the essence of Bellamy's life and asked that he continue the project. Morgan agreed but emphasized that progress on the book would be sporadic.[12]

In late 1938, Arthur Morgan, at age sixty, retreated to Yellow Springs, Ohio. For much of that year he prepared for and participated in the congressional investigation of TVA. That inquiry lasted from May to December, and the final report appeared a few months later. In early 1939, as the investigation concluded, Morgan turned his attention back to the Bellamy project. In a January 11, 1939 letter to Houghton Mifflin, Morgan explained that he had completed half of the book manuscript and expected to finish the second half in the next three or four months. That fall, Morgan submitted a portion of the manuscript to Houghton Mifflin for an initial review. The publisher reacted positively to the submission and encouraged the completion of the manuscript in 1940. In fact, Houghton Mifflin listed the book on their forthcoming titles list.[13]

Unlike previous Bellamy scholars and biographers, Morgan had access to a collection of Bellamy's journals, notebooks, personal and professional correspondence, and unpublished essays. The Bellamy family allowed Morgan full use of these materials during his research. Morgan concluded that the variety and depth of the private collection supported much more than just a single biographical treatment of Bellamy. Immersed in the details of Bellamy's life, ideas, and work, by 1940, Morgan was involved in several writing projects related to Bellamy.

Morgan's first published writing on Edward Bellamy appeared in 1940, but it was not the anticipated biography. This nearly fifty-page book, *The*

Religion of Solidarity, published by the Antioch Bookplate Company (a company started by Morgan), included a preface by Morgan and a previously unpublished essay by Bellamy. Morgan's main purpose in publishing the scarce essay was to share with readers a concise, direct, and illuminating statement of the overall philosophy of Edward Bellamy, in Bellamy's own words. According to Morgan, the essay, written by Bellamy at age twenty-four, captured the "best single statement we possess as to his general concept of life and of the nature of things."[14] Morgan hoped the ideals described in the essay would promote the relevance of Bellamy and generate interest for his forthcoming biography.

By 1940, Morgan concluded that Bellamy was much more than a social reformer or a utopian writer; instead, he was a philosopher. In the preface to *The Religion of Solidarity*, Morgan explained that the multiple threads of Bellamy's writings, activism, and views formed a cohesive philosophy. Morgan explained that Bellamy's view of life rested on how humans related to the universe, to society, and to themselves. According to Morgan, Bellamy was a rebel who rejected accepted knowledge and human logic in favor of analysis, intuition, and appraisal. As a result, Bellamy placed humans in control of their individual destinies and their collective environment. Morgan explained that Bellamy offered a unique perspective because he "examined the maze of life as from a great height." In the search for universal truth, Bellamy questioned the reasons behind accepted beliefs, learned behavior, and the organization of modern society.[15]

The Bellamy essay itself was a product of its time, full of Victorian Era allusions to nature, health, life, death, and human emotions. Written in 1874, "The Religion of Solidarity" discussed the inter-relationships between individual and social identity. Bellamy argued that human morality and self-sacrifice resulted in a tendency for social solidarity rather than individuality. That assertion, Bellamy believed, limited the ability of individuals to question their existence, society, religion, and future. Bellamy did not favor individuality over solidarity. Rather, he believed that individual analysis should occur before collective decisions about society were made. In 1887, Bellamy returned to his personal notebook containing the essay and added a note of explanation. After thirteen years of reflection, Bellamy explained that the essay "represents the germ of what has been ever since my philosophy of life." Due to the importance of the essay, he instructed that the philosophical treatise be read to him on his deathbed.[16]

Because of limited the print run, *The Religion of Solidarity* made few repercussions. In June 1941, *The New England Quarterly* ran a short review of the book. Despite the book's "obscuring religious jargon," the reviewer believed that the message to consider both individual and societal needs had great significance for readers.[17] For Morgan, the short book demonstrated his belief that Bellamy had relevance to the modern world as well, and Morgan continued approaching his subject from numerous perspectives, all with a sympathetic pen.

Morgan's research into different components of Bellamy's life resulted in expansion of the scope and length of his biography project. In early 1940, he explained to Houghton Mifflin that the manuscript would cover Bellamy's ideological and philosophical influences, rather than just listing Bellamy's social views and accomplishments. As a result, Morgan explained that the manuscript would exceed the agreed upon 150,000 word estimate. Houghton Mifflin cautioned Morgan to keep close to the word limit and to consider that the book would be targeted for popular audiences. Morgan responded saying that the book should appeal to both scholars and general readers.[18]

At that point, Morgan revealed to the publisher that his research led him to other areas of utopian thought and writing, which would deserve additional chapters in the swelling biography. In particular, Morgan wanted to explore the possible real connections between the Incan civilization in Peru and the utopian civilization described in Sir Thomas More's classic book *Utopia,* first published in 1516. Scholars discounted More's description of the New World as clever fiction designed to criticize the English monarchy, but Morgan determined that More's story was based on factual evidence.[19]

Morgan's research into Bellamy's life led to a larger study of the development of utopian thought. The crux of Morgan's evolving argument was that achieving a utopian state—a planned society where resources were equally shared, peace replaced war, and poverty eliminated—was possible in the twentieth century, as proven by the past success of New World civilizations. According to Morgan, the failure of the Incan empire was because it relied on a dictatorship rather than a democracy. Thus, the Spanish conquistadors conquered the Incans by capturing and executing their top leader. But with a democratic system, Morgan believed that a modern utopia could exist and thrive. With the gathering storm clouds of war in Europe and in the Pacific, Morgan believed that he had stumbled across a forgotten historical precedent that could be applied to solving the global problems of the early 1940s.[20]

Morgan's fascination with the connections among Thomas More's *Utopia,* Edward Bellamy's *Looking Backward,* and the history of utopian thought resulted in a second book-length project. By spring 1941, Morgan had completed five chapters of a proposed ten chapter book, tentatively titled "Utopias," and he mailed the material to Houghton Mifflin for review. He explained to the publisher that the publication of a book on the history of utopian development would boost the sales of the forthcoming, albeit long overdue, biography of Edward Bellamy. The publisher, however, quickly disagreed with Morgan and encouraged him to complete the Bellamy biography first. Morgan reassured the publisher that the primary project on Bellamy was nearly complete.[21]

In spring 1941, after eight years in the making, Morgan submitted the final chapters of the tentatively titled "The Life of Edward Bellamy" to Houghton Mifflin. Morgan's expanded focus on Bellamy's place in utopian history increased the size of the manuscript to over 200,000 words. On July 28, 1941, the editors at Houghton Mifflin sent Arthur Morgan a lengthy review of the manuscript. The reviewers reported that the length and excessive detail of the manuscript detracted from the book's intended premise—to describe and evaluate, for a wide range of readers, Bellamy's overall contributions to social and economic thought. The reviewers believed that the manuscript would only appeal to a small number of specialists and not to a broad book-buying audience. To remedy these issues, the report suggested creating two separate works. First, the reviewers recommended cutting the manuscript by fifty or sixty percent, to create a condensed book of approximately 100,000 words focused on the most significant details of Bellamy's life and contributions. Second, the extracted material and portions of the "Utopias" manuscript could form a second more scholarly and detailed book on Bellamy for later publication.[22]

On September 27, 1941, Morgan responded to the publisher's report. First, Morgan explained that the reason for the expanded manuscript had to do with his discovery of Bellamy's connections to previous utopian writings. Morgan clarified that the complexity of Bellamy's personality, interests, influences, and writings would be best served by one book (approximately 200,000 words, possibly as a two-volume set), but not two separate titles for different audiences. In an effort to establish Bellamy's undiscovered significance, Morgan articulated that Bellamy shaped the eugenics movement by questioning the theories of Charles Darwin, anticipated the behavioral theories of Sigmund Freud, and influenced the Theosophist movement of the late nineteenth century. Morgan argued that Bellamy's writings were, in fact, on par with the best works of James Joyce, Gertrude Stein, Robert Lewis Stevenson, and Henry David Thoreau. Of course, Morgan emphasized the significance of the industrial army described in *Looking Backward*, especially in light of the expansion of government in preparation for war. As possible audiences for the lengthy tome, Morgan listed Bellamy admirers, librarians, eugenicists, nature lovers, Theosophists, socialists, philosophers, and psychologists, but he did not mention general readers. Morgan concluded the letter saying that he would return the advance of $500 if they were no longer interested in the manuscript.[23]

On October 3, 1941, Houghton Mifflin responded to Morgan's letter. The publisher explained that the final manuscript was a much more expanded study of Bellamy than they had expected. Thus, without significant revisions and elimination of sections, they would be unable to publish the manuscript. Houghton Mifflin recommended that Morgan return the $500 advance and cancel their contract, so he would be free to seek another publisher.[24]

Not dissuaded, Morgan continued work on his extensive Bellamy study. Two years later, Morgan submitted a manuscript to Columbia University Press for consideration. On August 24, 1943, Columbia University Press sent Morgan a report that recommended publication with the condition that he reduce the length of the manuscript significantly. The report, which recommended eliminating 75,000 to 150,000 words from the text, indicates that Morgan added new material to the earlier manuscript before submitting it to Columbia University Press. This time, Morgan complied with the suggestions of the publisher and reduced the length of the manuscript, which went into production later that fall.[25]

In 1944, Columbia University Press published Arthur Morgan's *Edward Bellamy* with a list price of $5.00. At over four hundred pages, the book became the definitive biographical work on Bellamy, offering more detail on the utopian writer than any book before or since.[26] Morgan's tone proved overly sympathetic to Bellamy, comparing him to such luminaries as Sigmund Freud, Ralph Waldo Emerson, Henry David Thoreau, Nathaniel Hawthorne, Henry George, and Leonardo da Vinci. In the preface, Morgan explained that, "Bellamy was not just a utopian. His was one of the most ranging and penetrating minds America has produced." Morgan wanted to demonstrate the influence of Bellamy on the course of creating modern America. Morgan made it clear that Bellamy's influence went far beyond his most successful publication, *Looking Backward.* Morgan characterized Bellamy as a philosopher who possessed a vision of social and economic reform with modern day applications. Compared to other utopian writers, Bellamy's vision was practical and accessible to readers. Morgan explained that, "It was the genius of Edward Bellamy that he took Utopia out of the region of hazy dreamland and made it a concrete program for the actual modern world."[27]

Morgan structured his book into several distinct segments. First, the book summarized the basics of Bellamy's life, from his humble beginnings to his death at age forty-eight. As Morgan pointed out, Bellamy's family represented a long line of preachers, thinkers, philosophers, and rebels in thought. That legacy and the family's diversity of thought created an environment for intellectual curiosity to grow. As another important factor, Morgan placed the town of Chicopee Falls, Massachusetts, as a crucial part of young Bellamy's outlook. Morgan described the society of the small town as trapped in the middle of commercial and industrial transformation. That setting influenced Bellamy's understanding of social and economic problems of the nineteenth century. At the time of Bellamy's birth in 1850, Morgan explained, Chicopee Falls was "turbulently changing from a quiet New England village to an actively growing manufacturing town, with foreign quarters, slums, and strikes."[28]

The first chapters of the book traced Bellamy's formative years and his search for purpose. Morgan explained that as a young adult, Bellamy struggled in school and with several occupations because he was unable to find work that allowed him to make a positive contribution to society. He found only disappointment with law and journalism, settling on writing books and articles for much larger audience. In his writing, Bellamy took the greatest interest in organizing and structuring society for the greater good. As an example, Bellamy was a lifelong proponent of universal military service, even though his poor physical condition kept him out of West Point. Over the course of his adult life, Bellamy developed into a social philosopher who had definite ideas about how to best organize society. Those ideas, as best expressed in writings such as *Looking Backward* and *Equality*, brought Bellamy fame and interest from political groups, including the Nationalists, the Populists, and the Theosophists. Morgan concluded that Bellamy's only real weakness was poor health, which led to an early death and the loss of one of the greatest minds of modern America.[29]

In just over seventy pages, Morgan delivered an effective summary of Edward Bellamy's life, writings, and legacies. He included a large amount of quoted material from original and previously unavailable letters and notes written by Bellamy. These biographical sections could have been easily adapted and expanded for the purpose of a small book about Bellamy, which was the project that the original publisher and Morgan had set out to accomplish. However, Morgan's book was much more a comprehensive and comparative study, which reflected Morgan's views of important topics of the Progressive Era, such as urbanization, race, immigrants, labor, eugenics, and reforms. Morgan also moved Bellamy's ideas into the world of the early 1940s and the postwar period, making comments and connections on topics such as totalitarianism, the rise of the Soviet Union, and the failures of the New Deal.

The second segment of Morgan's book expanded the discussion of Bellamy's influences, beliefs, and personality. Morgan described Bellamy as a "rebel" who did not accept the common practices and traditions of late-nineteenth-century society. In particular, Bellamy realized that the social and economic system that he was a part of had put every class in bondage, and he sought freedom for them all. The industrial city was at the heart of that system, and instead Bellamy yearned for small communities, family life, and solitude. While Bellamy understood that working was a part of his society, he rejected the idea that a vocation was at the core of establishing self-worth and status in society. But unlike other philosophers of the period, such as Karl Marx, Bellamy did not believe in class warfare to bring about a change to society. Rather, Bellamy believed that all classes, not just the proletariat, would coalesce and demand a new economic and social system. The main driver for this transition, according to Bellamy, was the creation of an industrial army to provide for all the needs of all members of society.[30]

Another section of Morgan's book dealt with Bellamy's most significant writings. Morgan placed Bellamy's works within the context of the changes in American society during the late nineteenth century. Bellamy's writings reflected the industrial development and social upheaval of his time. He called for stronger public policy, coordinated planning for new development, and better use of the natural environment. Many of his works concluded that economic equality led to social equality. The transition from a competitive to a communal society would be accomplished and maintained by an industrial military organization. Morgan declared that Bellamy's writings offered a definite scheme of industrial reorganization, rather than a fairy tale of social perfection.[31]

Not surprisingly, Morgan devoted many pages of the book to the details of *Looking Backward.* Morgan declared that *Looking Backward* was the most significant utopian novel ever written, because it offered an exact plan for attaining economic and social equality. The other factor in the success of *Looking Backward* was its timing. Morgan believed that the publication of the book coincided with a dramatic shift in American society. Industrial strife and class violence marked that period, and Morgan believed that Bellamy's book provided realistic solutions to a more urban and modern populace. Morgan built on the concept of historian Frederick Jackson Turner by explaining that the book appeared just as the American "frontier" closed. The lack of new lands in the West to settle meant a "reduction of opportunity for the common man." The landscape of modern American was changing so rapidly during this period that people wanted some sort of realistic plan of organization, and according to Morgan, *Looking Backward* offered that blueprint. Morgan declared that, with *Looking Backward,* Bellamy "created a new world of social thought."[32]

The final segment of Morgan's book reviewed the overall responses to Bellamy and the legacies of his activism and writing. Morgan pointed out that the promise, or fear, that *Looking Backward* would lead to the elimination of private property was real during the late 1880s and early 1890s. Many political groups and social movements were attracted to Bellamy's ideas, including the Theosophists, the Christian Socialists, and the Populists. But the growth of the Nationalist Party was the most obvious reaction to Bellamy's utopian ideals. That political group espoused the "nationalization or municipalization of public services and branches of industry." Further, the Nationalists wanted to establish guaranteed rights for all members of society. Morgan attributed the social legislation of the Progressive Era and the New Deal to the early work of the Nationalists.[33]

Critics of *Looking Backward* were centered on Bellamy's industrial army as the sole means of production. Bellamy's detractors feared that the focus on military service and production would lead to the eradication of personal freedoms, an emphasis on militarism, and the replacement of democracy with some sort of communistic regime. Others charged that Bellamy's so-called enlightened society was based on totalitarian regimentation, which extinguished American liberties, such as free speech, press, expression, and religion. Morgan responded, however, that Bellamy designed his plan to centralize only the political and economic needs of society, without affecting personal freedoms. He argued that Bellamy's social blueprint promoted a mixed economy that included "co-operatives, publicly regulated private industry, public ownership in such fields as public utilities, and a residuum of subsistence industry." Finally, some critics found Bellamy's book to be a plagiarized amalgamation of nearly a dozen other utopian books. Morgan explained that, while Bellamy may have drawn inspiration of other works, he used those works "as bricks to build a house of his own design."[34]

Even though Morgan's book was sympathetic to its main character, he also offered his criticisms of Bellamy. Morgan believed that Bellamy underestimated the power of engrained cultural patterns and cultural lag time. While Bellamy lived his life with an open mind to new ideas, Morgan pointed out that Bellamy failed to realize that the vast majority of people in society held deep-seated beliefs that were slow to change. Other political movements and ideas of the period, such as a single tax plan, Marxist socialism, government regulation of private industry, the rise of cooperatives, and arguments for dual coinage further diluted the successful adaptation of Bellamy's philosophy. Even though Morgan believed that the timing for *Looking Backward* was ideal, he argued that Bellamy and other social thinkers of the late nineteenth century were far too impatient and ambitious with their timelines. More specifically, people who adhered to Bellamy's predictions expected enormous if not cataclysmic changes when the clock struck midnight on December 31, 1900, rather than more gradual, but still rapid, changes in society. And when those changes did not materialize, the movements lost momentum and either fell apart or merged into other causes.[35]

The importance of the small community remained central to Morgan's social planning, and thus he found Bellamy's centralized industrial army inadequate to meet local needs. According to Morgan, a large nationalized state "dissolved the intimate community groups" that produced the most successful contributors to society. Further, Morgan prized loyalty to family and community over all other loyalties, especially loyalty to the state. While Morgan recognized the importance of centralization in modern society, he believed that such centralization should be used to "protect the freedom of smaller units of society and of individuals." Morgan was not opposed to government regulation of certain sectors of society, but he opposed inefficient programs and ineffective administrators. Morgan highlighted this point, and vented his frustrations with directing the Tennessee Valley Authority, by saying, "The New Deal has poured many, many millions of dollars into settlement and co-operative relief projects, with a tragic record of waste and failure."[36]

Morgan believed that eugenic practice improved character and increased character development with each successive generation. He took the opportunity to discuss the importance of eugenics in both Bellamy's writings and the world of the 1940s. Bellamy's references to the topic of eugenics used the older term "stirpiculture." Morgan made clear that Bellamy endorsed the idea, saying that programs of social reform "must be accompanied by improvement in genetic quality." In *Looking Backward,* Bellamy wrote that a stable social and economic order depended on a sound eugenics program. In other works, Bellamy suggested that the unfit in society would not be allowed to reproduce, and some of the most violent or deviant individuals should be isolated from the rest of society. Morgan returned to the topic later in his biography, arguing that, with a sound eugenics policy, society could be remade to include those who were open minded to new ideas, resisted propaganda and authoritarian teaching, and demanded rapid social change.[37]

In the end, Morgan's overarching argument was that Edward Bellamy and his ideas constituted peculiarly American ideals. Bellamy's Nationalist plan reflected the social currents of the period. He believed that the interests of Americans in the late 1880s were more alike than they were dissimilar. Unlike class-based Marxist socialism, Bellamy relied on the solidarity of the middle class to lead a non-violent change to the social and economic structure. Morgan argued that that structure preserved the most important part of that society, rather than destroying it. Morgan avoided classifying Bellamy as a utopian. Instead he called Bellamy a social engineer (like Morgan) who developed a realistic, but not perfect, plan that reflected the American idealism of the modern era. And the influence of Bellamy, Morgan argued, could be seen in nearly every reform movement and progressive government initiative in the twentieth century. At certain points Morgan's book meandered into his philosophy and accomplishments, rather than solely describing the genius of Edward Bellamy.[38]

Morgan's biography received mostly positive reviews in the popular press and scholarly journals. The *New York Times* declared that the book was an "important spade-work book" on Bellamy. However, the reviewer explained that the book was uneven and did not provide a clear synthesis of Bellamy's thought and influence. The *New York Herald Tribune* was more favorable, saying that the book was "full of surprises and clues to American history."

Most notably, the reviewer pointed out that William Jennings Bryan adapted Bellamy's "I have seen humanity hanging on the cross" from *Looking Backward* and made it the closing line of his signature July 1896 "Cross of Gold" speech. A reviewer in the *Political Science Quarterly* agreed with Morgan's assessment that Bellamy's ideas influenced the world of the late nineteenth century. But the reviewer did not believe that the blueprint for a perfect society was applicable to the postwar world. Some reviews of the book came from more specialized fields. For example, a review in the *Journal of Forestry* argued that Bellamy was "one of America's most far-sighted conservationists." In the journal *Rural Sociology,* a reviewer said that the book had intellectual merits, but that "excesses of quotations and certain instances of repetitiousness" detracted from its readability. Overall, reviewers applauded Morgan for making such a substantial work on Bellamy available for the first time, but many also suggested that a more refined and synthetic work on Bellamy was still needed.[39]

In terms of Morgan's writing career, *Edward Bellamy* was his most detailed and lengthy project, and it created a corpus of extra material for other writing. In the preface of *Edward Bellamy,* Morgan addressed the areas not covered in the book, which he said would be included in forthcoming publications. This information indicated that Morgan did in fact trim material from his original manuscript. It also allowed Morgan to advertise his future Bellamy projects to readers, who might want more theoretical analyses of the utopian.[40]

Morgan followed the success of *Edward Bellamy* with three more books on related topics. The first was a self-published book called *Plagiarism in Utopia* (1944), which dealt with frequent charge that Edward Bellamy stole ideas from past utopian writers in order to create his blueprint for the perfect society. Morgan argued that Bellamy conceptualized and wrote *Looking Backward* with help of other utopian novels of the time. At just over thirty pages organized into two chapters, *Plagiarism in Utopia* was more of a pamphlet than a book. However, Morgan believed that this important topic related to Bellamy and the creation of *Looking Backward* deserved its own stand-alone source, rather than being incorporated into his lengthy biography *Edward Bellamy*.[41]

One of Morgan's more obscure publications, *Plagiarism in Utopia* focused on four books that critics most referred to as the unattributed sources for *Looking Backward.* Morgan reviewed the similarities of *Looking Backward*

After leaving TVA, Arthur Morgan wrote over a dozen books, including several focused on the life and philosophies of Edward Bellamy. Antiochiana, Antioch College.

with predecessor utopian novels starting with August Bebel's *Woman and Socialism* (1879). Some critics accused Bellamy of borrowing the economic model from Bebel's book, which also encouraged the takeover of private property by the state and the elimination of the profit system. The works of Bellamy and Bebel both described a social order where all members of society contributed their working years to the state, in exchange for the guarantees of personal freedom and the provision of all necessities throughout their entire lives. Acknowledging the similarities in the authors' broad concepts of utopia, Morgan argued that the same point of comparison could be made with utopian works of the past 2,500 years. More specifically, Morgan pointed out that Bebel's future utopia was set in Europe and did not reflect the American characteristics of an ideal society that Bellamy described.[42]

Morgan's book also discussed the similarities between *Looking Backward* and Laurence Gronlund's *The Cooperative Commonwealth* (1884). Several critics charged that Bellamy stole ideas from Gronlund's book, with their primary evidence that Bellamy read the book while completing his own manuscript. Once again, Morgan argued that, while there were broad similarities in the utopian concepts described in each book significant differences also existed in the details of attaining and maintaining the perfect society. Morgan also contended that Bellamy had not read the book prior to the publication of *Looking Backward.* Morgan emphasized the theme that utopian literature of the past was built and improved upon by new works, stating that, even if Bellamy had gleaned ideas from *The Cooperative Commonwealth,* "he should no more be blamed for such use . . . than was Shakespeare for taking current tales and turning them into immortal literature."[43]

Other critics charged that Bellamy borrowed from Etienne Cabet's *Voyage en Icarie* (1840) to write *Looking Backward.* Just like Bellamy's vision, Cabet based his utopia on a regimented state and complete industrialization of society. But different than most utopian novels that predated *Looking Backward,* Cabet's book placed great emphasis on the importance of technology to relieve drudgery. Morgan took issue with the comparisons, arguing that Cabet's book was based on the works of utopian writer and reformer Robert Owen. Again, Morgan returned to the argument that all utopians are influenced by their predecessors, and dismissed the charge of plagiarism.[44]

The majority of Morgan's *Plagiarism in Utopia* dealt with charges that Bellamy based *Looking Backward* on John Macnie's *The Diothas* (1883). Written by a mathematician at the University of North Dakota, this obscure utopian book had striking similarities to *Looking Backward,* most notably that in each story the heroine was named Edith, both books use the device of hypnotism to move forward in time, and the social systems in both books were nearly identical. Even more specific, critics pointed out that the utopias described in both books included: government by the elders, semi-military organization of labor, no idleness but much leisure, elimination of the profit motive and of commerce, few laws and no lawyers, incentives of honor instead of money, grandeur in public buildings, community of economic goods, science in high repute, universal public education, common eating places, and free choice of vocations.

Critics believed that Bellamy and Macnie were acquaintances and exchanged drafts and ideas before publication of their works. In fact, in the concluding chapter of *The Diothas,* Macnie referred to an anonymous friend "E_____" who offered inspiration on the structure and personality of a utopian society.[45]

Despite the similarities between the two books, Morgan believed that Bellamy's *Looking Backward* was a unique work that may have been influenced by *The Diothas,* but not ripped from the pages of Macnie's obscure book. Morgan explained that Bellamy had been writing about many of the ideas in both books, such as universal service in an industrial army and an equal social order without class distinctions, many years prior to the publication of *The Diothas.* Further, important differences in the books existed, especially Macnie's prediction that the utopian transformation in society would take 7,600 years, instead of just over 100 years as presented in Bellamy's work. Next, Morgan examined the theory that Bellamy and Macnie were acquainted and may have influenced each other's work. Morgan found that the sketch of a friend named "E____," described at the end of *The Diothas,* had similarities to the life of Edward Bellamy, but overall there were too many inaccuracies to confirm Bellamy as Macnie's anonymous friend. Morgan did not discount the possibility that Bellamy and Macnie corresponded with each other in the early 1880s. However, Morgan pointed out that, in the end, "the product of one is an almost unknown book, scarcely even sought by collectors; the other had been one of the greatest inspirations to a new social order that two centuries have produced."[46]

Morgan's short book *Plagiarism in Utopia* expanded on Bellamy's place in the utopian tradition. Rather than copying and adapting past works, Morgan believed that Bellamy took the most valuable components of hundreds of utopian books and theologians, and created a much more advanced and realistic vision of the future. Because of the small print run, the book did not attract reviews or any kind of scholarly attention, but Morgan's purpose in publishing the book was more to make his research on charges of plagiarism available for Bellamy's critics.[47]

In 1945, Morgan's next book on Bellamy appeared. As a supplement to encourage sales of the full-scale biography *Edward Bellamy,* King's Crown Press (a division of Columbia University Press) published *The Philosophy of Edward Bellamy.* This nearly 100-page book contained a reprint of Bellamy's "The Religion of Solidarity" essay and four topical essays with unpublished Bellamy material related to different components of the writer's philosophy. In the preface, Morgan explained that the success of *Looking Backward* focused Bellamy on social and political causes, and obscured his larger philosophical view of humanity and the modern world. Morgan's main purpose for the book was to dissect Bellamy's method of thinking and then to construct Bellamy's broad philosophy of life.[48]

Morgan centered much of *The Philosophy of Edward Bellamy* on the ideas in the previously published "The Religion of Solidarity" essay, especially the concept of Bellamy as a rebel. Building on the theme of religious thought, he included a chapter on the connections between Bellamy and ancient Indian philosophy, especially Hinduism. Another chapter detailed Bellamy and his attitude toward Christianity, saying that at a young age Bellamy's inquisitive nature led him to question many of the principles of Christianity. In both chapters, Morgan pointed out that later in life Bellamy declared that many conventional religions were trapped in a hostile social system that affected teachings, beliefs, and traditions. Throughout these sections, Morgan expanded his argument about Bellamy as a rebel of religious conformity.[49]

The two remaining chapters in the book dealt with Bellamy's philosophical view of human nature and happiness. According to Morgan, Bellamy believed that most members of society sought happiness, but were often hampered in their quest by internal guilt (nemesis), social mores, and the inability to overcome past actions. Contrary to Morgan's own efforts to establish moral codes in his own career, Bellamy believed that arbitrary systems of ethics or morals over societies only resulted in people becoming "disillusioned, cynical, and pessimistic over the possibility of ethical living." Instead, Bellamy suggested that the removal of economic factors in society allowed individuals to overcome these largely mental challenges.[50]

Morgan's short book argued that Bellamy's writings on religion, ethics, economics, and social reform formed an interdependent philosophy of life. He declared that Bellamy's philosophy and method of thinking about the nature of life was "saner, better balanced and more fundamental than Freud, more penetrating and more objective."[51] Such bold statements and publicity for Morgan's larger study of Bellamy attracted scholarly reviewers to *The Philosophy of Edward Bellamy*. The reviews were positive, with detailed discussion of Bellamy's "The Religion of Solidarity" essay. Several reviewers noted Morgan's important observation that Bellamy's early writings reflected the influence of transcendentalist writers such as Henry David Thoreau, Herman Melville, and Ralph Waldo Emerson. Although reviewers found Morgan's style to be sympathetic to Bellamy, they agreed that the publication of such obscure writings led to a fuller understanding of Bellamy's worldview and new perspectives on the potential future society described in *Looking Backward*.[52]

In 1946, the University of North Carolina Press published *Nowhere Was Somewhere: How History Makes Utopias and How Utopias Make History,* Morgan's last book dealing with topics of utopianism and Edward Bellamy. As noted earlier, in the early 1940s, Morgan compiled several chapters of a proposed book on the New World connections to the utopian civilization described in More's 1516 book *Utopia,* and this book was the completed version. *Nowhere Was Somewhere* combined the history of the utopian tradition in writing with tangible examples of successful civilizations, or utopias, which existed at different times and places throughout history. Morgan defined the concept of a utopia as an evolutionary process of social advancement, rather than a complete attainment of a perfect society. In many ways, Morgan connected utopianism to the Progressivism of the early twentieth century—gradual progress through uplift, scientific methods, and social improvement—which marked most of his professional career. Further, he believed that imagining the future depended on learning from the successes and failures of past utopias.[53]

The main part of Morgan's *Nowhere Was Somewhere* supported the theory that More's *Utopia* was a record of an actual trip to Peru, rather than a fictitious story. Previous scholars and popular audiences discounted this connection because More's book was published a decade before Francisco Pizarro's conquest of the Incas. However, Morgan reviewed historical information about the post-Columbian voyages to the New World and argued that there had been European contact with the Incas before Pizarro. Specifically, Morgan believed that More's character Raphael Hythloday visited Peru during an unrecorded voyage in 1503 by Amerigo Vespucci. Further, Morgan's most unusual assertion was that Hythloday returned from Peru by reaching India on a balsawood ship, commonly used by the Incas. Vespucci's unrecorded voyage and the details of other early South American expeditions were obscured from the historical record, Morgan believed, because the Portuguese were secretive with the details of their colonial exploits. While he did not prove that other voyages occurred or if a sailor named Hythloday existed, Morgan pointed out that, prior to the publication of More's book, at least three well-documented visits to Peru by European explorers occurred.[54]

After setting the historical precedent of early voyages to Peru prior to Pizarro and prior to the publication of *Utopia,* Morgan described the undeniable connections between the utopian society in More's book and the Incan Empire. He revealed parallels between the Incas and the society described in Bellamy's *Looking Backward.* Morgan explained that the Incan civilization developed into a complex economic, social, and political empire all without European influences. A centralized state controlled Incan society and featured mandatory service to the state, no private ownership of land, an economy based on goods rather than currency, a vast network of public works, communal agricultural production, and few laws. Morgan believed that More based the imaginary society described in *Utopia* on the actual society in Peru before Pizarro's arrival and conquest.[55]

The second part of Morgan's exploration of utopias, both real and imaginary, focused on the progression of utopian writing and concepts. He believed that utopian writers built upon the concepts of their predecessors and the most influential works emerged from the most advanced societies. Morgan reviewed utopian works from early civilizations, such as the Greeks, the Romans, the Hebrews, and the Chinese. Specifically, he pointed to Plato's *Republic* as the best and most widely known utopian work of its era, but it was certainly not the first book of its kind. Morgan returned to More's *Utopia* as another key work in the utopian tradition, because it defined a Western European perspective on organizing society, just as explorers began to colonize the New World. While many utopian works followed More's 1516 book, Morgan argued that the next significant work that advanced utopian thought was Edward Bellamy's *Looking Backward* in 1888. As part of that progression, Morgan believed that Bellamy represented the American perspective on organizing a more industrial society.[56]

Even though Morgan admired many of the described utopias, he noted flaws and suggested his own directions for structuring society. He believed that humans achieved utopian societies through change, progress, and social enlightenment over the course of decades, rather than through a rapid change or through centuries of development. Too many utopian works suggested unrealistic periods of transition, and were also too prescriptive on how that change might take place. As with his other books on utopianism, Morgan warned that regimentation in a centralized society resulted in great dissatisfaction and apathy in the population. Further, reliance on a strong central power over society historically resulted in dictatorships or military regimes. Instead, Morgan called for a central yet reserved governing body that would provide social unity without extinguishing the individual qualities of diversity, freedom, and initiative. To improve the quality of the members of society, Morgan called for the practice of eugenics. Through genetic engineering and selective human breeding, Morgan believed that enlightened societies would identify and propagate the most desirable characteristics in their ranks. Finally, Morgan pointed to the lessons of the utopians on how best to structure society as a way to understand the challenges of the future, especially how to use atomic energy for the betterment of society.[57]

Morgan's *Nowhere Was Somewhere* received decent reviews. Reviewers discounted Morgan's overarching theory about More's *Utopia* being based on direct observation of the Incan empire (the balsawood boat theory was especially criticized). The book reviewers took the most interest in Morgan's challenge of using utopian ideas to structure the postwar atomic world. One reviewer stated that, "Never was there a time in human history when imagination, invention, and idealism were more urgently needed than at the present moment, as we enter upon the atomic age with all of its social, economic, and political implications for the future of mankind." Perhaps just as important, Morgan's book articulated for scholarly and popular audiences his definition of a utopia as a society undergoing gradual social change, improvement, and enlightenment, rather than as an achievable and static state of perfection.[58]

Morgan's writings on Edward Bellamy and utopianism had their literary shortcomings, but his five works contributed to the literature on those subjects. The most significant of the books, *Edward Bellamy*, became a cornerstone biography of the utopian writer. His lengthy treatment of Bellamy relied on family material and previously unknown original sources. Perhaps more significant, Morgan's utopian writings explained much about his own definitions of the small community, character, education, and social reform. By committing his various thoughts on Bellamy to print, Morgan revealed the enormous influence that Bellamy had upon his own life and his vision. His administrative style, his high moral standards, his belief in human improvement (one individual and one community at a time), his belief in eugenics, and his reliance on the small community were all themes from the works of Edward Bellamy. Perhaps most importantly, Morgan believed deeply in the ability of individuals to create a more equal and enlightened society.

Morgan's utopian writings came at a time of great invention for the engineer. His familiar Yellow Springs home-base served as an incubator for new community building on the national and international stages. As he wrote *Edward Bellamy* and other books in literary solitude, Morgan heard the call of other important causes. At the end of World War II, with his TVA years well behind him, Morgan embarked on new battles and projects. This final phase of his career featured some of his most productive and overlooked accomplishments.

8

I SEE A VILLAGE

In the spring of 1973, Arthur Morgan arrived at the Andrew Johnson Hotel in Knoxville, Tennessee. At age ninety-five, Morgan's hearing, eyesight, and mobility had declined, but his interest in TVA had not waned. He had just completed a lengthy book-length study of the early TVA and wanted to see first-hand the reality of his past work. Nearly forty years earlier at the same location, Morgan met with David Lilienthal and H. A. Morgan to parse out TVA responsibilities; this trip would be a homecoming for Arthur Morgan. He greeted the hotel receptionist that morning saying, "It's good to be back." After over three and a half decades since his untimely departure from TVA, Morgan wanted one last look at the reality of his early vision.[1]

In the days that followed, Morgan met with a wide range of TVA officials, administrators, and employees throughout East Tennessee, and distributed preliminary drafts of *The Making of TVA,* his last book, published the next year, to interested parties. The response to Morgan was remarkable; everyone from the clerks to TVA board chairman Aubrey Wagner wanted to meet Morgan and pay tribute to his 1930s accomplishments. After several days of friendly meetings, discussions, and local touring, Morgan and his party departed Knoxville and headed north to the model town of Norris. Although TVA auctioned off the town in 1948 to a private consortium, who then sold lots to residents, Norris still had most of its original characteristics. Morgan met with several TVA foresters and residents, and concluded the brief visit by driving past his former residence in the town. Following his visit, Morgan reported that, "I was greatly encouraged by the direction and the rate of progress of TVA activities, and of the high level of interest that I found."[2]

Morgan's bittersweet return to Knoxville in 1973 served as an important point of closure and reflection on his TVA career. He came away from the visit with the clear indication that his early planning and promotion had not been in vain. The monumental dams and river improvements alone were more than nearly any twentieth century American engineer could claim. The inner-workings of the 1970s TVA still had clear marks from Morgan's hand. His accomplishments in forging labor policy, setting administrative standards, launching employee training programs, and establishing a system of personnel management stood the test of time for TVA. Still, Morgan expressed disappointment in the agency's lack of social and regional planning. His ethical and personal clash with David Lilienthal some forty years prior clouded his assessments of the agency and his own accomplishments.

Morgan highlighted his dissatisfaction with TVA in his last book, *The Making of TVA*. In the book he recounted his conflicts with Lilienthal, his disdain for big business, the absence of character in government service, and his version of the 1938 removal saga. He was most critical of Roosevelt for allowing the mission of TVA to drift away from their original agreements and expectations, and for becoming influenced by what he considered to be the self-centered motives of David Lilienthal. Morgan explained that he attempted to exclude criticism of Lilienthal from the book, but by doing so he would be unable to explain the realities of their working relationship. In the end, Morgan believed that his direction for TVA truly represented the public interest and that his fellow board members were much more politically concerned with their decisions and, thus, acted more for the private interest. While the book criticized Lilienthal's motives and character, Morgan admitted that the power director matured into a respected citizen and public servant. In fact, the book announced that Lilienthal fulfilled most of objectives and values that Morgan sought for TVA and for America. Overall, Morgan explained that, "In spite of the difficulties I encountered, those years of opportunity and challenge in the early life of the TVA provided one of the most significant experiences of my professional career."[3]

The book concluded with a discussion of the need for a universal ethical code, not unlike the 1930s mandate that Morgan proposed for TVA employees or his 1920s behavioral regulations for Antioch students. Morgan based his code on honesty, integrity, and self-denial. He also listed eugenic conscience as part of the code and called the inheritance of the most desirable traits an essential part of "any good social order."[4] Decades after his first conceptualization of ethical standards and moral character, Morgan had hardly changed his ideas about how to structure a more efficient, moral, and productive society.

While Morgan's rigidity remained firm after leaving TVA in 1938, he distanced himself from the difficult experience and registered some of his most fulfilling accomplishments. From the 1940s until the 1970s, Morgan embarked on a new career period, which combined his skills as a water-control engineer, educator, community builder, and national figure. In 1940, he founded the non-profit Community Service, Inc., to coordinate his various efforts from Yellow Springs. As the most recognizable resident of the town, Morgan worked with the students and administrators of Antioch College, founded small industries, and worked on other community-based initiatives. His life as a consultant took him across the globe, most notably to advise several African nations on engineering projects and to offer educational advice to the Indian government. Back in the United States, he helped the Seneca Nation in upstate New York in their battle with the U.S. Army Corps of Engineers. In all of these endeavors, Morgan continued his efforts to build small self-supporting communities. Morgan's work on the community of Mitraniketan in Kerala, India, became his most successful and fulfilling project—far surpassing his designs for Norris, Tennessee.

Such an active post–TVA career distanced Morgan from his 1930s disappointments. That diversity of accomplishment in areas somewhat out of the mainstream also relegated Morgan's contributions to the sidelines of historical studies, which have all but ignored Morgan after he left TVA. Yet, Morgan's most significant accomplishments as an educator and community builder occurred following his sacking by Roosevelt. Further, in this final period of Morgan's career and life, he came closest to establishing the principles of ethics, community, and honesty in several small communities of his design. TVA may have represented a period when he was in the national spotlight, but it did not and should not fully define the man. Morgan's brief return to TVA in the spring of 1973 allowed closure on an important part of his career. However, TVA stands as just one high point of many other high points in Morgan's seven decades of public service.

After World War II, the United States began a period of readjustment to a peacetime society. By 1946, expected prosperity, economic confidence, American ingenuity, and international influence replaced the doom that marked the decade-long Great Depression and over four years of savage warfare on numerous fronts. Veterans returned to redefine a nation, scores of women who toiled in wartime industries left the workplace, colleges and universities swelled with incoming students, and large groups of African Americans left their tenant farms for industrial jobs in northern cities. While the postwar economy brought prosperity and opportunity for many, not all Americans benefited. In the decades that followed, the nation struggled with issues of equality along racial, cultural, religious, gender, economic, and class lines. During this period, the culmination of a long civil rights movement for African Americans brought an end to segregation of public facilities, but these changes did not create an equal society.[5]

On the global stage, after World War II the United States emerged as one of the superpowers representing democracy and freedom abroad. The Soviet Union and its numerous satellite territories represented the opposing force of communism. For the next forty years, these two superpowers with opposing ideologies waged a Cold War, through surrogate military actions in secondary locations such as Cuba, Korea, and Vietnam, intense stockpiling of nuclear and chemical weapons, and a space race. Domestically, the fear of a nuclear war and the Soviets created a Cold War culture that permeated politics, the economy, and American society for decades. Fear of communist takeover abroad and communist infiltration from within weighed heavily on the minds of most Americans. Somehow, the standoff between ideologies and nations never resulted in nuclear war. By the late 1980s, the Cold War ended; historians are still measuring the effects of that decades-long struggle.[6]

While Arthur Morgan was not a central figure in determining the larger shifts in American society and culture during the second half of the twentieth century, he was involved in smaller more grassroots ways. In the postwar decades, he emerged as an expert and consultant both at home and abroad. Following his removal from TVA and the conclusion of a lengthy investigation of TVA, Morgan moved from Tennessee back to Ohio. Once in Yellow Springs, the sixty-year-old embarked on several projects that promoted small

In May 1963, Morgan led a 600-person parade in Yellow Springs to protest a local barber's refusal to cut the hair of African Americans. Antiochiana, Antioch College.

communities, local industries, and groups with unique needs. He strengthened his ties to Antioch College, served as an occasional lecturer, and published essays in *Antioch Notes.* He fought oppression locally. For example, in May 1963, Morgan led a 600-person parade in Yellow Springs to protest a local barber's refusal to cut the hair of African Americans.[7] Morgan also joined his wife Lucy as an active Quaker. True to his reputation and style, Morgan voiced his opinions, even if he knew his ideas would be met with opposition.

Launching his first post–TVA project of significance, in the summer of 1939 the American Friends Service Committee contacted Morgan about the feasibility of relocating Jewish and Spanish refugees in Mexico. Beginning in the late 1930s, Jewish refugees established small communities in Mexico City and surrounding towns. Morgan and other Quaker representatives traveled to Mexico to talk to government officials and visit leaders of fledgling Jewish communities. That fall, Morgan and other members of their exploratory committee issued a report stating that significant Jewish resettlement in Mexico would be difficult because of political, economic, and cultural reasons. Morgan recommended that the committee explore other areas in

Central America, especially Honduras. This effort was the first of many international consultations that Morgan accepted after his TVA tenure.[8]

Morgan's Friends connections resulted in other projects and initiatives during the war years. He demonstrated support for the Allies during World War II, but he also worked with those who refused to serve in the military. During the war, the federal government imprisoned several thousand conscientious objectors, while others chose to participate in alternative service. In 1944, Morgan organized a correspondence course for imprisoned conscientious objectors titled "The Community." Morgan spoke out about the persecution of those who did not willingly serve in the military. His short essay in *Antioch Notes,* "The Conscientious Objector," urged readers to have tolerance for those who were philosophically opposed to war. Morgan argued that even though conscientious objectors appeared to be unpatriotic, they were in fact offering different solutions to global problems. Tolerance for opposing opinions, Morgan believed, led to great social advances, even though he had not followed that advice at many points in his career.[9]

In the closing days of the war, Morgan spoke out against mandatory military service during peacetime. He took issue with congressional proposals for a universal compulsory military training program for young men. Morgan believed that such indoctrination and emphasis on the military endangered the best qualities of American life, and "would deeply affect education, social and industrial life, and resources for other needs." Morgan argued that the nation was engaged in a fight for choice, democracy, and peace, but that creating a standing military in the postwar would only lead to more wars and an erosion of American rights and democracy abroad. The growing importance of the military in postwar planning also concerned Morgan. The style of training at the nation's top military school, West Point, drew Morgan's ire. He explained that the program of regimentation at West Point created a caste of military subjects who were devoid of original thinking and contributed little to solving postwar problems, short of using excessive force. As a potential solution to the national debate, Morgan suggested that, if universal military service were instituted, the structure of the training program must be under complete and permanent civilian control.[10]

Morgan's wartime writings about mandatory military service occurred at the same time that he published his biography of Edward Bellamy. His criticisms of Edward Bellamy's industrial army and the problems of regimentation in society described in *Looking Backward* spilled over into Morgan's writings on the role of the military in postwar America. Those wartime writings also reflected Morgan's long-time criticisms of the U.S. Army Corps of Engineers. Morgan stated that the short-sighted and unoriginal planning of flood control projects by the Corps of Engineers were caused by inadequate training at West Point and other military institutions. In particular, Morgan believed that top officers in the Corps of Engineers, trained at West Point, had mismanaged flood control works on the Mississippi River for decades. Morgan's criticisms of the Corps of Engineers grew more public in the following decades.[11]

In the early 1940s, Morgan focused his efforts on defining and building small communities. Morgan believed that intimate community life in America was disappearing and that a displaced and isolated urban experience was becoming the norm. He believed that such an urban transformation represented societal decline, saying that, "A hardy, moral, thrifty people accumulates resources, becomes urbanized, and develops a climax of culture, wealth, and power; then it becomes flabby, corrupt, decadent, and sinks to weak obscurity."[12] In an effort to reclaim the charms of the small town and rural setting, Morgan defined his vision of the small community. He described the small community as the seedbed of civilization, where fundamental human traits such as integrity, good will, tolerance, and open-mindedness formed. Families constituted the main unit of small communities. He observed that the most desirable personality and character traits were transmitted and preserved within a small community environment. That setting, Morgan believed, imparted values of trust, sympathy, and planning for the greater good. But according to Morgan, these positive traits were not part of urban life and their absence contributed to global warfare. To support the economic and resource needs of the small community, Morgan promoted the importance of cooperatives, small industries and businesses, and cooperation between communities.[13]

Morgan spread his message of the small community through Community Service, Inc. Founded in 1940 and based in Yellow Springs, this non-profit enterprise helped small communities, educated the public through publications and lectures, and offered financial assistance for community-based projects. The mission of Community Service, Inc., was to "stimulate a general awareness of the value of the community as a basic social institution, of the importance of working at the grass roots of society, and of the dependence of a democracy upon the strength of local institutions." The organization served as a clearing house of information and advice for active communities and community groups, such as "local government agencies, civic clubs, cooperatives, and business and labor groups."[14] In the following decades, Community Service, Inc., expanded its efforts and sponsored dozens of projects worldwide.[15]

Morgan wrote and lectured extensively on the importance of the small community. Morgan's research and first writings on small communities occurred at the same time that he was producing books on Edward Bellamy and utopian topics. He did not encourage people to start utopian communities in a traditional sense, but utopian thought influenced his conceptualization of the small community and how to best execute those plans. The small community, Morgan believed, served as the basis for American culture, where people had the best access to services, opportunities, education, and an environment that advanced human ingenuity. His 1942 book *The Small Community: Foundation of Democratic Life, What It Is and How to Achieve It* was a prescriptive guidebook for establishing the structure of a small community. Morgan described how the small community had been relegated to the backburner of American life. He explained: "In modern times the small community has played the part of an orphan in an unfriendly world. It has been despised, neglected, exploited, and robbed. The cities have skimmed off the cream of its young population. Yet the small community supplied the lifeblood of civilization, and neglect of it has been one of the primary reasons for the slowness and the interrupted course of human progress. It is high time that the fundamental significance of the small community be recognized."[16] The book, which reads much like a rural sociology textbook, outlined how to manage a community, with details on operating a community council, suggestions on maintaining a strong local economy, options for providing residents with social and health services, and how to maintain a proper level of ethical behavior.[17]

His follow-up book on community building, *The Community of the Future and the Future of Community* (1957), echoed many of these same general principles and suggestions. But it went even further, arguing that small communities were more than just a collection of structures and people. Instead, Morgan explained that, "the informal spirit of community is the vital social spirit that inhabits and gives life to the formal organizations of society." He believed that the spirit and connectedness of the small community could be combined with many of the positive attributes of urban life to form the community of the future. To build these more productive and enlightened communities, Morgan emphasized the need for social controls, a stable economy driven more by needs than profits, representative government, and an educational system tailored to the talents of the students. In the end, he emphasized that the small community was one part of the larger societal puzzle of the future, saying, "A good community seeks not only balance and good proportion within itself, but it will seek to be an effective and valuable element within a larger society. It will seek to keep its own unique character, and to make its own unique contributions."[18]

Small businesses were crucial to Morgan's small community paradigm. Morgan believed that small industries, owned and operated by residents of the small community, would produce specialized goods that would allow small communities to be economically stable and nationally competitive with big businesses. As a way to perpetuate the community, Morgan explained that small industries would provide younger residents with practical on-the-job training and, later, economic incentives to stay in the community. In *A Business of My Own* (1946), Morgan outlined numerous possibilities for establishing small industries, in fields such as medicine, fine arts, engineering, food processing, agriculture, and handicrafts. He emphasized the importance of developing a mixed economy, training skilled laborers, and using cooperatives to distribute goods outside the community. The book reviewed how to research markets and strategies for obtaining startup loans for small businesses. Morgan believed that returning veterans would be interested in returning to their hometowns and starting their own small businesses.[19]

In the book *Industries for Small Communities* (1953), Morgan outlined the growth of industries in Yellow Springs, Ohio. He reviewed successful ventures in areas such as printing, fine arts, agriculture, metalworking, and landscape architecture. Morgan argued, long before many business leaders and government officials, that large industries were a good fit for small communities since these communities offered a dependable workforce, strong schools, and often nearby natural resources. But he reminded readers that profits and production were not the primary reasons to start or attract industries. Rather, Morgan believed that suitable and sustainable industries were a necessary part of his larger plan for a small community. He concluded the book with the observation: "America is still a long way from achieving a philosophy of community, or a clear picture of what qualities make a good community, or an understanding of how to manage affairs to bring the kind we do want. At best we are still feeling our way. Yet certain fundamentals of good living conditions are becoming clear. If we keep those well in mind we may adjust ourselves and our communities to a wide range of changing conditions, and yet keep and steadily increase the essential community values."[20]

Morgan's writings on the small community reflected his own experience with building communities and his ongoing research and writing on utopian thought. Under the right conditions, cooperation would displace competition and benefit all members of the community. He also believed that small communities, just like utopias, were part of gradual social evolution rather than the attainment of a static state of perfection. In all of his community-related works, Morgan declared that the small community prepared the leaders of tomorrow, provided the goods that allowed cities to rise and prosper, and, most importantly, transferred the most desirable characteristics and traditions to future generations. As for the future, Morgan envisioned that a string of successful small communities would coalesce into a "great community." In time, his great community would replace the impersonal and unethical urban world that Morgan detested.[21]

Morgan's philosophies about the small community encouraged the advancement, and often rebirth, of small rural localities. He envisioned building a society where students learned practical skills, cooperation, respect for others, and the importance of community. At the end of World War II, Morgan looked to developing nations for the chance to establish small communities. In turn, developing nations looked for well-known experts like Morgan to provide assistance in building and rebuilding their societies.

Because of his transformative programs at Antioch during the 1920s, Arthur Morgan maintained an international reputation as an educational expert and consultant. In the late 1940s, that notoriety led Morgan to India to help restructure the educational system. That initial consultation resulted in Morgan's deep commitment to building a small community in Kerala, India. His efforts to rebuild the community of Mitraniketan reflected much of his lifelong social, educational, and community philosophy.[22]

The end of World War II marked the final days of many colonial empires. In August 1947, after nearly two hundred years of occupation, Indians won freedom from the British, albeit in the form of two separate countries. In India, in addition to restructuring the government and economy, the newly elected Indian National Congress focused on education. The most pressing educational issue, addressed but never solved by the British, was how to provide social education for illiterate adults and universal, free, and compulsory education for all school-age children. To tackle these and other educational concerns, the new government created a separate Ministry of Education, split into five bureaus: school education; higher education; language, literature, and the arts; scholarships; and planning.[23]

In addition to the Ministry of Education, the Indian government created a number of committees to determine methods to improve educational needs specific to India. One of these committees was the Universities Education Commission, which met for the first time in 1948. The new government invited Indians, as well as international experts, to participate. Arthur Morgan was a member of this committee, and during the next year he visited numerous rural communities and Indian universities to assess India's educational structure. During these visits, Morgan observed that a great number of young Indian men and women were uneducated and permanently tied to their villages. And he saw that the few villagers who attended the urban universities seldom returned to their rural homes to educate others. Morgan's solution to this problem was to have the Indian government establish rural universities.[24]

Morgan's efforts on the commission proved valuable, as rural universities with much-needed agricultural centers soon dotted India. With the conclusion of the committee's work in 1950, Morgan returned to Yellow Springs. In early 1954, Morgan attended the Quakers' Society of Friends General Conference in Cape May, New Jersey, and met a young Indian student. That meeting reinitiated Morgan's connection to Indian education and began his involvement with a community building project that Morgan considered his most significant endeavor.[25]

K. Viswanathan, known as Viswan, was a twenty-seven-year-old from a small village in Travancore (present day Kerala) on the southwestern coast of India. Viswan hoped to reorganize the educational system in his small Indian village. At the 1954 conference, Morgan and Viswan got along famously, and Morgan invited Viswan to stay with him in Yellow Springs. Viswan accepted Morgan's invitation and spent the summer with the Morgans.

Although fifty years and different cultures separated the two, Viswan and Morgan shared the belief that community and practical education were vital to the development of the individual.[26]

Born in 1928, Viswan grew up near the village of Vellanad (population twelve thousand). His family was from one of the lower castes, the Ezhave who are engaged in weaving and also tapping coconut and palm trees for liquor. Belonging to one of the lowest castes, his family struggled for generations to maintain dignity. At an early age, Viswan understood the denial of his legal and social rights, and found inspiration from spiritual leader Sri. Narayana Guru. By the 1920s, Guru called for a casteless society, reforms in religious practices, and better education for the oppressed. Guru's movement changed the social structure of the region later called Kerala. Viswan attended high school in nearby Nedumangad and became deeply interested in writer, poet, and educator Rabindranath Tagore. The writings and teachings of Mahatma Gandhi further influenced him.[27]

Upon graduation, Viswan longed to attend Tagore's Santiniketan in the far northeast part of India. For a low-caste family to send a son to such a prestigious and distant school was a challenge, but his parents made it possible by mortgaging the family home. Viswan studied diverse subjects at Santiniketan for four years but did not pursue a degree. He criticized the privileged population and the "unconcerned spirit" among the university's students. Viswan then traveled to Sevagram and briefly attended Gandhi's school. He was interested in Gandhi's teachings, but the poor cultural quality of the institution, along with the school's tendency to deify Gandhi, disappointed Viswan.[28]

In 1952, dissatisfied with India's educational system, Viswan used Quaker connections to travel extensively in the United States and Europe. To support his trip to study rural life and education, Viswan agreed to work on farms and stay with Quakers while abroad. The next year, Viswan arrived in the United States and spent the rest of 1953 working in factories, farms, and cooperatives throughout the eastern part of the country. In early 1954, Viswan attended the Society of Friends Conference in Cape May, where he met Arthur Morgan.[29]

The two men admired Gandhi's educational teachings, particularly his belief that reforming the individual could influence social change. Gandhi taught that practical experiences would develop the intelligence of a child more quickly than only teaching, reading, and writing. Instead of teaching children either academics or a trade, Gandhi believed that the practical and the abstract should be combined for more effective education of the individual. This method of instruction, "whole education," encouraged students to be skilled in both academic subjects as well as some sort of craft to stimulate the local economy. According to Gandhi, this kind of instruction would strengthen the communities in the thousands of rural villages across the nation. In experiments with this system during the 1930s, Gandhi claimed that students developed a sense of purpose, concentration, promptness, perseverance, and perhaps most importantly morals. He also noted that with "whole education," students cooperated instead of competed.[30]

Gandhi's philosophies served as the starting point for many of Morgan's and Viswan's discussions. The two men shared mutual respect for their educational philosophies and approaches to pedagogy. Despite Morgan's departure from Antioch in the 1930s, the school continued with a work-study program and practical curriculum well into the 1950s. Viswan found that programs at Antioch prepared students for vocational trades and community concerns better than the methods used in India. Morgan admired Viswan's belief that education involved the active participation of children and adolescents in the common life of the family and community. For Viswan, education incorporated everything related to the full development of personality—health, economic life, academic study, social life, and ethical and aesthetic values. The combination of education and community, beginning in early childhood, fascinated Morgan and connected well to his writings about the small community. Together, their philosophies held that education was a lifelong endeavor and that the best instruction combined practical skills and academic knowledge.[31]

As a college president, Morgan created a curriculum based on practical experience and liberal arts, and while as a student Viswan learned that academic education must be supplemented by real-life situations. With the perspectives of both administrator and student, Viswan and Morgan combined their experiences and philosophies, and designed a community-based education project. Viswan was interested in returning to his rural village to establish a school that combined academics, practical education, and community involvement. The school would be the center of the new community, which would support itself with local agriculture and small industries. Morgan understood Viswan's strong dedication to reorganizing his native village and was impressed with Viswan's character, educational goals, and aspirations to rebuild his Indian home. By gathering private funds for the project, Morgan saw the opportunity to undertake an educational and societal project free from governmental or academic bureaucracy and regimentation. Near the end of Viswan's summer stay in Yellow Springs, the two agreed that Community Service, Inc., would coordinate and fund the project. With Viswan's direction and Morgan's financial support, the proposed community would put their educational theories into practice on a grand scale.[32]

In December 1955, after three years abroad, Viswan returned to India and surveyed the conditions of his native village of Vellanad. Viswan's return to his home coincided with a major political upheaval. Vellanad was in the state of Travancore, but with the States Reorganization Act of 1956, the Indian government merged this territory and several neighboring provinces into a larger state called Kerala. Although the smallest of the Indian states, Kerala was one of the most densely populated, averaging 1,200 people per square mile. The Indian president appointed a governor to serve as head of the state, and democratic elections resulted in a slate of new legislators. A principal reason for this merger was to unite all of the Malayalam speakers into one political unit. Malayalam was the main language of the state, but Hindi, Tamil, and English were also common. As for religious membership, although the Hindus were the largest denomination, together the Christians (mostly Orthodox and Catholic) and Muslims accounted for forty percent of the population. Another change in the new state was the emergence of the Communist Party of India as a dominant force in Kerala's government, but its ascendancy had little effect on Mitraniketan.[33]

During the 1950s, the state funded the building of a large number of schools, universities, libraries, and educational facilities. Although the government sponsored these programs, Viswan was less interested in mass education and more concerned with providing students individualized curricula, which combined practical skills and academic subjects. In the spring of 1956, Viswan broke ground for his community about two miles from Vellanad. At the same time Morgan raised awareness for Viswan's work by sending Community Service, Inc., supporters a "Friends of Viswan" newsletter. During fifty years of public service and several professional careers, Morgan amassed countless friends, political allies, and wealthy philanthropists. Morgan used his connections to help fund Viswan, but both men hoped that their experiment would become self-supporting.[34]

Viswan's initiative began as a local effort to educate the oppressed castes, but it expanded to include other social groups. He began his work by visiting

K. Viswanathan with Arthur and Lucy Morgan. Antiochiana, Antioch College.

five families and recruited seven children to start his primary-level school within the new community. Voluntary classes met outside on most week-nights, weekends, and during holidays, covering basic skills such as reading and writing. Even with buildings still under construction and a lack of accreditation, by the end of the year the enrollment at Viswan's informal school reached two hundred. By December 1956, Viswan and four friends completed a community building on the property. It housed a small library, lodging for guests, a meeting room, and space for several school classrooms. The structure itself cost $300, and with the purchases of various school-related materials, Viswan's funds were severely depleted. Near the end of 1956, Morgan informed supporters of Viswan's progress and immediate needs. He estimated that for the community to survive Viswan would need an annual promise of $1,000 from Community Service, Inc.[35]

As Morgan secured financial support and Viswan recruited new workers and students, 1957 proved to be a successful year. The school's enrollment increased to nearly three hundred students, which prompted Viswan to establish more organization. He created a three-person governing board known as the Executive Council and organized an open forum session, called the General Council, to discuss community concerns. The close interaction between instruction and application transformed teachers and students into residents of a small community. Viswan wanted the community to remain informal, with few rigid rules and regulations, but he realized that without some kind of administrative structure the experiment would crumble. As one of their first acts, in June 1957, the General Council named the community "Mitraniketan," Sanskrit for "An Abode of Friends." As Morgan and Viswan intended, the school was the center of Mitraniketan.[36]

Viswan was interested in educating children between the ages of six and sixteen. He believed that with proper guidance and environment, the lower-caste children could be as intelligent and active as higher-caste children. A typical day's curriculum included: cloth spinning; general knowledge consisting of biography, history, and geography; language study of Hindi, Malayalam, and English; mathematics; health and hygiene; manual work such as gardening; and elementary science. Teachers used hands-on approaches to instruction, and when possible, the teachers invited specialists to direct lessons. Unlike other schools, the teachers lived in the community as equal partners in the experiment. Their work was wholly voluntary and their contributions affected both the students and the community. India's climate allowed for most of the classes to be held outside in the shade of trees, while meetings took place in the community center. In the first year, a small volunteer staff of twenty, consisting of college students and Viswan's friends, taught and performed two to four hours of manual work daily. Several staff members had training in village development, as well as specialized skills such as spinning, weaving, bookbinding, notebook-making, and beekeeping.[37]

The next year, J. Dudley Dawson, the vice-president of Antioch College, visited Mitraniketan for a week. What Dawson saw impressed him, and he remarked, "There is an air of creativeness, freedom, self-discipline, friendliness, and purposefulness about the whole proceeding. . . ." Dawson observed Viswan working with the children of the community. On an informal basis, children would have talks, plays, songs, and technical discussions with youth leaders or teachers. Viswan's informal approach gave students a sense of purpose, self-confidence, and occupational skills. With the help of an American professor at the nearby agricultural college in Trivandrum (a college started after Morgan's 1948 suggestion), Dawson also assessed the physical plant. From these observations, Dawson reported to Morgan and Viswan that Mitraniketan needed major agricultural improvements.[38]

In summer 1958, Morgan informed supporters that Mitraniketan needed more money to purchase land and agricultural equipment. With Morgan's reassurance, in August Viswan purchased fifteen acres of land adjoining the community for $4,000. The new property included four acres of wetland for the production of rice and eleven dry acres for the community's chief farm and cash crop, tapioca macaroni. Also known as cassava, the tropical root crop contains a superior quality of starch and can be produced quite inexpensively. On their farm the community also maintained small groves of banana, coconut, mango, and cashew nut trees. With enough funds to cover well over half the initial cost, in November Morgan forwarded Viswan $1,500, and he completed the purchase. By the next year, the newly acquired lands were fully cultivated.[39]

In early 1960, Viswan sent the Kerala government a lengthy outline explaining education at Mitraniketan. To develop his school further, Viswan needed a state license to operate a full-time private school. Viswan applied for a permit in the late 1950s but was denied on the grounds that he lacked adequate financial support.[40] In March 1960, Viswan had an interview with the governor and the education minister of Kerala to discuss his reapplication. He explained that Mitraniketan was more than just a school; it was a rural community center offering facilities for agricultural, industrial, and educational activities. Viswan reviewed the history of the community and emphasized his strong devotion to the project. He stated that his school was designed to instruct from infancy to adulthood through "effective liberal education suited to enrich rural life." Viswan explained that once agricultural, industrial, and vocational training became part of the secondary curriculum, the school would be raised to the university level. As for teachers and students, Viswan listed a lengthy process for their selection, and closed his presentation by saying that Mitraniketan was financially secure, with physical assets of approximately $12,000.[41]

Viswan knew that consideration of his application would take many months, if not a few years. To increase his chances for accreditation, Viswan developed relationships with professors at nearby Trivandrum University and with government officials. In early 1960, he accepted the Indian government's invitation to administer a local system of cooperative banks (credit unions). The next year, Viswan founded a regional farm cooperative program to control fertilizer use and tapioca production. He also established a spinning and weaving cooperative called the Khadi Society, which produced homespun cloth. In 1961, the Indian government rewarded Viswan's regional work by recognizing Mitraniketan as a Service Cooperative Multipurpose Society. This endorsement made government funds available to financially support the cooperative aspects of Mitraniketan, but Viswan refused this assistance, believing that, if he accepted funding from the government, he would lose significant independence in the project. Two years later the state government granted Viswan a license to operate a primary school at Mitraniketan.[42]

In the United States, Morgan remained active in generating publicity for the project. In 1962, Morgan wrote a book about Mitraniketan called *It Can Be Done in Education.* Published by Community Service, Inc., the book explained the purposes of the community and was designed to attract new supporters, either to teach or to contribute. The book outlined the importance of character development, practical instruction, open inquiry, a holistic approach to education, community life, and actual experience with economic processes. He included chapters on Tagore and Gandhi, and made comparisons between their teachings and Viswan's educational philosophies. Morgan also pushed contributors to fund Viswan $10,000 annually for staff salaries and operating expenses, and to supply an additional request of $35,000 to improve the community. Morgan explained to supporters that the extra funding was needed to purchase more land, install indoor plumbing, prepare to harness electric power (from a line three miles away), and increase staff and teacher salaries. But most importantly, Morgan wanted

$6,000 of the requested sum to go towards improving the primary education program. Contibutors answered Morgan's call, and during the first half of 1964, donations totaled over $12,000.[43]

In early 1965, Morgan organized a nonprofit foundation to support the bulk of the community's fundraising efforts. In February, Community Service, Inc., established an Overseas Committee to oversee the funding of Mitraniketan. Their board of directors included six members and was headquartered in Washington, D.C. Later that year, the Indian government officially recognized and incorporated Mitraniketan as a nonprofit community, making Indian contributions tax deductible and Western funds tax-free.[44]

Even though selling excess tapioca and other crops generated some income for the community, Morgan pushed for the development of small industries. Small enterprises such as coconut oil processing, hand pounding of rice, carpentry, leatherworking, brickmaking, and bookbinding existed, but in March 1965, Morgan challenged donors to support a publishing firm at Mitraniketan. Nearly all Indians who spoke Malayalam, about fifteen to twenty million, were in Kerala, but the state had no educational publishing firms. With Kerala's high literacy rates, Morgan saw an ideal opportunity to educate millions and generate much-needed income for the community.[45]

That summer, Morgan and Community Service, Inc., secured approximately $15,000 from donors to cover the purchase of a printing plant. Viswan then chose a nearby industrial site and bought the property, building, two presses, and roughly six tons of type in Hindi, Malayalam, and English. In August, Morgan received enough funds from international donors to complete the purchase. Printing operations began with the help of Morgan's grandson, Lee Morgan. With Lee's assistance, Viswan hoped to publish both scientific and literary materials. As for labor, Lee and Viswan employed a large number of teenagers interested in learning the printing trade. By the next year, Mitraniketan's printing plant churned out published material. In August, the plant published a monthly newsletter describing community events called the *Mitraniketan Marg*.[46]

In 1966, Mitraniketan marked its tenth full year of existence. To celebrate, Morgan planned to visit Mitraniketan in early 1967. This trip would be Morgan's first visit to the community that, through fundraising efforts and support, he had helped found. At the same time, Richard Kaplan, a filmmaker and Antioch College alumnus, was making a documentary about Arthur Morgan. For the ending, Kaplan wanted footage from Morgan's first visit to Mitraniketan to show how that project epitomized of his lifelong aspiration—to build a self-supporting community based on cooperative learning and practical education. So Kaplan and an assistant traveled with Morgan to document the journey and to finish the film.[47]

In early 1967, eighty-nine-year-old Arthur Morgan embarked on an extensive six-week trip, which included engineering consulting in a few African nations before arriving in Kerala. On February 6, Morgan's small entourage arrived at Mitraniketan. Morgan first noticed the area's beautiful surroundings and remarked that the physical plant was "more than I had expected." He found the fifty acres of land well kept and was pleased to see nearly every corner of the steep terraced hillsides planted with tapioca and other crops. He was further impressed with the cleanliness of the grounds and the solidly constructed buildings and houses.[48]

More importantly, at Mitraniketan, Morgan found that education was top priority. That year, the community prepared to add both seventh and eighth grades to the school, and Viswan showed Morgan where they planned to build a two-year high school in the future. Morgan found that education at Mitraniketan was an informal venture, and that the teachers and students were open and friendly. He was most impressed with the children's resourcefulness and their respect for their teachers, and noted that in the community-based environment the students were receptive to learning. Morgan was amazed at the large number of students of all ages working in the community. Their work was part of the curriculum, but more importantly, it significantly contributed to the community and trained the students for future occupations. At Mitraniketan, Morgan observed that learning and working created a vibrant community.[49]

After the trip, Morgan reported in the March newsletter that Mitraniketan exceeded his expectations and that working with Viswan was one of the major accomplishments in his life. Still Morgan realized that no full assurance of Viswan's continued success existed. As serious hazards for the next decade, Morgan pointed to Viswan's often poor health due to being overworked, political upheavals, and the inability to find new supporters. Morgan continued to recruit volunteers to work and teach at Mitraniketan, but his involvement with the community decreased in 1970, when he resigned as executive director of Community Service, Inc., and passed the reigns of leadership to his son Griscom Morgan.[50]

Morgan's work with the Mitraniketan project provides important insights into his educational and community philosophy. Morgan believed that small communities, where students learned practical skills, cooperation, respect for others, and the importance of community, were the answer to the modern world's ills. Mitraniketan was the living embodiment of Morgan's educational and societal philosophy. His community education initiative in India was vital to the success of Mitraniketan. While Morgan helped others realize their goals, the project fulfilled his lifelong dream of building a small community with facets of morality, education, and cooperation. The success with Mitraniketan also revealed that, in his later years, Morgan became more flexible about letting others develop their vision through his vision. Morgan pointed to Mitraniketan's success as his most notable accomplishment, and the beginning of a larger grassroots movement of community development, practical education, and moral reawakening.[51]

Morgan's first professional accomplishments came as a water-control engineer. His successes with his private engineering firm, directorship of the Miami Conservancy District, and chairmanship of the Tennessee Valley Authority earned him professional respect and national notoriety. Over the course of his career, he focused on planning, promoting, and directing engineering projects, and delegated much of the actual designing, drafting, and fine-tuning work to other engineers. By the 1950s, Morgan's notoriety rested on his accomplishments as an educator, administrator, and writer. However, in the postwar period, Morgan quietly maintained an international reputation as a water-control engineer.

Morgan commanded a great deal of respect for his water-control engineering projects and expertise. In 1953, the American Society of Civil Engineers made Morgan an honorary member for his decades of engineering contributions. Morgan also served as an international engineering consultant to many developing nations in Africa and the Far East. In fact, the model of regional development and water-control engineering that Morgan endorsed in Ohio and Tennessee during the early part of the twentieth century continued to be replicated in China and Latin America.[52]

In addition to his other writing projects, Morgan revisited his engineering projects and produced several books. The first of these books, *The Miami Conservancy District* (1951), provided great detail on the first water-control engineering project that brought him to the national stage. The book described the importance of approaching a flood control problem from a regional perspective, rather than focusing on local, county, and state divisions. The last of Morgan's books to recollect his engineering prowess was *The Making of TVA* (1974). As previously mentioned, Morgan's efforts to document his TVA experiences were clouded by time, the long-standing disagreements with his fellow TVA board members, and the decades of change in the agency's mission. But the book made clear many of Morgan's contributions to flood control, community planning, and regional development.[53]

A few years before Morgan's book on TVA, he published a book critical of the engineering practices of the U.S. Army Corps of Engineers. The book *Dams and Other Disasters: A Century of the Army Corp of Engineers in Civil Works* (1971) argued that the Corps of Engineers relied on a training system that did not prepare their engineers for civil engineering work. As reflected in his 1940s articles about mandatory military service, Morgan believed that West Point pedagogy was a flawed approach to building expertise and original thinking. Morgan's book provided details of poorly planned and often disastrous projects that cost taxpayers millions of dollars. He was particularly critical of their work on the Mississippi River, which had not brought significant relief from flooding on the main channel or its tributaries.[54] In the end, Morgan held the Corps of Engineers responsible for environmental ruin, rather than reclamation, because of their propensity to ignore the opinions of other engineers, and let traditional practices prevail. In addition, Morgan criticized the Corps of Engineers for their reliance on high dams. He favored flood control systems that featured low dams and other improvements, which Morgan believed offered greater control of reservoirs, navigation channels, and excess floodwaters.[55]

Morgan had long-standing disagreements with the methods and authority of the Corps of Engineers. Throughout the twentieth century, he openly denounced the Corps of Engineers through speeches, newspaper articles, and essays. The engineering projects directed by his private company were caught in the crosshairs of the Corps of Engineers. Further, the Corps of Engineers opposed many of Morgan's plans for dams and river improvements on the Tennessee River. In the 1950s, Morgan resurrected his ongoing disagreements with the Corps of Engineers by working with the Seneca Indians to stop the building of a high dam. That struggle brought Morgan back to the national stage briefly, and his work to stop the building of the Kinzua Dam represented an important highlight of his engineering career.

Before European colonization, the Seneca Indians controlled much of western New York and Pennsylvania. In 1794, George Washington's personal emissary Timothy Pickering signed a peace treaty with the Seneca. That treaty recognized the Seneca as an independent nation and established title to their New York lands; it also transferred millions of acres to the federal government. After the 1794 treaty and well into the nineteenth century, the Seneca continued to lose their lands to speculators, negotiators, land companies, politicians, and United States Indian commissioners. By the time of the Civil War, the federal government confined the Seneca to four reservations. Three of the reservations were located near Buffalo—at Buffalo Creek, Cattaraugus, and Tonawanda. The fourth reservation, the Allegany tract, encompassed nearly 30,000 acres and was located along the banks of the Allegheny River in southwestern New York and northwestern Pennsylvania.[56]

The growth of the city of Pittsburgh depended on the Allegheny River. By the twentieth century, the need to control flooding in the city's central business district reached a tipping point. Between 1900 and 1936, over fifty floods struck Pittsburgh, but it was the "great St. Patrick's day flood" of 1936 that provided sufficient impetus and justification for government involvement in flood control. In metropolitan Pittsburgh alone, this devastating flood resulted in the deaths of forty-seven people and approximately $50 million in damage. In total, losses in the Pittsburgh district reached $95 million and destruction in the upper Ohio River Valley totaled nearly $200 million. After the 1936 flood, Pittsburgh's business leaders joined with the region's political leaders to form an effective lobby. Their efforts led to the passage of the Copeland Omnibus Flood Control Act of 1936, which provided for the construction of nine reservoirs in the upper Allegheny River Valley.[57]

With the passage of the Copeland Act in 1936, President Roosevelt pushed for the upper Allegheny River project to be controlled by a resource-planning board instead of the Corps of Engineers. However, the Pittsburgh flood-control groups designated the Corps of Engineers to complete the work, as they only wanted flood control and not a "New Deal" style project. The Corps of Engineers designed nine dams and, by 1952, had completed six of them. One of the uncompleted projects was a high dam planned for the main channel of the river just south of Kinzua, Pennsylvania, near the Senecas'

Allegany Indian reservation. The proposed high dam was designed to rise 220 feet from the bedrock (181 feet from the valley floor) and control a watershed area of nearly 2,200 square miles. The expense of such a massive project, which was over 200 miles upriver from Pittsburgh, combined with the expected dislocation of hundreds of Seneca Indians from their ancestral homeland made the project unlikely if not impractical.[58]

Then, in the spring of 1956, the highest flood recorded in the upper Allegheny River Valley since 1865 struck Warren, Pennsylvania, a city less than ten miles downstream from the proposed Kinzua Dam site. Property damage for the town of Warren was estimated at $2.5 million. The flood rekindled support for a high dam, and proponents pressured Congress to appropriate funds for its construction. These supporters believed that the Kinzua Dam would halt future flooding in the region, open the river to more industry, and create new recreation areas. However, the building of the dam would displace approximately 1,800 Seneca Indians from their reservation and violate the terms of the Senecas' 1794 treaty with the United States.[59]

Seneca leaders concluded that legal action would be the only way to halt the building of the dam and preserve their homeland. In the fall of 1956, the Seneca hired a lawyer, Edward E. O'Neil. He planned to file an injunction to keep the engineers off the reservation lands, but the Seneca knew that if passed, the injunction was only a temporary measure and not a solution to their problems. With the possibility of losing the legal battle, the Seneca recognized the need to combat the high dam proposal by developing an alternative water-control scheme for the area. To design and evaluate the feasibility of another plan, the Seneca hired two private engineers to research the possibilities.[60]

Seneca Nation president Cornelius V. Seneca followed a recommendation from the Society of Friends and hired Arthur Morgan as a consultant. The Seneca were intrigued with Morgan's varied career of water-control projects, educational reform, and especially his interest in small communities and small cultures. Further, Morgan was successful in limiting the involvement of the Corps of Engineers in his own engineering projects. The second engineer was one of Morgan's engineering associates, Barton M. Jones, who during his tenure with TVA designed and built the first TVA dam, Norris Dam. The Seneca instructed the two engineers to design and propose an alternative dam site or river-control project that would not involve the flooding of their land.[61]

Arthur Morgan with Seneca president George Heron, and unidentified woman, at the Seneca Reservation in the late 1950s. Antiochiana, Antioch College.

In late 1956, Morgan and Jones met with top Seneca leaders to discuss possible alternatives to the high dam proposal. Cornelius Seneca recommended that they explore a water diversion approach. This scheme involved building a channel to Lake Erie, which would divert floodwaters away from the Allegheny during periods of heavy rain. Although the plan had limitations, especially the cost of building such a channel, Morgan agreed that the diversion scheme was valid and worth further study. After the meeting, Cornelius Seneca announced that unless a suitable alternative was found, the Seneca would withdraw their objection to the construction of the Kinzua Dam.[62]

In May 1957, after six months of study, the two engineers developed an alternate plan for controlling floodwater in the upper Allegheny River Valley.

Their plan involved rerouting the floodwaters of the Allegheny River to Lake Erie through a long diversion channel through the Conewango basin. Morgan asserted that the Kinzua project presented only a narrow river channel to be closed by one dam in a specific place, whereas the nearby Conewango basin was unique. Conewango was a large irregular glacial basin with a long northern margin that stretched into New York not far from Lake Erie. Further, Morgan noted that the basin had a ready-made channel for an outlet through the deep pre-glacial gorge of Cattaraugus Creek and that one of the creek's branches flowed into Lake Erie. From these early studies Morgan concluded that the Conewango basin offered several alternative solutions to the Kinzua Dam. According to Morgan, the diversion plan would save the government $30 million, offer more comprehensive flood protection to the Allegheny Valley, and preserve the integrity of the Seneca Nation and the reputation of the United States.[63]

From their detailed research, Morgan alleged that the Corps of Engineers overlooked the possibility of the Conewango reservoir for the storage of floodwater and that they avoided acknowledging the oversight. According to Morgan, the Corps of Engineers disregarded the Conewango basin because it was a glacial excavation and not a river valley. Morgan pointed out that, because the glacial depression was more extensive than the river valley, the proposed Conewango reservoir would have had four times as much capacity for water storage as the waters behind the Kinzua Dam. If further storage were needed, then Morgan's reservoir would have much greater capacity.[64]

On May 10, 1957, with the alternative Conewango plan in hand, the opponents of the Kinzua Dam appeared before the Public Works subcommittee of the House Appropriations Committee. The contingent included the Seneca Nation's president Cornelius Seneca, attorney Edward O'Neil, engineering consultant Arthur Morgan, and representatives from the Indian Rights Association, the Society of Friends, the Association on American Indian Affairs, and various sportsmen's clubs from the Allegheny River Valley region.[65]

Morgan and Jones devised ten preliminary plans for the Conewango-Cattaraugus alternative, and at the May subcommittee meeting they submitted plan six for consideration. This plan utilized a glacial depression lying to the west of the Senecas' Allegany Indian Reservation. This plan called for a diversion canal to be built from the Allegheny River to the Conewango Creek Valley, which would be used as a storage reservoir and an outlet to Lake Erie. Floodwaters on the Allegheny could then be diverted into the

Conewango reservoir for storage. However, if the reservoir were full, the excess water would empty into Lake Erie. In effect, the plan would periodically change the course of the Allegheny River to run northwest rather than south. By changing the direction of the Allegheny, the downriver city of Pittsburgh would be better protected from flooding, and a new recreation area would develop around the new Conewango reservoir.[66]

Morgan emphasized to the subcommittee that it was a "folly" for the government to commit over $100 million to a project without studying alternatives, particularly when the project involved breaking a treaty and removing hundreds of Seneca from their reservation. Morgan also pointed out that the Kinzua site was perhaps the poorest location on the river to build a dam. He strengthened this line of argument by stating that the Kinzua site was over two hundred miles from the city it was designed to protect, and that the Allegheny River itself was never the main cause of Pittsburgh's downtown flooding. Further, Morgan asserted that the proposed dam would only control one-fifth of the Allegheny River Valley watershed.[67]

In his presentation to the subcommittee, Morgan compared both proposals. Morgan submitted that the Kinzua Dam would control floods from areas above the dam site, maintain a constant water flow for the Allegheny River, and provide recreational benefit above the dam. In comparison, Morgan's diversion plan would make available the same storage amount for river control as at Kinzua Dam, secure complete removal of floodwater from the upper Allegheny, and create a much more extensive, and thus much more valuable, recreation area.[68]

Morgan also took the opportunity to explain the plight of the Seneca to the subcommittee. As the Senecas' Allegany reservation was in a narrow river valley, Morgan pointed out that the Kinzua Dam would flood nearly all the habitable land and leave only steep mountainsides, effectively destroying the entire reservation. In contrast, Morgan's diversion plan would keep the reservation "above-water" and actually protect Seneca lands from annual flooding. In their defense, Morgan emphasized that the Seneca still had a treaty with the United States government which entitled them to full and permanent ownership of their lands. Morgan concluded his report by saying that the United States government should not be committed to the Kinzua project by an initial appropriation until a dependable and thorough comparison of other possibilities had been made. Further, he asked that the subcommittee provide an impartial, disinterested comparison of the two alternatives.[69]

Morgan's return to Capitol Hill to testify for the Seneca was a far cry from his last congressional appearance during the TVA investigation in 1938. This time, Morgan used data, reports, and charts to strengthen his arguments. His purpose was simple: to provide an alternative engineering plan that would protect the Seneca and non-Seneca from floodwaters in the most efficient and inexpensive way. Morgan delivered a compelling argument for his alternative proposal before the subcommittee, and two years later he returned to make yet another plea for the Seneca.

In response to Morgan's proposal for an independent comparison of the two proposals, Corps of Engineers representatives circulated the rumor that Morgan was a characterless, selfish, irresponsible publicity seeker who aimed to discredit the Corps of Engineers for mere personal reasons. To battle this negative publicity and to further the Senecas' cause, Morgan appealed directly to Pittsburgh business leaders. However, the financial community informed Morgan, in no uncertain terms, that the Corps of Engineers was the final source of authority. As the Corps of Engineers had already constructed six dams on the Allegheny River, the Pittsburgh leaders endorsed the Kinzua plan and announced that Morgan's alternative plan was too expensive and unnecessary.[70]

On August 30, 1957, Edward O'Neil filed an injunction against the Corps of Engineers. The document established that the Seneca were a semi-sovereign corporate body entitled to their lands. Further, O'Neil claimed that the Corps of Engineers' Kinzua Dam project violated the 1794 Pickering Treaty and the legal rights of the Seneca Nation. The next month, Seneca representatives requested that the government mediate the dispute between the Corps of Engineers and Morgan by hiring an impartial, independent firm to determine the feasibility of Morgan's Conewango reservoir proposal. To answer these demands, in October 1957, the Appropriation Committee of the House ordered the Corps of Engineers to make a comparison of the two proposals. Later that month, Colonel R. E. Smyser, division engineer of the Ohio River Division of the Corps of Engineers in Cincinnati, and the Seneca reached an agreement. In the understanding, the Corps of Engineers pledged to contract the independent civilian engineering firm of Tippetts-Abbett-McCarthy-Stratton (TAMS) in New York to review, reevaluate, and compare the Kinzua plan and Morgan's Conewango plan.[71]

Following the agreement, Morgan learned that TAMS was founded by a former director of civil works for the Corps of Engineers, Brig. Gen. James H.

Stratton; that three of the partners were ex-Corps of Engineers members; and that for twenty years the Corps of Engineers had been the most significant client of the firm. Morgan was convinced that the Corps of Engineers had undue influence over TAMS and that the firm would avoid embarrassing its main client. He wanted to help the Seneca in their fight against the Kinzua Dam, but Morgan also saw an opportunity to confront the Corps of Engineers. To relieve the Seneca of any financial responsibilities, in late 1957 Morgan resigned as consulting engineer. For the next five years, Morgan worked on behalf of the Seneca without compensation, covered his own expenses, and chose his own experts. Although not officially employed by the Seneca, Morgan was the sole public representative for the Seneca Indians into the early 1960s. As a reward for his service, in late 1957, the Seneca Nation of Indians of New York State made Morgan an honorary member.[72]

On April 1, 1958, after five months of study, the engineers at TAMS completed their comparison study, which supported the Corps of Engineers' Kinzua plan. During their comparison, the TAMS firm estimated that the Kinzua Dam would have a capacity of storage for control of 500,000 acre feet. In comparison, the report estimated that the Conewango Reservoir would have a total storage for river control of 2.5 million acre feet and a net storage of 2 million acre feet. Despite many positive facts gathered on the Conewango proposal, the Corps reported that "the additional investment [for Conewango] could not be justified on the basis of additional benefits that can now be evaluated." The engineers at TAMS reported that Morgan's alternative diversion scheme for the Conewango basin would cost from 25 to 38 percent more than the Kinzua project. Their report also explained that Morgan's plan required the submersion of from 51 percent to 108 percent more land than the Kinzua plan. In terms of the human factor, the TAMS report concluded that Morgan's plan called for the dislocation of from 150 to 180 more people than the Kinzua project. Finally, on the point of water-control, the Corps concluded that the additional storage for river control in the alternative proposal was unnecessary and not economically feasible. The TAMS report left the impression that Morgan's Conewango plan was too expensive, too massive in scope, and too destructive because too many people, nearly all non-Seneca, would be dislocated.[73]

Morgan responded to the TAMS report in an April 24, 1958, letter to Gen. Emerson C. Itschner of the Corps of Engineers, in which he stressed that the Kinzua Dam was a poorly conceived proposal with limited possibilities for flood control. Further, Morgan pointed out that, as the town of Salamanca, New York, was above the dam site, the amount of flood water to be held behind the dam was severely limited. In terms of relative cost, Morgan insisted that the TAMS engineers significantly overestimated the Conewango proposal; actually, the two plans were nearly comparable in value. Morgan also emphasized that the Conewango plan was superior to the Kinzua plan because it allowed for more abundant storage capacity, which would create a permanent lake more than five times larger than the proposed Kinzua reservoir and would enable the government to respect the treaty with the Seneca Indians. Morgan ended the letter by encouraging the Corps of Engineers to reevaluate the TAMS report and give the two proposals further consideration.[74]

Following his May 1958 letter, Morgan released a public statement concerning the TAMS report and the differences in the Kinzua and Conewango proposals. Similar to his Itschner letter, Morgan emphasized that the Kinzua proposal was a compromise limited by storage capacity, whereas the Conewango proposal had three times the capacity. Morgan also pointed out that the concrete and steel needed to build the Kinzua Dam would be much more expensive than the materials needed for the series of earthen dams proposed for the Conewango project. In his conclusion, Morgan emphasized that the permanent lake at the Conewango site would cover fourteen square miles, more than five times larger than the lake at Kinzua, thus making the recreational benefits of the Conewango proposal economically superior.[75]

In both the letter and the public statement, Morgan addressed the human element of the TAMS report by stating that, actually, many more persons would be displaced by Kinzua than by Conewango. He claimed that, with the completion of the Kinzua Dam, the Senecas would have to move their villages altogether, while, if the Conewango plan were implemented, the towns in the Conewango basin would only have to move the low-lying parts of the villages to adjoining higher areas. Morgan also argued that the TAMS report ignored the fact that the Kinzua Dam would provide protection for only half the estimated maximum flood levels and that the Conewango Reservoir would care for nearly all flood contingencies. Overall, Morgan concluded that TAMS filled their report with misleading information, so that Congress and the public would be unaware of vital information—data that was necessary to understand the benefits of Morgan's plan.[76]

Morgan noted that although the two reservoir sites were not far apart, they were different geologically. The Kinzua site, which was just south of past glacial action, especially the southern part where nearly all the construction work for the dam was located, was mountainous, with rocks protruding through the thin soil. The Corps estimated that moving this material would cost about $1.00 per cubic yard. In marked contrast, the Conewango basin was an area of intense glacial action. Glacial forces had once ground significant mountain chains into sand, clay, and gravel. Morgan determined that nine-tenths of the materials to be encountered in the Conewango excavation would be these three easily moved materials. Due to the ease of excavating sand, clay, and gravel, Morgan estimated that most of the heavy earth work could be completed for less than $0.30 per cubic yard.[77]

Frequently, in their concern to oppose Morgan's Conewango proposal and because of international relations, the Corps of Engineers stated that it would not be possible to divert water into the international waters of Lake Erie without full coordination and cooperation with Canada. Yet Morgan estimated that, in the highly unlikely event that the entire rainfall of a maximum storm on the upper Allegheny River watershed were put into Lake Erie all in an instant, the excess water would raise Lake Erie's level less than three inches.[78]

In July 1958, Morgan released yet another public statement comparing the Kinzua and Conewango proposals. This statement emphasized the significance of the town of Salamanca to both flood-control schemes. Morgan pointed out that the nearby town of Salamanca limited the storage capacity of the Kinzua Dam, and if maximum storage were attained, the town would be flooded. With a populated area at risk of flooding, Morgan deemed the Kinzua proposal impractical and hazardous for the town of Salamanca.[79]

In the fall of 1958, the courts halted the project. After repeated urging from Pennsylvania congressman John Saylor (R), the House Appropriations Committee restricted further expenditures for the Kinzua project until the settlement of the Senecas' appeal. Earlier that year, the United States District Court for the District of Columbia began deliberating the Senecas' case. On April 14, the district court ruled that the engineers could take the Senecas' land by the right of public purpose. Judge Joseph McGarraghy ruled that Congress knew that it was breaking the treaty when it appropriated money for the construction of a dam in late 1956. Further, McGarraghy argued that a federal-Indian treaty could not rise above the power of Congress to legislate. In effect, this ruling meant that, if the United States government negotiated and made a treaty, they could also break that agreement.[80]

On November 25, 1958, in what proved to be the last major rendering by a federal court in the Kinzua Dam matter, the three judges of the United States Court of Appeals for the District of Columbia unanimously affirmed Judge McGarraghy's decision and denied the Seneca an injunction against the Corps of Engineers. Citing congressional and previous testimony, the court found that Congress was aware of what it was doing to the Indians and their lands when it had appropriated funds for the proposed dam in late 1956.[81]

The legal battle continued as the Seneca petitioned to have their case heard before the Supreme Court. But because of the two previous verdicts, in early 1959 the Supreme Court refused to hear the Senecas' case. With the appeal turned back, the Corps of Engineers pushed for further appropriations for their proposal. At the same time, Morgan prepared for another series of subcommittee hearings scheduled for May 1959. Both the Seneca and the Corps of Engineers knew that Morgan's Conewango proposal was all that stood between the Allegany Indian Reservation and inundation.[82]

In May 1959, Morgan returned to Washington, D.C., to present his Conewango plan at meetings of the subcommittee on Public Works of the House and Senate Committees on Appropriations. In his statement, Morgan once again compared the Kinzua plan and his Conewango proposal. Morgan also stated that the TAMS report was biased toward the Corps of Engineers and therefore inaccurate. He implied that the independent report had been unduly influenced by the Corps of Engineers, but unlike his previous congressional appearances, he did not make charges of unethical misconduct. Instead, Morgan relied on data, and compared the economic and human losses of Kinzua with the numerous advantages of Conewango.[83]

For the rest of 1959, Morgan continued promoting the alternative proposal, and nearly a year later he was given yet a third opportunity to convince a congressional subcommittee of the dangers of Kinzua. Just as he had done in 1957 and 1959, on April 7 and 8, 1960, Arthur Morgan appeared before the subcommittee on Public Works of the House and Senate Committees on Appropriations with his alternative reservoir proposal. On April 7, 1960, Morgan restated the undisputed facts of the TAMS report. First, the TAMS engineers reported that the Kinzua Dam would protect Pittsburgh from moderate flooding, but they also found that the Conewango plan would fully protect

Pittsburgh from a flood three times greater. Morgan also pointed out that, as the TAMS report never actually listed the estimated cost to build the Kinzua Dam, the comparison of costs between the two proposals was completely unfounded. Further, on the issue of cost, he emphasized that, because the Kinzua site was in an active river valley, it would take several costly seasons to move tons of earth into the area and to finish the concrete section amid the frequent flooding. Morgan ended the day of testimony by saying that an impartial analysis of his Conewango plan had never been conducted.[84]

On the second day of testimony, Morgan focused on bigger issues. He first explained that, as the Kinzua Dam would not end the threat of flooding to Pittsburgh, other reservoirs would have to be built. However, if the Conewango reservoir were built, flooding in the Allegheny River Valley would be virtually eliminated, thus making other reservoirs unnecessary. Once again Morgan spoke of the inaccuracies of the TAMS report and accused the Corps of Engineers of intentionally dismissing the superior Conewango proposal. In his concluding statement, Morgan said that, by approving and building the Kinzua Dam, the Corps of Engineers and the United States government would make a "colossal blunder."[85]

Despite another bold presentation, Morgan's request for reprieve remained unanswered. Almost two months later, on May 25, 1960, with a vote of 398 to 18, the House of Representatives passed a $4.5 million appropriation bill for the construction of Kinzua Dam. Four months later, in September 1960, preliminary construction at the Kinzua site began. On October 22, 1960, Pennsylvania governor David Lawrence delivered the major address at the groundbreaking ceremony for the Allegheny River Reservoir at Kinzua, Pennsylvania. He hailed the project as the "first great stride to bring flood protection to millions of homes and thousands of industries in six states." Further, Lawrence praised the Corps of Engineers for their objective research and their concern for all groups in the affected area. The governor concluded by saying that Kinzua Dam was an example of good government, whereby the needs of humanity were fulfilled through cooperation and trust.[86]

By the beginning of 1961, construction at the Kinzua site was fully underway. Realizing the immediacy of the situation, Arthur Morgan took new approaches to stopping the project. Morgan first wrote to President John F. Kennedy to request an impartial comparison of the two existing proposals.

In the March 14 letter, Morgan informed the recently inaugurated president of the history of the Kinzua struggle and the Senecas' desperate situation. In the March letter, Morgan outlined the Senecas' Pickering Treaty, the reservoir proposals, the geography and geology of the two sites, the history of the Corps of Engineers in the Allegheny River Valley, and the disadvantages of the Kinzua project. Morgan concluded the letter by asking Kennedy to halt the Kinzua Dam project until a competent and wholly impartial comparison of the two plans could be made.[87]

In a brief reply later that year, Kennedy announced that he refused to halt the Kinzua Dam construction because the need for flood protection was "real and immediate."[88] Morgan received no further response or action from President Kennedy, so he decided to go to a larger audience. On December 28, 1961, in his final public appeal on the matter, Morgan appeared on NBC's morning talk show "Today" and reviewed the Kinzua Dam controversy. During the twenty minute interview session, NBC reporter Hugh Downs questioned Morgan about the Conewango alternative for the Allegheny River Valley, the Kinzua Dam proposal, and the Seneca Indians. Morgan briefly described his lifelong career in flood control engineering and how he had become involved in the Kinzua matter. Then Hugh Downs asked Morgan about the two proposals designed to control flooding in the Allegheny Valley. Morgan explained the purpose, scope, and facts of each proposal; although he questioned the validity and integrity of the TAMS report, Morgan emphasized that his goal was to provide the best plan for flood control and not simply to slander the Corps of Engineers. Like his congressional testimony, Morgan focused on the facts and the possible outcomes of the two proposals. He presented the advantages of his Conewango plan, such as cost, effectiveness, and practicality, and compared it to the poorly conceived and inferior Kinzua plan. Morgan also intertwined the issue of flood control with the plight of the Seneca. He quoted his April 1960 subcommittee testimony as he emphasized that the construction of the Kinzua Dam would be a "colossal blunder."[89]

Although Morgan's appearance on the "Today" show created publicity and attention, this last action symbolized the end for all serious appeals against the Kinzua Dam. Following Morgan's television appearance, no significant public outcry for the cause emerged and no new hearings were scheduled. By 1962, with the Kinzua Dam under construction, Morgan exhausted nearly all alternative appeals and had also reached a final impasse with the Corps of Engineers and the United States government. With few options remaining, in 1963, Arthur Morgan officially withdrew from the battle against the Kinzua Dam and the Corps of Engineers. The next year the government awarded the Seneca $15 million for their land and relocated nearly 700 Seneca Indians to nearby communities. In 1965, the waters behind the Kinzua Dam claimed over 10,000 acres of land from the Seneca Indian Nation.[90]

Though the end result was the same, the story of the Kinzua Dam would have been much different without the presence of Arthur Morgan. As chief engineer and main representative for the Seneca Indians, Morgan intelligently utilized data to present his Conewango proposal as a better alternative to the Kinzua Dam. His efforts between 1956 and 1962 delayed the building of the Kinzua Dam, but more importantly, his rejected Conewango proposal revealed to the public gigantic errors that existed in the United States government's public policy, relations with Native Americans, and close relationship with the Corps of Engineers.[91]

Just as Morgan's work with the Seneca ended, he focused attention on developing a small community in the mountains of Western North Carolina. Throughout his career, Morgan established several communities based on practical education and character building. Beginning with the idea of Jacob's Pillow project in 1915, Morgan always envisioned establishing his own educational based community. His work with Moraine Park School, Antioch College, and Mitraniketan were successful attempts at combining practical education and the small community. However, those projects did not involve Morgan's ownership of the property, his preferences on the selection of the community members, and an educational curriculum that he controlled.[92]

Morgan's development of the Celo Community near Burnsville, North Carolina, represented many of the realities and pitfalls of community building. In the early 1930s, just as Morgan prepared to lead the Tennessee Valley Authority, he began talking to other Quakers about building a rural community to educate and train unemployed youth. With financial backing for the project from publisher William H. Regnery, Morgan sent his son Griscom Morgan to investigate available property in the mountains of the

Appalachian South. The younger Morgan located a large tract of land near Burnsville, North Carolina, about fifty miles from Asheville, that could support subsistence agriculture, small industries, and possibly mining.[93]

In the summer of 1938, just as Morgan prepared for the TVA investigation, the press reported on Morgan's "Quaker colony" in North Carolina. Reporters suggested that Morgan's project was more of a speculative economic venture than a community building project, but Morgan denied the claims and insisted that he intended to use the property to educate students. On December 28, 1938, Morgan formalized his plans for the new property by incorporating it as the Celo Community, Inc. The purpose of the entity was to promote general education and vocational guidance, subsistence agriculture, economic development, and create a planned community in the vicinity of Celo, North Carolina.[94]

Because of multiple obligations, Morgan left most of the work of creating Celo to others. In 1939, the directors of Celo identified families and leaders to take residence at the new location. The first residents of Celo built structures, improved the land, and began shaping the purpose of the community. Because of a lack of infrastructure, services, structures, and subpar agricultural production, the early years of Celo were difficult. The community also had a high turnover rate of families, but Celo grew. Morgan later recalled that during the 1940s he gave little time to assess the progress at Celo. However, he pointed out the problems with Celo, most notably that many of the selected residents did not have the backgrounds and interests to make a rural cooperative society successful. Morgan believed that Celo evolved into a community that depended more on external communities than on its own capabilities, resources, and expertise.[95]

The Celo community expanded and contracted during the 1940s and 1950s, becoming a haven for pacifists, Quakers, and nonconformists. Morgan remained a distant supporter of Celo, and, in the late 1950s, his son Ernest and daughter-in-law Elizabeth organized summer camps for high school and college students. The success of those summer camps led to the establishment of the Arthur Morgan School in 1962 within the Celo community. The integration of the school into the life of the community represented what Morgan had hoped to do with the Jacob's Pillow project nearly fifty years prior. The Celo community and the Arthur Morgan School continued to flourish and represented the kind of educational based community that Morgan helped establish at Mitraniketan.[96]

On October 11, 1974, Arthur Morgan and his granddaughter Faith Morgan Odiorne boarded a plane destined for St. Cloud, Minnesota. Morgan was returning to the place of his youth to receive a distinguished alumni award from St. Cloud State College (now St. Cloud University). At age ninety-six, Morgan's poor health confined him to a wheelchair, but his mind was as sharp as ever. Morgan's visit coincided with the school's homecoming activities. That weekend Morgan rode in a parade, attended the school's homecoming football game, and attended an alumni banquet where he was recognized for his lifetime of service. Upon receiving the award Morgan made a brief speech. Morgan treated the audience to details of his 1897 trip down the Mississippi River and out West in search of adventure. He closed the speech by recommending that students take the time to explore the world and to find their purpose in life.[97]

Near the end of Morgan's visit to St. Cloud, he returned to his boyhood home at 812 7th Avenue. Despite his poor eyesight, Morgan pointed out trees and ferns that he had planted as a boy. He also noted the roof on the back side of the house that he used to slide down from his bedroom window before running off into the woods to explore. The next morning, the two Morgans returned to Yellow Springs. This brief homecoming trip would be the last significant trip of Arthur Morgan's life.[98]

Apart from the occasional consultation or trip, Morgan spent most of the 1970s in Yellow Springs, surrounded by friends and family. With the help of a system of magnifying glasses and hearing devices, Morgan continued to communicate and write. Morgan resumed work on an autobiography, which was never published, and talked with scholars about his TVA years. He also began working on a new book about his educational philosophy, which he called "wholemanism," but dropped the project to take care of his wife Lucy, who suffered a stroke. Morgan moved his wife of sixty years to a nursing home in Xenia, Ohio, where he visited her regularly. She passed away in 1972. Morgan spent the next few years working on a few writing projects, local initiatives, and the transfer of his papers (which were stored in a nearby barn loft) to the Antioch College library. On November 16, 1975, at age ninety-seven, Arthur Morgan died. The next summer, Antioch College held a two-day convocation in his honor. Following the events, two of Morgan's

Morgan Boulder located outside of Glen Helen Nature Preserve, Yellow Springs, Ohio. Antiochiana, Antioch College.

great-grandchildren interred his and his wife's ashes at the base of a large rock, named Morgan Boulder, at the entrance to the Glen Helen Nature Preserve just across the street from the Antioch College campus.[99]

CONCLUSION

Over the course of nearly a century, Arthur Morgan recorded a long list of professional accomplishments. His peers and admirers recognized his achievements through numerous awards, honorary degrees, and accolades. Morgan established small communities across the globe, with his contributions to the small town of Yellow Springs, Ohio, as perhaps the most significant. His engineering works and reclamation projects scattered across the country were his most recognizable and tangible achievements, even though his name was seldom affixed to plaques or dedication markers. These often revolutionary public works have stood the test of time to prevent flooding, loss of life, and saved untold millions in property damages. As an author, Morgan published over a dozen books and countless articles on a wide range of topics, including engineering, utopian thought, and the small community. Finally, Morgan kept a close network of family and friends, who were a central part of his personal life. Many of those associates still reminisce about Morgan's kind demeanor, concern for others, and zest for life, more than his professional achievements.

Despite Morgan's wide-ranging professional accomplishments, outside of Yellow Springs, Dayton, and the Miami River Valley of Ohio, Arthur Morgan is not well-known. Those who recognize the name either align him with Antioch College or TVA. Concerning both institutions, however, Morgan is not the central figure. There is not a building on the Antioch College campus named for Morgan, only the nearby Arthur Morgan house (where he and Lucy lived for many years) which is now a bed-and-breakfast a few blocks from campus. But there are hints of Morgan's connections across the campus, including the Morgan Papers housed on the second floor of the Olive Kettering Library. Similarly, there are few obvious Morgan connections to the dozens of TVA structures and projects. No TVA buildings or dams were ever named in his honor—a proposed but never completed "superdam" to control the watersheds of Ohio and Cumberland Rivers might have been named for Morgan.[1] One possible reason for his omission from TVA lore was David Lilienthal's successful promotion of TVA through his wildly successful book, *TVA: Democracy on the March* (1944), which downplayed Morgan's early contributions.[2] More likely, Morgan's untimely departure from TVA in 1938 explains why his early contributions to the agency have been glossed over for decades.

The most obvious evidence of Morgan's legacy includes a series of small communities that bear his markings. The Arthur Morgan School in Celo, North Carolina, continues to attract students and teachers from across the country to experience a unique style of practical education. In Kerala, India, the Mitraniketan community has grown and thrived since the late 1950s, with continued support from international organizations like Community Service, Inc. His most celebrated and known community, the town of Norris, Tennessee, remains a vibrant part of Anderson County, Tennessee. The author once visited the local historical society just across from the Norris post office and asked about Arthur Morgan, the first chairman of TVA. The volunteer at the desk smiled and said, "Oh you must mean David Lilienthal, he founded this town." Despite such confusion, just beneath the surface there is still a great deal of tangible evidence of Morgan's influence on communities like Norris and the design of dozens of TVA dams.

A lack of scholarly and popular attention is another reason why Morgan has been relegated to the footnotes and sidelines of history. Only a few scholars tackled Morgan's life and career and with varying results. Roy Talbert's *FDR's Utopian* (1987) remains the only scholarly work focused on Morgan, but it lacks depth after Morgan left the Tennessee Valley and does not address the vision that Morgan developed over his lifetime. Talbert provided an overview of Morgan's TVA and engineering career, but his book fell short of fully evaluating Morgan and the undeniable influence of Edward Bellamy on the engineer. Further, his definition of Morgan as a utopian is not an accurate portrayal of a complex reformer with a late nineteenth-century social vision that looked to the past to shape and improve the future.

The fuller picture and stronger analysis of Morgan begins with understanding his vision, which is most apparent in his writings. Two of Morgan's books best articulated the details of his vision for organizing a rapidly changing society. In *The Long Road,* published in 1936 during some of his most tense moments with TVA, Morgan outlined the importance of character in organizing society. He believed that in order to move the country forward, and out of the Great Depression, Americans must rely on building strong character and communities, and not depend on the government or business to solve modern problems. Morgan announced that past reliance on these later institutions led to poor social health, cultural malnourishment, and "political pellagra." As the cure, Morgan suggested "social vitamins" and character building.[3]

In *The Long Road,* Morgan articulated his definition of good character and how to achieve it. Morgan believed that character depended on three elements. First, individuals must have a purposefulness and direction that fulfills larger societal aims. Second, he stated that there must be "good will and the skilled and disciplined drive of desire which presses toward the realization of aims and purposes."[4] Finally, Morgan believed that ethical or moral quality would lead enlightened individuals to make wholesome choices that benefitted the individual and society. Later in the book, Morgan explained that establishing a moral code was an essential part of reinforcing elements of character, and, if followed, the code would lead to great social advancement.[5]

Although the ethical code described in *The Long Road* was less defined than the code Morgan proposed for TVA, it included some specific ways to build character and indicated which attributes to emphasize. He explained that methods of building of strong character included: "the defining and clarifying of purposes and motives, the development of integrity and open-dealing, the increase of self-discipline, the tempering of body and spirit to endure hardship, the growth of courage, the practice of tolerance, the habit of acting for the general good, and the growth of human understanding and of neighborly affection and regard."[6]

Morgan also included the importance of eugenic conscience as a method to pass along the most enlightened traits to future generations. In an unfortunate analogy, Morgan described how Minnesota dairyman increased their milk and butter production by breeding cattle with certain characteristics. He explained that the process of selecting superior cattle for breeding was not unlike the way that humanity perpetuated those with the most desirable characteristics. Yet Morgan also pointed out the dangers of selective breeding, saying that the process of natural selection, mutations, and adaptations often made the most superior cattle, and possibly humans, vulnerable.[7]

Like later works, *The Long Road* pointed to the small community as the way to build a society with strong character. Morgan believed that the intimate nature of small communities promoted the "qualities of good will, fair dealing, and unselfish cooperation."[8] Further, small industries, rather than big businesses that focused primarily on profits, provided residents with employment, income, skills, and the principle of self-sufficiency. Again Morgan railed against urban areas. He believed that urban settings were "industrially regimented," and that only the most wealthy city dwellers had real opportunities for advancement. As a sharp contrast, Morgan called for the creation of a community character that could only be nurtured in smaller, non-urban settings.[9]

The book revealed Morgan's frustrations with TVA and his vision for organizing society. His call for stronger American character, rather than more government assistance, occurred just as other New Deal programs were scrapped. Morgan believed that the way to recover from the economic crisis was to start rebuilding the social structure with strong principles, character, and communities. He explained that social evolution was possible through an ongoing process of character and community enrichment. Even though Morgan blamed political and business leaders for many of the problems with modern society, he invited them to lead the nation toward a stronger American character and a more enlightened society. Morgan's delivery and audience may have changed, but his message of improving American character stayed the same. He was still a moralist with a vision.[10]

In 1957, Morgan published *Search for Purpose,* which further explained his social vision. This book continued with the themes of character building, cooperation, ethical codes, and eugenics as the way to advance mankind, but Morgan approached these topics in a much more subdued and somewhat non-proscriptive fashion. The numerous analogies and light writing tone made the book digestible for casual readers. With TVA far behind him and the global community seeking his advice, Morgan assumed the role of a philosopher focused on how to best organize society in the atomic age. Morgan explained that individuals must identify their individual purpose in life and seek out the experiences and opportunities to fulfill that purpose. With a strong sense of purpose at the individual and community levels, Morgan believed that new patterns of social organization would emerge.[11]

Morgan began *Search for Purpose* by explaining that the postwar world was experiencing a great transition. Advances in technology, scientific thought, and the spread of democracy across the globe rendered many existing patterns of life inadequate for the atomic age. At the same time, Morgan recognized that the challenges of the postwar period provided new opportunities for restructuring society. Capturing the context of the time, Morgan referred to the threat of atomic war and the possibility of annihilation of the human race. Morgan advised readers not to be afraid of falling bombs, but to be more concerned about the character of scientists and politicians. The implications of potential atomic warfare, Morgan believed, would result in a rebirth of strong character in the area of public policy and improved international relations.[12]

With the Cold War as the backdrop, Morgan reviewed the steps needed to promote human survival and progress. First, he described the importance of human mastery over the physical world. Morgan explained that humans were high-functioning animals capable of free will and choice. With that biological perspective, Morgan discussed human evolution, mutations, natural selection, the transmission of knowledge, and the need to control the natural environment. Morgan connected these topics to global issues such as population growth, urban problems, the development of the third world, and limiting the effects of cataclysmic events such as flooding, famine, and pandemics. He believed that these challenges could be overcome with new technology, international cooperation, and global planning.[13]

Second, Morgan emphasized the need for strong character in the atomic age. In order to build character, Morgan believed that society must identify and embrace clear values. He listed purposeful social values, including "honesty in dealing with associates, acting for the long-time general good rather than for one's personal good where there is conflict between the two; carrying one's share of the social load; [and] maintaining one's physical and mental health."[14] Once identified, Morgan believed that societal values would be translated into codes of ethical and moral behavior. According to Morgan, social codes would lead to a greater purposefulness in individuals, would improve character, and would "provide a way for accelerating evolution" of society.[15]

Finally, Morgan described the importance of eugenic practice in building strong purposeful and contributing members of society. Building on his approach that humans were animals, Morgan believed that the advancement and evolution of the human race depended on the intentional transmission of knowledge and strong traits of character from one generation to the next. Eugenic practice would also eliminate less desirable traits such as mental and physical illness. Even more directly, Morgan wrote that "in eugenics we have few misgivings when we prevent the reproduction of near idiots." He recognized the dangers of eugenics, citing the Nazis' efforts for racial betterment through genocide, but he believed that, with the proper development, eugenic practices gave society a genetic conscience. For Morgan, eugenics was a way to control society, and he viewed the theories and practices as a simple genetic responsibility to advance the human race. He predicted that in "the coming years eugenic research, education and policy may lead to rapid and sustained improvement of human quality, and tragedy from inadequacy of human genetic inheritance may largely disappear."[16]

Eugenics was a constant thread in Morgan's writings beginning in the 1920s. Unlike many others who abandoned eugenics after the atrocities of World War II, Morgan held on to the idea that the practice of better and selective breeding would result in a better world. However, at no point in Morgan's career did he actually execute any eugenics research on actual living beings. Morgan was not a scientist. Rather, he was a promoter of the concept, and in his later years he hoped that the scientific community would return to the components of eugenic thought as a way to improve the science of genetics.

Other components of Morgan's social philosophies and vision were part *of Search for Purpose.* He spoke of the importance of small communities as the seedbed of civilization and social change. Morgan mentioned the importance of cooperation, rather than competition, in modern society. While he did not make direct references to Edward Bellamy, he did explain that past utopian authors had predicted wonderful human achievements. However, Morgan was quick to point out that advances in technology and communication had far outstripped the predictions made by past utopians. In the end, Morgan explained that the quest for an ideal pattern of society was an innate trait for humans. His purpose in life was to explore ways to advance and achieve a much more enlightened society.[17]

Books such as *The Long Road* and *Search for Purpose* revealed many of the details of Morgan's vision for organizing society. While that vision was sometimes unclear and changed over time, Morgan believed that a more enlightened society was possible with a series of steps. As the means to achieve that vision, Morgan called for the development of small communities, scientific planning, practical education, social reform, moral and ethical codes, character building, and eugenic practices. In each of his careers, Morgan promoted each of these "steps" on the pathway to a better tomorrow.

Morgan also believed that the opportunity to restructure society was at the individual level, and not from governments, schools, or business leaders. Strong character and moral purpose in life, he believed, depended on individual choice. He hoped to win the hearts and minds of modern Americans through his writings and his various community-based projects. But oddly, his influence as a social philosopher and community builder was greater in the third world than in the United States.

Morgan's vision was influenced by three important components. First, the scientific and cultural discussions of the late nineteenth century made a significant impression on Morgan. Instead of adopting his mother's strong religious devotion, Morgan found much greater solace in science, by immersing himself in the intellectual debates of the time, including topics such as evolution, natural selection, and genetics. An adherent of the early conservation movement, Morgan took great interest in the natural world, and he spent much of his life reclaiming and protecting undeveloped lands. His reliance on science and technology to solve human problems led him to the emerging field of water-control engineering and reclamation. Although a poor student in the traditional sense, Morgan overcame his lack of education through practical experience and a self-directed curriculum. Morgan emerged from the late nineteenth century with a moral compass, a fascination with scientific solutions to modern problems, and a growing vision for structuring society.

Second, the reforms and reformers of the Progressive Era made a significant impression on Morgan. During the first decades of the twentieth century Morgan developed his professional footing as a water-control engineer and drainage expert. But more than just building dams and flood control projects to control the physical environment, he began experimenting with other ways to use science and public works to improve society. Morgan searched for solutions to modern problems, such as Americanizing immigrants, exposing corruption and waste, protecting natural environments, promoting peace during times of war, and providing students with practical education. Like other Progressive Era reformers, Morgan embraced eugenics as a scientific method for improving the gene pool. He believed that eugenic practices would eliminate less desirable traits and create future generations with strong character, morality, and ethical convictions. Unlike other Progressive Era leaders who favored urban reform, Morgan focused on improving smaller, more rural communities through his projects. Morgan's brand of reform was fully aligned with the Progressive Era and he carried out his later work with the same approaches of improvement through social uplift, elimination of waste, scientific methods to improve efficiency, and social planning.

Finally, Edward Bellamy had significant influence on Morgan. Bellamy's writings and utopian philosophies directly affected Morgan's belief that a more enlightened society was possible through a natural evolution of individual character. Rather than a sudden change in the social fabric, Morgan's plan was gradual. Much of his vision had strong parallels to the future described in Edward Bellamy's utopian novel *Looking Backward,* a book that Morgan considered one of the most transformative works in American history. Morgan was not solely driven by Bellamy's ideals, but the connection clarifies how Morgan envisioned structuring society.

Morgan's complex plans for restructuring society reveals that he was more of a reformer with a vision than a utopian. Morgan took great interest in the concept of utopia, wrote extensively about the history of utopianism, and admired the work of Edward Bellamy. However, those traits should not define Morgan as a utopian. Unlike utopians, Morgan did not want to create separate communities bent on perfectionism, communal living, and isolation from the modern world. Instead, Morgan was a reformer with a unique vision—complete with manifold practical problems that would need to be worked out over a possibly long period of time—for building a new society, which was based on shaping one small community at a time.

Like other visionaries Morgan's achievements, actions, and declarations were littered with dichotomies. Many times he undercut his own successes. His style, judgment, and personality frequently conflicted with the task at hand. Most importantly, Morgan had difficulty in altering his plans, especially when he convinced himself that he was right. And when he was sure he was right, he grew stubborn, turned inward, and could not be moved. Moreover, he could characterize those who developed differing views, not only as wrong, but as malicious, unethical, and merely self-interested. Morgan best defined his sense of rightness, saying that, "By rightness I mean a conduct of life which is in accordance with the nature of things. We strive to approach rightness by search for the truth—by following the truth wherever it may lead, regardless of the consequences."[18]

Morgan's style of leadership repelled some, especially after long exposure to it, but he attracted others to his cause. And those who were drawn to Morgan were loyal, competent, and hard working. Throughout the twentieth century, Morgan worked in several professional fields. He led each initiative with the zeal of a visionary, but in reality he often served as an administrator or manager, which required great skill and the ability to compromise. As he advanced in his career, Morgan's sense of his own rightness grew stronger, which sometimes weakened his ability to lead projects and work with others who had differing opinions. Morgan elaborated on his ability to make decisions which he knew were ethically right, saying, "I often find well-meaning, simple-minded people greatly confused over ethical issues which seems very clear to me, and some of my friends may find me in similar confusion. My own policy is to do my best, and then not to worry over past mistakes."[19]

Morgan's engineering career and management of projects revealed many of his personality traits and flaws. Morgan was a professional engineer, more specifically a water-control engineer. At the turn of the twentieth century, young Morgan settled on a career in an emerging field that fit well with the efforts of Progressive Era leaders to control the environment, improve efficiency, and make better use of natural resources for industrial purposes. Despite his lack of formal engineering education, he stumbled into a field that was still based on an apprentice system of practical experience. He learned what he needed to know about water-control engineering by reading the professional literature, listening to leaders of projects (including his father), and, most importantly, plodding through flooded swamps throughout the South. Morgan learned enough of the advanced mathematics needed to design reclamation plans and earthworks. His flair for the work and attention to detail resulted in successful projects and the opportunity to leave the fieldwork to his employees.

During the first decade of the twentieth century, Morgan achieved enough status as a water-control engineer to take some risks with larger projects. His work as a drainage consultant for the government introduced Morgan to management, directing multiple teams of surveyors and engineers, and the bureaucracy of government work. Morgan's small and successful campaign to expose corruption during a survey of the Florida Everglades justified his growing sense of rightness and his distaste for government service. The latter reality led him back into private practice, where he had much more flexibility and control over his professional advancement. But the Miami flood of 1913 placed him in the spotlight and gave him another opportunity for public service.

In the 1910s, Morgan served as the lead engineer and spokesperson for the Miami Conservancy District. The unique design of the earthworks earned him accolades from the professional engineering community. But perhaps more unique, the Miami Conservancy District demonstrated the potential for regional planning in public works projects. Morgan did not see political boundaries in his engineering projects, and during the process of legally establishing the Miami Conservancy District, he had to deal with public opinion and some opposition. Unlike later periods in his career, he did not let his sense of rightness displace his ability to work with and talk to others who did not share his opinion. Morgan grew to detest politics and the political process, but during the mid-1910s he was an effective force and worked with many public officials and leaders to make the Miami Conservancy District a reality.

Morgan's growing sense of social responsibility placed him alongside other reformers of the period. Like many Progressive Era leaders who owned a business, Morgan took great interest in improving his workers. He offered recent immigrants the chance to work on his engineering teams, with the intention of familiarizing them and their families with American traditions and practices. With the Miami Conservancy District, Morgan provided his workers with elaborate camps at each of the major project sites. The large investment in the camps drew criticism, but Morgan effectively argued that such facilities would result in greater productivity from the workforce. Although temporary, the model villages represented his first attempt to build small communities that could be regulated and controlled. While directing the Miami Conservancy District, Morgan practiced civic involvement by supporting national efforts during World War I and then taking a leadership role in the League to Enforce Peace. By the early 1920s, Morgan completed a water-control system to protect Dayton and surrounding communities from future flooding, but he had also established himself as a national figure and an innovator.

Morgan returned to the spotlight in 1933 when he accepted Franklin D. Roosevelt's offer to direct the Tennessee Valley Authority. Even though Morgan voted for Herbert Hoover, an engineer, in the 1933 presidential election, he was taken by Roosevelt's charisma and New Deal vision.[20] During the next five years Morgan designed and directed an expansive water-control project across seven states. Morgan's engineering work with TVA was notable and impressive, but much of the speed of the projects was due to the fact that Morgan relied on lengthy studies of the Tennessee River Valley completed by the U.S. Army Corps of Engineers during the 1920s. Certainly Morgan added his own unique touch to the dams and other water-control works needed to control the Tennessee River basin, but because Morgan did not have to start the engineering work of TVA from scratch, he focused his attention elsewhere.

One of Morgan's focus areas during the early TVA period was the building of the town of Norris, Tennessee. Expanding on his idea for workers of the Miami Conservancy District, Morgan wanted Norris to be a permanent community that was self-sustainable and replicable. Because of the great scale of plans for the community, Morgan faced significant criticism for the costs associated with building Norris. The town was completed, but no other such permanent towns were built at TVA dam sites. Because of other TVA challenges, Morgan had little time to build on the success of Norris, but the town represented his first permanent built community.

The intersection of engineering and politics was most apparent during Morgan's TVA tenure. During the 1930s, the political landscape changed rapidly to meet the needs of the Great Depression. Even though Roosevelt promised Morgan that TVA would be free of politics, Morgan knew that such a promise could not be kept. The complex process of securing land, removing residents, relocating graves and gravesites, and starting construction projects for TVA involved political support at the local, state, and national levels. Morgan was most convincing when he was discussing his engineering proposals, but when he veered into other areas, such as electric power policy and social planning, he encountered significant opposition. Morgan's inability to collaborate and communicate with his fellow TVA board members was due to a combination of his poor skills as a politician and his growing sense of righteousness that made the actions of others—particularly David Lilienthal—seem like betrayals. The flurry of the New Deal and the demands of the Great Depression pushed Morgan the engineer into a political realm, where he appeared outdated, out-of-touch, and impractical.

After TVA, Morgan emerged as an engineering consultant with a strong message of regional and social planning. He supplied advice to many nations, and his private engineering practice completed projects across the United States. Morgan's work with the Seneca Indian Nation represented his last significant engineering consultation. Although removed from a drafting table for many years, Morgan capitalized on the opportunity to discredit one of his old foes, the U.S. Army Corps of Engineers. His brief return to the spotlight did not stop the building of the Kinzua Dam, but it demonstrated Morgan's ability to effectively argue for his engineering designs before a national and congressional audience, his devotion to eliminating waste, and his distaste for the political process.

Throughout his career, Morgan directed much of his intellectual curiosity and professional opinions to the printed page. Morgan wrote professional engineering essays and popular articles as a young man, but during his Antioch presidency, Morgan focused his philosophy into brief essays and addresses appearing in the serial publication *Antioch Notes.* Allegedly, Franklin and Eleanor Roosevelt first learned about Morgan's accomplishments in education because they read *Antioch Notes.* He wrote over one hundred essays on varied topics, including religion, government, international relations, values, eugenics, and developing a sense of purpose in life. Later, Morgan developed many of those topics into lengthier articles or books.

During the 1930s, Morgan used his notoriety to publish a number of articles about TVA in national publications. His books on engineering topics, such as the Miami Conservancy District and TVA, were also designed to promote and record Morgan's involvement and perspective. Perhaps his most unique written contributions were a series of books related to Edward Bellamy and the utopian thought of the late nineteenth century. The books were part history and part philosophy. Following Morgan's utopian writing phase, he published widely on the topics of community building, social values, and practical education.

Morgan wrote at a prolific pace and generated an impressive body of work. He wrote for a select popular and professional audience, never with the intention of creating bestsellers. In fact, many of his books were printed by the Antioch Press, a small industry that he founded. Morgan's engineering titles were dense, with mathematical details, charts, and figures, while his essays in *Antioch Notes* were basic and digestible. His style was direct and often written in the first person, the content was readable, and he had a specific audience in mind for each work. Morgan grew as a writer, and throughout this career he used the printed word to promote his initiatives and interests.

During his career, Morgan recorded significant accomplishments as an educator, which often ran parallel to his engineering work and community building initiatives. Similar to his rise within the engineering profession, Morgan became an educational expert without any formal training or even a college degree. His self-education informed the brand of practical education that he promoted through his years at Antioch and in numerous speeches, essays, and books on education.

In the late 1910s, Morgan organized several educational initiatives in the Miami River Valley, but his ascendancy to the presidency of Antioch College in 1919 symbolized his commitment to developing practical education programs and education reform. Morgan started strong at Antioch. He recruited top faculty, ambitious students, wealthy supporters, and board members who initially supported Morgan's leadership. His new educational order was based on practical education, work-study assignments in off-campus enterprises, and an open academic curriculum. Morgan later remarked that Antioch combined technical education and the liberal arts into something he called cultural education. He explained that, "The position which Antioch has taken is that *the aim of cultural education* should be to introduce the student to all the major fields of human interest and concern, so that he can read and think and act appropriately in every field."[21]

Within a few years, Morgan reorganized the school, improved the physical plant, and attracted national attention. As the school thrived, Morgan grew disenchanted with the experiment and even demanded to dismantle what he had created. Part of his dissatisfaction was his own isolation from the Antioch community. By the end of the 1920s, his dictatorial style of leadership, his inability to compromise, and his sense of rightness isolated him from the students, faculty, and supporters. By the early 1930s, Morgan longed for a new challenge and an exit from the rigors of being a college president. His opportunity to lead TVA was fortuitous. When he departed for TVA, Morgan left behind a much more stable institution, which would most likely have closed in the early 1920s without his direction.

Following Morgan's Antioch tenure, he did not formally return to a college or university as an employee or as an appointed leader. Instead, he focused his thoughts on educational practice and leadership into a variety of speeches, articles, and books. He also became an educational consultant for small communities. Morgan succeeded as an educational philosopher, arguing for student-centered education and practical experience over traditional rote approaches to teaching. Even if he did not invent work-study as an educational concept, his program at Antioch provided students with new ways to gain real-world experience. Morgan's tenure at Antioch was overshadowed by his administrative style, an inability to compromise, and his tendency to isolate himself. Unlike a private business with employees, colleges or universities have a different workforce with more varied objectives. The engineers and work crews who worked for Morgan in the 1910s were not the same as the academic faculty and the inquisitive students in Yellow Springs. Morgan's inability to connect with many of his constituents at Antioch led to disappointment and his desire to return to engineering.

Morgan's work as an engineer and educator contributed to experiments with community building. As a young professional and Progressive Era reformer, he took great interest in improving society by building small self-sustaining communities. His first real community building experience came with the labor camps of the Miami Conservancy District. Morgan went far beyond the traditional designs of temporary labor camps with the hope that the villages would become permanent. He started with the same formula when he planned the town of Norris, Tennessee, and greatly expanded his designs. Even though Antioch College was an existing community when Morgan arrived in Yellow Springs in 1919, he literally transformed the campus. He viewed the work at Antioch the same way that he viewed a dam project and the nearby worker villages, saying in 1924 that, "Antioch is an engineering job. While we rejoice in what we have done, it is but a promise, a suggestion of what can be."[22]

In the postwar period, Morgan wrote and spoke mostly about the importance of the small community and how to achieve a better society through community planning. His rhetoric resonated beyond the United States, especially in third world countries where colonialism had ended and where there was great potential for democracy and rebuilding societies. The challenge, however, was great, and Morgan acknowledged the difficult work, saying: "The work of community building is slow, arduous, and sometimes drearily parsimonious of emotional satisfactions. To one who has lived in the self-hypnotic world of reform, dreams of grandeur, the day-by-day and year-by-year work of creative living in a small community may seem painfully unrewarding. Yet it is there society is made. The great reformer cannot succeed except where the long hard work of community building had preceded, and has created a soil in which his seed can grow. But when the slow hard work had been done and the great community had come into being, the gates of hell cannot prevail against it."[23]

Morgan's community building projects in North Carolina, India, and elsewhere included the necessary infrastructure to provide the inhabitants with modern comforts. But more than just homes, streets, and electricity, Morgan's small communities were about people. He wanted to populate his communities with people who possessed strong character, morality, and ethics—traits that he wanted to transfer to future generations. At several points in his career, Morgan called for the creation of ethical codes to guide and govern the members of his small communities. However, that suggestion usually resulted in significant opposition from the people most affected. Such suggestions indicated that Morgan took a paternalistic view of people in his communities, workers on his engineering projects, and the students and faculty on his campus. Morgan also recommended that small industries could keep communities self-sufficient, economically viable, and provide practical education to youth. That educational component, as first demonstrated at Antioch, was the necessary key to unlock the potential of each community. Some of these small industries succeeded, but few, if any, were capable of supporting the needs of all members of the community.

Throughout his career, Morgan founded many communities and local industries. However, his greatest weakness as a community builder was that he seldom remained an active member or supporter of his own initiatives. In many ways, his primary focus was founding a school, establishing a program, or building a community, and once the initial phase was completed, he became a distant advocate. His inability to allow others to develop their own ideas, which might in fact conflict with his ideas, was another reason for his distance from his own successes. This trend was also apparent in other areas of Morgan's career, especially his comparatively brief stints as leader at Antioch in the 1920s and with the Tennessee Valley Authority in the 1930s.

Throughout his life, Morgan dabbled in many things, with mixed results. He was a successful engineer, a poor politician, an often mediocre administrator, a social planner, a community builder, an educator with limited formal education, and a writer. Finally, he was a person with common flaws. He succeeded in some areas; he failed in others. Remembered by most for his TVA tenure, he quietly recorded significant accomplishments in the postwar years as a philosopher, consultant, and global planner.

Despite limited scholarly and popular recognition for Morgan's contributions, he continues to have modern day relevance. Morgan's call for a more enlightened society through individual character development, small community networks, focus on the family, peace and cooperation, and hands-on education fits well into modern day discussions about twenty-first century challenges. Similar to Edward Bellamy, Morgan's early predications for the future may not have come to fruition. But in fact, during the twentieth century, advances in technology, science, and communication far eclipsed what Morgan and Bellamy once imagined.

A dreamer, a visionary, and a designer, Morgan's approach to organizing society revolved around a unique vision that was firmly grounded in the past. With a reform agenda from the late nineteenth century, Morgan was clearly a man of a former time. His vision went far beyond the TVA dams and small communities that Morgan designed and constructed. Instead, Morgan's purpose was to build a more enlightened society, one individual at a time. However, his vision of gradual change clashed with a lengthy and fast moving period of change.

Arthur Morgan was much more than an early leader of the Tennessee Valley Authority. Instead he represented a complex reformer with a unique social vision to build a better world. His rigid adherence to that vision often undercut his own successes. Morgan's accomplishments remain notable and relevant, even if most of them remain hidden underneath the surface of history. More importantly, Morgan's vision offers significant insights into the motivations, influences, and results of reformers of the early twentieth century. Unlike his contemporaries, he carried forward the reform spirit of the Progressive Era and his unique vision for society into a later period of unprecedented change in American history.

Selected Bibliography

MANUSCRIPT COLLECTIONS, PAPERS, AND GOVERNMENT RECORDS

Florida

University of Florida, Gainesville, P. K. Yonge Library of Florida History, Special Collections
    Arthur E. Morgan Collection

Georgia

National Archives and Records Administration—Southeast Region (Atlanta)
    Record Group 8, Records of the Bureau of Agricultural Engineering
    Record Group 142, Records of the Tennessee Valley Authority

Maryland

National Archives at College Park
    Record Group 8, Records of the Bureau of Agricultural Engineering
    Record Group 16, Records of the Office of the Secretary of Agriculture

Massachusetts

Houghton Library, Harvard University
    Arthur Ernest Morgan Papers Concerning Edward Bellamy, 1912–1944

New Jersey

Seeley G. Mudd Manuscript Library, Princeton University
    David E. Lilienthal Papers

New York

Franklin D. Roosevelt Library and Museum, Hyde Park
    President's Official Files
    President's Personal Files

Ohio

Antioch College, Yellow Springs
    Antioch College Archives
    Arthur E. Morgan Papers
    Ernest Morgan Papers

Miami Conservancy District, Dayton
Employee Records

The Ohio State University, Columbus
William Oxley Thompson Papers

Wright State University, Dayton
Miami Conservancy District Records, 1897–1980

Pennsylvania

Allegheny College, Meadville
Ida M. Tarbell Collection, 1890–1944

Tennessee

University of Tennessee, Knoxville, Special Collections Library
Howard A. Bridgman Diary, 1936
Harry A. Curtis Papers
Harcourt Morgan Papers

Tennessee State Library and Archives, Nashville
Jo Conn Guild Collection

Tennessee Valley Authority, Knoxville
Corporate Library
Office of General Counsel

COURT CASES

Ashwander, et al., v. Tennessee Valley Authority, et al. U.S. Supreme Court. 297 U.S. 288. 1936.

Condemnation Case v. C. A. Harris, et al. 1937.

Morgan v. Tennessee Valley Authority, et al. U.S. Supreme Court. 312 U.S. 701. 1938.

Morgan v. Tennessee Valley Authority, et al. U.S. Circuit Court of Appeals. 115 Fed. 2d. 990. 1940.

Morgan v. Tennessee Valley Authority, et al. U.S. District Court. 28 Supp. 732. 1939.

Seneca Nation of Indians v. Wilber M. Brucker. District of Columbia, District Court. 1958.

Tennessee Electric Power Company v. TVA 306 U.S. 118. 1939.

Tennessee Electric Power Company, et al., v. Tennessee Valley Authority, et al. U.S. District Court, 228. 1936.

Tennessee Electric Power Company, et al., v. Tennessee Valley Authority, et al. U.S. Supreme Court 27. 1938.

Tennessee Valley Authority v. Ashwander, et al. U.S. Circuit Court of Appeals. 78 F.2d 578. 1935.

Tennessee Valley Authority, et al., v. The Tennessee Electric Power Company, et al. U.S. Circuit Court of Appeals 7606. 1937.

GOVERNMENT DOCUMENTS

Statutes at Large. 1887, 1898, 1904, 1907. Washington, D.C.: Government Printing Office.

Tennessee Valley Authority. *The Norris Project: A Comprehensive Report on the Planning, Design, Construction, and Initial Operations of the Tennessee Valley Authority's First Water Control System.* Technical report no. 1. Washington, D.C.: Government Printing Office, 1940.

———. *TVA Employee Relationship Policy 1935.* Knoxville: TVA, 1935.

U.S. Congress. *Hearings Before the Joint Committee on the Investigation of the Tennessee Valley Authority.* 14 parts. Washington, D.C.: Government Printing Office, 1939.

———. *Investigation of the Tennessee Valley Authority: Report of the Joint Committee on the Investigation of the Tennessee Valley Authority.* Washington, D.C.: Government Printing Office, 1939.

U.S. Department of Agriculture. *Annual Reports of the Department of Agriculture.* 1899, 1900, 1902, 1904, 1907. Washington, D.C.: Government Printing Office.

———. *Experiment Station Record, 1910.* Washington, D.C.: Government Printing Office, 1910.

———. *Irrigation and Drainage Investigations of the Office of Experimental Stations.* Washington, D.C.: Government Printing Office, 1904.

U.S. House. *Everglades of Florida, Hearings Before the Committee on Expenditures in the Department of Agriculture.* 42 parts. Washington, D.C.: Government Printing Office, 1912.

———. *Expenditures in the Department of Agriculture.* 62nd Cong., 2nd sess., 1912. Misc. Repts. 1207, Serial 6133. Washington, D.C.: Government Printing Office, 1912.

U.S. President. *Removal of a Member of the Tennessee Valley Authority.* Washington, D.C.: Government Printing Office, 1938.

U.S. Senate. *Everglades of Florida: Acts, Reports, and Other Papers, State and National, Relating to the Everglades of the State of Florida and Their Reclamation.* Washington, D.C.: Government Printing Office, 1911.

MEMOIRS AND OTHER PRIMARY SOURCES

After a Year: Moraine Park School, 1917–1918. Dayton: Moraine Park School, 1918.

Alger, William R. *The Solitudes of Nature and of Man: Or, the Loneliness of Human Life.* Boston: Roberts Brothers, 1867.

American Eugenics Society. *American Eugenics, Proceedings of the Annual Meeting and Round Table Conferences of the American Eugenics Society, May 7, 1936.* New York: American Eugenics Society, 1936.

———. *A Eugenics Program for the United States.* New York: American Eugenics Society, ca. 1935.

Auger, Tracy B. "The Planning of the Town of Norris." *American Architect* 148 (April 1936): 19–26.

Barrows, John Henry ed., *The World's Parliament of Religions: An Illustrated and Popular Story of the World's First Parliament of Religions, Held in Chicago in Connection with the Columbian Exposition of 1893.* 2 vols. Chicago: The Parliament Publishing Company, 1893.

Bebel, August. *Woman and Socialism.* 1879. English translation, New York: Socialist Literature Company, 1910.

Bellamy, Charles. *The Breton Mills: A Romance.* New York: G. P. Putnam's Sons, 1880.

———. *The Way Out: Suggestions for Social Reform.* New York: G. P. Putnam's Sons, 1884.

Bellamy, Edward. *Equality.* New York: D. Appleton and Company, 1897.

———. "How I Came to Write 'Looking Backward.'" *The Nationalist* 1 (May 1889): 1–4.

———. "How I Wrote 'Looking Backward.'" *Ladies Home Journal* 2 (April 1894): 2.

———. *Looking Backward, 2000–1887.* Boston: Ticknor and Company, 1888. Reprint, New York: Oxford University Press, 2007.

———. "Looking Forward." *The Nationalist* 2 (December 1889): 1–4.

———. *The Religion of Solidarity.* Yellow Springs: Antioch Bookplate Company, 1940.

Bellamy, Joseph. *The Works of Joseph Bellamy, D.D., First Pastor of the Church in Bethlehem, Conn., With a Memoir of His Life and Character.* 2 vols. Boston: Doctrinal Tract and Book Company, 1853.

Boyd, Alan W. "The Tennessee Valley Litigation." *Indiana Law Journal* 11 (October 1935): 368–75.

Brownell, Baker, and Frank Lloyd Wright. *Architecture and Modern Life.* New York: Harper and Brothers, 1937.

Cabet, Etienne. *Voyage en Icarie.* Paris, 1848.

"Churchless Norris." *The Christian Century* 51 (November 14, 1934): 1448–49.

Clapp, Gordon R. *The TVA: An Approach to the Development of a Region.* Chicago: University of Chicago Press, 1955.

Commonwealth and Southern Corporation. *The Commonwealth and Southern Corporation and Its Subsidiary Companies, A Public Utility Holding Company Group, Outline of History and Development.* New York: Commonwealth and Southern Corporation, 1935.

Complete Presidential Press Conferences of Franklin D. Roosevelt. 25 vols. New York: DeCapo Press, 1972.

Cox, James M. *Journey Through My Years.* New York: Simon And Schuster, 1946.

Darwin, Charles. *The Formation of Vegetable Mould, Through the Action of Worms, with Observations on their Habits.* London: J. Murray, 1881.

———. *On the Origin of Species.* London: J. Murray, 1859.

Dewey, John. "Bellamy's Utopia." *Common Sense* 3 (April 1934): 6–7.

Draper, Earle S. "The New Town of Norris, Tennessee." *The American City* 48 (December 1933): 67–68.

———. "The TVA Town of Norris, Tennessee." *American Planning and Civic Annual* 5 (1934): 208–9.

———. "TVA's Yardstick for Housing." *The Architectural Forum* 63 (September 1935): 162–70.

Draper, W. *The Conflict Between Religion and Science.* New York: D. Appleton and Company, 1875.

Drummond, Henry. *The Ascent of Man.* New York: James Pott and Company, 1894.

Enforced Peace: Proceedings of the First Annual National Assemblage of the League to Enforce Peace, Washington, May 26–27, 1916. New York: League to Enforce Peace, 1916.

Farley, James A. *Behind the Ballots: The Personal History of a Politician.* New York: Harcourt, Brace and Company, 1938.

Gittleman, David. "A Yankee's Way to Utopia (On the 50th Anniversary of Edward Bellamy's 'Looking Backward')." *Unity* 116 (February 3, 1936): 206–9.

Grant, Madison. *The Passing of the Great Race: Or the Racial Basis of European History.* New York: Charles Scribner's Sons, 1916.

Gronlund, Laurence. *The Cooperative Commonwealth: In Its Outlines An Exposition of Modern Socialism.* Boston: Lee and Shepard, 1884.

A Handbook of American Private Schools, 1920. Boston: Porter E. Sargent, 1920.

Hanna, Alfred Jackson, and Kathyrn Abbey Hanna. *Lake Okeechobee: Wellspring of the Everglades.* Indianapolis: Bobbs-Merrill Company, 1948.

Henderson, Charles Hanford. *Education and the Larger Life.* New York: Houghton Mifflin Company, 1902.

Hobart, Nathaniel. *Life of Emanuel Swedenborg: With Some Account of His Writings, Together with a Brief Notice of the Rise and Progress of the New Church.* Boston: Allen and Goddard, 1831.

Hover, John C., Joseph D. Barnes, et al., eds. *Memoirs of the Miami Valley.* 3 vols. Chicago: Robert O. Law Company, 1919.

Ickes, Harold L. *The Secret Diary of Harold Ickes.* 3 vols. New York: Simon and Schuster, 1953–1955.

The Industrial Commission of Ohio. *Preliminary Survey of Labor Camps in Ohio.* Columbus: The Industrial Commission of Ohio, 1917.

Johnson, Rossiter, ed., *A History of the World's Columbian Exposition Held in Chicago in 1893.* 4 vols. New York: D. Appleton and Company, 1898.

Kahoe, Walter. *Arthur Morgan: A Biography and Memoir.* Moylan, Pa.: The Whimsie Press, 1977.

Lilienthal, David E. *The Journals of David E. Lilienthal.* 7 vols. New York: Harper and Row, 1964–1983.

———. *TVA: Democracy on the March.* New York: Harper and Brothers, 1944.

Macnie, John. *The Diothas, Or a Far Look Ahead.* New York: G. P. Putnam's Sons, 1883.

Mitchell, Jonathan. "Utopia—Tennessee Valley Style." *The New Republic* 76 (October 18, 1933): 272–74.

Mitchell, William B. "St. Cloud in the Territorial Period." In *Collection of the Minnesota Historical Society,* Volume 12. St. Paul: Minnesota Historical Society, 1908.

Morgan, Arthur E. "The Antioch Plan: Training for Administration and Proprietorship at a Small College." *Engineering News Record* 86 (January 20, 1921): 108–11.

———. "Building Up an Engineering Organization—With Special Reference to the Selection of Men." *Engineering News Record* 79 (September 20, 1917): 552–53.

———. *A Business of My Own.* Yellow Springs, Ohio: Community Service, Inc. 1953.

———. "Community." *Antioch Notes* 28 (November 15, 1950).

———. "The Community: The Seed Bed of Society." *Atlantic Monthly* 169 (February 1942): 225–26.

———. *The Community of the Future and the Future of Community.* Yellow Springs, Ohio: Community Service, Inc., 1957.

———. *A Compendium of Antioch Notes.* Yellow Springs, Ohio: Kahoe and Company, 1930.

———. "The Conscientious Objector." *Antioch Notes* 18 (November 1, 1940).

———. *Dams and Other Disasters: A Century of the Army Corp of Engineers in Civil Works.* Boston: Porter Sargent, 1971.

———. "Does the Punishment Fit the Crime?" *Engineering News* 67 (February 22, 1912): 359–60.

———. "The Duty to Adventure." *Antioch Notes* 7 (January 15, 1930).

———. "Education: The Mastery of the Arts of Life." *Atlantic Monthly* 121 (March 1918): 337–46.

———. *Education for Engineers.* Yellow Springs, Ohio: Antioch Press, 1955.

———. *Edward Bellamy.* New York: Columbia University Press, 1944.

———. "Ethical Origins." *Antioch Notes* 7 (December 1, 1929).

———. "Ethics." *Antioch Notes* 7 (February 1, 1930).

———. *The Great Community.* Chicago, Ill.: Human Events Associates, 1946.

———. *Industries for Small Communities: With Cases from Yellow Springs.* Yellow Springs, Ohio: Community Service, Inc., 1953.

———. *It Can Be Done in Education.* Yellow Springs, Ohio: Community Service, Inc., 1962.

———. "Little Industry in the Community." *Journal of Educational Sociology* 27 (December 1953): 160–62.

———. *Log of the TVA.* New York: Survey Associates, Inc., 1936.

———. *The Long Road.* Washington, D.C.: The National Home Library Foundation, 1936.

———. *The Making of the TVA.* Buffalo: Prometheus Books, 1974.

———. *The Miami Conservancy District.* New York: McGraw Hill, Inc., 1951.

———. "The Miami Valley Flood-Protection Work." *Engineering News* 77 (January 11, 1917): 62–65.

———. "The Military Mind and Peacetime Training." *Progressive Education* 23 (October 1945): 28–31.

———. "Morality." *Antioch Notes* 4 (December 1, 1926).

———. "More Concerning Mr. Elliott's Dismissal: The Engineering Plans for Draining the Florida Everglades." *Engineering News* 67 (March 28, 1912): 601–2.

———. "New Light on Lincoln's Boyhood. *Atlantic Monthly* 125 (1920): 208–18.

———. "The Next Four Years in the TVA." *The New Republic* 89 (January 6, 1937): 290–94.

———. *Nowhere was Somewhere: How History Makes Utopias and How Utopias Make History.* Chapel Hill: University of North Carolina Press, 1946.

———. *Observations.* Yellow Springs, Ohio: Antioch Press, 1968.

———. *The Philosophy of Edward Bellamy.* New York: King's Crown Press, 1945.

———. *Plagiarism in Utopia: A Study of the Utopian Tradition With Special Reference to Edward Bellamy's Looking Backward.* Yellow Springs, Ohio: The author, 1944.

———. "A Policy for the Mississippi." *Annals of the American Academy of Political and Social Science* 135 (January 1928): 50–56.

———. *A Preliminary Report on the St. Francis Valley Drainage Project in Northeastern Arkansas.* Washington, D.C.: Government Printing Office, 1909.

———. "Public Ownership of Power." *Atlantic Monthly* 160 (September 1937): 339–46.

———. *Purpose and Circumstance.* Yellow Springs, Ohio: Kahoe and Company, 1928.

———. *Report of the Chief Engineer, Arthur Morgan: Submitting a Plan for the Protection of the District from Flood Damage.* 3 vols. Dayton: Miami Conservancy District, 1916.

———. *Report on the St. Francis Valley Drainage Project in Northeastern Arkansas.* Washington, D.C.: Government Printing Office, 1911.

———. *Search for Purpose.* London: C. A. Watts and Company, Ltd., 1957.

———. *The Seed Man: Or, Things in General.* Yellow Springs, Ohio: Antioch Press, 1932.

———. *The Small Community, Foundation of Democratic Life: What it is and How to Achieve it.* New York: Harper and Brothers, 1942.

———. "Social Methods of the Tennessee Valley Authority." *Journal of Educational Sociology* 8 (January 1935): 261–65.

———. "Sociology in the TVA." *American Sociological Review* 2 (April 1937): 157–65.

———. "The Tennessee Valley Authority." *The Scientific Monthly* 38 (January 1934): 64–72.

———. "A Time to Be Careful." *Antioch Notes* 22 (February 15, 1945).

———. "The Trouble With Utopia." *This Week, Magazine of the New York Herald,* November 28, 1948, 6–7, 30.

———. "Universal Compulsory Military Training." *Antioch Notes* 22 (January 15, 1945).

———. "Vitality and Formalism in Government." *Social Forces* 13 (October 1934): 1–6.

Morgan, Arthur, and S. H. McCrory. *Preliminary Report Upon the Drainage of the Lands Overflowed by the North and Middle Forks of the Forked Deer River and the Rutherford Fork of the Obion River in Gibson County, Tennessee.* Nashville: State Geological Survey, 1910.

Morgan, Ernest. *Arthur Morgan Remembered.* Yellow Springs, Ohio: Community Service, Inc., 1991.

———. *Dealing Creatively with Life: The Life Adventure of Ernest Morgan.* New York: Barclay House, 1999.

———, comp. "The Morgan Heritage, Early Letters from Arthur Morgan to his Son Ernest." Pamphlet, ca. 1990s.

Morgan, Lucy Griscom. *Finding His World: The Story of Arthur E. Morgan.* Yellow Springs, Ohio: Kahoe and Company.

———. *Pioneering Days at Antioch.* Yellow Springs, Ohio: Antioch Press, 1947.

Moraine Park School: A Statement of Policy, 1922–1923. Dayton: Moraine Park School, 1922.

Moutoux, John T. "The TVA Builds a Town." *The New Republic* 77 (January 31, 1934): 330–31.

Nationalist, Volume 1. 1889. Reprint, New York: Greenwood Reprint Corp., 1968.

The New Nation, Volume 1. 1891. Reprint, New York: Greenwood Reprint Corp., 1968.

Nordau, Max. *Degeneration.* Trans. from 2nd ed. of the German ed. 5th ed. New York: D. Appleton and Company, 1895.

Norris, George. *Fighting Liberal: The Autobiography of George W. Norris.* New York: MacMillan Company, 1945.

Owen, Marguerite. *The Tennessee Valley Authority.* New York: Praeger Publishers, 1973.

Owen, Robert. *The Book of the New Moral World.* New York: G. Vale, 1845.

Pestalozzi, Johann Heinrich. *Leonard and Gertrude.* Trans. Philadelphia: Robert Carr, 1801.

Phillips, C. N. *The Story of the Miami Conservancy District.* Dayton: Miami Conservancy District, 1922.

Poe, J. Charles. "The Morgan-Lilienthal Feud." *Nation* 143 (October 3, 1936): 385–86.

Pritchett, C. Herman. *The Tennessee Valley Authority: A Study in Public Administration.* Chapel Hill: University of North Carolina Press, 1943.

Richberg, Donald. *My Hero: The Indiscreet Memoirs of an Eventful but Unheroic Life.* New York: Putnam, 1954.

Rosenman, Samuel I., comp. *The Public Papers and Addresses of Franklin D. Roosevelt.* 13 vols. New York: Random House, 1938–1950.

Shipley, Mrs. John B. "Bebel's Bricks or Bellamy's?" *Liberty* 7 (June 21, 1890): 3.

Slutz, Frank. *Moraine Park School, an Educational Laboratory.* Bulletin no. 5. Washington, D.C.: Progressive Education Association, April 1912.

Still, Andrew Taylor. *Autobiography of Andrew T. Still.* 1897. Reprint, New York: Arno Press, 1972.

Tarbell, Ida M. "Morgan of Antioch: An Engineer's Great Contribution to the Training of Useful Americans." *Collier's* 69 (June 3, 1922): 7–8, 20–21, 23.

———. *The Nationalizing of Business, 1878–1898.* New York: The Macmillan Company, 1936.

———. "New Dealers of the 'Seventies: Henry George and Edward Bellamy." *Forum and Century* 92 (September 1934): 133–39.

Tennessee Electric Power Company. *A Compilation of Facts Regarding the Growth and Development of Tennessee With a Forecast of the Future Through the Utilization of the State's Most Valuable Natural Resource—Waterpower.* Chattanooga: The Tennessee Electric Power Company, 1925.

Tiffany, Francis B., comp. *General Statues of Minnesota, Supplement 1917.* St. Paul: West Publishing Company, 1918.

The WPA Guide to Minnesota. Reprint. St. Paul: Minnesota Historical Society, 1985.

Wright, James O. *Why Was Wright's Report Suppressed.* Tallahassee: T. J. Appleyard, 1911.

NEWSPAPERS AND OTHER PERIODICALS

The American Economic Review, 1946

The American Historical Review, 1946

The American Journal of Sociology, 1947

The Annals of the American Academy of Political and Social Science, 1946

Antioch College Bulletin, 1921, 1925

Antioch Notes, 1926–1950

The Antiochian, 1931

Business Weekly, 1934

Chattanooga News, 1933

Chicago Tribune, 1934

Christian Register, 1932

Columns, 2004

Congressional Record, 1911

Daily Texarkanian, 1912

Dayton Daily Herald, 1918

Dayton Daily Journal, 1918

Dayton Daily News, 1918

Dayton News, 1918

Engineering News, 1912–1920

Engineering News Record, 1917–1920

Hamilton Daily Journal, 1918

Journal of Forestry, 1945

The Journal of Philosophy, 1946

The Journal of Political Economy, 1947

Knoxville News Sentinel, 1936, 1938

Labor Review, 1918

Memphis Commercial Appeal, 1912

The Miami Conservancy Bulletin, 1918–1919

Middletown Daily Journal, 1918

Middletown Daily News-Signal, 1918

Mitraniketan Marg, 1966

The Nation, 1921, 1936, 1961

National Whirligig, 1936

New England Quarterly, 1941, 1946

The New Republic, 1921, 1922, 1933, 1934, 1937, 1964

New York Herald Tribune, 1945

New York Times, 1912, 1933–1939, 1945, 1946, 1975

The Outlook, 1926

Political Science Quarterly, 1945

Public Works, 1920

Rural Sociology, 1945

Seed World, 1948

Sidney Daily Journal, 1918

St. Cloud Times, 1956

Troy Daily News, 1918

Washington Post, 1933

The World's Work, 1921

SECONDARY SOURCES

Abrams, George H. J. *The Seneca People.* Phoenix: Indian Tribal Series, 1976.

Arnold, Joseph L. *The New Deal in the Suburbs: A History of the Greenbelt Town Program, 1935–1954.* Columbus: The Ohio State University Press, 1971.

Atkinson, Henry A. *Theodore Marburg: The Man and His Work.* New York: Morton Littman Printing Company, 1951.

Barde, Robert E. "Arthur E. Morgan, First Chairman of TVA." *Tennessee Historical Quarterly* 30 (September 1971): 299–314.

Barnard, Ellsworth. *Wendell Willkie: Fighter for Freedom.* Marquette: Northern Michigan University Press, 1966.

Barnes, Joseph. *Willkie: The Events He Was Part of, the Ideas He Fought For.* New York: Simon and Schuster, 1952.

Bartlett, Ruhl F. *The League to Enforce Peace.* Chapel Hill: University of North Carolina Press, 1944.

Becker, Carl M., and Patrick B. Nolan. *Keeping the Promise: A Pictorial of the Miami Conservancy District.* Dayton, Ohio: Landfall Press, 1988.

———. "They Gathered at the River: The Miami Conservancy District." *Timeline* 6 (October/November 1989): 34–47.

Bernstein, Irving. *The Lean Years: A History of the American Workers, 1920–1933.* Baltimore: Penguin, 1966.

Bertuca, David J., comp. *The World's Columbian Exposition: A Centennial Bibliographic Guide.* Westport, Conn.: Greenwood Press, 1996.

Biggers, Jeff. *From the Dusty Soil: The Story of Mitraniketan, Community Education and Development in Rural India.* Kerala, India: Mitraniketan Printers and Publishers, 1996.

Blake, Nelson Manfred. *Land into Water—Water into Land: A History of Water Management in Florida.* Tallahassee: University Presses of Florida, 1980.

Blanke, David. *The 1910s.* Westport, Conn.: Greenwood Press, 2002.

Blum, John Morton. *V Was For Victory: Politics and American Culture During World War II.* New York: Harcourt Brace Jovanovich, 1976.

Bowman, Sylvia E. *Edward Bellamy.* Boston: Twayne Publishers, 1986.

———. *The Year 2000: A Critical Biography of Edward Bellamy.* New York: Bookman Associates, 1953.

———, et al. *Edward Bellamy Abroad: An American Prophet's Influence.* New York: Twayne Publishers, 1962.

Brinkley, Alan. *The End of Reform: New Deal Liberalism in Recession and War.* New York: Alfred A. Knopf, 1995.

Bureau of the Census. *Historical Statistics of the United States: Colonial Times to 1970.* Washington, D.C: Government Printing Office, 1975.

Burg, David F. *Chicago's White City of 1893.* Lexington: The University Press of Kentucky, 1976.

Callahan, North. *TVA: Bridge Over Troubled Waters.* New York: A. S. Barnes and Company, 1980.

Cashman, Sean Dennis. *America in the Gilded Age: From the Death of Lincoln to the Rise of Theodore Roosevelt.* 2nd ed. New York: New York University Press, 1988.

Chadha, Yogesh. *Rediscovering Gandhi.* London: Century, 1997.

Chafe, William H. *The Unfinished Journey: America Since World War II.* New York: Oxford University Press, 1995.

Chambers, John Whiteclay, II. *The Tyranny of Change: America in the Progressive Era, 1900–1917.* New York: St. Martin's Press, 1980.

Chatfield, Charles. *The American Peace Movement: Ideals and Activism.* New York: Twayne Publishers, 1992.

Chitnis, Suma, and Philip G. Altbach, eds. *Higher Education Reform in India: Experience and Perspectives.* New Delhi, India: Sage Publications, 1993.

Clark, Burton R. *The Distinctive College: Antioch, Reed, and Swarthmore.* Chicago: Aldine Publishing Co., 1970.

Conkin, Paul. *Tomorrow a New World: The New Deal Community Program.* Ithaca: Cornell University Press, 1959.

Corwin, R. David. "Dilemma of the Iroquois." *Natural History* 6 (June–July 1967): 6–7, 60–66.

Cremin, Lawrence A. *The Transformation of the School: Progressivism in American Education, 1876–1957.* New York: Alfred A. Knopf, 1964.

Crichton, Judy. *America 1900: The Turning Point.* New York: Henry Holt and Company, 1998.

Crunden, Robert M. *Ministers of Reform: The Progressives' Achievement in American Civilization, 1889–1920.* New York: Basic Books, 1982.

Dalton, Dennis. *Mahatma Gandhi: Nonviolent Power in Action.* New York: Columbia University Press, 1993.

Davis, Kenneth S. *FDR: Into the Storm, 1937–1940.* New York: Random House, 1993.

Dictionary of American Biography, Supplement Four, 1946–1950. New York: Charles Scribner's Sons, 1974.

Doran, William A. "Early Hydroelectric Power in Tennessee." *Tennessee Historical Quarterly* 27 (Spring 1968): 72–82.

Dowdy, G. Wayne. *Mayor Crump Don't Like It: Machine Politics in Memphis.* Jackson: University Press of Mississippi, 2006.

Downs, Robert B. *Horace Mann: Champion of Public Schools.* New York: Twayne Publishers, Inc., 1974.

Drowne, Kathleen, and Patrick Huber. *The 1920s.* Westport, Conn.: Greenwood Press, 2004.

Droze, Wilmon Henry. *High Dams and Slack Waters: TVA Rebuilds a River.* Baton Rouge: Louisiana State University Press, 1965.

Dutta, Krishna, and Andrew Robinson. *Rabindranath Tagore: The Myriad-Minded Man.* London: Bloomsburg, 1995.

The Edward Bellamy Association of New York. New York: Edward Bellamy Association of New York, ca. late 1933.

Edward Bellamy Speaks Again! Articles—Public Addresses—Letters. Kansas City, Mo.: Peerage Press, 1937.

Edwards, Rebecca. *New Spirits: Americans in the Gilded Age, 1865–1905.* New York: Oxford University Press, 2006.

Edwardson, Mickie. "Three Chapters Concerning the Career of James Lawrence Fly at TVA (part of a proposed biography)." Unpublished manuscript, ca. 1990s.

Egan, Timothy. *The Worst Hard Times: The Untold Story of Those Who Survived the Great American Dust Bowl.* Boston: Houghton Mifflin Company, 2006.

The Egyptians Yearbook, 1982–1983. Memphis, Tenn.: The Egyptians, 1983.

Engs, Ruth Clifford. *The Eugenics Movement: An Encyclopedia* (Westport, Conn.: Greenwood Press, 2005.

Field, Gregory B. "'Electricity for All': The Electric Home and Farm Authority and the Politics of Mass Consumption, 1932–1935." *Business History Review* 64 (Spring 1990): 32–60.

Flanagan, Maureen A. *America Reformed: Progressives and Progressivisms, 1890s–1920s.* New York: Oxford University Press, 2007.

Franke, Richard W., and Barbara H. Chasin. *Kerala: Radical Reform as Development in an Indian State.* San Francisco, Calif.: Institute for Food and Development Policy, 1991.

Gaddis, John Lewis. *The Cold War: A New History.* New York: Penguin Press, 2005.

Gannon, Anthony B. "Vision or Obsession? Arthur E. Morgan and the Superdam." *Register of the Kentucky Historical Society* 97 (January 1999): 45–82.

Gardner, Howard. *Frames of Mind: The Theory of Multiple Intelligences.* New York: Basic Books, Inc., 1983.

———. *Multiple Intelligences: The Theory in Practice.* New York: Basic Books Inc., 1993.

Gelderman, Carol. *Henry Ford: The Wayward Capitalist.* New York: St. Martin's Press, 1989.

Goldberg, David J. *Discontented America: The United States in the 1920s.* Baltimore, Md.: The Johns Hopkins University Press, 1999.

Goldberg, Ronald Allen. *America in the Twenties.* Syracuse, N.Y.: Syracuse University Press, 2003.

Goodwyn, Lawrence. *The Populist Moment: A Short History of the Agrarian Revolt in America.* New York: Oxford University Press, 1978.

Gordon, John Steele. *An Empire of Wealth: The Epic History of American Economic Power.* New York: Harper Perennial, 2005.

Gosse, Philip. *The Pirates' Who's Who: Giving Particulars of the Lives and Deaths of the Pirates and Buccaneers.* Reprint. Glorieta, N.Mex.: Rio Grande Press, Inc., 1988.

Graham, Otis L., Jr. *An Encore for Reform: The Old Progressives and the New Deal.* New York: Oxford University Press, 1967.

Graham, Patricia Albjerg. *Progressive Education, From Arcady to Academe: A History of the Progressive Education Association, 1919–1955.* New York: Teachers College Press, 1967.

Grant, Nancy L. *TVA and Black Americans: Planning for the Status Quo.* Philadelphia: Temple University Press, 1990.

Gray, Aelred J. "The Maturing of a Planned New Town—Norris, Tennessee." *Tennessee Planner* 32 (1974): 1–25.

Gray, Aelred J., and David A. Johnson. *The TVA Regional Planning and Development Program: The Transformation of an Institution and Its Mission.* Burlington, Vt.: Ashgate Publishing Company, 2005.

Groh, George W. *The Black Migration: The Journey to Urban America.* New York: Weybright and Talley, 1972.

Halacy, D. S., Jr. *1936: The Picture Story of an Unforgettable Year.* New Rochelle, N.Y.: Arlington House Publishers, 1974.

Haller, Mark H. *Eugenics: Hereditarian Attitudes in American Thought.* New Brunswick, N.J.: Rutgers University Press, 1963.

Hartford, Ellis F. *Our Common Mooring.* Athens: University of Georgia Press, 1941.

Hauptman, Laurence M. *Conspiracy of Interests: Iroquois Dispossession and the Rise of New York State.* Syracuse, N.Y.: Syracuse University Press, 1999.

———. *The Historic Background to the Present Day Seneca Nation—Salamanca Lease Controversy: The First Hundred Years, 1851–1951.* Albany: State University of New York, 1985.

———. *The Iroquois Struggle for Survival: World War II to Red Power.* Syracuse, N.Y.: Syracuse University Press, 1986.

Hawley, Ellis W. *The Great War and the Search for a Modern Order, A History of the American People and Their Institutions, 1917–1933.* New York: St. Martin's Press, 1979.

Henderson, Richard B. *Maury Maverick: A Political Biography.* Austin: University of Texas Press, 1970.

Herr, Stephen R. *Connected Thoughts: A Reinterpretation of the Reorganization of Antioch College in the 1920s.* New York: University Press of America, Inc., 1997.

Hicks, George L. *Experimental Americans: Celo and Utopian Community in the Twentieth Century.* Urbana: University of Illinois Press, 2001.

Hobday, Victor C. *Sparks at the Grassroots: Municipal Distribution of TVA Electricity in Tennessee.* Knoxville: University of Tennessee Press, 1969.

Hofstadter, Richard. *The Age of Reform: From Bryan to FDR.* New York: Vintage Books, 1955.

Hubbard, Preston. *Origins of the TVA: The Muscle Shoals Controversy, 1920–1932.* New York: W.W. Norton and Company, 1961.

Hunt, John Gabriel, ed. *The Essential Franklin Delano Roosevelt.* New York: Gramercy Books, 1995.

Husain, S. Abid. *The Way of Gandhi and Nehru.* London: Asia Publishing House, 1959.

Jaycox, Faith. *The Progressive Era.* New York: Facts on File, 2005.

Josephy, Alvin M., Jr. "Cornplanter, Can You Swim?" *American Heritage* 20 (December 1968): 4–9, 106–110.

Kennedy, David M. *Freedom from Fear: The American People in Depression and War, 1929–1945.* New York: Oxford University Press, 1999.

Kent, Noel Jacob. *America in 1900.* Armonk, N.Y.: M. E. Sharpe, 2000.

Kevles, Daniel J. *In the Name of Eugenics: Genetics and the Uses of Human Heredity.* New York: Alfred A. Knopf, 1985.

King, Judson. *The Conservation Fight: From Theodore Roosevelt to the Tennessee Valley Authority.* Washington, D.C.: Public Affairs Press, 1959.

Klein, Philip S., and Ari Hoogenbom. *A History of Pennsylvania.* University Park: Pennsylvania State University Press, 1980.

Knapp, Joseph G. *The Advance of American Cooperative Enterprise, 1920–1945.* Danville, Ill.: Interstate Printers and Publishers, Inc., 1973.

Kuehl, Warren F. *Hamilton Holt: Journalist, Internationalist, Educator.* Gainesville: University of Florida Press, 1960.

Kyle, John H. *The Building of TVA: An Illustrated History.* Baton Rouge: Louisiana State University Press, 1958.

Kyvig, David E. *Daily Life in the United States, 1920–1939: Decades of Promise and Pain.* Westport, Conn.: Greenwood Press, 2002.

Lacey, Robert. *Ford: The Men and the Machine.* Boston: Little, Brown, and Company, 1986.

Lawson, Arthur. "Has the President an Inherent Power of Removal of His Non-Executive Appointees?" *Tennessee Law Review* 16 (April 1940): 259–90.

Laughlin, Henry A. "Ferris Greenslet." *Proceedings of the Massachusetts Historical Society.* Third Series, 72 (October 1957–December 1960), 379–84.

Layton, Edwin T., Jr. *The Revolt of the Engineers: Social Responsibility and the American Engineering Profession.* Cleveland: Case Western Reserve, 1971.

Leuba, Clarence J. *A Road to Creativity: Arthur Morgan, Engineer, Educator, Administrator.* North Quincy, Mass.: Christopher Publishing House, 1971.

Leuchtenburg, William E. *Franklin D. Roosevelt and the New Deal, 1932–1940.* New York: Harper and Row, 1963.

———. "Norris and the 'Seven Little TVAs.'" *Journal of Politics* 14 (August 1952): 418–41.

Lief, Alfred. *Democracy's Norris: The Biography of A Lonely Crusade.* New York: Stackpole Sons, 1939.

Link, Arthur S. *Woodrow Wilson and the Progressive Era, 1910–1917.* New York: Harper and Brothers, 1954.

Link, Arthur S., and Richard L. McCormick. *Progressivism.* Arlington Heights, Ill.: Harlan Davidson, 1983.

Lowitt, Richard. *George W. Norris: The Persistence of a Progressive, 1913–1933.* Urbana: University of Illinois Press, 1971.

———. *George W. Norris: The Triumph of a Progressive, 1933–1944.* Urbana: University of Illinois Press, 1978.

Lubove, Roy, ed. *Pittsburgh.* New York: Franklin Watts, 1976.

Majors, William R. "Gordon Browning and Tennessee Politics." *Tennessee Historical Quarterly* 28 (Spring 1969): 57–69.

Maney, Patrick J. *The Roosevelt Presence: A Biography of Franklin Delano Roosevelt.* New York: Twayne Publishers, 1992.

McCraw, Thomas K. *Morgan Versus Lilienthal: The Feud Within the TVA.* Chicago, Ill.: Loyola University Press, 1970.

———. *TVA and the Power Fight: 1933–1939.* New York: J. B. Lippincott Co., 1971.

McDonald, Michael J., and John Muldowny. *TVA and the Dispossessed: The Resettlement of Population in the Norris Dam Area.* Knoxville: University of Tennessee Press, 1982.

McElvaine, Robert S. *The Great Depression: America, 1929–1941.* New York: Times Books, 1993.

McGerr, Michael. *A Fierce Discontent: The Rise and Fall of the Progressive Movement in America, 1870–1920.* New York: Free Press, 2003.

McKenna, Marian C. *Franklin Roosevelt and the Great Constitutional War: The Court Packing Crisis of 1937.* New York: Fordham University Press, 2002.

Mehon, A. Sreedhara. *A Survey of Kerala History.* Kottayam, India: Sahitya Pravarthaka Co-operative Society, 1967.

Messerli, Jonathan. *Horace Mann: A Biography.* New York: Alfred A. Knopf, 1972.

Miller, Nathan. *New World Coming: The 1920s and the Making of Modern America.* New York: Scribner, 2003.

Miller, Timothy. *The Quest for Utopia in Twentieth Century America.* 2 vols. Syracuse, N.Y.: Syracuse University Press, 1998.

Miller, William D. *Memphis During the Progressive Era, 1900–1917.* Memphis, Tenn.: Memphis State University Press, 1957.

———. *Mr. Crump of Memphis.* Baton Rouge: Louisiana State University Press, 1964.

Minton, John Dean. *The New Deal in Tennessee, 1932–1938.* New York: Garland Publishing, Inc., 1979.

Mooney, Jack. *Printers in Appalachia: The International Printing Pressmen and Assistants' Union of North America, 1907–1967.* Bowling Green, Ohio: Bowling Green State University Popular Press, 1993.

Mukerji, S. N. *History of Education in India (modern period).* Fifth ed. Baroda, India: Acharya Book Depot, 1966.

Nandy, Ashis. *The Illegitimacy of Nationalism: Rabindranath Tagore and the Politics of Self.* Oxford, Eng.: Oxford University Press, 1994.

The National Cyclopaedia of American Biography. 63 vols. New York: James T. White and Company, 1892–1984.

Neuberg, Richard L., and Stephen B. Khan. *Integrity: The Life of George W. Norris.* New York: Vanguard Press, 1937.

Neuse, Stephen M. *David Lilienthal: The Journey of an American Liberal.* Knoxville: University of Tennessee Press, 1996.

Newman, George Charles. *Leadership and the Politics of Innovative Change: Antioch College Under Arthur E. Morgan.* Toledo, Ohio: University of Toledo, 1981.

Noggle, Burl. *Into the Twenties: The United State from Armistice to Normalcy.* Urbana: University of Illinois Press, 1974.

Nossiter, T. J. *Communism in Kerala: A Study in Political Adaptation.* Berkeley: University of California Press, 1982.

Nurick, Aaron J. *Participation in Organizational Change: The TVA Experience.* New York: Praeger Publishers, 1985.

Ordover, Nancy. *American Eugenics: Race, Queer Anatomy, and the Science of Nationalism.* Minneapolis: University of Minnesota Press, 2003.

Painter, Nell Irvin. *Standing at Armageddon: The United States, 1877–1919.* New York: W. W. Norton and Company, 1987.

Parayil, Govindan, ed. *Kerala: The Development Experience, Reflections on Sustainability and Replicability.* New York: St. Martin's Press, 2000.

Parrish, Michael E. *Anxious Decades: American in Prosperity and Depression, 1920–1941.* New York: W. W. Norton, 1992.

Patai, Daphne, ed. *Looking Backward, 1988–1888: Essays on Edward Bellamy.* Amherst: University of Massachusetts Press, 1988.

Paul, Charles H. *A Brief History of the Engineers' Club of Dayton.* Dayton: National Cash Register Company, 1942.

Pickens, Donald K. *Eugenics and the Progressives.* Nashville, Tenn.: Vanderbilt University Press, 1968.

Pickles, George W. *Drainage and Flood-Control Engineering.* New York: McGraw Hill, 1941.

Pritchard, Erin E., ed. *TVA Archaeology: Seventy-Five Years of Prehistoric Site Research.* Knoxville: University of Tennessee Press, 2009.

Pritchett, C. Herman. *The Roosevelt Court: A Study in Judicial Politics and Values, 1937–1947.* Chicago: Quadrangle, 1948.

Proctor, Samuel. *Napoleon Bonaparte Broward: Florida's Fighting Democrat.* Gainesville: University of Florida Press, 1950.

Purcell, Aaron D. "Collaboration and the Small Community: Arthur Morgan and the Mitraniketan Project in Kerala." *The Historian* 65 (Spring 2003): 641–64.

———. "The Engineering of Forever: Arthur E. Morgan, the Seneca Indians, and the Kinzua Dam." *New York History* 78 (July 1997): 309–36.

———. "Plumb Lines, Politics, and Projections: The Florida Everglades and the Wright Report Controversy." *Florida Historical Quarterly* 80 (Fall 2001): 161–97.

———. "Power to the People: David Lilienthal Founds TVA's Electric Power Policy, 1933." *The Journal of East Tennessee History* 70 (1998): 90–108.

———. "Pursuing Peace: Arthur Morgan and Ohio's League to Enforce Peace, 1915–1920" *Ohio History* 109 (Winter–Spring 2000): 24–46.

———. "Reclaiming Lost Ground: Arthur Morgan and the Miami Conservancy District Labor Camps." *The Historian* 64 (Winter 2002): 367–90.

———. "Struggle Within, Struggle Without: The TEPCO Case and the Tennessee Valley Authority, 1936–1939." *Tennessee Historical Quarterly* 61 (Fall 2002): 194–210.

———. "Suppressed Currents: The 'Fool Report' and the Early Tennessee Valley Authority." *The Journal of East Tennessee History* 74 (2002): 69–83.

———. "Undermining the TVA: George Berry, David Lilienthal, and Arthur Morgan." *Tennessee Historical Quarterly* 57 (Fall 1998): 168–89.

———. *White Collar Radicals: TVA's Knoxville Fifteen, the New Deal, and the McCarthy Era.* Knoxville: University of Tennessee Press, 2009.

Rauchway, Eric. *Murdering McKinley: The Making of Theodore Roosevelt's America.* New York: Hill and Wang, 2003.

Read, Hadley. *Partners With India: Building Agricultural Universities.* Urbana: University of Illinois, 1974.

Rorty, James. "TVA's H. A. Morgan." *The Commonweal* 48 (June 18, 1948): 226–30.

Rosier, Paul C. "Dam Building and Treaty Breaking: The Kinzua Dam Controversy, 1936–1958." *The Pennsylvania Magazine of History and Biography* 69 (October 1995): 345–68.

Schlesinger, Arthur M., Jr. *The Age of Roosevelt.* 3 vols. Boston: Houghton Mifflin Company, 1957–1960.

Sealander, Judith. *Grand Plans: Business Progressivism and Social Change in Ohio's Miami Valley, 1890–1929.* Lexington: The University Press of Kentucky, 1988.

Selden, Steven. *Inheriting Shame: The Story of Eugenics and Racism in America.* New York: Teachers College Press, 1999.

Selznick, Philip. *TVA and the Grass Roots: A Study in the Sociology of Formal Organization.* Berkley: University of California Press, 1949.

Singh, Amrik, and Philip G. Altbach, eds. *The Higher Learning in India.* Delhi, India: Vikas Publishing House, 1974.

Smith, Ronald M. "The Politics of Pittsburgh Flood Control, 1936–1960." *Pennsylvania History* 44 (January 1977): 3–24.

States of Our Union: Kerala. Delhi, India: Ministry of Information and Broadcasting, 1968.

Stevenson, Elizabeth. *Babbitts and Bohemians: The American 1920s.* New York: Macmillan, 1967.

Swidler, Joseph C., and Robert H. Marquis. "TVA in Court: A Study of TVA's Constitutional Litigation." *Iowa Law Review* 32 (January 1947): 296–338.

Talbert, Roy, Jr. "Arthur E. Morgan's Social Philosophy and the Tennessee Valley Authority." East Tennessee Historical Society's *Publications* 41 (1969): 86–99.

———. *FDR's Utopian: Arthur Morgan of the TVA.* Jackson: University of Mississippi Press, 1987.

———, ed. "Arthur E. Morgan's Ethical Code for the Tennessee Valley Authority." East Tennessee Historical Society's *Publications* 40 (1968): 119–27.

Taylor, Walter. "The Treaty We Broke." *Nation* 193 (September 2, 1961): 120–21.

Thomas, John L. *Alternative America: Henry George, Edward Bellamy, Henry Demarest Lloyd and the Adversary Tradition.* Cambridge, Mass.: Harvard University Press, 1983.

Traxel, David. *1898: The Birth of the American Century.* New York: Alfred A. Knopf, 1998.

Vohra, Ranbir. *The Making of India: A Historical Survey.* Second ed. Armonk, N.Y.: M. E. Sharpe, 2001.

Wallace, Louis D., ed. *Makers of Millions: Not for Themselves, But For You.* Nashville: Tennessee Department of Agriculture, 1951.

Weibe, Robert. *The Search for Order, 1877–1920.* Westport, Conn.: Greenwood Press, 1967.

Wehle, Louis B. *Hidden Threads of History: Wilson Through Roosevelt.* New York: The MacMillan Company, 1953.

White, Ronald C., Jr., and C. Howard Hopkins. *The Social Gospel: Religion and Reform in Changing America.* Philadelphia: Temple University Press, 1976.

Whitman, Willson. *David Lilienthal: Public Servant in a Power Age.* New York: Henry Holt and Company, 1948.

Why They Came: The Story of Yellow Springs, Ohio. Yellow Springs, Ohio: Yellow Springs Centennial Committee, 1956.

Woodcock, George. *Kerala: A Portrait of the Malabar Coast.* London: Faber, 1967.

Young, William H., and Nancy K. Young. *The 1930s.* Westport, Conn.: Greenwood Press, 2002.

Zucker, Norman L. *George W. Norris: Gentle Knight of American Democracy.* Urbana: University of Illinois Press, 1966.

PAPERS, THESES, AND DISSERTATIONS

Bryant, John. "Man With a Dream." Term Paper, Antioch College, 1961.

Cigliano, Jan Elizabeth. "Norris, Tennessee: America's Forgotten TVA New Town." Master's thesis, George Washington University, 1982.

Coelho, Anthony. "David Eli Lilienthal: Pragmatic Liberal at the Crossroads." Term Paper, Brown University, 1973.

Creiger, Sharon E. "Lake of Perfidy." Term Paper, Antioch University, Putney, Vt., 1967.

Gietschier, Steven Philip. "William Oxley Thompson and the League to Enforce Peace in Ohio." PhD diss., The Ohio State University, 1971.

Lee, Allen Burridge. "The Kinzua Dam Project: A Case Study of the Politics of Flood Control." PhD diss., University of Pittsburgh, 1959.

Naylor, Richard Allen. "Arthur E. Morgan's Philosophy of Work-Study at Antioch College: A Progressive Reformer's Response to Reconstructing the Relationship Between Work and Education in the Community." PhD diss., State University of New York at Albany, 1987.

Purcell, Aaron D. "Building Dams, Burning Bridges: Conflicting Philosophies on the Tennessee Valley Authority Board, 1933–1939." Master's thesis, University of Louisville, 1996.

Talbert, Roy Jr. "Beyond Pragmaticism: The Story of Arthur E. Morgan." PhD diss., Vanderbilt University, 1971.

———. "The Human Engineer: Arthur E. Morgan and the Launching of the Tennessee Valley Authority." Master's thesis, Vanderbilt University, 1967.

Wong, Soo Mun Theresa. "Making the Mekong: Nature, Region, Postcoloniality." PhD diss., The Ohio State University, 2010.

FILMS, INTERNET RESOURCES, AND OTHER MEDIA

America 1900. Produced by David Grubin, written by Judy Crichton and David Grubin. David Grubin Productions, Inc. Film for *The American Experience,* WGBH, 1998.

"Arthur Morgan Institute for Community Solutions," at http://www.communitysolution.org/about.html.

"Dance Heritage Coalition," at http://danceheritage.org.

I See A Village: The Arthur Morgan Story. Richard Kaplan. Richard Kaplan Productions, 1968.

"Jacob's Pillow Dance School and Festival," at http://www.jacobspillow.org/festival/index.asp;

"Ida M. Tarbell Collection, 1890–1944," at https://dspace.allegheny.edu/handle/10456/13708

"Tennessee Valley Authority Act," at http://www.tva.gov/abouttva/pdf/TVA_Act.pdf

"Today." NBC television. December 28, 1961.

Notes

INTRODUCTION

1. Donald S. Harrington, "The Greatest American of Our Time: Arthur E. Morgan—Human Engineer," December 14, 1975, 1–2, 18, Arthur E. Morgan Papers, Antiochiana, Antioch College, Yellow Springs, Ohio (hereafter cited as Morgan Papers). Researchers interested in locating cited material in the Morgan Papers should be aware that boxes and folders are not numbered sequentially. Instead, the Morgan Papers are arranged by logical series (either by chronological periods in Morgan's life, subjects or projects, or formats), various sub-series, and often lengthy folder titles, which were too elaborate and lengthy to include in the notes. The unpublished finding aid to the Morgan Papers is available at Antiochiania, Antioch College.

2. *Complete Presidential Press Conferences of Franklin D. Roosevelt* (New York: DeCapo Press, 1972), 1:288; *New York Times,* May 20, 1933.

3. *New York Times,* November 17, 1975; Gerald R. Ford to Ernest Morgan, November 18, 1975, Morgan Papers.

4. Edward Bellamy's most significant work, *Looking Backward, 2000–1887* (Boston: Ticknor and Company, 1888), is a fictional story of a young nineteenth-century Bostonian who wakes up 113 years into the future to discover a much different and more perfect world. Bellamy's novel influenced generations of Americans from the late Victorian Era through the Information Age

5. Lucy Griscom Morgan, *Finding His World: The Story of Arthur E. Morgan* (Yellow Springs: Kahoe and Company, 1927); Clarence J. Leuba, *A Road to Creativity: Arthur Morgan, Engineer, Educator, Administrator* (North Quincy, Mass.: Christopher Publishing House, 1971); Walter Kahoe, *Arthur Morgan: A Biography and Memoir* (Moylan, Pa.: The Whimsie Press, 1977).

6. See Thomas K. McCraw, *Morgan Versus Lilienthal: The Feud Within the TVA* (Chicago, Ill.: Loyola Univ. Press, 1970); Thomas K. McCraw, *TVA and the Power Fight: 1933–1939* (New York: J. B. Lippincott Co., 1971); Roy Talbert Jr., "The Human Engineer: Arthur E. Morgan and the Launching of the Tennessee Valley Authority" (master's thesis, Vanderbilt University, 1967); Roy Talbert Jr., *FDR's Utopian: Arthur Morgan of the TVA* (Jackson: Univ. of Mississippi Press, 1987); Wilmon Henry Droze, *High Dams and Slack Waters: TVA Rebuilds a River* (Baton Rouge: Louisiana State Univ. Press, 1965); Robert E. Barde, "Arthur E. Morgan, First Chairman of TVA," *Tennessee Historical Quarterly* 30 (September 1971): 299–314.

7. Burton R. Clark, *The Distinctive College: Antioch, Reed, and Swarthmore* (Chicago: Aldine Publishing Co., 1970); Stephen R. Herr, *Connected Thoughts: A Reinterpretation of the Reorganization of Antioch College in the 1920s* (New York: Univ. Press of America, Inc., 1997); George Charles Newman, *Leadership and the Politics of Innovative Change: Antioch College Under Arthur E. Morgan* (Toledo, Ohio: Univ. of Toledo, 1981).

8. Talbert, *FDR's Utopian,* xii–xiii.

9. Because *Looking Backward* has gone through innumerable reprints and editions, this book uses a readily available version for direct text citations. Edward Bellamy, *Looking Backward, 2000–1887* (repr., New York: Oxford University Press, 2007), 193.

10. For a general overview of the reforms for the Progressive Era see, Richard Hofstadter, *The Age of Reform: From Bryan to FDR* (New York: Vintage Books, 1955). In *An Encore for Reform: The Old Progressives and the New Deal* (New York: Oxford University Press, 1967), Otis L. Graham Jr. created a sample of 400 Progressive Era reformers and their connections to the New Deal. He argued that by the 1930s many of the reformers opposed the New Deal and those who supported Roosevelt were more focused on urban problems. Similarly, Arthur Morgan, who was not included in the sample, grew antagonistic of the New Deal. But unlike the reformers described in Graham's work, Morgan focused on rural reform and community building in the decades that followed the New Deal.

1. A PERILOUS JOURNEY

1. Arthur E. Morgan Diary, 1900, Morgan Papers.

2. Morgan Diary, 1900; Kahoe, *Arthur Morgan,* 16–19; Talbert, *FDR's Utopian,* 12, 16.

3. See Robert Weibe, *The Search for Order, 1877–1920* (Westport, Conn.: Greenwood Press, 1967); David Traxel, *1898: The Birth of the American Century* (New York: Alfred A. Knopf, 1998); Rebecca Edwards, *New Spirits: Americans in the Gilded Age, 1865–1905* (New York: Oxford Univ. Press, 2006); Nell Irvin Painter, *Standing at Armageddon: The United States, 1877–1919* (New York: W.W. Norton and Company, 1987); Sean Dennis Cashman, *America in the Gilded Age: From the Death of Lincoln to the Rise of Theodore Roosevelt,* 2nd ed. (New York: New York Univ. Press, 1988).

4. Judy Crichton, *America 1900: The Turning Point* (New York: Henry Holt and Company, 1998), 201, 211–19, 256, 285–86; *America 1900,* produced by David Grubin, written by Judy Crichton and David Grubin (David Grubin Productions, Inc., film for *The American Experience,* WGBH, 1998); Noel Jacob Kent, *America in 1900* (Armonk, N.Y.: M. E. Sharpe, 2000), 118.

5. Crichton, *America 1900,* 296.

6. Morgan Diary, 1893, 1900.

7. Kahoe, *Arthur Morgan,* 3; Arthur E. Morgan, "Notes on My Birthplace," 20 March 1976, Morgan Papers.

8. Kahoe, *Arthur Morgan,* 3–5; Arthur E. Morgan, "Notes on Parents," May 14, 1972, Morgan Papers; *The WPA Guide to Minnesota* (repr., St. Paul: Minnesota Historical Society, 1985), 256.

9. Morgan, *Finding His World,* 18; Kahoe, *Arthur Morgan,* 4, 8; Ernest Morgan, comp., "The Morgan Heritage, Early Letters from Arthur Morgan to his Son Ernest," pamphlet, ca. 1990s, 1, in author's possession. Also available in the Ernest Morgan Papers, Antiochiana, Antioch College.

10. Morgan, "Early Letters," 1–2; Arthur E. Morgan, "Notes Concerning the Origin of Interest in Antioch, 17 January 1945," 2, Morgan Papers; Talbert, *FDR's Utopian,* 6; Kahoe, *Arthur Morgan,* 4, 8.

11. Quote from Morgan, "Notes on Parents"; Morgan, *Finding His World,* 16.

12. Quote from Morgan, "Notes on Parents"; Kahoe, *Arthur Morgan,* 3; Morgan, *Finding His World,* 16; Talbert, *FDR's Utopian,* 9.

13. Quote from Morgan, "Notes on Parents"; Kahoe, *Arthur Morgan,* 1–3.

14. Kahoe, *Arthur Morgan,* 3.

15. Quote from Morgan, "Notes on Parents"; Talbert, *FDR's Utopian,* 9.

16. Quotes from Morgan, "Notes on Parents."

17. Quotes from Morgan, "Notes on Parents"; Kahoe, *Arthur Morgan,* 5.

18. Quote from Morgan, "Notes on Parents."

19. Quote from Kahoe, *Arthur Morgan,* 137.

20. Quote from Ibid., 137–38.

21. Ibid., 8–9.

22. In the 1970s educators and psychologists developed distinct learning styles and applied them to dealing with students. The four main categories included verbal-visual, non-verbal-visual,

auditory, and kinesthetic learning. During the 1980s, Howard Gardner, a professor of education at Harvard, took these categories of learning one step forward with the theory of multiple intelligences. See Howard Gardner, *Frames of Mind: The Theory of Multiple Intelligences* (New York: Basic Books, Inc., 1983); Howard Gardner, *Multiple Intelligences: The Theory in Practice* (New York: Basic Books, 1993).

23. Arthur E. Morgan, "My View of Life at the Age of 87," ca. 1965, Morgan Papers; Kahoe, *Arthur Morgan,* 7.

24. Morgan Diary, 1893; Kahoe, *Arthur Morgan,* 10–11; David J. Bertuca, comp., *The World's Columbian Exposition: A Centennial Bibliographic Guide* (Westport, Conn.: Greenwood Press, 1996), xix–xxi; David F. Burg, *Chicago's White City of 1893* (Lexington: The Univ. Press of Kentucky, 1976), xii–xiii, 224.

25. H. Dharmapala's major address on Buddhism is reprinted in John Henry Barrows, ed., *The World's Parliament of Religions: An Illustrated and Popular Story of the World's First Parliament of Religions, Held in Chicago in Connection with the Columbian Exposition of 1893* (Chicago: The Parliament Publishing Company, 1893), 2:862–80.

26. Morgan Diary, 1893; Morgan, "My View of Life at the Age of 87," ca. 1965; Kahoe, *Arthur Morgan,* 11; Burg, *White City,* 264–69.

27. Burg, *White City,* 262; Charles Darwin, *On the Origin of Species* (London: J. Murray, 1859).

28. Rossiter Johnson, ed., *A History of the World's Columbian Exposition Held in Chicago in 1893* (New York: D. Appleton and Company, 1898), 4:229, 413–16, 435–41, 459; Burg, *White City,* 262.

29. Barrows, *World's Parliament,* 2:1316–25; Johnson, *History of the Exposition,* 311–17.

30. First quote from Henry Drummond, *The Ascent of Man* (New York: James Pott and Company, 1894), 7; Morgan quotes from Morgan, "My View of Life at the Age of 87," ca. 1965; Morgan Diary, 1894.

31. Morgan, "My View of Life at the Age of 87," ca. 1965; *WPA Guide to Minnesota,* 258; William B. Mitchell, "St. Cloud in the Territorial Period," in *Collection of the Minnesota Historical Society,* Vol. 12 (St. Paul: Minnesota Historical Society, 1908), 639–40; *St. Cloud Times,* 30 June 1956; "Facts About the St. Cloud Library Taken from the Stearns County History, Compiled in 1915 by W.B. Mitchell," undated typescript, in Morgan Papers.

32. Arthur E. Morgan, "Books I Have Read," ca. 1897, Morgan Papers; Morgan Diaries, 1893–1897; Talbert, *FDR's Utopian,* 10–11; W. Draper's *The Conflict Between Religion and Science* (New York: D. Appleton and Company, 1875); Charles Darwin, *The Formation of Vegetable Mould, Through the Action of Worms, with Observations on their Habits* (London: J. Murray, 1881); William R. Alger, *The Solitudes of Nature and of Man: Or, the Loneliness of Human Life* (Boston: Roberts Brothers, 1867); Nathaniel Hobart, *Life of Emanuel Swedenborg: With Some Account of His Writings, Together with a Brief Notice of the Rise and Progress of the New Church* (Boston: Allen and Goddard, 1831).

33. Quote from Morgan Diary, 1896; Talbert, *FDR's Utopian,* 45; Max Nordau, *Degeneration,* trans. from 2nd ed. of the German ed. (5th ed., New York: D. Appleton and Company, 1895); Bellamy, *Looking Backward.*

34. Morgan, *Edward Bellamy,* 9; Philip Gosse, *The Pirates' Who's Who: Giving Particulars of the Lives and Deaths of the Pirates and Buccaneers* (repr., Glorieta, N.Mex.: Rio Grande Press, Inc., 1988), 47–48.

35. Joseph Bellamy, *The Works of Joseph Bellamy, D.D., First Pastor of the Church in Bethlehem, Conn., With a Memoir of His Life and Character* (Boston: Doctrinal Tract and Book Company, 1853), 1:viii–x; Arthur E. Morgan, *Edward Bellamy* (New York: Columbia University Press, 1944), 14–16.

36. Morgan, *Edward Bellamy,* 5–8, 16–17; John L. Thomas, *Alternative America: Henry George, Edward Bellamy, Henry Demarest Lloyd and the Adversary Tradition* (Cambridge: Harvard Univ. Press, 1983), 28.

37. Morgan, *Edward Bellamy,* 8, 18–20, 24–27, 30–33, 36–38, 41–48; Sylvia E. Bowman, *Edward Bellamy* (Boston: Twayne Publishers, 1986), 1–6; Thomas, *Alternative America,* 27–28.

38. Morgan, *Edward Bellamy,* 57–58; Bowman, *Edward Bellamy,* 7–9.

39. Edward Bellamy, *The Religion of Solidarity* (Yellow Springs: Antioch Bookplate Company, 1940), 43, 24–26, 31, 36–38, 40; Thomas, *Alternative America,* 86–88; Morgan, *Edward Bellamy,* 203.

40. Bowman, *Edward Bellamy,* 17–23.

41. Morgan, *Edward Bellamy,* 204–12; Weibe, *Search for Order,* 12–17, 27.

42. Morgan, *Edward Bellamy,* 213–22; Charles Bellamy, *The Breton Mills: A Romance* (New York: G. P. Putnam's Sons, 1880); Charles Bellamy, *The Way Out: Suggestions for Social Reform* (New York: G. P. Putnam's Sons, 1884); Thomas, *Alternative America,* 356–60.

43. Morgan, *Edward Bellamy,* 223–27; Edward Bellamy, "How I Came to Write 'Looking Backward,'" *The Nationalist* 1 (May 1889): 1–4; Edward Bellamy, "How I Wrote 'Looking Backward,'" *Ladies Home Journal* 2 (April 1894): 2; Thomas, *Alternative America,* 238–40.

44. Bellamy, *Looking Backward,* 5–11, 29, 148.

45. Ibid., 12–23.

46. Ibid., 31–42, 110, 149.

47. Ibid., 51, quote on 52, 82–83, 119–21, 134–41, 176

48. Ibid., 150–55.

49. Ibid., 179–87, quote on 182, 190–94.

50. Thomas, *Alternative America,* 262–65; Morgan, *Edward Bellamy,* 188.

51. Edward Bellamy, "Looking Forward," *The Nationalist* 2 (December 1889): quote on 1, 1–4; Thomas, *Alternative America,* 266–67, 274–75; Morgan, *Edward Bellamy,* 247–60.

52. Frederic Cople Jaher, "Introduction," in *Nationalist, Volume 1, 1889* (New York: Greenwood Reprint Corp., 1968); Thomas, *Alternative America,* 267–69.

53. See, Lawrence Goodwyn, *The Populist Moment: A Short History of the Agrarian Revolt in America* (New York: Oxford Univ. Press, 1978).

54. Frederic Cople Jaher, "Introduction," in *The New Nation, Volume 1, 1891* (New York: Greenwood Reprint Corp., 1968); Thomas, *Alternative America,* 271–76; Edward Bellamy, *Equality* (New York: D. Appleton and Company, 1897).

55. Kahoe, *Arthur Morgan,* 133, 146, 165; Talbert, *FDR's Utopian,* 10; Morgan, *Finding His World,* 25.

56. Morgan, *Finding His World,* quote on 26; Leuba, *A Road to Creativity,* 47–48.

57. Morgan, *Finding His World,* 27–30; Kahoe, *Arthur Morgan,* 14–15; Leuba, *Road to Creativity,* 50, 59.

58. Quote from Morgan, *Finding His World,* 31.

59. Morgan, *Finding His World,* 33–34.

60. Arthur E. Morgan to Jessie Morgan, [July 1898], Morgan Papers; Morgan, *Finding His World,* 35–43; Kahoe, *Arthur Morgan,* 15–18; Talbert, *FDR's Utopian,* 16.

61. Arthur E. Morgan to Jessie Morgan, [July 1898], Morgan Papers; Kahoe, *Arthur Morgan,* 17–18; Morgan, *Finding His World,* 46; Talbert, *FDR's Utopian,* 12–13.

62. Morgan, *Finding His World,* 49; Leuba, *Road to Creativity,* 61; Talbert, *FDR's Utopian,* 12; Kahoe, *Arthur Morgan,* 18.

63. Morgan Diary, 1900; Kahoe, *Arthur Morgan,* 18–19; Morgan, *Finding His World,* 52–55.

64. Morgan, *Finding His World,* 57; Morgan Diary, 1900.

65. Morgan, *Finding His World,* 63.

66. Morgan Diary, 1900.

2. FINDING HIS WORLD

1. Carl M. Becker and Patrick B. Nolan, "They Gathered at the River: The Miami Conservancy District" *Timeline* 6 (October/November 1989): 35–36; "The Flood of March–April, 1913,

on the Ohio River and Its Tributaries," *Engineering News* 69 (April 10, 1913): 751–53; "Flood Devastation at Dayton, Ohio," *Engineering Record* 67 (April 12, 1913): 403–404; "Dayton After the Flood," *Engineering News* 69 (April 24, 1913): 865–67; Aaron D. Purcell, "Reclaiming Lost Ground: Arthur Morgan and the Miami Conservancy District Labor Camps" *The Historian* 64 (Winter 2002): 367.

2. Quote from Arthur E. Morgan, "Broken Threads, Engineering I," undated, 68, Morgan Papers; Arthur E. Morgan, *The Miami Conservancy District* (New York: McGraw Hill, Inc., 1951), 151.

3. Leuba, *Road to Creativity,* 106; Purcell, "Reclaiming Lost Ground," 369–70.

4. Arthur S. Link and Richard L. McCormick, *Progressivism* (Arlington Heights, Ill.: Harlan Davidson, 1983), 1–2, 21; John Whiteclay Chambers II, *The Tyranny of Change: America in the Progressive Era, 1900–1917* (New York: St. Martin's Press, 1980), 238–45; Robert M. Crunden, *Ministers of Reform: The Progressives' Achievement in American Civilization, 1889–1920* (New York: Basic Books, 1982), ix.

5. Michael McGerr, *A Fierce Discontent: The Rise and Fall of the Progressive Movement in America, 1870–1920* (New York: Free Press, 2003), 315; Maureen A. Flanagan, *America Reformed: Progressives and Progressivisms, 1890s-1920s* (New York: Oxford Univ. Press, 2007), 283–86.

6. Eric Rauchway, *Murdering McKinley: The Making of Theodore Roosevelt's America* (New York: Hill and Wang, 2003), xi–xiii.

7. Kahoe, *Arthur Morgan,* 20.

8. Quote from Morgan Diary, 1901; Morgan, *Edward Bellamy,* 287; Bellamy, *Equality,* iii.

9. Quotes from Morgan Diary, 1901.

10. Quotes from Morgan Diary, 1901; Morgan Diary, 1900.

11. Quotes from Morgan Diary, 1901; Morgan Diary, 1900; see also Ronald C. White Jr., and C. Howard Hopkins, *The Social Gospel: Religion and Reform in Changing America* (Philadelphia: Temple Univ. Press, 1976).

12. Quotes from Morgan Diary, 1901.

13. Quotes from Morgan Diary, 1901.

14. Quote from Morgan, "Broken Threads," 1–2; Kahoe, *Arthur Morgan,* 22; Lebua, *Road to Creativity,* 73.

15. Morgan, "Broken Threads," 2–5; Kahoe, *Arthur Morgan,* 22–23; Arthur E. Morgan, "Youthful Experiences as a Timber Cruiser," 1972, Morgan Papers.

16. Morgan, "Broken Threads," 3; Kahoe, *Arthur Morgan,* 23, 28.

17. Morgan, "Broken Threads," quote on 102, 6–7; Talbert, *FDR's Utopian,* 22; George W. Pickles, *Drainage and Flood-Control Engineering* (New York: McGraw Hill, 1941), 7; Kahoe, *Arthur Morgan,* 26.

18. Morgan, "Broken Threads," 7–8; Kahoe, *Arthur Morgan,* 26–27.

19. Kahoe, *Arthur Morgan,* 27–28; Talbert, *FDR's Utopian,* 24.

20. Kahoe, *Arthur Morgan,* 27–28; Lebua, *Road to Creativity,* 80.

21. Kahoe, *Arthur Morgan,* 28; Lebua, *Road to Creativity,* 80; Francis B. Tiffany, comp., *General Statues of Minnesota, Supplement 1917* (St. Paul, Minn.: West Publishing Company, 1918), 575.

22. "Arthur E. Morgan, President Morgan Engineering Company," 1915; "Service Record of Arthur E. Morgan," ca. 1920, all in Morgan Papers; Kahoe, *Arthur Morgan,* 28–29; Lebua, *Road to Creativity,* 81–82; Talbert, *FDR's Utopian,* 24.

23. Morgan, *Finding His World,* 78; Kahoe, *Arthur Morgan,* 29; Talbert, *FDR's Utopian,* 23; Andrew Taylor Still, *Autobiography of Andrew T. Still* (1897; repr., New York: Arno Press, 1972).

24. Quote from Arthur E. Morgan to Ernest Morgan, December 18, 1905, in "The Morgan Heritage;" Talbert, *FDR's Utopian,* 23; Lebua, *Road to Creativity,* 81; Kahoe, *Arthur Morgan,* 29–30.

25. "The Morgan Heritage;" Kahoe, *Arthur Morgan,* 30; Morgan, *Finding His World,* 78; Talbert, *FDR's Utopian,* 25.

26. Kahoe, *Arthur Morgan,* 29; Morgan, *Finding His World,* 79; Lebua, *Road to Creativity,* 81–82.

27. "Hatch Act (Agricultural Experiment Stations)" *Statutes at Large,* chap. 314, 24 (1887): 440; "Department of Agriculture Appropriations for 1898" *Statutes at Large,* chap. 85, 30 (1898): 335; *Annual Reports of the Department of Agriculture for the Fiscal Year Ended June 30, 1899* (Washington, D.C.: Government Printing Office, 1899), xxxv–xxxvi; *Annual Reports of the Department of Agriculture for the Fiscal Year Ended June 30, 1900* (Washington, D.C.: Government Printing Office, 1900), 200–201; U.S. Department of Agriculture, *Irrigation and Drainage Investigations of the Office of Experimental Stations* (Washington, D.C.: Government Printing Office, 1904), 5–6; Talbert, *FDR's Utopian,* 25; Aaron D. Purcell, "Plumb Lines, Politics, and Projections: The Florida Everglades and the Wright Report Controversy," *Florida Historical Quarterly* 80 (Fall 2001): 166.

28. *Annual Report of the Department of Agriculture for the Fiscal Year Ending June 30, 1902* (Washington, D.C.: Government Printing Office, 1902), 294; *Annual Report of the Department of Agriculture for the Fiscal Year Ending June 30, 1904* (Washington, D.C.: Government Printing Office, 1904), 501; USDA, *Irrigation and Drainage Investigations,* 6; *Annual Report of the Department of Agriculture for the Fiscal Year Ending June 30, 1907* (Washington, D.C.: Government Printing Office, 1908), 700–701, 710–11; "Department of Agriculture Appropriations for 1904," *Statutes at Large,* chap. 1486, 33 (1904): 294; "Department of Agriculture Appropriations for 1907" *Statutes at Large,* chap. 2907, 34 pt. 1 (1907): 1279; Purcell, "Plumb Lines," 167.

29. "Charles G. Elliott," *The National Cyclopaedia of American Biography* (New York: James T. White and Company, 1931), 21:287–88; U.S. House, *Everglades of Florida, Hearings Before the Committee on Expenditures in the Department of Agriculture* (Washington, D.C.: Government Printing Office, 1912), 17:773; Purcell, "Plumb Lines," 167.

30. Morgan, "Broken Threads," 12; Morgan, *Finding His World,* 79; Talbert, *FDR's Utopian,* 25.

31. Morgan, "Broken Threads," 13; Morgan, *Finding His World,* 79–80; "Service Record," Morgan Papers.

32. "Service Record," Morgan Papers; Kahoe, *Arthur Morgan,* 33; Lebua, *Road to Creativity,* 86.

33. Quote from Arthur E. Morgan to Ernest Morgan, May 31, 1908, in "The Morgan Heritage."

34. Quote from Morgan, *Finding His World,* 84, 1–3, 88–89; Ernest Morgan, "About Lucy Morgan," October 1986, Morgan Papers; Talbert, *FDR's Utopian,* 27.

35. Quotes from Arthur E. Morgan to Ernest Morgan, February 12, 1909, in "The Morgan Heritage;" Morgan, *Finding His World,* 85; Arthur E. Morgan, "New Light on Lincoln's Boyhood, *Atlantic Monthly* 125 (1920): 208–18; Arthur E. Morgan, "New Light on Lincoln's Boyhood," ms. draft, Morgan Papers.

36. Kahoe, *Arthur Morgan,* 33–35; Lebua, *Road to Creativity,* 86–87; Arthur E. Morgan, *Report on the St. Francis Valley Drainage Project in Northeastern Arkansas* (Washington, D.C.: Government Printing Office, 1911), 7–8.

37. U.S. Department of Agriculture, *Experiment Station Record, 1910* (Washington, D.C.: Government Printing Office, 1910), 190; Arthur E. Morgan, *A Preliminary Report on the St. Francis Valley Drainage Project in Northeastern Arkansas* (Washington, D.C.: Government Printing Office, 1909), 1–31; Morgan, *Report on the St. Francis Valley Drainage Project,* 54–56; Kahoe, *Arthur Morgan,* 35.

38. Arthur E. Morgan, "The Florida Everglades Incident," 1954, 21–22, Box 1 Arthur E. Morgan Collection, University of Florida, Gainesville; W. M. Hays to Arthur E. Morgan [appointment letter], December 17, 1907; E. W. Allen to W. M. Hays, June 23, 1909; Personal Departmental Record for Arthur E. Morgan, [ca. 1911], folder 2, Everglades 1913 (Morgan), Box 6, Miscellaneous Papers; "Arthur E. Morgan," [ca. 1912], folder 4, A. E. Morgan, Box 8, Miscellaneous Papers, Record Group 16, Records of the Office of the Secretary of Agriculture, National Archives at College Park, Maryland (hereafter cited as NACP); James O. Wright, *Why Was Wright's Report Suppressed* (Tallahassee: T. J. Appleyard, 1911), 9; U.S. House, *Hearings,*

17:792, 9:337, and 12:503; Lebua, *Road to Creativity,* 87–88; Kahoe, *Arthur Morgan,* 167; Purcell, "Plumb Lines," 176.

39. Alfred Jackson Hanna and Kathyrn Abbey Hanna, *Lake Okeechobee: Wellspring of the Everglades* (Indianapolis: Bobbs-Merrill Company, 1948), 122; Charles G. Elliott, "Drainage Investigations, 1904, By C.G. Elliott, Engineer, U.S. Department of Agriculture, in Charge," in U.S. Senate, *Everglades of Florida: Acts, Reports, and Other Papers, State and National, Relating to the Everglades of the State of Florida and Their Reclamation* (Washington, D.C.: Government Printing Office, 1911), 94–97; Purcell, "Plumb Lines," 168.

40. Hanna, *Lake Okeechobee,* 122–27; Samuel Proctor, *Napoleon Bonaparte Broward: Florida's Fighting Democrat* (Gainesville: Univ. of Florida Press, 1950), 220–24, 240; Charles Elliott to Napoleon Broward, February 28, 1903; first quote from Napoleon Broward to Charles Elliott, March 3, 1905; Charles Elliott to Napoleon Broward, March 10, 1905; second quote from Charles Elliott to Elwood Mead, January 6, 1905 [*sic* 1906]; Napoleon Broward to James Wilson, January 16, 1906; James Wilson to Napoleon Broward, January 26, 1906, all in Box 3, Record Group 8, Records of the Bureau of Agricultural Engineering, NARA–Southeast Region, Atlanta, Georgia (hereafter cited as NARA–SE); Purcell, "Plumb Lines," 168–69. Sources in Record Group 8 are divided between National Archives facilities in College Park, Maryland and Atlanta, Georgia.

41. Morgan, "Florida Everglades Incident," 21–22; Napoleon Broward to James Wilson, June 28, 1906, 1–5; Napoleon Broward to Edward [*sic*] Mead, June 29, 1906, all in Box 3, RG 8, NARA–SE; E. W. Allen to Charles Elliott, July 21, 1906 [L-3 1/2], Box 2, RG 16, NACP; U.S. House, *Hearings,* 17:829, 18:837; Purcell, "Plumb Lines," 171.

42. Quote from James Wright to Charles Elliott, February 29, 1908, Box 3, RG 8, NARA–SE; James Wilson to A. C. True, March 14, 1908; James Taliaferro to James Wilson, March 12, 1908; James Wilson to James Taliaferro, March 14, 1908; James Taliaferro to James Wilson, March 14, 1908, all in Box 2, RG 16, NACP; Hanna, *Lake Okeechobee,* 128; Purcell, "Plumb Lines," 172–73.

43. First quote from Charles Elliott to James Wright, March 17, 1908; second quote from James Wright to Charles Elliott, March 30, 1908; James Wright to Charles Elliott, April 6, 1908, all in Box 3, RG 8, NARA–SE; Hanna, *Lake Okeechobee,* 128; Purcell, "Plumb Lines," 173–75.

44. Wright, "Extract From a Report," February 25, 1909, in Senate, *Everglades, Acts, and Other Papers,* 130–37; Morgan, "Florida Everglades Incident," 22; Wright, *Why Was Report Suppressed,* 8; U.S. House, *Hearings,* 17:792; Purcell, "Plumb Lines," 175–76.

45. Morgan, "Florida Everglades Incident," 22; U.S. House, *Hearings,* 9:341–45, 12:508–9; A. D. Morehouse to Harold Wheeler, September 8, 1909, Box 3, RG 8, NARA–SE; Purcell, "Plumb Lines," 176–77.

46. Morgan, "Florida Everglades Incident," 22–23; U.S. House, *Hearings,* 9:348–51, 386–87; 10:397–98; 17:793, 797–99; Purcell, "Plumb Lines," 177.

47. Morgan, "Florida Everglades Incident," 23; U.S. House, *Hearings,* 9:351–53; 10:387, 405; 17:799–802; Purcell, "Plumb Lines," 177–78.

48. "Announcement of the Morgan Engineering Company," ca. 1910, Morgan Papers; Lebua, *Road to Creativity,* 95–96.

49. Quote from "Announcement of the Morgan Engineering Company;" Morgan, *Finding His World,* 94; Kahoe, *Arthur Morgan,* 40.

50. Morgan Engineering Company, "A Statement of the Recent Practice of the Engineering Company, February 1912," Morgan Papers; Arthur E. Morgan and S. H. McCrory, *Preliminary Report Upon the Drainage of the Lands Overflowed by the North and Middle Forks of the Forked Deer River and the Rutherford Fork of the Obion River in Gibson County, Tennessee* (Nashville, Tenn.: State Geological Survey, 1910), 21; Kahoe, *Arthur Morgan,* 40–44.

51. Charles Warren Hunt to Arthur E. Morgan, May 4, 1910, Morgan Papers; Kahoe, *Arthur Morgan,* 46, 168.

52. William D. Miller, *Memphis During the Progressive Era, 1900–1917* (Memphis, Tenn.: Memphis State Univ. Press, 1957), 148–49; William D. Miller, *Mr. Crump of Memphis* (Baton Rouge: Louisiana State Univ. Press, 1964), 77–81; G. Wayne Dowdy, *Mayor Crump Don't Like*

It: Machine Politics in Memphis (Jackson: Univ. Press of Mississippi, 2006), 7–11; *The Egyptians Yearbook, 1982–1983* (Memphis, Tenn.: The Egyptians, 1983), iv; Talbert, *FDR's Utopian,* 28–29.

53. Morgan, "Florida Everglades Incident," 23; Wright, *Why Was Report Suppressed,* 10–11; U.S. House, *Hearings,* 6:237–38, 252; 7:256–59; 17:803–5; Purcell, "Plumb Lines," 178–82.

54. U.S. Senate, *Everglades, Acts, and Other Papers,* 5; "To Be Printed as a Public Document A Compilation of Acts, Reports, and Other Papers, State and National, Relating to the Reclamation of the Everglades," (S. Res. 120, S. Doc. 89) 62nd Cong., 1st sess., *Congressional Record,* 47 (August 5, 1911), 3669; U.S. Senate, *Hearings,* 7:262; 19:949–52; 21:1042; Wright, *Why Was Report Suppressed,* 12; Drainage Investigations Division, "Memorandum Concerning Senate Document 89, 62nd Congress, 1st Session, Entitled 'Everglades of Florida,'" December 7, 1911, 1–4, Box 25, RG 8, NACP);; Hanna, *Lake Okeechobee,* 158; Purcell, "Plumb Lines," 183–85.

55. "Florida Land Sale Inquiry," *New York Times,* February 7, 1912; Frank Clark to James Wilson, October 26, 1911; Frank Clark to James Wilson, December 20, 1911; James Wilson to Frank Clark, December 21, 1911; Frank Clark to James Wilson, January 6, 1912, all in Box 2, RG 16, NACP; Nelson Manfred Blake, *Land into Water—Water into Land: A History of Water Management in Florida* (Tallahassee: Univ. Press of Florida, 1980), 117; Purcell, "Plumb Lines," 186.

56. First quote from Arthur E. Morgan to A. C. True, February 12, 1912, Box 25, RG 8, NACP; second and third quotes from Arthur E. Morgan to James Wilson, January 29, 1912, Morgan Papers; Morgan, "Florida Everglades Incident," 21, 24–26; Purcell, "Plumb Lines," 186–87.

57. "Everglades Reclaimed," *New York Times,* February 15, 1912; Arthur E. Morgan to Frank Clark, February 7, 1912, Morgan Papers; Purcell, "Plumb Lines," 187–88.

58. "Says U.S. Employees Aided Land Schemes," *Memphis Commercial Appeal,* February 7, 1912; "Another Wiley Case May Be Developed," *Memphis Commercial Appeal,* February 8, 1912; "Morgan Defends Engineers Elliott; Declares Drainage Chief Blameless," *Daily Texarkanian,* February 9, 1912; Purcell, "Plumb Lines," 188.

59. Arthur E. Morgan, "Does the Punishment Fit the Crime?" *Engineering News* 67 (February 22, 1912): 359–60; Arthur E. Morgan, "More Concerning Mr. Elliott's Dismissal: The Engineering Plans for Draining the Florida Everglades," *Engineering News* 67 (March 28, 1912): 601–2; A. L. Dabney, Jacob A. Harman, and Isham Randolph, "The Charges Against Mr. C. G. Elliott, Late Chief of Drainage Investigations, Department of Agriculture," *Engineering News* 67 (June 6, 1912): 1092; W. C. Hammatt, "The Defense of Mr. C. G. Elliott," *Engineering News* 67 (June 27, 1912): 1235; Morgan, "Florida Everglades Incident," 27; Purcell, "Plumb Lines," 189, 192.

60. Morgan, "Florida Everglades Incident," 27; U.S. House, *Hearings,* 9:391; 10:410–11, 414; Purcell, "Plumb Lines," 188–89.

61. U.S. House, *Expenditures in the Department of Agriculture,* 62nd Cong., 2nd sess., 1912. Misc. Repts. 1207, Serial 6133 (Washington, D.C.: Government Printing Office, 1912), 1–15; "Everglades Charges Fail," *New York Times,* August 31, 1912; Hanna, *Lake Okeechobee,* 144–45; Purcell, "Plumb Lines," 192–95.

62. Becker and Nolan, "They Gathered at the River," 36; Morgan, *The Miami Conservancy District,* 152–69; "Flood-Prevention Investigations in Ohio," *Engineering Record* 68 (July 12, 1913): 38–39; "The Ohio Flood Prevention and Water Conservancy Bill," *Engineering News* 71 (February 5, 1914): 322; S. H. Ankeney, "Securing Popular Support for a Great Project," *Engineering Record* 70 (December 12, 1914): 646–48; Purcell, "Reclaiming Lost Ground," 367–68.

63. Morgan, *Miami Conservancy District,* 176–85; Leuba, *Road to Creativity,* 106.

64. Morgan, *Miami Conservancy District,* 201–3.

65. Ibid., 204–12.

66. Arthur E. Morgan, *Report of the Chief Engineer, Arthur Morgan: Submitting a Plan for the Protection of the District from Flood Damage* (Dayton: Miami Conservancy District, 1916), 1:13; Becker and Nolan, "They Gathered at the River," 36; Morgan, *Miami Conservancy District,* 211–13, 222–23; Purcell, "Reclaiming Lost Ground," 368; Morgan, *Finding His World,* 95.

67. Morgan, *The Miami Conservancy District,* 229–39, 272–73; Morgan, *Report of the Chief Engineer,* 1:17–19; "Miami Conservancy Plans are Completed," *Engineering Record* 73 (March 11,

1916): 348; "Final Flood-Protection Plan for Miami Valley," *Engineering News* 75 (April 6, 1916): 674–75; H. M. Crittenden, "The Battle Over the Miami Flood-Prevention Plans," *Engineering News* 76 (November 9, 1916): 906–10.

68. Morgan, *The Miami Conservancy District,* 238–40.

69. Quote in Morgan, *The Miami Conservancy District,* 245; Miami Flood-Prevention Plan Approved by Court," *Engineering News* 76 (November 30, 1916): 1055.

70. "Miami Flood-Prevention Plans Sustained," *Engineering Record* 74 (December 2, 1916): 673; Arthur E. Morgan, "The Miami Valley Flood-Protection Work," *Engineering News* 77 (January 11, 1917): 62–65; Purcell, "Reclaiming Lost Ground," 368.

3. REFORM IN PROGRESS

1. Quote from Morgan, *Finding His World,* 100; Ernest Morgan, *Arthur Morgan Remembered* (Yellow Springs: Community Service, Inc., 1991), 38.

2. Arthur S. Link, *Woodrow Wilson and the Progressive Era, 1910–1917* (New York: Harper and Brothers, 1954), 223–24, 229–30, 249.

3. Link, *Woodrow Wilson,* 226, 236–37; Faith Jaycox, *The Progressive Era* (New York: Facts on File, 2005), 426–47; David Blanke, *The 1910s* (Westport, Conn.: Greenwood Press, 2002), 7.

4. Link, *Woodrow Wilson,* 136–37; Jaycox, *The Progressive Era,* 426–27; Donald K. Pickens, *Eugenics and the Progressives* (Nashville, Tenn.: Vanderbilt Univ. Press, 1968), 49–51, 86–88; George W. Groh, *The Black Migration: The Journey to Urban America* (New York: Weybright and Talley, 1972), 49–52.

5. Arthur E. Morgan, "An Experiment in Educational Engineering," 1917, Morgan Papers.

6. Kahoe, *Arthur Morgan,* 50; Leuba, *Road to Creativity,* 105; Talbert, *FDR's Utopian,* 42.

7. Charles H. Paul, *A Brief History of the Engineers' Club of Dayton* (Dayton: National Cash Register Company, 1942); Kahoe, *Arthur Morgan,* 168.

8. Charles Chatfield, *The American Peace Movement: Ideals and Activism* (New York: Twayne Publishers, 1992), 30; Warren F. Kuehl, *Hamilton Holt: Journalist, Internationalist, Educator* (Gainesville: Univ. of Florida Press, 1960), 126–29; Henry A. Atkinson, *Theodore Marburg: The Man and His Work* (New York: Morton Littman Printing Company, 1951), 147–48; Aaron D. Purcell, "Pursuing Peace: Arthur Morgan and Ohio's League to Enforce Peace, 1915–1920" *Ohio History* 109 (Winter-Spring 2000): 24.

9. "Unsigned draft letter [Arthur E. Morgan]," November 1915; Frederick H. Rike to Arthur E. Morgan, February 5, 1916; "Minutes of March 2, 1916 Meeting of the Ohio Branch of the League to Enforce Peace," all in Morgan Papers; Steven Philip Gietschier, "William Oxley Thompson and the League to Enforce Peace in Ohio" (PhD diss., The Ohio State Univ., 1971), 7–9; Purcell, "Pursuing Peace," 24–25, 27–30.

10. Ruhl F. Bartlett, *The League to Enforce Peace* (Chapel Hill: Univ. of North Carolina Press, 1944), 48–49; *Official Program: First Annual Assemblage of the League to Enforce Peace,* May 26–27, 1916, in Morgan Papers; *Enforced Peace: Proceedings of the First Annual National Assemblage of the League to Enforce Peace, Washington, May 26–27, 1916* (New York: League to Enforce Peace, 1916), 192; Talbert, *FDR's Utopian,* 40; Purcell, "Pursuing Peace," 30–32.

11. Morgan, "About Lucy Morgan," Morgan Papers; Quote from Leuba, *Road to Creativity,* 135; Morgan, *Finding His World,* 1, 86.

12. Quotes in Leuba, *Road to Creativity,* 51.

13. Morgan, *Finding His World,* 96–97; Kahoe, *Arthur Morgan,* 50.

14. Morgan, *Finding His World,* 94–95, 98; Leuba, *Road to Creativity,* 50–51.

15. Quotes in Arthur E. Morgan, "Notes for Prospectus for a School at Jacob's Pillow, Massachusetts, About 1916," Morgan Papers.

16. Quotes in Ibid.

17. "Morgan's Notes on Jacob's Pillow," July 10, 1970, Morgan Papers; Talbert, *FDR's Utopian,* 39; "Jacob's Pillow Dance School and Festival," at http://www.jacobspillow.org/festival/index.

asp; Finding Aid for "Jacob's Pillow Dance Festival Archives, 1915–2000" available through the Dance Heritage Coalition at http://danceheritage.org.

18. Leuba, *Road to Creativity*, 135; Talbert, *FDR's Utopian*, 42; Kahoe, *Arthur Morgan*, 50.

19. Arthur E. Morgan, "An Outline of a Proposed Boys' School for Which a Headmaster or Teacher is Being Sought," ca. 1916; Arthur E. Morgan to Charles Eliot, September 27, 1916, all in Morgan Papers. Morgan listed the following books as having a great influence on his educational theory: Johann Heinrich Pestalozzi, *Leonard and Gertrude* (trans., Philadelphia: Robert Carr, 1801); Charles Hanford Henderson, *Education and the Larger Life* (New York: Houghton Mifflin Company, 1902).

20. Charles Eliot to Arthur E. Morgan, September 1916; Arthur E. Morgan to Charles Eliot, September 27, 1916; Charles Eliot to Arthur E. Morgan, October 9, 1916; "Statement of Progress, Moraine Park School, Dayton," May 3, 1917; Arthur E. Morgan to Lloyd Marcus, September 29, 1947, all in Morgan Papers; *A Handbook of American Private Schools, 1920* (Boston, Mass.: Porter E. Sargent, 1920), 319; Leuba, *Road to Creativity*, 135–37.

21. "Statement of Progress," May 3, 1917; "Moraine Park School—Dayton, Ohio, Enrolment for School Year, 1917–1918"; Frank Slutz, "Outline of the General Policy of the School at Dayton, Ohio," ca. 1917, all in Morgan Papers; Frank Slutz, *Moraine Park School, an Educational Laboratory*, bulletin no. 5 (Washington, D.C.: Progressive Education Association, April 1912), 1–2; "Moraine Park School: A Progressive Education," *Columns* (February 2004): 3–4; John C. Hover, Joseph D. Barnes, et al., eds., *Memoirs of the Miami Valley* (Chicago: Robert O. Law Company, 1919), 2:162–63; *After a Year: Moraine Park School, 1917–1918* (Dayton: Moraine Park School, 1918), 1–2.

22. *Moraine Park School: A Statement of Policy, 1922–1923* (Dayton: Moraine Park School, 1922), 1–2; Hover and Barnes, *Memoirs*, 2:161–62; "Moraine Park School," 4; Morgan to Marcus, September 29, 1947, Morgan Papers.

23. Arthur E. Morgan, "Education: The Mastery of the Arts of Life," *Atlantic Monthly* 121 (March 1918): 338–43, 346; Talbert, *FDR's Utopian*, 43.

24. Morgan, *Miami Conservancy District*, 272–74.

25. Morgan, *Miami Conservancy District*, 248–55; "Flood Control Work in the Miami Conservancy District," *Public Works* 48 (February 14, 1920): 95; C. N. Phillips, *The Story of the Miami Conservancy District* (Dayton, Ohio: Miami Conservancy District, 1922), 10–15.

26. Purcell, "Reclaiming Lost Ground," 368–69; Judith Sealander, *Grand Plans: Business Progressivism and Social Change in Ohio's Miami Valley, 1890–1929* (Lexington: The Univ. Press of Kentucky, 1988), 76–77; Becker and Nolan, "They Gathered at the River," 37.

27. Morgan, *Miami Conservancy District*, 386–87; Purcell, "Reclaiming Lost Ground," 373.

28. The Industrial Commission of Ohio, *Preliminary Survey of Labor Camps in Ohio* (Columbus: The Industrial Commission of Ohio, 1917), 5–6, 9–14, 16, 18–22; Purcell, "Reclaiming Lost Ground," 373.

29. Morgan, *Miami Conservancy District*, 387; Arthur E. Morgan, "Miami Conservancy District Camp Communities," July 12, 1920, 1, Morgan Papers; Purcell, "Reclaiming Lost Ground," 373.

30. Purcell, "Reclaiming Lost Ground," 371; Arthur E. Morgan, *The Small Community, Foundation of Democratic Life: What It Is and How to Achieve It* (New York: Harper and Brothers, 1942).

31. Edwin T. Layton Jr., *The Revolt of the Engineers: Social Responsibility and the American Engineering Profession* (Cleveland, Ohio: Case Western Reserve, 1971), 109–27; Talbert, *FDR's Utopian*, 26, 30, 54; Purcell, "Reclaiming Lost Ground," 372.

32. Arthur E. Morgan to the National Housing Association, January 14, 1918; Arthur E. Morgan to W. F. Walker, February 28, 1918; Arthur E. Morgan to Department of Sociology, University of Michigan, January 8, 1918, all in Miami Conservancy District Records, 1897–1980, Wright State University, Dayton, Ohio (hereafter cited as MCD Records); "Construction Camps Model Towns on Miami Flood Works," *Engineering News Record* 81 (September 26, 1918): 578;

"Sewage Treatment at the Miami Conservancy Camps," *Engineering News Record* 85 (August 19, 1920): 361; Purcell, "Reclaiming Lost Ground," 375.

33. Arthur E. Morgan to Porter-Shirley, January 14, 1918, MCD Records; Arthur E. Morgan, "Miami Conservancy District Camp Communities," July 12, 1920; Arthur E. Morgan, "Report: The Old and New Order," August 27, 1918, Morgan Papers; Purcell, "Reclaiming Lost Ground," 375.

34. "Construction Camps on Miami Flood Works," 576–77; "The Camps," *The Miami Conservancy Bulletin* 1 (August 1918): 12–13; Morgan, "Camp Communities," July 12, 1920, Morgan Papers; Arthur E. Morgan, "General Order #11, Terms for Renting Cottages and Room in Bunkhouses," May 8, 1918, MCD Records; Purcell, "Reclaiming Lost Ground," 376.

35. "Construction Camps on Miami Flood Works," 577; "The Camps," 12–13; Morgan, "Camp Communities," July 12, 1920, Morgan Papers; Arthur E. Morgan to A. M. McKay, April 26, 1918; Arthur E. Morgan to F. C. Williams, July 24, 1918; Morgan, "Terms for Renting," May 8, 1918, all in MCD Records; Purcell, "Reclaiming Lost Ground," 377.

36. "Construction Camps on Miami Flood Works," 577; Morgan, "Camp Communities," July 12, 1920, Morgan Papers; Arthur E. Morgan, "A Corporation With a Stomach," ca. January 1918, MCD Records; Purcell, "Reclaiming Lost Ground," 377.

37. "Construction Camps on Miami Flood Works," 577–78; "Medical Inspection at Miami Camps Checks Influenza," *Engineering News Record* 82 (January 28, 1919): 197; "The Camps," 14; Morgan, "Camp Communities," July 12, 1920, 6–7, 14; "Inventory of Building and Building Equipment at the Five Conservancy Damsites," ca. 1920, all in Morgan Papers; Morgan, *Miami Conservancy District,* 389–91; Purcell, "Reclaiming Lost Ground," 377.

38. C. N. Phillips to C. W. Porter-Shirley, December 30, 1918, MCD Records. This document refers to the "black mess" receiving supplies, which implies that there were separate facilities for African American employees. Purcell, "Reclaiming Lost Ground," 378.

39. Becker and Nolan, "They Gathered at the River,'" 36; Leuba, *Road to Creativity,* 106–107; Arthur E. Morgan, "Building Up an Engineering Organization—With Special Reference to the Selection of Men," *Engineering News Record* 79 (September 20, 1917): 552–53; Purcell, "Reclaiming Lost Ground," 378.

40. C. W. Porter-Shirley, "Number of Applications on File," April 18, 1918; C. W. Porter-Shirley, "Employees on Various Features (Estimated)," April 18, 1918, MCD Records; Purcell, "Reclaiming Lost Ground," 378–79.

41. "Conservancy Employe[e]s Housed at Dam Sites," *Troy Daily News,* February 16, 1918; "Labor Problem Confronts Board," *Troy Daily News,* February 2, 1918; Purcell, "Reclaiming Lost Ground," 379–80.

42. Morgan to Michigan Sociology Department, January 8, 1918; Arthur E. Morgan to C. W. Porter-Shirley, January 14, 1918; Arthur E. Morgan to S. S. Marquis, January 22, 1918, all in MCD Records; Sealander, *Grand Plans,* 77; Purcell, "Reclaiming Lost Ground," 380.

43. International Employment Bureau to C. W. Porter-Shirley, April 3, 1918; C. W. Porter-Shirley to International Employment Bureau, April 9, 1918; C. W. Porter-Shirley, "Employment Sources," April 18, 1918; Porter-Shirley, "Employees on Various Features," April 18, 1918; Porter-Shirley, "Number of Men on Each Job," April 18, 1918, all in MCD Records; Purcell, "Reclaiming Lost Ground," 380.

44. Arthur E. Morgan to A. W. Freeman, April 27, 1918; A. W. Freeman to Arthur E. Morgan, May 1, 1918; A. W. Freeman to W. M. Smalley, June 12, 1918; "Attachment Dealing with De-Lousing," June 7, 1918, all in MCD Records; "Physician Appointed for Conservancy District," *Troy Daily News,* April 19, 1918; "Dr. Smalley is New Conservancy District Physician," *Dayton News,* April 16, 1918; Purcell, "Reclaiming Lost Ground," 380.

45. C. W. Porter-Shirley to Elmer S. Forbes, April 22, 1918; C. W. Porter-Shirley to Clapp, Nordstrom and Riley, May 13, 1918; C. W. Porter-Shirley to H. H. Forbes, May 18, 1918, all in MCD Records; "1,250 Employed By Conservancy Directors in Flood Protection Work," *Hamilton*

Daily Journal, May 13, 1918; "Many Employed on Flood Work," *Middletown Daily Journal,* May 15, 1918; "Flood Prevention Work Progressing Rapidly," *Troy Daily News,* May 9, 1918; Purcell, "Reclaiming Lost Ground," 381.

46. C. W. Porter-Shirley to I. Podrube, June 6, 1918; Clapp, Nordstrom and Riley to C. H. Locher, June 20, 1918; C. W. Porter-Shirley to Joseph Kugler, June 24, 1918, all in MCD Records; Purcell, "Reclaiming Lost Ground," 381.

47. Morgan, *Miami Conservancy District,* 399–401; Carl M. Becker and Patrick B. Nolan, *Keeping the Promise: A Pictorial of the Miami Conservancy District* (Dayton, Ohio: Landfall Press, 1988), 135; Sealander, *Grand Plans,* 79; Arthur E. Morgan, "A Labor Policy for the Miami Conservancy District: Adopted by the Board of Directors, June 21, 1918," Morgan Papers; Purcell, "Reclaiming Lost Ground," 381.

48. Morgan, *Miami Conservancy District,* 402–3; Becker and Nolan, *Keeping the Promise,* 135; Sealander, *Grand Plans,* 79; "Faulty Labor Policy of Miami Conservancy District," *Labor Review* (newsletter copy), July 19, 1918, MCD Records; Purcell, "Reclaiming Lost Ground," 381–82.

49. "Walkout is Hampering Conservancy Work," *Troy Daily News,* July 11, 1918; "Strike Delays Flood Work," *Hamilton Daily Journal,* July 11, 1918; "Strike Has No Bad Effect on Dam Contracts," *Dayton Daily Herald,* July 11, 1918; "Walk Out Hinders Conservancy Work, Officials Assert," *Dayton Daily Journal,* July 11, 1918; "100 Conservancy Workmen Quit," *Dayton Daily News,* July 11, 1918; Sealander, *Grand Plans,* 79–80; Purcell, "Reclaiming Lost Ground," 382.

50. "Morgan Makes a Statement," *Hamilton Daily Journal,* July 18, 1918; :"Open Shop: Policy Will Be Followed in Employing Conservancy District Help," *Middletown Daily News-Signal,* July 18, 1918; "Conservancy Board for the Open Shop," *Sidney Daily Journal,* July 18, 1918; "Declare 'Closed Shop' Policy is Impossible," *Dayton Daily News,* July 17, 1918; "Will Maintain an Open Shop," *Dayton Daily Journal,* July 13, 1918; Morgan, *Miami Conservancy District,* 407; Sealander, *Grand Plans,* 80; Purcell, "Reclaiming Lost Ground," 382.

51. Arthur E. Morgan to J. E. Barlow, February 13, 1919; "Rates for Transportation of Men," ca. July 1918, all in MCD Records; Sealander, *Grand Plans,* 80; Purcell, "Reclaiming Lost Ground," 382.

52. Morgan, "Camp Communities," July 12, 1920, 9–10, Morgan Papers; Purcell, "Reclaiming Lost Ground," 384.

53. Morgan, "Camp Communities," July 12, 1920, 10–11, Morgan Papers; "Six Months Progress of the Camp Community Associations," *The Miami Conservancy District Bulletin* 1 (June 1919): 172–74; "The Taylorsville Community Association," *The Miami Conservancy District Bulletin* 1 (January 1919): 94–95; "The Constitution and By-Laws of the Taylorsville Community," ca. November 1918, 1–3, MCD Records; Morgan, *Miami Conservancy District,* 392; "Construction Camp Community Association Like Commission Government," *Engineering News Record* 82 (January 30, 1919): 235; Purcell, "Reclaiming Lost Ground," 384.

54. Morgan, *Miami Conservancy District,* 393; "Construction Camp Community Association," 235; Arthur H. Kent, "Englewood Versus Taylorsville on Camp Organization," *Miami Conservancy Bulletin* 1 (March 1919): 126–27; Arthur H. Kent, "Riverside Community Organization," February 15, 1919, 1–2, MCD Records; Purcell, "Reclaiming Lost Ground," 384.

55. Morgan, *Miami Conservancy District,* 386–87, 393–94, 397–98; "Six Months Progress," 173; Morgan, "Camp Communities," July 12, 1920, 11, Morgan Papers; "Effect of Dry Wave on Conservancy Camps," *Miami Conservancy Bulletin* 2 (September 1919): 20; C. W. Porter-Shirley to C. C. Chambers, January 18, 1919; Arthur A. Hauck to O. N. Floyd, March 1, 1919, all in MCD Records; Purcell, "Reclaiming Lost Ground," 384–85.

56. A. O. Aulabaugh to Arthur A. Hauck, January 29, 1919; H. L. Fruend to C. W. Porter-Shirley, December 9, 1918, MCD Records; Morgan, *Miami Conservancy District,* 389; Morgan, "Camp Communities," July 12, 1920, 15, Morgan Papers; "The Conservancy Schools," *Miami Conservancy Bulletin* 1 (November 1918): 56–57; "Construction Camps Model Towns," 578; "Opening of Conservancy Schools," *Miami Conservancy Bulletin* 2 (September 1919): 31; Sealander, *Grand Plans,* 80; Purcell, "Reclaiming Lost Ground," 386.

57. Morgan, *Miami Conservancy District,* 389; "Night Schools Started at the Camps," *Miami Conservancy Bulletin* 1 (November 1918): 57; Morgan, "Camp Communities," July 12, 1920, 15, Morgan Papers; Purcell, "Reclaiming Lost Ground," 387.

58. The Community War Chest Association of Dayton to Arthur E. Morgan, April 24, 1918; C. W. Porter-Shirley to Thomas F. Kelly, April 30, 1918; C. W. Porter-Shirley to William Marchant, May 1, 1918; C. W. Porter-Shirley to [William Marchant], May 21, 1918; C. W. Porter-Shirley to F. C. Williams, June 3, 1918; Thomas F. Kelly to C. W. Porter-Shirley, June 20, 1918; C. W. Porter-Shirley to Thomas F. Kelly, June 24, 1918, all in MCD Records; Purcell, "Reclaiming Lost Ground," 386.

59. Gietschier, "Thompson and the League," 18; Edward Deeds to Arthur E. Morgan, February 27, 1918, Morgan Papers; Talbert, *FDR's Utopian,* 40; Purcell, "Pursuing Peace," 37–38.

60. Arthur E. Morgan to William Thompson, May 8, 1918, Box: Office of the President (RG 3/e/26/40), William Oxley Thompson Papers, The Ohio State University, Columbus, Ohio; Arthur E. Morgan to Charles Thwing, May 18, 1918; Arthur E. Morgan to William Short, May 27, 1918; William Short to Arthur E. Morgan, June 1, 1918; Arthur E. Morgan to Charles Thwing, June 3, 1918; Arthur E. Morgan to William Short, June 3, 1918, all in Morgan Papers; Gietschier, "Thompson and the League," 20–21; Purcell, "Pursuing Peace," 38–39.

61. Gietschier, "Thompson and the League," 28; Bartlett, *League to Enforce Peace,* 114; Purcell, "Pursuing Peace," 39.

62. Gietschier, "Thompson and the League," 32–33; Daniel Ryan to Arthur E. Morgan, April 3, 1919, Morgan Papers; Purcell, "Pursuing Peace," 39–40.

63. Gietschier, "Thompson and the League," 34–35; Bartlett, *League to Enforce Peace,* 126–27; Purcell, "Pursuing Peace," 41.

64. Frederick Rike to Arthur E. Morgan, May 14, 1919; Tom Jones Meek to Arthur E. Morgan, May 15, 1919; Arthur E. Morgan to Frederick Rike, May 16, 1919; Felix Held to Arthur E. Morgan, May 16, 1919; Arthur E. Morgan to Felix Held, May 17, 1919; Arthur E. Morgan to Felix Held, May 26, 1919; Felix Held to Arthur E. Morgan, May 28, 1919; Irwin Smith to Arthur E. Morgan, June 17, 1919; Arthur E. Morgan to Herbert Houston, July 14, 1919, all in Morgan Papers; Purcell, "Pursuing Peace," 41.

65. Arthur E. Morgan to William Short, November 12, 1919; Arthur E. Morgan to William Short, December 30, 1919; Herbert Houston to Arthur E. Morgan, April 19, 1921; Arthur E. Morgan to Herbert Houston, April 23, 1921, all in Morgan Papers; Purcell, "Pursuing Peace," 43–44.

66. Arthur E. Morgan, "Mitraniketan Newsletter," November 1963, 2, Morgan Papers; Purcell, "Pursuing Peace," 45–46.

67. Robert B. Downs, *Horace Mann: Champion of Public Schools* (New York: Twayne Publishers, Inc., 1974), 57–75, 107–18; Jonathan Messerli, *Horace Mann: A Biography* (New York: Alfred A. Knopf, 1972), 365–72; *Why They Came: The Story of Yellow Springs, Ohio* (Yellow Springs, Ohio: Yellow Springs Centennial Committee, 1956), 14.

68. Clark, *Distinctive College,* 14–18; Downs, *Horace Mann,* 137.

69. Herr, *Connected Thoughts,* 45; Clark, *Distinctive College,* 18–19.

70. Lucy Griscom Morgan, *Pioneering Days at Antioch* (Yellow Springs, Ohio: Antioch Press, 1947), 1; Morgan, "Notes on Interest in Antioch," January 17, 1945, 11–12, Morgan Papers; Kahoe, *Arthur Morgan,* 53; Leuba, *Road to Creativity,* 143; Clark, *Distinctive College,* 19.

4. EDUCATING THE COMMUNITY

1. Quotes from Arthur E. Morgan to Anna Wiley Morgan, August 17, 1919, Morgan Papers.
2. Quotes from Ibid.
3. Ibid.
4. Quotes from Morgan to Morgan, August 17, 1919; H. L. Mencken to H. W. Van Loon, May 22, 1921, all in Morgan Papers.

5. John Steele Gordon, *An Empire of Wealth: The Epic History of American Economic Power* (New York: Harper Perennial, 2005), 298–99; David E. Kyvig, *Daily Life in the United States, 1920–1939: Decades of Promise and Pain* (Westport, Conn.: Greenwood Press, 2002), 21–27, 37–38; Burl Noggle, *Into the Twenties: The United State from Armistice to Normalcy* (Urbana: Univ. of Illinois Press, 1974), 153–54.

6. Kathleen Drowne and Patrick Huber, *The 1920s* (Westport, Conn.: Greenwood Press, 2004), xix–xx, 136–37, 144; Michael E. Parrish, *Anxious Decades: American in Prosperity and Depression, 1920–1941* (New York: W.W. Norton, 1992), x; Gordon, *Empire of Wealth,* 307–9; Kyvig, *Daily Life,* 50–54.

7. Drowne and Huber, *The 1920s,* 143; Noggle, *Into the Twenties,* 168–70; Elizabeth Stevenson, *Babbitts and Bohemians: The American 1920s* (New York: Macmillan, 1967), 70–74.

8. Gordon, *Empire of Wealth,* 299; Noggle, *Into the Twenties,* 163–67; Ronald Allen Goldberg, *America in the Twenties* (Syracuse, N.Y.: Syracuse Univ. Press, 2003), 168–70; Ellis W. Hawley, *The Great War and the Search for a Modern Order: A History of the American People and Their Institutions, 1917–1933* (New York: St. Martin's Press, 1979), 58.

9. Kyvig, *Daily Life,* 19–24; David J. Goldberg, *Discontented America: The United States in the 1920s* (Baltimore, Md.: The Johns Hopkins Univ. Press, 1999), 1–3, 60–65; Noggle, *Into the Twenties,* 159–60; Nathan Miller, *New World Coming: The 1920s and the Making of Modern America* (New York: Scribner, 2003), 13.

10. Frank D. Slutz, "Suggestions by Mr. Frank D. Slutz for College Curriculum for Antioch College Cooperating with Industry, June 30, 1919," Morgan Papers.

11. Quote from Antioch College Board of Trustees, "Minutes of Meetings," August 3, 1919, Antioch College Archives; Herr, *Connected Thoughts,* 48–50; Clark, *Distinctive College,* 19; Richard Allen Naylor, "Arthur E. Morgan's Philosophy of Work-Study at Antioch College: A Progressive Reformer's Response to Reconstructing the Relationship Between Work and Education in the Community" (PhD diss., State Univ. of New York at Albany, 1987), 86, 88–89.

12. Herr, *Connected Thoughts,* 48–49; Arthur E. Morgan, "The College Budget," ca. summer 1919; Conklin, "Report on Antioch College Buildings," September 15, 1919, all in Morgan Papers; Naylor, "Work-Study at Antioch," 85–90; Newman, *Innovative Change,* 24–26; Morgan, *Arthur Morgan Remembered,* 38.

13. Newman, *Innovative Change,* 26–27; Clark, *Distinctive College,* 23.

14. Newman, *Innovative Change,* 27–28; Clark, *Distinctive College,* 23.

15. Arthur E. Morgan to the Board of Trustees of Antioch College, April 13, 1920, Morgan Papers; Herr, *Connected Thoughts,* 54–56; Clark, *Distinctive College,* 24.

16. Lawrence A. Cremin, *The Transformation of the School: Progressivism in American Education, 1876–1957* (New York: Alfred A. Knopf, 1964), 117–23; Hawley, *The Great War,* 143; Noggle, *Into the Twenties,* 175–76.

17. Patricia Albjerg Graham, *Progressive Education, From Arcady to Academe: A History of the Progressive Education Association, 1919–1955* (New York: Teachers College Press, 1967), 8–12; Hawley, *The Great War,* 143; Noggle, *Into the Twenties,* 176.

18. Graham, *Progressive Education,* 17; Cremin, *Transformation of the School,* 240.

19. Graham, *Progressive Education,* 20–24, 32; Cremin, *Transformation of the School,* 243–47; "Progressive Education Association Aims," [brochure], ca. 1920, Morgan Papers.

20. Arthur E. Morgan to [Progressive Education Association], ca. spring 1920; Arthur E. Morgan, "Progressive Education Association Address, Boston," August 6, 1920; Arthur E. Morgan, "Hopes for the Progressive Education Association," ca. summer 1920, Morgan Papers; Slutz, *Moraine Park School,* 1–8.

21. Quote from Arthur E. Morgan to Gertrude Stevens Ayres, November 18, 1920, Morgan Papers.

22. Quote from "Digest of the Second Annual Convention of the Progressive Education Association," 1921, 8; "Record of the Morning Session of the Progressive Education Association, Engineer's Club," April 2, 1921, Morgan Papers; Graham, *Progressive Education,* 166.

23. Morgan, "PEA Address, Boston," August 6, 1920, handwritten note on cover page, Morgan Papers; Talbert, *FDR's Utopian,* 44; Graham, *Progressive Education,* 85–89, 163–64; Cremin, *Transformation of the School,* 269–73.

24. Arthur E. Morgan, "The Reorganization Program for Antioch College," July 6, 1920, Morgan Papers; Herr, *Connected Thoughts,* 56; "The Antioch Plan, Announcement 1921–1922" *Antioch College Bulletin* 17 (April 1921): 1–21.

25. Arthur E. Morgan to the Antioch College Board of Trustees, September 24, 1920; Arthur E. Morgan, "The Plan for the New Antioch," December 1920, all in Morgan Papers; Clark, *Distinctive College,* 24–25.

26. Arthur E. Morgan to Charles Eliot, February 11, 1921; Charles Eliot to Arthur E. Morgan, February 14, 1921; Arthur E. Morgan to Hendrick W. Van Loon, April 21, 1921; Hendrick W. Van Loon to Arthur E. Morgan, April 23, 1921; Arthur E. Morgan to Hendrick W. Van Loon, May 3, 1921; Hendrick W. Van Loon to Arthur E. Morgan, May 6, 1921, all in Morgan Papers; Clark, *Distinctive College,* 25; Talbert, *FDR's Utopian,* 53–54.

27. Quote from H. L. Mencken to Hendrick W. Van Loon, May 22, 1921, Morgan Papers; Naylor, "Work-Study at Antioch," 93–95, 103–6, 219–21; "General Catalogue, 1925–1926," *Antioch College Bulletin* 20 (July 1925): 139–50; Talbert, *FDR's Utopian,* 54.

28. Arthur E. Morgan, "The Antioch Curriculum," ca. 1921, Morgan Papers; Herr, *Connected Thoughts,* 86, 96; Clark, *Distinctive College,* 28; Newman, *Innovative Change,* 90–91.

29. Arthur E. Morgan, "The Antioch Plan: Training for Administration and Proprietorship at a Small College," *Engineering News Record* 86 (January 20, 1921): 108–11; Herr, *Connected Thoughts,* 69, 91; Talbert, *FDR's Utopian,* 50–51; Hawthorne Daniel, "Arthur E. Morgan's New Type of College, *The World's Work* 41 (February 1921): 405–9; "The Antioch Plan," *The New Republic* 27 (July 20, 1921): 205–6; Dickinson S. Miller, "The Antioch Idea," *Nation* 113 (September 7, 1921): 263.

30. Herr, *Connected Thoughts,* 83–86; Talbert, *FDR's Utopian,* 53; Newman, *Innovative Change,* 32–34; Clark, *Distinctive College,* 29–30.

31. Arthur E. Morgan, "Antioch College: Progress of College Plan up to December 1, 1921," December 16, 1921, Morgan Papers.

32. George Marvin, "The Answer of Antioch: Does Education Educate?" *The Outlook,* 142 (February 10, 1926): 211–13; Arthur Ruhl, "The Antioch Idea at Work," *The New Republic* 30 (May 24, 1922): 373–75; Ida M. Tarbell, "Morgan of Antioch: An Engineer's Great Contribution to the Training of Useful Americans," *Collier's* 69 (June 3, 1922): 7–8, 20–21, 23; Talbert, *FDR's Utopian,* 52–56, 64; Newman, *Innovative Change,* 52–55; Herr, *Connected Thoughts,* 127.

33. Quotes from Arthur E. Morgan, "Notes for a Fifteen Minute Talk on Factors Responsible for the Success of the Miami Conservancy District," Ohio State University Natural Resources Seminar, February 6, 1962, Morgan Papers.

34. Arthur E. Morgan to Board of Directors, Miami Conservancy District, August 31, 1921; Arthur E. Morgan to *The Dayton News,* August 27, 1921, 1–2; Miami Conservancy District to Arthur E. Morgan, February 1, 1922, all in Morgan Papers; Morgan, *Miami Conservancy District,* 420–23; Sealander, *Grand Plans,* 82; Purcell, "Reclaiming Lost Ground," 387–88.

35. Purcell, "Reclaiming Lost Ground," 388; Kahoe, *Arthur Morgan,* 18; Morgan, *Arthur Morgan Remembered,* 43.

36. Quote from Arthur E. Morgan, "Morality," *Antioch Notes* 4 (December 1, 1926); Arthur E. Morgan, "Ethical Origins," *Antioch Notes* 7 (December 1, 1929); Arthur E. Morgan, "What I Think of Tobacco," ca. early 1920s, Morgan Papers; Talbert, *FDR's Utopian,* 56–57, 60–61; Morgan, *Arthur Morgan Remembered,* 48.

37. Quote from Arthur E. Morgan, "Notes on My Life Outlook," September 7, 1967, Morgan Papers; Arthur E. Morgan, "The Duty to Adventure," *Antioch Notes* 7 (January 15, 1930); Arthur E. Morgan, "Ethics," *Antioch Notes* 7 (February 1, 1930); Talbert, *FDR's Utopian,* 56–57.

38. Morgan, "Duty to Adventure;" Morgan, "Ethics;" Talbert, *FDR's Utopian,* 82, 84.

39. Morgan, "Morality;" Talbert, *FDR's Utopian,* 57–58.

40. Morgan, "Morality;" Morgan, "Ethical Origins;" Arthur E. Morgan, "One Hundred Years from Now," January 20, 1924, Morgan Papers.

41. Mark H. Haller, *Eugenics: Hereditarian Attitudes in American Thought* (New Brunswick, N.J.: Rutgers Univ. Press, 1963), 3–6; Pickens, *Eugenics and the Progressives,* 8–13; Daniel J. Kevles, *In the Name of Eugenics: Genetics and the Uses of Human Heredity* (New York: Alfred A. Knopf, 1985), 8.

42. Haller, *Eugenics,* 104, 149; Pickens, *Eugenics and the Progressives,* 49–50; Madison Grant, *The Passing of the Great Race: Or the Racial Basis of European History* (New York: Charles Scribner's Sons, 1916); Nancy Ordover, *American Eugenics: Race, Queer Anatomy, and the Science of Nationalism* (Minneapolis, Minn.: Univ. of Minnesota Press, 2003), 4–7, 13, 24–25, 141, 195.

43. Kevles, *In the Name of Eugenics,* 97, 100; Haller, *Eugenics,* 62–63, 133–39, 155; Ordover, *American Eugenics,* 137–41; Pickens, *Eugenics and the Progressives,* 32, 127.

44. Pickens, *Eugenics and the Progressives,* 51–53; Steven Selden, *Inheriting Shame: The Story of Eugenics and Racism in America* (New York: Teachers College Press, 1999), 4–15, 22–23; Ruth Clifford Engs, *The Eugenics Movement: An Encyclopedia* (Westport, Conn.: Greenwood Press, 2005), 5–8, 85; Talbert, *FDR's Utopian,* 58.

45. Ohio Race Betterment Association, "Race Betterment: A Symposium," *Brush Foundation Publication no. IV,* 7, in Morgan Papers; Talbert, *FDR's Utopian,* 59.

46. Ellsworth Huntington to Arthur E. Morgan, ca. November 1935; Ellsworth Huntington to Arthur E. Morgan, January 24, 1936; Arthur E. Morgan to Ellsworth Huntington, February 1, 1936; Ellsworth Huntington to Arthur E. Morgan, February 21, 1936; Frederick Osborn to Arthur E. Morgan, March 25, 1936; Ellsworth Huntington to Arthur E. Morgan, April 1, 1936, all in Morgan Papers; American Eugenics Society, *A Eugenics Program for the United States* (New York: American Eugenics Society, ca. 1935), 4–5, 8–16.

47. George Reid Andrews to Arthur E. Morgan, April 3, 1936; Arthur E. Morgan, "Eugenics and Social Inheritance," in American Eugenics Society, *American Eugenics, Proceedings of the Annual Meeting and Round Table Conferences of the American Eugenics Society, May 7, 1936* (New York: American Eugenics Society, 1936), quote on 17, 11–12, 20; George Reid Andrews to Arthur E. Morgan, May 11, 1936, all in Morgan Papers.

48. Ellsworth Huntington to Arthur E. Morgan, May 13, 1936, Morgan Papers.

49. Morgan, *Edward Bellamy,* 158–63.

50. Herr, *Connected Thoughts,* 132–33, 142; Newman, *Innovative Change,* 40, 63; Clark, *Distinctive College,* 38.

51. Herr, *Connected Thoughts,* 143–47.

52. Talbert, *FDR's Utopian,* 61.

53. Morgan, "One Hundred Years from Now," January 20, 1924, Morgan Papers.

54. Quote from Ibid.

55. Ibid.

56. Ibid.

57. Quotes from Ibid.

58. Ibid.

59. Newman, *Innovative Change,* 58–62, 71–74; Herr, *Connected Thoughts,* 165–67, 174–79, 207–8, 213–16.

60. Newman, *Innovative Change,* 52–54, 73–74; Arthur E. Morgan to Charles Eliot, July 12, 1920, Morgan Papers; Naylor, "Work-Study at Antioch," 155–57; Talbert, *FDR's Utopian,* 60, 64; Arthur E. Morgan, *Industries for Small Communities: With Cases from Yellow Springs* (Yellow Springs, Ohio: Community Service, Inc., 1953), 43–50, 72–73.

61. Quotes from Arthur E. Morgan to Lucy Morgan, March 7, 1928, Morgan Papers; Talbert, *FDR's Utopian,* 63–64.

62. Arthur E. Morgan, "A Letter to the Faculty Written at Cintra, Portugal," Fall 1931, Morgan Papers, quotes from 1, 5, 42.

63. First quote, Arthur E. Morgan to Lucy Morgan, March 25, 1932; other quotes from Arthur E. Morgan, "An Effort to Express My Outlook and Life Purpose," January 6, 1932; Antioch Faculty to Arthur E. Morgan, December 22, 1932, all in Morgan Papers; *The Antiochian* December 14, 1931; Talbert, *FDR's Utopian,* 65.

64. Arthur E. Morgan, "Remarks on Proposed New Program for Antioch College," May 4, 1932, Morgan Papers.

65. Arthur E. Morgan, *The Seed Man: Or, Things in General* (Yellow Springs, Ohio: Antioch Press, 1932); Talbert, *FDR's Utopian,* 66–67.

66. Quote from Arthur E. Morgan, "The Seed Man or Things in General: A Play in Eleven Scenes," January 1932, Morgan Papers; Morgan, *The Seed Man*; "An Antioch Play," *Christian Register,* 111 (July 21-28, 1932): 457; "The Seed Man," *Seed World,* 63 (November 7, 1948): 56-57; Talbert, *FDR's Utopian,* 67.

67. Morgan Engineering Company, "Report on Water Resources, Muskingum Drainage Area," 1931, 1:1–6, 109, in Morgan Papers; Talbert, *FDR's Utopian,* 83.

68. Arthur E. Morgan, "Recollections Concerning the TVA," June 15, 1971, 3, Morgan Papers; Talbert, *FDR's Utopian,* 83. In June 1933, the Morgan Engineering Company became the chief engineer of the Muskingum Conservancy District project. Carl Bock to Board of Directors, Muskingum Watershed Conservancy District, July 19, 1933, Morgan Papers.

5. VALLEY OF VISIONS

1. Arthur E. Morgan, "Recollections of FDR for Posterity," May 1966; Morgan, "Recollections Concerning the TVA," June 15, 1971, 4, all in Morgan Papers.

2. Quotes in Arthur E. Morgan, *The Making of the TVA* (Buffalo: Prometheus Books, 1974), 6–7; Morgan, "Recollections," 4; Aaron D. Purcell, "Building Dams, Burning Bridges: Conflicting Philosophies on the Tennessee Valley Authority Board, 1933–1939" (master's thesis, Univ. of Louisville, 1996), 84–85, 100–102.

3. Arthur E. Morgan to Mrs. Franklin D. Roosevelt, April 11, 1931; Mrs. Franklin D. Roosevelt to Arthur E. Morgan, April 15, 1933, all in Morgan Papers; James M. Cox, *Journey Through My Years* (New York: Simon And Schuster, 1946), 176; Kahoe, *Arthur Morgan,* 6; Purcell, "Building Dams," 98–99.

4. Quote in *The Public Papers and Addresses of Franklin D. Roosevelt,* comp. Samuel I. Rosenman (New York: Random House, 1938), 1:659.

5. Kyvig, *Daily Life,* 180–91; William E. Leuchtenburg, *Franklin D. Roosevelt and the New Deal, 1932–1940* (New York: Harper and Row, 1963), 1–3; Robert S. McElvaine, *The Great Depression: America, 1929–1941* (New York: Times Books, 1993), 66, 134–35.

6. David M. Kennedy, *Freedom from Fear: The American People in Depression and War, 1929–1945* (New York: Oxford Univ. Press, 1999), 118–29; Preston Hubbard, *Origins of the TVA: The Muscle Shoals Controversy, 1920–1932* (New York: W.W. Norton and Company, 1961), 312–13; Judson King, *The Conservation Fight: From Theodore Roosevelt to the Tennessee Valley Authority* (Washington, D.C.: Public Affairs Press, 1959), 254.

7. George Norris, *Fighting Liberal: The Autobiography of George W. Norris* (New York: MacMillan Company, 1945), 156–61; Alfred Lief, *Democracy's Norris: The Biography of A Lonely Crusade* (New York: Stackpole Sons, 1939), 152–55; Richard Lowitt, *George W. Norris: The Persistence of a Progressive, 1913–1933* (Urbana: Univ. of Illinois Press, 1971), 22.

8. King, *Conservation Fight,* 77, 83–84, 95; Hubbard, *Origins of TVA,* 3–4; Richard L. Neuberg and Stephen B. Khan, *Integrity: The Life of George W. Norris* (New York: Vanguard Press, 1937), 205.

9. King, *Conservation Fight,* 98–99, 121–22; Hubbard, *Origins of TVA,* 28–29; Lowitt, *Norris, Persistence,* 200, 203; Carol Gelderman, *Henry Ford: The Wayward Capitalist* (New York: St. Martin's Press, 1989), 248–49; Robert Lacey, *Ford: The Men and the Machine* (Boston: Little, Brown, and Company, 1986), 211–14.

10. Khan, *Integrity,* 222; Norman L. Zucker, *George W. Norris: Gentle Knight of American Democracy* (Urbana: Univ. of Illinois Press, 1966), 121–23; Lowitt, *Norris, Persistence,* 247; Hubbard, *Origins of TVA,* 233–35, 292–301; C. Herman Pritchett, *The Tennessee Valley Authority: A Study in Public Administration* (Chapel Hill: Univ. of North Carolina Press, 1943), 12–13.

11. Quote in *Public Papers of FDR,* 1:888–89; Lowitt, *Norris, Persistence,* 552–53, 558–59, 567; Pritchett, *Tennessee Valley Authority,* 29; Hubbard, *Origins of TVA,* 314.

12. *Public Papers of FDR,* 1:122–23; Arthur E. Morgan to Franklin D. Roosevelt, April 12, 1933; quote in Franklin D. Roosevelt to Arthur E. Morgan, April 18, 1933, all in TVA microfilm, Morgan Papers; Lief, *Democracy's Norris,* 414–17; Richard Lowitt, *George W. Norris: The Triumph of a Progressive, 1933–1944* (Urbana: Univ. of Illinois Press, 1978), 16–19.

13. Lowitt, *Norris, Triumph,* 18; Talbert, *FDR's Utopian,* 87–88; Kahoe, *Arthur Morgan,* 72–73; Lief, *Democracy's Norris,* 417; Morgan, *Making of the TVA,* 18–19.

14. Lowitt, *Norris, Triumph,* 22; "Tennessee Valley Authority Act," available at http://www.tva.gov/abouttva/pdf/TVA_Act.pdf; Marguerite Owen, *The Tennessee Valley Authority* (New York: Praeger Publishers, 1973), 16–18; Aaron D. Purcell, *White Collar Radicals: TVA's Knoxville Fifteen, the New Deal, and the McCarthy Era* (Knoxville: Univ. of Tennessee Press, 2009), 4–5; Louis B. Wehle, *Hidden Threads of History: Wilson Through Roosevelt* (New York: The MacMillan Company, 1953), 157.

15. "TVA Act;" Morgan to Roosevelt, April 12, 1933; Roosevelt to Morgan, April 18, 1933, all in TVA microfilm, Morgan Papers; Talbert, *FDR's Utopian,* 91–92.

16. *Complete Presidential Press Conferences,* 1:288. Despite Morgan's new TVA responsibilities and his dissatisfaction with Antioch College, he remained president of Antioch College until April 1935. See, Arthur Morgan to Homer Corry, April 27, 1935, Morgan Papers.

17. *New York Times,* May 20, 1933; Arthur E. Morgan to Marvin McIntyre, May 30, 1933, Morgan Papers; Arthur E. Morgan to Marvin McIntyre, notes from phone conversation, 3 or 4 June, 1933, in Box 3, RG 142, Records of the Tennessee Valley Authority, NARA–SE; Talbert, *FDR's Utopian,* 90–95; McCraw, *Morgan vs. Lilienthal,* 12, 17–18; Morgan, *Making of the TVA,* 20–23; David E. Lilienthal, *The Journals of David E. Lilienthal* (New York: Harper and Row, 1964), 1:32–34; Stephen M. Neuse, *David Lilienthal: The Journey of an American Liberal* (Knoxville: Univ. of Tennessee Press, 1996), 62–63.

18. McCraw, *TVA and the Power Fight,* 40–41; Arnold Kruckman, "Unpublished article about H. A. Morgan," July 21, 1933, Harcourt Morgan Papers, University of Tennessee Special Collections, Knoxville, Tennessee (hereafter cited as Harcourt Morgan Papers); James Rorty, "TVA's H. A. Morgan," *The Commonweal* 48 (June 18, 1948): 228; Purcell, "Building Dams," 104–5.

19. McCraw, *TVA Power Fight,* 40; Harcourt Morgan, "Tentative Definition of the Common Mooring," Harcourt Morgan Papers; Ellis F. Hartford, *Our Common Mooring* (Athens: Univ. of Georgia Press, 1941), 27–28; Mouzon Peters, "The Story of Dr. Harcourt Morgan," book V in *Makers of Millions: Not for Themselves, But For You,* ed. Louis D. Wallace (Nashville: Tennessee Department of Agriculture, 1951), 39; Purcell, "Building Dams," 105.

20. Neuse, *David Lilienthal,* 1–3, 12–13, 20–21, 25; Lilienthal, *Journals,* 1:1, 3, 9–10, 14–15, 33–34; Anthony Coelho, "David Eli Lilienthal: Pragmatic Liberal at the Crossroads" (Term paper, Brown University, 1973), 3, available at the TVA Corporate Library, Knoxville, Tennessee; Purcell, "Building Dams," 107–9.

21. Donald Richberg, *My Hero: The Indiscreet Memoirs of an Eventful but Unheroic Life* (New York: Putnam, 1954), 126–27; Willson Whitman, *David Lilienthal: Public Servant in a Power Age* (New York: Henry Holt and Company, 1948), 6–9; McCraw, *Morgan vs. Lilienthal,* 21–22; Neuse, *David Lilienthal,* 44, 47–50, 63–65; Purcell, "Building Dams," 110–12.

22. Morgan, *Making of the TVA,* 6–7; Kenneth S. Davis, *FDR: Into the Storm, 1937–1940* (New York: Random House, 1993), 166; Roy Talbert Jr., "Arthur E. Morgan's Social Philosophy and the Tennessee Valley Authority," East Tennessee Historical Society's *Publications* 41 (1969): 86–90; Purcell, *White Collar Radicals,* 5.

23. McCraw, *TVA and the Power Fight,* 40–41; Morgan, "Definition of the Common Mooring," Harcourt Morgan Papers; Hartford, *Our Common Mooring,* 37–39, 60–63; Purcell, *White Collar Radicals,* 5.

24. McCraw, *Morgan vs. Lilienthal,* 23; Neuse, *David Lilienthal,* 71; Coelho, "Lilienthal, Pragmatic Liberal," 16; Purcell, *White Collar Radicals,* 6.

25. *New York Times,* June 4 and June 5, 1933; *Washington Post,* June 11, 1933; Neuse, *David Lilienthal,* 63.

26. Quote from Arthur E. Morgan, "Memorandum of a Visit of Arthur E. Morgan with Postmaster General Farley, Wednesday, June 7, 1933," 3–4, TVA microfilm, Morgan Papers; Morgan, *Making of the TVA,* 9–13; James A. Farley, *Behind the Ballots: The Personal History of a Politician* (New York: Harcourt, Brace and Company, 1938), 232–33; Talbert, *FDR's Utopian,* 97; Purcell, "Building Dams," 114.

27. Arthur E. Morgan, "Memorandum of a Conference with President Roosevelt, June 8, 1933," 1–5; Arthur E. Morgan, "Memorandum of a Second Visit of Arthur E. Morgan with Postmaster General Farley, Saturday afternoon, about 11:30, June 10, 1933," 3, 5, all in TVA microfilm, Morgan Papers; Talbert, *FDR's Utopian,* 99–100; Purcell, "Building Dams," 114–15.

28. *Washington Post,* June 11, 1933; "Minutes of the First Meeting of the Board of Directors of the Tennessee Valley Authority, June 16, 1933," TVA Office of General Counsel, Knoxville, Tennessee; McCraw, *Morgan vs. Lilienthal,* 26–27; Talbert, *FDR's Utopian,* 101–2; Aaron D. Purcell, "Power to the People: David Lilienthal Founds TVA's Electric Power Policy, 1933," *The Journal of East Tennessee History* 70 (1998): 96.

29. Lilienthal, *Journals,* 1:39; McCraw, *Morgan vs. Lilienthal,* 27; Purcell, "Power to the People," 97.

30. Lilienthal, *Journals,* 1:39; McCraw, *Morgan vs. Lilienthal,* 27; Purcell, "Power to the People," 97.

31. Purcell, "Power to the People," 97–98; Talbert, *FDR's Utopian,* 102–3.

32. Arthur E. Morgan, "Memorandum of a talk between Arthur E. Morgan, and Mr. Willkie, President of the Commonwealth and Southern Corporation, at the University Club, New York, Wednesday Evening, June 28, 1933," David E. Lilienthal Papers, Seeley G. Mudd Manuscript Library, Princeton University, Princeton, N.J. (hereafter cited as Lilienthal Papers); Purcell, "Power to the People," 98; McCraw, *TVA and the Power Fight,* 53–54.

33. Arthur E. Morgan to Wendell Willkie, July 12, 1933; Wendell Willkie to Arthur E. Morgan, July 15, 1933, all in Lilienthal Papers; Purcell, "Power to the People," 98–99; McCraw, *TVA and the Power Fight,* 54–55.

34. Arthur E. Morgan to David Lilienthal, "Penciled Memorandum," [ca. July 10 or 15, 1933], Lilienthal Papers; Talbert, *FDR's Utopian,* 139–40.

35. David Lilienthal to Arthur E. Morgan, July 21, 1933, Lilienthal Papers.

36. Purcell, "Power to the People," 99; Paul David Interview, November 20, 1990, [transcript] 2–4, University of Kentucky and Pi Sigma Alpha, American Political Science Association Oral History Project, Antioch College; Talbert, *FDR's Utopian,* 110; Roy Talbert Jr., ed., "Arthur E. Morgan's Ethical Code for the Tennessee Valley Authority," East Tennessee Historical Society's *Publications* 40 (1968): 119.

37. Arthur E. Morgan, "An Ethical Code for the Staff of the Tennessee Valley Authority," July 15, 1933, 1–8, Morgan Papers; Talbert, "Morgan's Moral Code," 121–27; Kahoe, *Biography and Memoir,* 76–77, 85–86.

38. *New York Times,* August 2, 1933; Talbert, *FDR's Utopian,* 102–3, 115–16; Harold L. Ickes, *The Secret Diary of Harold Ickes* (New York: Simon and Schuster, 1953), 1:119; Purcell, "Building Dams," 130–31.

39. Michael J. McDonald and John Muldowny, *TVA and the Dispossessed: The Resettlement of Population in the Norris Dam Area* (Knoxville: Univ. of Tennessee Press, 1982), 219–20; Aelred J. Gray, "The Maturing of a Planned New Town—Norris, Tennessee" *Tennessee Planner* 32 (1974): 2; *New York Times,* August 6, 1933; Purcell, "Building Dams," 129–31; Jan Elizabeth Cigliano, "Norris, Tennessee: America's Forgotten TVA New Town" (master's thesis, George Washington Univ., 1982), 7.

40. Quote from Morgan, *Making of the TVA,* 88–89.

41. Harcourt Morgan and David Lilienthal, "Memorandum on Organization," August 3, 1933, 1–6, Lilienthal Papers; Purcell, "Power to the People," 101.

42. "Minute Entry—August 5, 1933," Lilienthal Papers; "TVA Board Minutes, 5 August 1933," TVA microfilm, Morgan Papers; *New York Times,* August 11, 1933; Talbert, *FDR's Utopian,* 104; Pritchett, *The Tennessee Valley Authority,* 155–56; Purcell, "Power to the People," 101; Purcell, "Building Dams," 130.

43. Arthur E. Morgan to H. A. Morgan and David Lilienthal, August 14, 1933, Lilienthal Papers; Purcell, "Power to the People," 100–101.

44. David Lilienthal, "Memorandum in Opposition to Proposal of Chairman A. E. Morgan for Territorial Division Agreement and 'Cooperation' between Tennessee Valley Authority and Private Utilities," August 16, 1933; David Lilienthal, "Principles for a Power Policy," August 16, 1933; David Lilienthal, "A Plan of Action for Carrying out the Power Program," August 17, 1933, all in Lilienthal Papers; Purcell, "Power to the People," 101–2.

45. "TVA Power Policy Summary," David Lilienthal's personal copy, Lilienthal Papers; Talbert, *FDR's Utopian,* 144; Roy Talbert Jr., "Beyond Pragmaticism: The Story of Arthur E. Morgan" (PhD diss., Vanderbilt Univ., 1971), 194; Purcell, "Power to the People," 102–103; Purcell, "Building Dams," 129.

46. McDonald and Muldowny, *TVA and the Dispossessed,* 127–29, 155–58, 175, 195, 220–21; Tennessee Valley Authority, *The Norris Project: A Comprehensive Report on the Planning, Design, Construction, and Initial Operations of the Tennessee Valley Authority's First Water Control System,* technical report no. 1 (Washington, D.C.: Government Printing Office, 1940), 12, 19, 63–65, 173–76; Erin E. Pritchard, ed., *TVA Archaeology: Seventy-Five Years of Prehistoric Site Research* (Knoxville: Univ. of Tennessee Press, 2009), 18–20; Aelred J. Gray and David A. Johnson, *The TVA Regional Planning and Development Program: The Transformation of an Institution and Its Mission* (Burlington, Vt.: Ashgate Publishing Company, 2005), 14–15.

47. Gray and Johnson, *TVA Regional Planning,* 12–15; TVA, *The Norris Project,* 174–75; Gray, "Planned New Town," 3–7; Tracy B. Auger, "The Planning of the Town of Norris," *American Architect* 148 (April 1936): 22; Cigliano, "Norris, Tennessee," 63–64; John H. Kyle, *The Building of TVA: An Illustrated History* (Baton Rouge: Louisiana State Univ. Press, 1958), 16–17.

48. Gray, "Planned New Town," 9; Earle S. Draper, "The TVA Town of Norris, Tennessee," *American Planning and Civic Annual* 5 (1934): 208; Earl S. Draper, "The New Town of Norris, Tennessee," *The American City* 48 (December 1933): 67; Auger, "The Planning of the Town of Norris," 22.

49. Aaron D. Purcell, "Suppressed Currents: The 'Fool Report' and the Early Tennessee Valley Authority," *The Journal of East Tennessee History* 74 (2002): 70.

50. Morgan, *Making of the TVA,* 133; Pritchett, *TVA Public Administration,* 177; Purcell, "Suppressed Currents," 74–75; Russell S. McBride, "Confidential Report," [ca. October 1933], Harry A. Curtis Papers, University of Tennessee Special Collections, Knoxville, Tennessee (hereafter cited as Curtis Papers).

51. McBride, "Confidential Report," Curtis Papers; Purcell, "Suppressed Currents," 75.

52. Quote in Harry A. Curtis to Russell S. McBride, December 19, 1933; Russell S. McBride, "Letter proposed for transmittal to Dr. Morgan and the other members of the Tennessee Valley Authority," December 15, 1933, all in Curtis Papers; Purcell, "Suppressed Currents," 75–76.

53. Droze, *High Dams and Slack Waters,* 21; Pritchett, *Tennessee Valley Authority,* 35–36; Purcell, "Power to the People," 108.

54. Arthur E. Morgan, "General Program Report for the Tennessee Valley Authority," 22 Dec. 1933, TVA microfilm, Morgan Papers; Talbert, *FDR's Utopian,* 106.

55. Quote from *New York Times,* August 6, 1933; *New York Times,* October 28, 1933; Talbert, *FDR's Utopian,* 106–7.

56. *New York Times,* December 3, 1933; Jonathan Mitchell, "Utopia—Tennessee Valley Style," *The New Republic* 76 (18 October 1933): 272.

57. *Chattanooga News,* November 9, 1933; November 11, 1933; November 13, 1933; Mitchell, "Utopia—Tennessee Valley Style," 272–73.

58. Arthur E. Morgan, "Vitality and Formalism in Government," *Social Forces* 13 (October 1934): 4; Arthur E. Morgan, "Social Methods of the Tennessee Valley Authority," *Journal of Educational Sociology* 8 (January 1935): 263–64; Arthur E. Morgan, "The Tennessee Valley Authority," *The Scientific Monthly* 38 (January 1934): 65, 71; Arthur E. Morgan, "Sociology in the TVA," *American Sociological Review* 2 (April 1937): 164.

59. Morgan, "The Tennessee Valley Authority," 68.

60. McDonald and Muldowny, *TVA and the Dispossessed,* 221; Gray, "Planned New Town," 5, 7; Auger, "The Planning of the Town of Norris," 24; John T. Moutoux, "The TVA Builds a Town," *The New Republic* 77 (January 31, 1934): 331.

61. Earle S. Draper, "TVA's Yardstick for Housing" *The Architectural Forum* 63 (September 1935): 162–70; Moutoux, "The TVA Builds a Town," 330; *New York Times,* November 26, 1933; Scott Sanders to Aaron D. Purcell, December 8, 2009, e-mail in author's possession; Cigliano, "Norris, Tennessee," 91–93; Talbert, *FDR's Utopian,* 116–17.

62. Morgan, *Arthur Morgan Remembered,* 68–69; *Chicago Tribune,* November 5, 1934; "Churchless Norris," *The Christian Century* 51 (November 14, 1934): 1448–49; Talbert, *FDR's Utopian,* 120–21.

63. Quote from *New York Times,* November 17, 1934; *Chicago Tribune,* November 17, 1934; Ickes, *Secret Diary,* 1:225; Baker Brownell and Frank Lloyd Wright, *Architecture and Modern Life* (New York: Harper and Brothers, 1937), 67; Cigliano, "Norris, Tennessee," 74.

64. *New York Times,* January 26, 1934; Joseph G. Knapp, *The Advance of American Cooperative Enterprise, 1920–1945* (Danville, Ill.: Interstate Printers and Publishers, Inc., 1973), 327–28; Pritchett, *Tennessee Valley Authority,* 129–30; Purcell, "Building Dams," 177–78.

65. Knapp, *American Cooperative Enterprise,* 328–29; *New York Times,* January 26, 1934; Purcell, "Building Dams," 178.

66. Gray, "Planned New Town," 9; McDonald and Muldowny, *TVA and the Dispossessed,* 224; North Callahan, *TVA: Bridge Over Troubled Waters* (New York: A. S. Barnes and Company, 1980), 30; Kyle, *Building of TVA,* 15; Purcell, "Building Dams," 184–85.

67. TVA, *TVA Employee Relationship Policy 1935* (Knoxville, Tenn.: TVA, 1935), 4; Nancy L. Grant, *TVA and Black Americans: Planning for the Status Quo* (Philadelphia: Temple Univ. Press, 1990), 19, 37–39; Purcell, *White Collar Radicals,* 10.

68. Morgan, *Making of the TVA,* 124–26; Purcell, "Building Dams," 132–33; Talbert, *FDR's Utopian,* 118–20; Callahan, *TVA Bridge,* 35.

69. TVA, *Employee Relationship Policy, 1935,* 2–9; Pritchett, *The Tennessee Valley Authority;* Purcell, *White Collar Radicals,* 43.

70. See Joseph L. Arnold, *The New Deal in the Suburbs: A History of the Greenbelt Town Program, 1935–1954* (Columbus: The Ohio State Univ. Press, 1971); Paul Conkin, *Tomorrow a New World: The New Deal Community Program* (Ithaca: Cornell Univ. Press, 1959).

71. Knapp, *American Cooperative Enterprise,* 338–40; Owen, *Tennessee Valley Authority,* 28–30; Purcell, "Building Dams," 172–74, 180.

72. Gregory B. Field, "'Electricity for All': The Electric Home and Farm Authority and the Politics of Mass Consumption, 1932–1935," *Business History Review* 64 (Spring 1990): 34–35, 38, 47–49; David E. Lilienthal, "National Home and Farm Electrification Program: Proposed by the Tennessee Valley Authority," November 21, 1933, Lilienthal Papers; "TVA Appliances," *Business Weekly,* (March 17, 1934), 10; Neuse, *David Lilienthal,* 86–88; Purcell, "Building Dams," 164–68.

73. "Contract Between Tennessee Valley Authority and Commonwealth and Southern Corporation," *TVA Press Release,* January 5, 1934, Jo Conn Guild Collection, Tennessee State Library and Archives, Nashville, Tennessee (hereafter cited as Jo Conn Guild Collection, TSLA); Lilienthal, *Journals,* 1:713–15; McCraw, *Morgan Versus Lilienthal,* 43; Joseph Barnes, *Willkie: The Events He Was Part of, the Ideas He Fought For* (New York: Simon and Schuster, 1952), 64–65, 69, 74; Neuse, *Lilienthal: American Liberal,* 82; Talbert, *FDR's Utopian,* 144–45; McCraw, *Power Fight,*

65; Aaron D. Purcell, "Struggle Within, Struggle Without: The TEPCO Case and the Tennessee Valley Authority, 1936–1939," *Tennessee Historical Quarterly* 61 (Fall 2002): 195–96; Purcell, "Power to the People," 104–8.

74. Joseph C. Swidler and Robert H. Marquis, "TVA in Court: A Study of TVA's Constitutional Litigation," *Iowa Law Review* 32 (January 1947): 305–9; McCraw, *Power Fight,* 112–13; Alan W. Boyd, "The Tennessee Valley Litigation," *Indiana Law Journal* 11 (October 1935): 368–75; "Opinion of the Court," *Tennessee Valley Authority et al. v. Ashwander et al.* U.S. Circuit Court of Appeals, 78 F.2d 578 (1935), 3–15; *Ashwander et al. v. Tennessee Valley Authority et al.,* 297 U.S. 288 (1936); Purcell, "Struggle Within, Struggle Without," 196.

75. Arthur E. Morgan to Harcourt Morgan, August 3, 1934, Harcourt Morgan Papers; Purcell, "Building Dams," 174.

76. Field, "Electricity for All," 52; Purcell, "Building Dams," 170–71, 183.

77. Neuse, *David Lilienthal,* 95–96; Talbert, *FDR's Utopian,* 153–55; McCraw, *Morgan Versus Lilienthal,* 50–51; McCraw, *TVA and the Power Fight,* 88–89.

78. Quote from Arthur E. Morgan, "Relations with the President (Rough Draft Continued)," July 5, 1938, 5–7, TVA microfilm, Morgan Papers; Morgan, *Making of the TVA,* 167; Ickes, *Secret Diary,* 1:566; McCraw, *TVA and the Power Fight,* 88; Purcell, "Building Dams," 191–92.

79. Morgan, "Relations with the President," July 5, 1938, 7, TVA microfilm, Morgan Papers; Lilienthal, *Journals,* 1:61–62; Purcell, "Building Dams," 192.

80. McCraw, *TVA and the Power Fight,* 88; Leuba, *Road to Creativity,* 189; Purcell, "Building Dams," 314–15.

6. THE LONG ROAD CUT SHORT

1. Quote from *New York Times,* March 5, 1936; Lowitt, *Norris, Persistence,* 122–23; *Knoxville News Sentinel,* March 4, 1936.

2. Quotes from Howard A. Bridgman Diary, 1936, 64, University of Tennessee Special Collections, Knoxville, Tennessee.

3. *Knoxville News Sentinel,* March 4 and 5, 1936; Droze, *High Dams and Slack Waters,* 45–47; Talbert, *FDR's Utopian,* 126.

4. William E. Leuchtenburg, "Norris and the 'Seven Little TVAs,'" *Journal of Politics* 14 (August 1952): 418–19.

5. Kennedy, *Freedom From Fear,* 222–23, 288–89, 384–85, 392–402; Bureau of the Census, *Historical Statistics of the United States: Colonial Times to 1970* (Washington, D.C.: Government Printing Office, 1975), 135; D. S. Halacy Jr., *1936: The Picture Story of an Unforgettable Year* (New Rochelle, N.Y.: Arlington House Publishers, 1974), 24–25; Timothy Egan, *The Worst Hard Times: The Untold Story of Those Who Survived the Great American Dust Bowl* (Boston: Houghton Mifflin Company, 2006) 9–10; William H. Young and Nancy K. Young, *The 1930s* (Westport, Conn.: Greenwood Press, 2002), xviii–xix, 7.

6. Kennedy, *Freedom From Fear,* 324–25; C. Herman Pritchett, *The Roosevelt Court: A Study in Judicial Politics and Values, 1937–1947* (Chicago: Quadrangle, 1948), 5–7; Arthur M. Schlesinger Jr., *The Politics of Upheaval* (Boston, Mass.: Houghton Mifflin Company, 1960), 252–60, 274–83, 487–88; Leuchtenburg, *FDR and the New Deal,* 144–47, 170–71; Marian C. McKenna, *Franklin Roosevelt and the Great Constitutional War: The Court Packing Crisis of 1937* (New York: Fordham Univ. Press, 2002), 101–3, 131–35.

7. Purcell, "Struggle Within, Struggle Without," 196.

8. Morgan, "Relations with the President," July 5, 1938, 7–8, TVA microfilm, Morgan Papers; Morgan, *Making of the TVA,* 167.

9. Schlesinger, *Politics of Upheaval,* 365; Purcell, "Building Dams," 193; McCraw, *Morgan Versus Lilienthal,* 55.

10. David E. Lilienthal to George Norris, May 4, 1936, Lilienthal Papers; Neuse, *David Lilienthal,* 96; McCraw, *Morgan Versus Lilienthal,* 54–55; McCraw, *TVA and the Power Fight,* 115.

11. Arthur E. Morgan to Franklin D. Roosevelt, May 1936, TVA microfilm, Morgan Papers; McCraw, *Morgan Versus Lilienthal,* 55.

12. Lilienthal, *Journals,* 1:61–62.

13. Quote from Franklin D. Roosevelt to Arthur E. Morgan, May 15, 1936, TVA microfilm, Morgan Papers; Morgan, *Making of the TVA,* 167–68.

14. *New York Times,* May 19, 1936; Arthur E. Morgan to Franklin Roosevelt, May 18, 1936; Morgan, "Relations with the President," July 5, 1938, 11–12, all in TVA microfilm, Morgan Papers.

15. Swidler and Marquis, "TVA in Court;" McCraw, *TVA and the Power Fight,* 104; "Bill of Complaint for an Injunction and Other Relief in Chancery Court of Knox County, Tennessee, 29 May 1936," in *Tennessee Electric Power Company et al. v. Tennessee Valley Authority et al., Transcript of Record, Volume I,* U.S. Supreme Court 27 (1938), 1–28; "Pending Litigation (Concerning the Sale of Surplus Electricity)," November 25, 1936, all in TVA microfilm, Morgan Papers; *Tennessee Electric Power Company v. TVA* 306 U.S. 118 (1939); Purcell, "Struggle Within, Struggle Without," 197.

16. Tennessee Electric Power Company, *A Compilation of Facts Regarding the Growth and Development of Tennessee With a Forecast of the Future Through the Utilization of the State's Most Valuable Natural Resource—Waterpower* (Chattanooga: The Tennessee Electric Power Company, 1925), 5–6, 25; Arthur W. Crouch, comp., *The Tennessee Electric Power Company, 1860–1939,* 1:10–13, Jo Conn Guild Collection, TSLA; William A. Doran, "Early Hydroelectric Power in Tennessee," *Tennessee Historical Quarterly* 27 (Spring 1968): 74; Commonwealth and Southern Corporation, *The Commonwealth and Southern Corporation and Its Subsidiary Companies, A Public Utility Holding Company Group, Outline of History and Development* (New York: Commonwealth and Southern Corporation, 1935), 9, 11, 15, 35; Purcell, "Struggle Within, Struggle Without," 197–98.

17. "19 Utilities' Litigation (A Chronology)," November 1, 1937, TVA microfilm, Morgan Papers; Purcell, "Struggle Within, Struggle Without," 198.

18. U.S. Congress, *Hearings Before the Joint Committee on the Investigation of the Tennessee Valley Authority* (Washington, D.C.: Government Printing Office, 1939), 3:1152; Morgan, "Relations with the President," July 5, 1938, 11–13, TVA microfilm, Morgan Papers; Neuse, *David Lilienthal,* 97.

19. "Power Policy: Organization of Department of Electricity," 1938, Lilienthal Papers; Pritchett, *Tennessee Valley Authority,* 163–65; Congress, *Investigation,* 3:1152–54; Owen, *Tennessee Valley Authority,* 48.

20. Arthur E. Morgan to David Lilienthal, June 4, 1936, Box 84, RG 142, NARA–SE; McCraw, *Morgan Versus Lilienthal,* 60–61; Neuse, *David Lilienthal,* 97; Talbert, *FDR's Utopian,* 163.

21. Aaron D. Purcell, "Undermining the TVA: George Berry, David Lilienthal, and Arthur Morgan," *Tennessee Historical Quarterly* 57 (Fall 1998): 170.

22. "Berry Associates Deny 'Plot' on TVA," *New York Times,* August 18, 1938, 34; Arthur E. Morgan, "Notes on Conversation with W. H. Ford, Dayton, Ohio," May 16, 1938; Alexander Harris, "Direct Examination by Judge Morris," 8–9, all in TVA microfilm, Morgan Papers; Purcell, "Undermining the TVA," 171.

23. Jack Mooney, *Printers in Appalachia: The International Printing Pressmen and Assistants' Union of North America, 1907–1967* (Bowling Green, Ohio: Bowling Green State Univ. Popular Press, 1993): 27–30; Purcell, "Undermining the TVA," 170.

24. *Dictionary of American Biography, Supplement Four, 1946–1950* (New York: Charles Scribner's Sons, 1974), 74–75; Irving Bernstein, *The Lean Years: A History of the American Workers, 1920–1933* (Baltimore, Md.: Penguin, 1966), 511; *National Cyclopedia of American Biography,* 36:477; Schlesinger, *Politics of Upheaval,* 386; McCraw, *Morgan Versus Lilienthal,* 91; Talbert, *FDR's Utopian,* 177; Purcell, "Undermining the TVA," 170, 173.

25. W. N. Garrett, "Statement of fact within my own experiences relating to preparation and trial of Berry Marble Case," January 2, 1937; Arthur E. Morgan, "Berry Marble Case," ca. 1938, 11; Edwin C. Eckel to Carl A. Bock, March 25, 1935; Carl A. Bock to the TVA Board of Directors,

March 30, 1935; E. W. Cowling to George Collins, April 12, 1935, all in TVA microfilm, Morgan Papers; Purcell, "Undermining the TVA," 172.

26. George Berry to Arthur E. Morgan, April 22, 1935; Arthur E. Morgan to George Berry, April 26, 1935; John Snyder to Carl Bock, May 15, 1935; Carl Bock to John Snyder, July 2, 1935; Frank H. Towsley, "Marble Claims—Conferences of March 30, 1936," April 1, 1936, all in TVA microfilm, Morgan Papers; Talbert, *FDR's Utopian,* 181; Purcell, "Undermining the TVA," 172–73.

27. James S. Cullison to the TVA Board of Directors, June 2, 1936; Arthur E. Morgan to the TVA Board of Directors, June 17, 1936, all in TVA microfilm, Morgan Papers; Purcell, "Undermining the TVA," 174.

28. George Berry to David Lilienthal, June 26, 1936; William H. Ford, "Rough Draft of Sworn Statement," ca. 1937; Tennessee Valley Authority and Major George Berry and Associates, "Memorandum Stating a Conciliation Agreement," July 13, 1936, all in TVA microfilm, Morgan Papers; Pritchett, *Tennessee Valley Authority,* 19–95; Purcell, "Undermining the TVA," 174.

29. First and third quotes from "A. E. Morgan Absent as TVA Begins Vital Budget Parleys," *Knoxville News Sentinel,* July 14, 1936; second quote from J. Charles Poe, "The Morgan-Lilienthal Feud," *Nation* 143 (October 3, 1936): 386; Purcell, "Building Dams," 202–203; Neuse, *David Lilienthal,* 97–98.

30. Quotes from "Morgan Absent," *Knoxville News Sentinel,* July 14, 1936; Purcell, "Building Dams," 203–4; Neuse, *David Lilienthal,* 98.

31. Quote from David Lilienthal to Felix Frankfurter, August 2, 1936, Lilienthal Papers.

32. "News Behind the News," *The National Whirligig,* June 29, 1936.

33. Franklin Roosevelt to Arthur E. Morgan, July 11, 1936; Arthur E. Morgan to Franklin Roosevelt, July 25, 1936, all in TVA microfilm, Morgan Papers; Purcell, "Building Dams," 208–9.

34. Purcell, "Struggle Within, Struggle Without," 198; McCraw, *Morgan Versus Lilienthal,* 69, 77–78.

35. Quote from David Lilienthal to Felix Frankfurter, August 2, 1936, Lilienthal Papers; Purcell, "Building Dams," 210.

36. Quote from Lilienthal to Frankfurter, August 2, 1936, Lilienthal Papers; Purcell, "Building Dams," 210–11.

37. "TVA Board Meeting Minute Entry," August 3, 1936; "TVA Board Meeting Minute Entry," August 4, 1936; David Lilienthal, "Policy on Territorial Restriction," August 4, 1936, all in Lilienthal Papers; Arthur E. Morgan to Franklin Roosevelt, August 4, 1938, TVA microfilm, Morgan Papers; Purcell, "Building Dams," 211.

38. McCraw, *Morgan Versus Lilienthal,* 91–92; Talbert, *FDR's Utopian,* 177; Purcell, "Undermining the TVA," 174–75.

39. Arthur E. Morgan to George Berry, August 9, 1936; George Berry to Arthur E. Morgan, August 15, 1936, all in Morgan Papers; Purcell, "Undermining the TVA," 175.

40. Arthur E. Morgan to the TVA Board of Directors, August 26, 1936, TVA microfilm, Morgan Papers; Purcell, "Undermining the TVA," 175.

41. David Lilienthal to George Norris, August 7, 1936, Lilienthal Papers; Arthur E. Morgan to George Norris, August 13, 1936, TVA microfilm, Morgan Papers.

42. James McMullin, "News Behind the News," *New York Whirligig,* August 28, 1936; Arthur Krock, "The Internal Struggle in TVA Group," *New York Times,* August 18, 1936.

43. "Power Policy: The President's Pooling Conference of 1936," 1938, 163–64; David Lilienthal to Franklin Roosevelt, September 9, 1936, all in Lilienthal Papers; Franklin Roosevelt to Arthur E. Morgan, September 17, 1936; David E. Lilienthal to TVA Board of Directors, September 19, 1936, all in TVA microfilm, Morgan Papers; McCraw, *Morgan Versus Lilienthal,* 69–71; Purcell, "Building Dams," 214–16.

44. *New York Times,* October 1, 1936; George Fort Milton to George Norris, November 4, 1936; "The Hamilton Incident," 1–3, all in Lilienthal Papers; McCraw, *Morgan Versus Lilienthal,* 72; Purcell, "Building Dams," 218–19.

45. David Lilienthal to Robert La Follette, December 18, 1936, Lilienthal Papers; Lilienthal, *Journals*, 1:63–64; Purcell, "Building Dams," 219.

46. Quote from Wehle, *Hidden Threads of History*, 164–66; "Statement of Arthur E. Morgan, David E. Lilienthal, and Wendell L. Willkie," October 11, 1936, Lilienthal Papers; Purcell, "Building Dams," 216–17.

47. David Lilienthal to Wendell Willkie, October 13, 1936, Lilienthal Papers; Purcell, "Building Dams," 217–18.

48. Schlesinger, *Politics of Upheaval*, 642; Lowitt, *Triumph of a Progressive*, 159; Purcell, "Building Dams," 219.

49. Swidler and Marquis, "TVA in Court," 313; Wehle, *Hidden Threads of History*, 178; John J. Gore, "Order for Preliminary Injunction," December 22, 1936, in *Tennessee Electric Power Company, et al. v. Tennessee Valley Authority, et al.*, U.S. District Court, 228 (1936), TVA microfilm, Morgan Papers; "Order for Removal—June 15, 1936;" John J. Gore, "Memorandum Opinion on Application for Temporary Injunction—December 22, 1936," in *TEPCO v. TVA, Transcript*, 1:136, 260–62; Purcell, "Struggle Within, Struggle Without," 199.

50. James Fly to David Lilienthal, January 11, 1937; "Litigation Chronology," all in TVA microfilm, Morgan Papers; Purcell, "Struggle Within, Struggle Without," 199.

51. Wendell Willkie to Franklin Roosevelt, January 6, 1937, Lilienthal Papers; "Litigation Chronology," TVA microfilm, Morgan Papers; Purcell, "Struggle Within, Struggle Without," 199.

52. Arthur E. Morgan, "The Next Four Years in the TVA," *The New Republic* 89 (6 January 1937): 290–94; Arthur E. Morgan, "Dr. Morgan Pleads for 'Cooperation' with the Utilities," *New York Times*, January 17, 1937; "Norris Opens War of TVA Injunctions," *New York Times*, January 17, 1937; Purcell, "Struggle Within, Struggle Without," 199.

53. Lilienthal, *Journals*, 1:65–66; Purcell, "Struggle Within, Struggle Without," 199.

54. George Berry to Arthur E. Morgan, February 5, 1937; Arthur E. Morgan, "Testimony of Dr. A. E. Morgan in the Berry Marble Case," ca. 1937, all in TVA microfilm, Morgan Papers.

55. All quotes from Walter Kahoe, "Notes Taken at TVA Board Meeting Held February 24, 1937, in Arthur E. Morgan's Office," August 11, 1938, 1–5, Morgan Papers; Purcell, "Undermining the TVA," 175.

56. Kahoe, "Notes Taken at TVA Board Meeting," 6–11, Morgan Papers; Purcell, "Undermining the TVA," 175.

57. Morgan, "Berry Marble Case," 67–68; Arthur E. Morgan to the TVA Board of Directors, February 25, 1937; Harcourt Morgan and David Lilienthal to Arthur E. Morgan, March 25, 1937, all in TVA microfilm, Morgan Papers; Purcell, "Undermining the TVA," 175–76.

58. Arthur E. Morgan, "Summary of a statement by Arthur E. Morgan, Chairman of the Tennessee Valley Authority, in reply to public statements by Dr. H. A. Morgan and Mr. D. E. Lilienthal and by Senator George L. Berry concerning the Chairman's testimony in the Berry marble case," ca. March 1938, 3, Morgan Papers; Purcell, "Undermining the TVA," 176.

59. James L. Fly to the TVA Board of Directors, March 16, 1937; Morgan, "Testimony," 20–21, all in TVA microfilm, Morgan Papers; Purcell, "Undermining the TVA," 176.

60. "Brief of Complainants on Questions Suggested by the Court. Decision of the Sixth Circuit Court of Appeals, May 14, 1937," 1–18, in *Tennessee Valley Authority et al. v. The Tennessee Electric Power Company et al.*, U.S. Circuit Court of Appeals 7606 (1937), Jo Conn Guild Collection, TSLA; "Order Dissolving Preliminary Injunction—June 16, 1937," in *TEPCO v. TVA, Transcript*, I:285; Litigation Chronology," TVA microfilm, Morgan Papers; McCraw, *Power Fight*, 117; Purcell, "Struggle Within, Struggle Without," 201.

61. McCraw, *Power Fight*, 117–18; Patrick J. Maney, *The Roosevelt Presence: A Biography of Franklin Delano Roosevelt* (New York: Twayne Publishers, 1992), 90–95; Leuchtenburg, *FDR and the New Deal*, 232–38; Mickie Edwardson, "Three Chapters Concerning the Career of James Lawrence Fly at TVA (part of a proposed biography)," unpublished manuscript in author's possession, 48; Franklin D. Roosevelt, "Fireside Chat on Reorganization of the Judiciary," March 9, 1937, in *The Essential Franklin Delano Roosevelt*, ed. John Gabriel Hunt (New York:

Gramercy Books, 1995), 133–40; Wehle, *Hidden Threads of History,* 180–84, 208–211; Purcell, "Struggle Within, Struggle Without," 201.

62. Garrett, "Statement of Fact," January 2, 1937, TVA microfilm, Morgan Papers; U.S. Congress, *Investigation of the Tennessee Valley Authority: Report of the Joint Committee on the Investigation of the Tennessee Valley Authority,* (Washington, D.C.: Government Printing Office, 1939), 31, 37; *Condemnation Case v. C. A. Harris et al.* (1937); McCraw, *Morgan Versus Lilienthal,* 93–94, 129; Talbert, *FDR's Utopian,* 177–78; Pritchett, *Tennessee Valley Authority,* 197; William R. Majors, "Gordon Browning and Tennessee Politics," *Tennessee Historical Quarterly* 28 (Spring 1969): 63; Purcell, "Undermining the TVA," 176.

63. Arthur E. Morgan, "Public Ownership of Power," *Atlantic Monthly* 160 (September 1937): 339–45; Lilienthal, *Journals,* 1:69; Purcell, "Building Dams," 258–59.

64. Franklin Roosevelt to Arthur E. Morgan, September 3, 1937, Morgan Papers; Harcourt Morgan to Franklin Roosevelt, August 31, 1937; "Memorandum of Analysis of Articles By Dr. A. E. Morgan and Mr. Wendell Willkie, in *Atlantic Monthly,* September 1937," 1–8, Lilienthal Papers; Neuse, *David Lilienthal,* 100; Purcell, "Building Dams," 259–60.

65. Wehle, *Hidden Threads of History,* 185–86; "Litigation Chronology;" James Lawrence Fly, "The Files," November 17, 1937, 1–4; James Lawrence Fly, "The Files, Engineering in TEP Case—Conference with Dana Wood and James S. Bowman," 1–2; Arthur E. Morgan to James Lawrence Fly, December 14, 1937; James Lawrence Fly to Arthur E. Morgan, December 20, 1937; James Lawrence Fly to Arthur E. Morgan, December 29, 1937; James Lawrence Fly to Arthur E. Morgan, January 3, 1938; "Eighteen Utilities Case, The Chandler Report," 1–12, all in TVA microfilm, Morgan Papers; Swidler and Marquis, "TVA in Court," 314; Congress, *Investigation,* 3:1014–16; Neuse, *David Lilienthal,* 100–101; McCraw, *Morgan Versus Lilienthal,* 94; Purcell, "Struggle Within, Struggle Without," 201.

66. Harcourt Morgan and David Lilienthal to Franklin Roosevelt, November 19, 1937, Lilienthal Papers; Purcell, "Struggle Within, Struggle Without," 201–2.

67. George Berry, "Direct Examination," 5, TVA microfilm, Morgan Papers; Arthur E. Morgan, "Statement by Arthur E. Morgan Before the Joint Congressional Committee to Investigate the TVA, May 25, 1938, *Berry Case: Summary,*" May 25, 1938, 5, Morgan Papers; Purcell, "Undermining the TVA," 177.

68. Arthur E. Morgan to Len G. Broughton, December 19, 1937; James Lawrence Fly, "The Files, Conversation with Mr. Kampmeier," January 10, 1938, all in TVA microfilm, Morgan Papers; Congress, *Investigation: Report,* 36; McCraw, *Morgan Versus Lilienthal,* 97; Pritchett, *Tennessee Valley Authority,* 199; *New York Times,* December 21 and 23, 1937; Neuse, *David Lilienthal,* 101; Talbert, *FDR's Utopian,* 181; Purcell, "Undermining the TVA," 180.

69. David Lilienthal and Harcourt Morgan, "Statement of Vice Chairman Harcourt A. Morgan and Director David E. Lilienthal," December 22, 1937, TVA microfilm, Morgan Papers.

70. Arthur E. Morgan to TVA Board of Directors, December 22, 1937, TVA microfilm, Morgan Papers; Purcell, "Building Dams," 263–64.

71. Swidler and Marquis, "TVA in Court," 314–15; Purcell, "Struggle Within, Struggle Without," 202.

72. Charles E. Hoffman to Arthur E. Morgan, January 5, 1938; Arthur E. Morgan to the [TVA] Board of Directors, January 5, 1938; Forest Allen, "Board Meeting, January 5, 1938, About 10:15 A.M.,"1–2; Forest Allen, "Board Meeting, January 5, 1938, about 3:10 P.M.," 1–2; Forest Allen, "Board Meeting, January 5, 1938, [addition]," 1–2; "Transcript Taken at Board Meeting of January 5, 1938, by Marguerite L. Pritchett, Who Was Called in About 3:30 P.M., After the Meeting had Started, and Who Took Up at that Point," 1–2, 5–8, 13–17; W. J. Hayes to James Lawrence Fly, January 6, 1938, all in TVA microfilm, Morgan Papers; Purcell, "Struggle Within, Struggle Without," 203.

73. Harcourt Morgan and David Lilienthal to Franklin Roosevelt, January 18, 1938, Morgan Papers; Purcell, "Building Dams," 265–66.

74. "Opinion of the Court;" "Final Decree—Filed January 25, 1938," in *TEPCO v. TVA, Transcript,* 1:548, 551–65, 573; Swidler and Marquis, "TVA in Court," 315–16; Wehle, *Hidden Threads of History,* 186; Neuse, *David Lilienthal,* 102; Ellsworth Barnard, *Wendell Willkie: Fighter for Freedom* (Marquette: Northern Michigan Univ. Press, 1966), 119; Purcell, "Struggle Within, Struggle Without," 203.

75. "Notice of Appeal—Filed February 23, 1938;" "Petition for Appeal—Filed February 24, 1938," in *TEPCO v. TVA, Transcript,* 713–15; Neuse, *David Lilienthal,* 110; Purcell, "Struggle Within, Struggle Without," 203.

76. Arthur E. Morgan to Maury Maverick, February 14, 1938, Morgan Papers; McCraw, *Morgan Versus Lilienthal,* 99; Purcell, "Building Dams," 268.

77. All quotes from Morgan to Maverick, February 14, 1938, Morgan Papers; McCraw, *Morgan Versus Lilienthal,* 99; Purcell, "Building Dams," 268–70.

78. *New York Times,* March 2 and 3, 1938; Congress, *Investigation: Report,* 36–38; S. W. Luggan, Rush Strong, Len G. Broughton Jr., Commissioners, "To the Honorable George C. Taylor, District Judge: Report," 1–5, TVA microfilm, Morgan Papers; McCraw, *Morgan Versus Lilienthal,* 99; Purcell, "Building Dams," 270; Purcell, "Undermining the TVA," 180.

79. Lilienthal, *Journals,* 1:70–72; Purcell, "Building Dams," 271–72.

80. U.S. President, *Removal of a Member of the Tennessee Valley Authority* (Washington, D.C.: Government Printing Office, 1938), 16–17; Arthur E. Morgan to Franklin Roosevelt, March 9, 1938; Franklin Roosevelt to Arthur E. Morgan, March 9, 1938, all in Morgan Papers; Purcell, "Building Dams," 272–73.

81. "Short Summary of TVA Hearing Before the President," March 11, 1938, 1–2, Lilienthal Papers; Purcell, "Building Dams," 273.

82. "Short Summary of TVA Hearing," March 11, 1938, 3–6, Lilienthal Papers; President, *Removal of a Member of TVA,* 5–7; Purcell, "Building Dams," 274–75.

83. "Short Summary of TVA Hearing," March 11, 1938, 2, Lilienthal Papers; President, *Removal of a Member of TVA,* 15; Ickes, *Secret Diary,* 2:337; Purcell, "Building Dams," 274.

84. "Short Summary of TVA Hearing," March 11, 1938, 2, 6–10, Lilienthal Papers; Purcell, "Building Dams," 275–76.

85. "Short Summary of TVA Hearing," March 11, 1938, 2, Lilienthal Papers; President, *Removal of a Member of TVA,* 70–71; Purcell, "Building Dams," 276.

86. President, *Removal of a Member of TVA,* 75, 96; Talbert, *FDR's Utopian,* 191; Purcell, "Building Dams," 277–78.

87. President, *Removal of a Member of TVA,* 97–105; McCraw, *Morgan Versus Lilienthal,* 102; Purcell, "Building Dams," 279.

88. Franklin Roosevelt to Arthur E. Morgan, March 22, 1938; Arthur E. Morgan to Franklin Roosevelt, March 24, 1938; Tennessee Valley Authority, "Power of the President to Remove Director," April 15, 1938, all in Morgan Papers; Arthur E. Morgan to Harcourt Morgan, March 24, 1938; Arthur E. Morgan to TVA Board of Directors, March 24, 1938; Arthur E. Morgan to TVA Board of Directors, April 7, 1938, all in Box 84, RG 142, NARA–SE; *New York Times,* March 23, 1938; Lilienthal, *Journals,* 1:74; *Morgan v. Tennessee Valley Authority et al.,* U.S. District Court 28 Supp. 732 (1939); Purcell, "Building Dams," 279–80; McCraw, *Morgan Versus Lilienthal,* 131.

89. Quote from Richard B. Henderson, *Maury Maverick: A Political Biography* (Austin: Univ. of Texas Press, 1970), 170; McCraw, *Morgan Versus Lilienthal,* 103; Purcell, "Building Dams," 281.

90. Congress, *Investigation,* 1:6; Neuse, *David Lilienthal,* 106; Kahoe, *Arthur Morgan,* 111; Purcell, "Building Dams," 282.

91. Congress, *Investigation,* 1:96–97, 118–22; Purcell, "Building Dams," 282–83.

92. Congress, *Investigation,* 1:148–50, 158–60, 192–201, 222–29; Purcell, "Building Dams," 283–84.

93. Neuse, *David Lilienthal,* 106–7; Whitman, *David Lilienthal,* 46–47; Purcell, "Building Dams," 284–86.

94. Neuse, *David Lilienthal,* 107; Purcell, "Building Dams," 284–86.

95. Neuse, *David Lilienthal,* 105; Purcell, "Building Dams," 287.

96. Purcell, "Building Dams," 284–87.

97. TVA Opinion of the Supreme Court of the United States, in the *Tennessee Electric Power Company, et al., v. Tennessee Valley Authority, et al.* On Appeal from U.S. District Court for the Eastern District of Tennessee," February 3, 1939, 1–4, Jo Conn Guild Collection, TSLA; McCraw, *Power Fight,* 119, 136–37; Edwardson, "James Lawrence Fly," unpublished ms., 87–89; Wehle, *Hidden Threads of History,* 187; Neuse, *David Lilienthal,* 110; Lilienthal, *Journals,* 1:85; Barnard, *Wendell Willkie,* 121; Purcell, "Struggle Within, Struggle Without," 204–205.

98. Biddle, *In Brief Authority,* 58; Kahoe, *Arthur Morgan,* 115–16; *New York Times,* April 4, 1939; Congress, *Investigation: Report,* 237–39; Purcell, "Building Dams," 288.

99. *Morgan v. Tennessee Valley Authority, et al.,* U.S. Supreme Court 312 U.S. 701 (1941); *Morgan v. Tennessee Valley Authority, et al.,* U.S. Circuit Court of Appeals 115 Fed. 2d. 990 (1940); *Morgan v. Tennessee Valley Authority et al,* U.S. District Court 28 Supp. 732 (1939); Arthur Lawson, "Has the President an Inherent Power of Removal of His Non-Executive Appointees?" *Tennessee Law Review* 16 (April 1940): 259, 261, 272, 290; McCraw, *Morgan Versus Lilienthal,* 102–3, 131.

100. Roy Talbert and Thomas McCraw contended that the board split was based on differing power policies, rather than personalities. Purcell, "Building Dams," 290.

101. Roosevelt referred to Morgan as a "befuddled old man" just before the March 1938 White House meetings with the TVA directors. Lilienthal, *Journals,* 1:70.

7. REDISCOVERING THE UTOPIANS

1. Quote from Ferris Greenslet to Arthur E. Morgan, November 3, 1933, Morgan Papers; Henry A. Laughlin, "Ferris Greenslet," *Proceedings of the Massachusetts Historical Society,* Third Series, 72 (October 1957–December 1960), 379–84; Morgan, *Edward Bellamy,* 71.

2. Quote from Greenslet to Morgan, November 3, 1933, Morgan Papers.

3. First quote from Greenslet to Morgan, November 3, 1933; second quote from Ferris Greenslet to Arthur E. Morgan, November 24, 1933, all in Morgan Papers.

4. Arthur E. Morgan to Ferris Greenslet, December 4, 1933, Morgan Papers.

5. There were a number of books published in the 1930s focused on the writings of Edward Bellamy. See: *Edward Bellamy Speaks Again! Articles—Public Addresses—Letters* (Kansas City. Mo.: Peerage Press, 1937).

6. See Kennedy, *Freedom From Fear;* Alan Brinkley, *The End of Reform: New Deal Liberalism in Recession and War* (New York: Alfred A. Knopf, 1995); John Morton Blum, *V Was For Victory: Politics and American Culture During World War II* (New York: Harcourt Brace Jovanovich, 1976).

7. *The Edward Bellamy Association of New York* (New York: Edward Bellamy Association of New York, ca. late 1933), 1–7, Morgan Papers.

8. *Bellamy Association,* 1, 4; John Dewey, "Bellamy's Utopia," *Common Sense* 3 (April 1934): 6–7; David Gittleman, "A Yankee's Way to Utopia (On the 50th Anniversary of Edward Bellamy's 'Looking Backward')," *Unity* 116 (February 3, 1936): 206–9.

9. See Ida M. Tarbell, *The Nationalizing of Business, 1878–1898* (New York: The Macmillan Company, 1936).

10. George A. Kahn to Ida M. Tarbell, November 3, 1933; George A. Kahn to Ida M. Tarbell, November 22, 1933, all in Ida M. Tarbell Collection, 1890–1944, Pelletier Library, Allegheny College, Meadville, Pa., available online at https://dspace.allegheny.edu/handle/10456/13708 (hereafter cited as Tarbell Collection).

11. Ida M. Tarbell to George A. Kahn, November 6, 1933; George A. Kahn to Ida M. Tarbell, November 8, 1933; Ida M. Tarbell to George A. Kahn, November 9, 1933; George A. Kahn to Ida M. Tarbell, November 14, 1933; Ida M. Tarbell to George A. Kahn, November 21, 1933; George A. Kahn to Ida M. Tarbell, November 22, 1933; Marion Bellamy Earnshaw to Ida M.

Tarbell, December 19, 1933; George A. Kahn to Ida M. Tarbell, April 14, 1934; Ida M. Tarbell to George A. Kahn, April 25, 1934; Ida M. Tarbell to Mrs. Edward Bellamy, April 25, 1934; George A. Kahn to Ida M. Tarbell, August 14, 1934; Marion Bellamy Earnshaw to Ida M. Tarbell, September 2, 1934; Emma S. Bellamy to Ida M. Tarbell, September 18, 1934, all in Tarbell Collection, available online at: https://dspace.allegheny.edu/handle/10456/13708; Ida M. Tarbell, "New Dealers of the 'Seventies': Henry George and Edward Bellamy," *Forum and Century* 92 (September 1934): 133–39.

12. Arthur E. Morgan to Grace Smelo, January 2, 1934; Arthur E. Morgan to Charles Putnam, January 6, 1934; Arthur E. Morgan to Grace Smelo, January 6, 1934; Grace Smelo to Arthur E. Morgan, February 3, 1934; Arthur E. Morgan to Grace Smelo, March 16, 1934; Grace Smelo, "Report of Progress to Date on Bellamy Biography," undated [ca., summer 1934]; Arthur E. Morgan to Ira Rich Kent, January 7, 1935; Ferris Greenslet to Arthur E. Morgan, October 20, 1937; Ferris Greenslet to Arthur E. Morgan, October 25, 1937; Arthur E. Morgan to Ferris Greenslet, October 30, 1937, all in Morgan Papers.

13. Arthur E. Morgan to Ferris Greenslet, January 11, 1939; Arthur E. Morgan to Ferris Greenslet, January 28, 1939; Arthur E. Morgan to Ferris Greenslet, September 27, 1941; *Houghton Mifflin Booklist for 1940* (Boston: Houghton Mifflin, 1940), 14, all in Morgan Papers.

14. Bellamy, *Religion of Solidarity*, 4.

15. Ibid., 8.

16. Ibid., 43.

17. John Lyndenberg, review of *The Religion of Solidarity*, by Arthur E. Morgan, In *The New England Quarterly* 14 (June 1941): 417.

18. Ferris Greenslet to Arthur E. Morgan, January 5, 1940; Arthur E. Morgan to Ferris Greenslet, January 11, 1940, all in Morgan Papers.

19. Morgan to Greenslet, January 11, 1940, Morgan Papers.

20. Morgan to Greenslet, January 11, 1940, Morgan Papers; Talbert, *FDR's Utopian*, 197.

21. Thelma Berley to Ferris Greenslet, April 23, 1941; Ferris Greenslet to Arthur E. Morgan, May 20, 1941, all in Morgan Papers.

22. Morgan to Greenslet, September 27, 1941, Morgan Papers.

23. Ibid.

24. Ferris Greenslet to Arthur E. Morgan, October 3, 1941, Morgan Papers.

25. Charles G. Proffit to Arthur E. Morgan, August 24, 1943; Charles G. Proffit to Arthur E. Morgan, September 3, 1943, all in Morgan Papers.

26. Later works on Edward Bellamy include: Bowman, *Edward Bellamy;* Sylvia E. Bowman, et al., *Edward Bellamy Abroad: An American Prophet's Influence* (New York: Twayne Publishers, 1962); Sylvia E. Bowman, *The Year 2000: A Critical Biography of Edward Bellamy* (New York: Bookman Associates, 1953); Daphne Patai, ed., *Looking Backward, 1988–1888: Essays on Edward Bellamy* (Amherst: Univ. of Massachusetts Press, 1988).

27. Morgan, *Edward Bellamy*, v, ix.

28. Ibid., 6–8, 29.

29. Ibid., 31, 41, 47, 50–53, 58, 65–67, 69–71.

30. Ibid., 74, 76, 87, 92, 94–96, 136.

31. Ibid., 204–8, 211, 219–21, 224, 227.

32. Ibid., first quote on 210, second quote on 243, 172, 208, 210–12, 230, 243.

33. Ibid., quote on 258, 247, 249, 252, 284–85, 294–97.

34. Ibid., first quote on 333, second quote on 243, 239–43, 316–18, 320, 326, 330.

35. Ibid., quote on 304, 363–65.

36. Ibid., first quote on 342, second quote on 349, 344–45.

37. Ibid., quote on 159, 158–63, 341–42, 366.

38. Ibid., 244, 379–82, 389, 411, 416, 420.

39. *New York Times*, January 28, 1945; *New York Herald Tribune*, February 4, 1945; Louis Filler, review of *Edward Bellamy*, by Arthur E. Morgan, *Political Science Quarterly* 55

(September 1945): 468–70; Howard W. Beers, review of *Edward Bellamy,* by Arthur E. Morgan, *Rural Sociology* 10 (June 1945): 213; Bernard Frank, review of *Edward Bellamy,* by Arthur E. Morgan, *Journal of Forestry* 43 (August 1945): 613–14.

40. Morgan, *Edward Bellamy,* xv–xvii.

41. Arthur E. Morgan, *Plagiarism in Utopia: A Study of the Utopian Tradition With Special Reference to Edward Bellamy's Looking Backward* (Yellow Springs, Ohio: The author, 1944).

42. Morgan, *Plagiarism,* 3–4; August Bebel, *Woman and Socialism* (1879; English trans., New York: Socialist Literature Company, 1910); Mrs. John B. Shipley, "Bebel's Bricks or Bellamy's?" *Liberty* 7 (June 21, 1890): 3.

43. Morgan, *Plagiarism,* quote on 10, 5–6, 8; Laurence Gronlund, *The Cooperative Commonwealth: In Its Outlines An Exposition of Modern Socialism* (Boston, Mass.: Lee and Shepard, 1884).

44. Morgan, *Plagiarism,* 10–13; Etienne Cabet, *Voyage en Icarie* (Paris, 1848); Robert Owen, *The Book of the New Moral World* (New York: G. Vale, 1845).

45. Morgan, *Plagiarism,* quote on 29, 13–15, 29; John Macnie, *The Diothas, Or a Far Look Ahead* (New York: G. P. Putnam's Sons, 1883).

46. Morgan, *Plagiarism,* quote on 31, 16–17, 21, 27, 29.

47. Ibid., 33.

48. Arthur E. Morgan, *The Philosophy of Edward Bellamy* (New York: King's Crown Press, 1945), v–vi, 1–4.

49. Ibid., 28–29, 78–82, 85, 92.

50. Ibid., quote on 43, 35–36, 41, 65–66, 77.

51. Morgan, *Philosophy of Edward Bellamy,* quote on 1–2, 96.

52. Joseph L. Blau, review of *The Philosophy of Edward Bellamy,* by Arthur E. Morgan, *The Journal of Philosophy* 43 (June 1946): 331–34; Harry W. Laidler, review of *The Philosophy of Edward Bellamy,* by Arthur E. Morgan, *The American Economic Review* 36 (March 1946): 195–96; Bernard R. Bowron, review of *The Philosophy of Edward Bellamy,* by Arthur E. Morgan, *The New England Quarterly* 19 (March 1946): 123–25.

53. Arthur E. Morgan, *Nowhere was Somewhere: How History Makes Utopias and How Utopias Make History* (Chapel Hill: Univ. of North Carolina Press, 1946), 5–7, 10–14.

54. Ibid., 34–35, 80, 87, 187–88, 192, 195, 211–12.

55. Ibid., 20, 34–35, 39–40, 45–46, 54, 60, 212.

56. Ibid., 91, 114–15, 118–19.

57. Ibid., 12–13, 150, 156, 165–69.

58. Quote from Charles E. Merriam, review of *Nowhere was Somewhere,* by Arthur E. Morgan, *The American Journal of Sociology* 52 (May 1947): 546; Christina Stead, review of *Nowhere was Somewhere,* by Arthur E. Morgan, *New York Times,* August 11, 1946; Paul H. Douglas, review of *Nowhere was Somewhere,* by Arthur E. Morgan, *The Journal of Political Economy* 55 (August 1947): 389; Louis Filler, review of *Nowhere was Somewhere,* by Arthur E. Morgan, *The American Historical Review* 52 (October 1946): 97–98; J. O. Hertzler, review of *Nowhere was Somewhere,* by Arthur E. Morgan, *The Annals of the American Academy of Political and Social Science* 247 (September 1946): 196–97.

8. I SEE A VILLAGE

1. Quote from Margot Ensign, "Return to the Valley, June 1973," March 16, 1976, Morgan Papers.

2. Quote from Arthur E. Morgan to Friends at the TVA, June 19, 1973; Margot Ensign, "The TVA Revisited," May 15, 1984;" Ensign, "Return to the Valley, June 1973," March 16, 1976, all in Morgan Papers.

3. Quote from Morgan, *Making of the TVA,* xiv, 171, 181.

4. Ibid., quote on 197, 195–98.

5. See William H. Chafe, *The Unfinished Journey: America Since World War II* (New York: Oxford Univ. Press, 1995); Blum, *V Was For Victory;* Kennedy, *Freedom From Fear.*

6. See John Lewis Gaddis, *The Cold War: A New History* (New York: Penguin Press, 2005).

7. Kahoe, *Arthur Morgan,* 174.

8. "Report of Mexican Commission Appointed by the Jewish Joint Distribution Committee and the American Friends Service Committee," September 1, 1939; [Arthur E. Morgan], "The Jewish Community in Mexico," September 5, 1939; Arthur E. Morgan to Clarence Pickett, November 10, 1939, all in Morgan Papers.

9. Arthur E. Morgan, "The Conscientious Objector," *Antioch Notes* 18 (November 1, 1940); Kahoe, *Arthur Morgan,* 172.

10. Quote from Arthur E. Morgan, "Universal Compulsory Military Training," *Antioch Notes* 22 (January 15, 1945); Arthur E. Morgan, "A Time to Be Careful," *Antioch Notes* 22 (February 15, 1945); Arthur E. Morgan, "The Military Mind and Peacetime Training," *Progressive Education* 23 (October 1945): 28–31; Arthur E. Morgan, "Comments on Universal Compulsory Military Training," February 1945, Morgan Papers.

11. Morgan, "The Military Mind," 29; Morgan, "Comments on Universal Compulsory Military Training," February 1945, Morgan Papers.

12. Arthur E. Morgan, "Community," *Antioch Notes* 28 (November 15, 1950): 2.

13. [Arthur E. Morgan], "Community Service, Inc., Purposes and Program," 1941; "The Purposes of Community Service," 1961; John Bryant interview with Arthur E. Morgan, November 25, 1961, handwritten notes, all in Morgan Papers; Arthur E. Morgan, "The Community: The Seed Bed of Society," *Atlantic Monthly* 169 (February 1942): 225–26.

14. Quotes from [Morgan], "Community Service, Inc.," 1941, Morgan Papers; Kahoe, *Arthur Morgan,* 117; [Arthur E. Morgan], "Community Service, Inc., Purposes and Program," 1941, Morgan Papers.

15. Community Service, Inc., was renamed the Arthur Morgan Institute for Community Solutions. See http://www.communitysolution.org/about.html.

16. Morgan, *The Small Community,* 3.

17. Ibid.,12–19, 57.

18. Arthur E. Morgan, *The Community of the Future and the Future of Community* (Yellow Springs, Ohio: Community Service, Inc., 1957), first quote on 4, second quote on 144.

19. Morgan, *Industries for Small Communities,* 15–17; Arthur E. Morgan, *A Business of My Own* (Yellow Springs, Ohio: Community Service, Inc., 1953); Arthur E. Morgan, "Little Industry in the Community," *Journal of Educational Sociology* 27 (December 1953): 160–62.

20. Morgan, *Industries for Small Communities,* 107.

21. Morgan, *The Small Community;* Arthur Morgan, *The Great Community* (Chicago: Human Events Associates, 1946); Arthur E. Morgan, "The Trouble With Utopia" *This Week,* Magazine of the *New York Herald,* November 28, 1948, 6–7, 30.

22. Aaron D. Purcell, "Collaboration and the Small Community: Arthur Morgan and the Mitraniketan Project in Kerala," *The Historian* 65 (Spring 2003): 643–44.

23. Ranbir Vohra, *The Making of India: A Historical Survey,* second edition (Armonk, N.Y.: M. E. Sharpe, 2001), 185–87; S. N. Mukerji, *History of Education in India (modern period),* fifth edition (Baroda, India: Acharya Book Depot, 1966), 237–38; Purcell, "Collaboration and the Small Community," 646–47.

24. Suma Chitnis and Philip G. Altbach, eds., *Higher Education Reform in India: Experience and Perspectives* (New Delhi, India: Sage Publications, 1993), 91; Amrik Singh and Philip G. Altbach, eds., *The Higher Learning in India* (Delhi, India: Vikas Publishing House, 1974), 26–27, 336–37; Hadley Read, *Partners With India: Building Agricultural Universities* (Urbana: Univ. of Illinois, 1974), 17; Arthur E. Morgan, *It Can Be Done in Education* (Yellow Springs, Ohio: Community Service, Inc., 1962), 3; Leuba, *Road to Creativity,* 208–10; Purcell, "Collaboration and the Small Community," 647.

25. Purcell, "Collaboration and the Small Community," 647–48.

26. Arthur E. Morgan, "Introductory Letter—Viswan Newsletter," January 1965, Morgan Papers; Read, *Partners With India,* 41–85; Morgan, *It Can Be Done in Education,* 4; Purcell, "Collaboration and the Small Community," 648.

27. Recent historical surveys include: Krishna Dutta and Andrew Robinson, *Rabindranath Tagore: The Myriad-Minded Man* (London: Bloomsburg, 1995); Ashis Nandy, *The Illegitimacy of Nationalism: Rabindranath Tagore and the Politics of Self* (Oxford, Eng.: Oxford Univ. Press, 1994); Dennis Dalton, *Mahatma Gandhi: Nonviolent Power in Action* (New York: Columbia Univ. Press, 1993); and Yogesh Chadha, *Rediscovering Gandhi* (London: Century, 1997). Purcell, "Collaboration and the Small Community," 648.

28. Arthur E. Morgan, "A Biographical Note About K. Viswanathan," November 1963, Morgan Papers; Jeff Biggers, *From the Dusty Soil: The Story of Mitraniketan, Community Education and Development in Rural India* (Kerala, India: Mitraniketan Printers and Publishers, 1996), 28–29, 40, 45–50, 54–55; Purcell, "Collaboration and the Small Community," 649.

29. Arthur E. Morgan, "Viswan's Childhood," n.d.; John Bryant, "Man With a Dream" (term paper, Antioch College, 1961), 2, all in Morgan Papers; Biggers, *From the Dusty Soil,* 59–63; Purcell, "Collaboration and the Small Community," 649.

30. S. Abid Husain, *The Way of Gandhi and Nehru* (London: Asia Publishing House, 1959), 69–74; Purcell, "Collaboration and the Small Community," 649–50.

31. Arthur E. Morgan, "Viswanathan's Educational Philosophy," n.d.; Arthur E. Morgan, "Friends of Viswanathan," August 1962; Arthur E. Morgan, "Friends of Viswanathan," November 2, 1962; Morgan, "Viswan's Childhood," all in Morgan Papers; Purcell, "Collaboration and the Small Community," 650.

32. Morgan, "Biographical Note About Viswan," Morgan Papers; Morgan, *It Can Be Done in Education,* 4; Purcell, "Collaboration and the Small Community," 650–51.

33. A. Sreedhara Mehon, *A Survey of Kerala History* (Kottayam, India: Sahitya Pravarthaka Co-operative Society, 1967), 369–70; *States of Our Union: Kerala* (Delhi, India: Ministry of Information and Broadcasting, 1968), 5, 24–25; T. J. Nossiter, *Communism in Kerala: A Study in Political Adaptation* (Berkeley: Univ. of California Press, 1982), 7, 109; Richard W. Franke and Barbara H. Chasin, *Kerala: Radical Reform as Development in an Indian State* (San Francisco: Institute for Food and Development Policy, 1991), 51; Govindan Parayil, ed., *Kerala: The Development Experience, Reflections on Sustainability and Replicability* (New York: St. Martin's Press, 2000), 102–3; Purcell, "Collaboration and the Small Community," 651–52.

34. Morgan, "Biographical Note About Viswan," 3; Donald Helm, "History of Mitraniketan," April 18, 1964, 6–8; Arthur E. Morgan, "Friends of Community Services," 29 March 1956, all in Morgan Papers; Biggers, *From the Dusty Soil,* 89; Purcell, "Collaboration and the Small Community," 652.

35. Arthur E. Morgan, "Newsletter to Members," December 15, 1956, 3–4; Arthur E. Morgan, "Friends of Viswanathan," May 7, 1958, all in Morgan Papers; Purcell, "Collaboration and the Small Community," 652–53.

36. K. Viswanathan to Arthur E. Morgan, June 22, 1957; "Rules and Regulations of Mitraniketan," 1967, 1–5, all in Morgan Papers; Purcell, "Collaboration and the Small Community," 653.

37. Viswan to Morgan, June 22, 1957, Morgan Papers; Purcell, "Collaboration and the Small Community," 653–54.

38. Quote from J. Dudley Dawson to Arthur E. Morgan, February 9, 1958; Arthur E. Morgan, "Friends of Viswanathan," March 1958, all in Morgan Papers; Purcell, "Collaboration and the Small Community," 654.

39. Arthur E. Morgan, "Friends of Viswanathan: From the Report of Baij Nath Singh, September 1958," November 1958; Dawson to Morgan, February 9, 1958; Morgan, "Friends of Viswanathan," March 1959; Elizabeth Morgan and Ernest Morgan, "Friends of Viswanathan," July 1959, all in Morgan Papers; Purcell, "Collaboration and the Small Community," 655.

40. K. Viswanathan to Elizabeth Morgan and Ernest Morgan, March 18, 1960; Arthur E. Morgan, "Friends of Viswanathan," August 1963, all in Morgan Papers; Morgan, *It Can Be Done in Education,* 81–82; Purcell, "Collaboration and the Small Community," 655.

41. Quote from K. Viswanathan, "Mitraniketan: An Outline of the Proposed System for Rural Education," March 1960; K. Viswanathan to Arthur E. Morgan, March 18, 1960, all in Morgan Papers; Purcell, "Collaboration and the Small Community," 655–56.

42. K. Viswanathan to Arthur E. Morgan, January 9, 1960, 1; K. Viswanathan to Arthur E. Morgan, July 27, 1960; Arthur E. Morgan, "Friends of Viswanathan," November 1960; Elizabeth Morgan, "Friends of Viswanathan," March 1960; Arthur E. Morgan, "Friends of Viswanathan," ca. 1961; Arthur E. Morgan, "Friends of Viswanathan," August 1963, all in Morgan Papers; Morgan, *It Can Be Done In Education,* 97; Purcell, "Collaboration and the Small Community," 656–57.

43. Morgan, *It Can Be Done in Education,* 112–13; Arthur E. Morgan, "Friends of Viswanathan," November 2, 1962; Morgan, "Friends of Viswanathan," ca. 1962; Arthur E. Morgan, "Notes Concerning Mitraniketan," February 1963; Morgan, "Friends of Viswanathan," ca. 1963, all in Morgan Papers; Biggers, *From the Dusty Soil,* 115–17; Purcell, "Collaboration and the Small Community," 657–58.

44. Arthur E. Morgan, "Friends of Viswanathan," January 1965; Arthur E. Morgan, "Friends of Viswanathan," February 1965; David H. Scull, "Mitraniketan—At the Take-Off Point," October 1965, 15, all in Morgan Papers; Purcell, "Collaboration and the Small Community," 658.

45. Arthur E. Morgan, "Viswanathan Newsletter," March 1965; Arthur E. Morgan, "Viswanathan Newsletter," August 1965; Arthur E. Morgan, "A Multipurpose Undertaking," ca. 1962, 7; Arthur E. Morgan, "The Abode of Friends: Mitraniketan [brochure]," all in Morgan Papers; George Woodcock, *Kerala: A Portrait of the Malabar Coast* (London: Faber, 1967), 25; Purcell, "Collaboration and the Small Community," 658–59.

46. Morgan, "Viswanathan Newsletter," March 1965; Arthur E. Morgan, "Viswanathan Newsletter," August 1965; Arthur E. Morgan, "Friends of Viswanathan," ca. 1961; K. Viswanathan, "Mitraniketan: Past, Present, and Future in Brief," January 1966, 3, all in Morgan Papers; *Mitraniketan Marg* 1 (August 20, 1966): 1–12; Purcell, "Collaboration and the Small Community," 659.

47. Arthur E. Morgan to A. B. Shah, December 26, 1966; *I See A Village: The Arthur Morgan Story,* Richard Kaplan, Richard Kaplan Productions, 1968, all in Morgan Papers; Biggers, *From the Dusty Soil,* 139; Purcell, "Collaboration and the Small Community," 659.

48. Quote from Arthur E. Morgan, "Viswanathan Newsletter," February 1967, Morgan Papers; Purcell, "Collaboration and the Small Community," 659–60.

49. Morgan, "Viswanathan Newsletter," February 1967, Morgan Papers; Purcell, "Collaboration and the Small Community," 660.

50. Arthur E. Morgan, "Viswanathan Newsletter," March 1967; Arthur E. Morgan, "Chronology of Mitraniketan and AEM," 1967, all in Morgan Papers; Purcell, "Collaboration and the Small Community," 660–61.

51. Purcell, "Collaboration and the Small Community," 664.

52. The controversial Three Gorges Dam project in China is the best example of an international TVA–inspired project of water-control, electric power production, and regional development. See Soo Mun Theresa Wong, "Making the Mekong: Nature, Region, Postcoloniality" (PhD diss., The Ohio State Univ., 2010). Kahoe, *Arthur Morgan,* 121.

53. Morgan, *The Miami Conservancy District;* Morgan, *The Making of the TVA.*

54. Morgan published several articles, reports, and studies related to flood control of the Mississippi River and the Corps of Engineers. See Arthur E. Morgan, "A Policy for the Mississippi," *Annals of the American Academy of Political and Social Science* 135 (January 1928): 50–56.

55. Arthur E. Morgan, *Dams and Other Disasters: A Century of the Army Corp of Engineers in Civil Works* (Boston: Porter Sargent, 1971), ix–xi, xxiii.

56. Laurence M. Hauptman, *Conspiracy of Interests: Iroquois Dispossession and the Rise of New York State* (Syracuse, N.Y.: Syracuse Univ. Press, 1999), 88–92; Laurence M. Hauptman, *The*

Historic Background to the Present Day Seneca Nation—Salamanca Lease Controversy: The First Hundred Years, 1851–1951 (Albany: State Univ. of New York, 1985), 2–3; George H. J. Abrams, *The Seneca People* (Phoenix: Indian Tribal Series, 1976), 48–90; Aaron D. Purcell, "The Engineering of Forever: Arthur E. Morgan, the Seneca Indians, and the Kinzua Dam," *New York History* 78 (July 1997): 311–12.

57. Paul C. Rosier, "Dam Building and Treaty Breaking: The Kinzua Dam Controversy, 1936–1958," *The Pennsylvania Magazine of History and Biography* 69 (October 1995): 348; Roy Lubove, ed., *Pittsburgh* (New York: Franklin Watts, 1976), 193, 214; Purcell, "Engineering of Forever," 314.

58. Rosier, "Dam Building," 348–49; Allen Burridge Lee, "The Kinzua Dam Project: A Case Study of the Politics of Flood Control" (PhD diss., Univ. of Pittsburgh, 1959), 22–24; Purcell, "Engineering of Forever," 316–17.

59. Lee, "Kinzua Dam Project," 23, 25, 28; Purcell, "Engineering of Forever," 317–18.

60. Lee, "Kinzua Dam Project," 25; Purcell, "Engineering of Forever," 318–19.

61. Alvin M. Joseph, Jr., "Cornplanter, Can You Swim?" *American Heritage* 20 (December 1968): 106; Rosier, "Dam Building," 358; Purcell, "Engineering of Forever," 319.

62. Morgan, *Dams and Other Disasters*, 318; Purcell, "Engineering of Forever," 319–20.

63. Arthur E. Morgan and Barton M. Jones, "The Allegheny Reservoir Project: A Summation of the Diversion Canal Plan Diverting the Flood Waters of the Allegheny River into Lake Erie," May 1957, 1–4, Morgan Papers; Rosier, "Dam Building," 358–59; Morgan, *Dams and Other Disasters*, 323; Purcell, "Engineering of Forever," 321.

64. Morgan, *Dams and Other Disasters*, 83; Purcell, "Engineering of Forever," 321–22.

65. Rosier, "Dam Building and Treaty Breaking," 357–58; Purcell, "Engineering of Forever," 322.

66. Arthur E. Morgan, "Statement of Arthur Morgan for the Public Works Subcommittee of the House Appropriations Committee in Relation to the Hearing on May 10, 1957," May 10, 1957; Sharon E. Creiger, "Lake of Perfidy" (term paper, Antioch Univ., Putney, Vt., 1967), 6–7, all in Morgan Papers; Walter Taylor, "The Treaty We Broke," *Nation* 193 (September 2, 1961): 121; Lee, "Kinzua Dam Project," 38; Purcell, "Engineering of Forever," 322.

67. Morgan, "Statement, Public Works Subcommittee," May 10, 1957, 1, 7, Morgan Papers; Rosier, "Dam Building and Treaty Breaking," 358; Purcell, "Engineering of Forever," 322–24.

68. Morgan, "Statement, Public Works Subcommittee," May 10, 1957, 11, Morgan Papers; Purcell, "Engineering of Forever," 324.

69. Morgan, "Statement, Public Works Subcommittee," May 10, 1957, 12–13, Morgan Papers; Morgan, *Dams and Other Disasters*, 83, 325; Purcell, "Engineering of Forever," 324.

70. Morgan, *Dams and Other Disasters*, 363; Purcell, "Engineering of Forever," 324–25.

71. Edward E. O'Neil, "Petition for Injunction," August 30, 1957, 1–3, Morgan Papers; Morgan, *Dams and Other Disasters*, 83, 320–21, 325; Rosier, "Dam Building and Treaty Breaking," 366–67; Purcell, "Engineering of Forever," 325–26.

72. Morgan, *Dams and Other Disasters*, 319, 321; Rosier, "Dam Building and Treaty Building," 367; Constance Sontag, "Arthur Morgan: Biographical Sketch," March 19, 1968," Morgan Papers; Purcell, "Engineering of Forever," 326.

73. "TAMS: Allegheny River Reservoir, a Review of Authorized Plan and Alternatives for the U.S. Army Engineer Division, Ohio River, April 1958," Morgan Papers; Morgan, *Dams and Other Disasters*, quote on 84, 83–84, 325, 330–33; Laurence M. Hauptman, *The Iroquois Struggle for Survival: World War II to Red Power* (Syracuse, N.Y.: Syracuse Univ. Press, 1986), 113; Purcell, "Engineering of Forever," 326–27.

74. Arthur E. Morgan to Emerson C. Itschner, April 24, 1958, Morgan Papers; Purcell, "Engineering of Forever," 327.

75. Arthur E. Morgan, "A Statement Concerning the Relative Safety and Value of the Proposed Kinzua Reservoir on the Upper Allegheny and the Alternative, the Proposed Conewango Reservoir," May 1958, Morgan Papers; Purcell, "Engineering of Forever," 327–28.

76. Morgan, *Dams and Other Disasters*, 334–35, 340–42; Purcell, "Engineering of Forever," 328.

77. Morgan, *Dams and Other Disasters,* 351–52; Purcell, "Engineering of Forever," 328–29.

78. Morgan, *Dams and Other Disasters,* 329; Purcell, "Engineering of Forever," 329.

79. Arthur E. Morgan, "Comparison of the Proposed Kinzua Reservoir with the Proposed Conewango Reservoir on the Upper Allegheny as they would affect Salamanca," July 22, 1958, Morgan Papers; Purcell, "Engineering of Forever," 329.

80. *Seneca Nation of Indians v. Wilber M. Brucker,* District of Columbia, District Court (February 1958), Morgan Papers; Hauptman, *Iroquois Struggle for Survival,* 101, 118; Rosier, "Dam Building and Treaty Breaking," 367; Josephy, "Cornplanter," 106; Purcell, "Engineering of Forever," 329.

81. *Seneca Nation of Indians v. Wilber M. Brucker* (District of Columbia District Court of Appeals, April 1958), Morgan Papers; Hauptman, *Iroquois Struggle for Survival,* 101; Rosier, "Dam Building and Treaty Breaking," 367; Josephy, "Cornplanter," 106; Purcell, "Engineering of Forever," 330.

82. Petition for a Writ of Certiorari to the United States Court of Appeals for the District of Columbia Circuit Court (Supreme Court of the United States, Oct. 1958), Morgan Papers; Hauptman, *Iroquois Struggle for Survival,* 119; Purcell, "Engineering of Forever," 330.

83. Arthur E. Morgan, "A Comparison of the Kinzua Plan and the Conewango Plan for Control of the Upper Allegheny River: A Statement Presented to the Subcommittees of Public Works of the House and Senate Committees on Appropriations," May 5–6, 1959, 1–11, Morgan Papers; Purcell, "Engineering of Forever," 330.

84. Arthur E. Morgan, "Testimony of Arthur Morgan Concerning Upper Allegheny Flood Control Before Sub-Committee on Public Works of the House Appropriations Committee," April 7, 1960, 1–6; Arthur E. Morgan, "Testimony of Arthur Morgan Concerning Upper Allegheny Flood Control Before Sub-Committee on Public Works of the House Appropriations Committee," April 8, 1960, 1–4, all in Morgan Papers; Purcell, "Engineering of Forever," 330–31.

85. Morgan, "Testimony, Sub-Committee on Public Works, House Appropriations Committee," April 8, 1960, 1–4, Morgan Papers; Purcell, "Engineering of Forever," 331.

86. Ronald M. Smith, "The Politics of Pittsburgh Flood Control, 1936–1960," *Pennsylvania History* 44 (January 1977): 22; Hauptman, *Iroquois Struggle for Survival,* quote on 121, 120–21; Purcell, "Engineering of Forever," 331–32.

87. Arthur E. Morgan to John F. Kennedy, March 14, 1961, Morgan Papers; Purcell, "Engineering of Forever," 332.

88. Philip S. Klein and Ari Hoogenbom, *A History of Pennsylvania* (University Park: Pennsylvania State Univ. Press, 1980), 511; Purcell, "Engineering of Forever," 332.

89. "Today," NBC television, December 28, 1961, Antiochiana, Antioch College; Morgan to Kennedy, March 14, 1961, Morgan Papers; Purcell, "Engineering of Forever," 333–34.

90. R. David Corwin, "Dilemma of the Iroquois," *Natural History* 6 (June–July 1967): 62; "Lake of Perfidy," *The New Republic* 150 (April 18, 1964): 5; Rosier, "Dam Building and Treaty Breaking," 345; Purcell, "Engineering of Forever," 334–35.

91. Purcell, "Engineering of Forever," 335.

92. Morgan, *Arthur Morgan Remembered,* 88.

93. Arthur E. Morgan, "Notes from Memory by Arthur E. Morgan and Griscom Morgan on the Beginnings of Celo Community in North Carolina," October 7, 1957, Morgan Papers; George L. Hicks, *Experimental Americans: Celo and Utopian Community in the Twentieth Century* (Urbana: Univ. of Illinois Press, 2001), 73–74.

94. *Knoxville News-Sentinel,* July 24, 1938; "Certificate of Incorporation of Celo Community, Inc.," December 28, 1938, Morgan Papers.

95. Morgan, "Notes from Memory," October 7, 1957; "Transcription of Tape Made by Arthur E. Morgan, November 3, 1970, The Beginnings of the Celo Community," all in Morgan Papers; Hicks, *Experimental Americans,* 76–79.

96. Timothy Miller, *The Quest for Utopia in Twentieth Century America* (Syracuse, N.Y.: Syracuse Univ. Press, 1998), 1:157; Ernest Morgan, *Dealing Creatively with Life: The Life Adventure of*

Ernest Morgan (New York: Barclay House, 1999), 261–62; Hicks, *Experimental Americans,* 101–2; "Transcription of Tape Made by Arthur Morgan, November 3, 1970," Morgan Papers.

97. Margot Ensign, "Arthur Morgan's Last Trip," April 27, 1976, Morgan Papers.

98. Ibid.

99. Morgan, *Arthur Morgan Remembered,* 109–113; Kahoe, *Arthur Morgan,* 128; Talbert, *FDR's Utopian,* 200–201.

CONCLUSION

1. See Anthony B. Gannon, "Vision or Obsession?: Arthur E. Morgan and the Superdam," *Register of the Kentucky Historical Society* 97 (January 1999): 45–82.

2. David E. Lilienthal, *TVA: Democracy on the March* (New York: Harper and Brothers, 1944).

3. Arthur E. Morgan, *The Long Road* (Washington, D.C.: The National Home Library Foundation, 1936), 2–12.

4. Quote from Ibid., 42.

5. Ibid., 42–43, 59–60.

6. Quote from Ibid., 34.

7. Ibid., 59–64, 104–10.

8. Quote from Ibid., 92.

9. Ibid., 14, 92–94.

10. Ibid., 66, 76, 119.

11. Arthur E. Morgan, *Search for Purpose* (London: C. A. Watts and Company, Ltd., 1957), v–vi, 5.

12. Ibid., 3, 110, 118–19, 165, 189.

13. Ibid., vii, 38–40, 45, 88–91, 103, 147.

14. Quote from Ibid., 87.

15. Quote from Ibid., 51.

16. Ibid., first quote on 180, second quote on 8, 35, 101, 149–150, 158.

17. Ibid., 94, 102–103, 148–49, 177, 191.

18. Arthur E. Morgan, *Purpose and Circumstance* (Yellow Springs, Ohio: Kahoe and Company, 1928), 24.

19. Quote from Morgan, "Broken Threads," 101.

20. Morgan, "Recollections of FDR for Posterity," May 1966, Morgan Papers.

21. Arthur E. Morgan, *Education for Engineers* (Yellow Springs, Ohio: Antioch Press, 1955), 29.

22. Arthur E. Morgan, *A Compendium of Antioch Notes* (Yellow Springs, Ohio: Kahoe and Company, 1930), 24.

23. Arthur E. Morgan, *Observations* (Yellow Springs, Ohio: Antioch Press, 1968), 81.

Index

Page numbers in **boldface** refer to illustrations.